The Fehmarnbelt Fixed Link:

REGIONAL DEVELOPMENT PERSPECTIVES

CONTENTS

INTRODUCTION Christian Wichmann Matthiessen & Jacob Vestergaard	4
CHAPTER 1. THE FIXED FEHMARNBELT LINK: NEW DYNAMIC REGIONAL DEVELOPMENT IN NORTHERN EUROPE. SUMMARY Christian Wichmann Matthiessen	10
CHAPTER 2. MAPS AND FIGURES Petra Aulin, Jacek Rokicki & Signe Schilling	44
CHAPTER 3. INFRASTRUCTURE, TRANSPORT AND LOGISTICS Petra Aulin, Jacek Rokicki, Patrik Ryden, Signe Schilling, Lars Rostgaard Toft, Emmanouil Tranos & Morten Vedby	88
CHAPTER 4. THE ROLE OF THE CITIES – A GLOBAL PERSPECTIVE Christian Wichmann Matthiessen	114
CHAPTER 5. CROSS-BORDER LABOUR MARKET Johannes Bröcker, Hayo Herrmann & Artem Korzhenevych	150
CHAPTER 6. CROSS-BORDER MOBILITY: COMMUTING SCENARIOS FOR 2020 Johannes Bröcker, Hayo Herrmann & Artem Korzhenevych	202
CHAPTER 7. CLUSTERS IN THE ECONOMY: POTENTIAL NEW INTERACTION Hayo Herrmann & Christian Wichmann Matthiessen	238
CHAPTER 8. THE SCIENTIFIC WORLD: CENTRES, NETWORKS, DEVELOPMENT OPPORTUNITIES Søren Find, Christian Wichmann Matthiessen & Annette Winkel Schwarz	280
CHAPTER 9. THE FIXED LINK'S POTENTIAL EFFECTS ON HOUSE PRICES David Emanuel Andersson, Åke E. Andersson, Zoltan Kettinger & Oliver F. Shyr	330
CHAPTER 10. THE CULTURAL SECTOR Birgit Stöber	360
CHAPTER 11. GENERAL VALUES AND ATTITUDES AMONG YOUNG PEOPLE Ingvar Holmberg	384
GLOSSARY	432
ABOUT THE AUTHORS	436

A MAJOR NEW EUROPEAN REGION IS TAKING SHAPE

The fixed link across the Fehmarnbelt is currently one of the largest infrastructure investments in Northern Europe. It represents the third phase in the ongoing integration of Scandinavia and the European continent of which the first was the Storebælt link and the second was the Øresund Bridge.

With the decision by Germany and Denmark to build a fixed Fehmarnbelt link, the two nations not only embarked on a large scale project to improve the infrastructure of Northern Europe and reduce travel times, but also to stimulate economic, cultural and social development in the areas, regions and countries around the link. With the fixed Fehmarnbelt link, one of the world's mega projects in terms of logistics will be completed. "The missing Scandinavian links" will no longer be "missing".

The first stage of the Northern European integration project was completed with the opening in 1997/1998 of the fixed link across Denmark's Storebælt. This represented a huge leap into the future in terms of logistics and physical interaction between East and West Denmark. Although networks across Storebælt already existed, the new link enhanced the potential for co-operation between the various parts of Denmark very significantly.

By 2000, despite the fact that the Øresund Region's major cities provided excellent opportunities for integration, only some fairly weak networks had been established between Scania in Sweden and Zealand in Denmark. The opening of the Øresund Bridge, therefore, substantially improved networking across the Øresund waterway and, following a somewhat sluggish start, such links have been steadily growing ever since. In the same way, the fixed Fehmarnbelt link will considerably change our world although differences between the German and Scandinavian languages and the fact that the near areas are sparsely populated will constitute some barriers to the area's development. Nevertheless, the potential gains are great.

One thing is certain: as new infrastructure projects of this size have always resulted in major changes, the link will create growth and development. The links across the Bosporus are one example; others are the Eurotunnel and the construction of high speed rail lines in France and Spain. This is useful to remember as the development of economic, social and cultural links between Southern Scandinavia and Northern Germany accelerate.

The fixed Fehmarnbelt link will not only take over the transport services carried out by the ferries between Rødby and Puttgarden since 1963. No less important is the fact that new relations between the communities on both sides of the link will be forged – between Southern Zealand, Lolland and Falster in Denmark and Eastern Holstein in Germany as well as, further afield, between Copenhagen/the Øresund City and Hamburg. As a result, new trading opportunities, new forms of tourism, new jobs and new housing opportunities will arise. In turn, this will open up new regional development perspectives for the entire Fehmarnbelt Region. Already a range of contacts and partnerships are being formed between Denmark, Germany and Sweden for the purpose of exploiting the opportunities created by the fixed Fehmarnbelt link.

In 2009, Femern A/S established a group of Danish, German and Swedish academics under Professor Christian Wichmann Matthiessen from the University of Copenhagen. Each with their own area of expertise and experience, the academics were commissioned to analyse a range of development opportunities in Northern Europe following the opening of the fixed Fehmarnbelt link. The project is designed to provide inspiration to the many decision makers who, over the years ahead, will be involved in the gigantic process of change initiated by the Danish-German treaty on the fixed Fehmarnbelt link.

Christian Wichmann Matthiessen
University of Copenhagen

Jacob Vestergaard
Femern A/S

CHAPTER 1
THE FIXED FEHMARNBELT LINK: NEW DYNAMIC REGIONAL DEVELOPMENT IN NORTHERN EUROPE
SUMMARY

CHRISTIAN WICHMANN MATTHIESSEN

The treaty on the construction of a fixed Fehmarnbelt link was signed by the Danish and German governments on 3 September, 2008. The decision engendered strong focus on the development perspectives following the fixed link's completion in 2020. This book examines the potential for regional development in the Fehmarnbelt Region.

The Fehmarnbelt Region comprises the Zealand archipelago, Bornholm, Schleswig-Holstein, Hamburg and Scania. Parts of this publication also include Mecklenburg-Vorpommern, and when discussing major cities, Rostock.

Fehmarn was joined by a bridge to mainland Germany in 1963. Over the previous centuries, the large islands in the Zealand archipelago had become linked by the construction of bridges and tunnels. Amager in Copenhagen is hardly regarded as an island any longer, and Lolland and Falster are so closely linked that during the local government reforms in 2007, Guldborgsund Municipality was established across the Guldborg Sound. Zealand and Møn are linked by a bridge and the two islands are, in turn, connected to Falster by bridges and dams. The Zealand archipelago was joined to mainland Europe by

FIGURE 1.
TRAFFIC DEVELOPMENT ACROSS THE THREE STRAITS THAT SEPARATE THE ZEALAND ARCHIPELAGO FROM THE REST OF THE WORLD

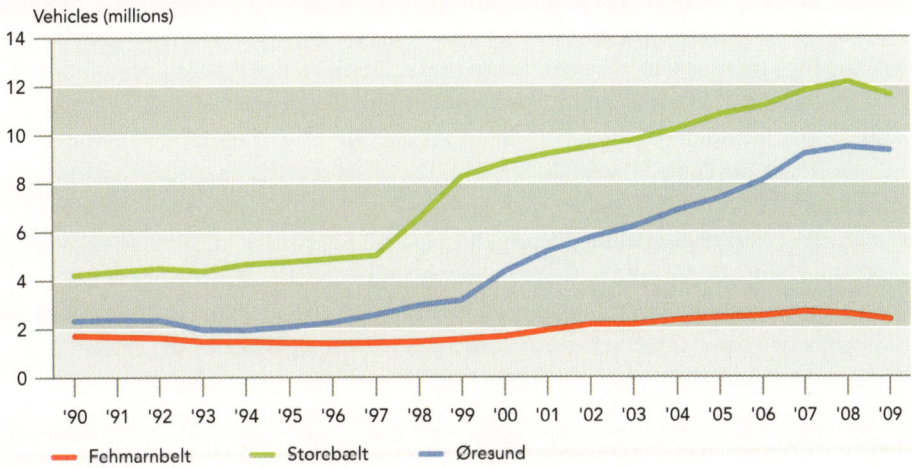

The figures in the diagram show traffic across the whole section. With regard to Storebælt, this means from Sjællands Odde to Tårs towards Jutland and Funen. The Øresund statistics comprise traffic from Elsinore – Helsingborg to Dragør – Limhamn. The statistics for Fehmarnbelt traffic include those from Rødbyhavn and Gedser to Northern Germany.

the opening of the Storebælt Bridge in 1998 while the fixed link between Zealand and the Scandinavian peninsula, the Øresund Bridge, was commissioned in 2000. The two latter systems have significantly changed the geographical reality for Southern Scandinavia.

What strikes you when you look at the diagram in Figure 1 are the traffic jumps following the opening of the fixed links. The traffic jump was significant after the opening of the Storebælt Bridge and developments subsequently entailed a new lasting growth regime. The reason was that a series of networks were already functioning and were ready to be employed in new and more value creating ways. Family ties were national, companies had Denmark as their market and the public sector, institutions and organisations were organised on a nationwide basis. What was needed was simply to change the logistics and localisation patterns.

There was also a traffic jump following the opening of the Øresund Bridge, but this took longer because there was no existing, well developed network to build on. Rather, developments following the Øresund Bridge can be described as something new where all localisation decisions were taken in the light of the fixed link as a reality, when logistics acquired new development opportunities and when new economies of scale were added to the agenda with their starting point in an overall Danish/Swedish metropolitan region.

The question is now how the transport picture at Fehmarnbelt will change. This publication is intended to respond to this question. We do not doubt that changes will occur and that the fixed Fehmarnbelt link will result in a traffic jump and new growth potential. We believe that in the short-term, this will be less dramatic than it was following the two other mega projects (the Storebælt and Øresund links) because there are no well established networks across the Fehmarnbelt or heavy centres near the future fixed link. By contrast, we believe that the project will create a new lasting growth regime based on its considerable value creating potential, particularly brought about by the establishment of new networks and because a new border regional framework calls for action.

THREE PERSPECTIVES WITHIN REGIONAL DEVELOPMENT

The basic analysis model is outlined in two simple diagrams where the diagram in Figure 2 shows the current situation, while the diagram in Figure 3 shows the potential interaction following the commissioning of a fixed link across the Fehmarnbelt.

Basically, there are three different perspectives for regional development. The first comprises the interaction between the major heavy centres, i.e. between Copenhagen-Malmö-Lund (the Øresund City) on the one side and especially Hamburg, but also between Kiel, Lübeck and Rostock on the other. Within this perspective, there are almost exclusively potential gains. The second perspective comprises those parts of the region that are close to the Fehmarnbelt. Here it is not only about potential winners, but also realising that once the fixed link is completed, jobs linked to the ferries and crossings will disappear, and that construction work will cease at the same time. The third perspective encompasses the other ferry towns, which will experience new tough competition.

The major cities will see new growth potential. First and foremost, this will apply to the Øresund City and Hamburg and secondly to Kiel, Lübeck and Rostock which, however, will see some negative development potential in that ferry services in these towns will be exposed to strong competition. The major cities will also see a strengthening of their cross-point function, which will make them more attractive as localisation targets for a wide range of companies. They themselves will be occupied by strengthening the interaction within areas that will create new value by exploiting both the complementary opportunities and supplementing each other's activities. They will be better positioned within the international

FIGURE 2.
SIMPLE MODEL OF ACTIVITIES AND INTERACTION
CURRENT SITUATION IN THE FEHMARNBELT REGION

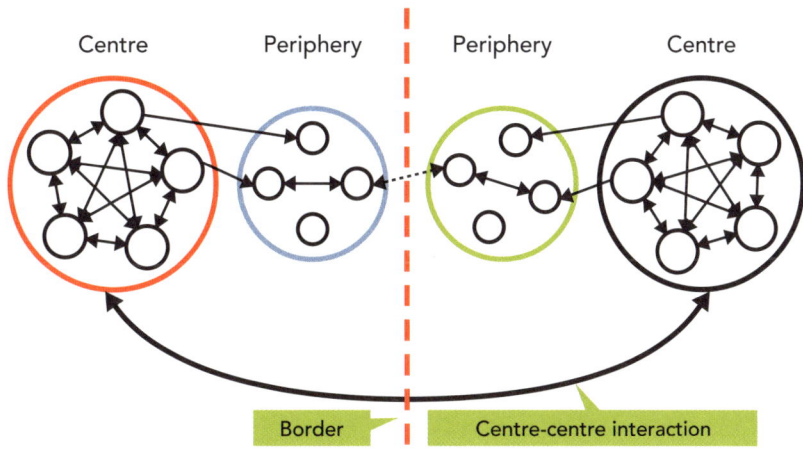

FIGURE 3.
SIMPLE MODEL OF ACTIVITIES AND INTERACTION
FUTURE SCENARIO IN THE FEHMARBELT REGION

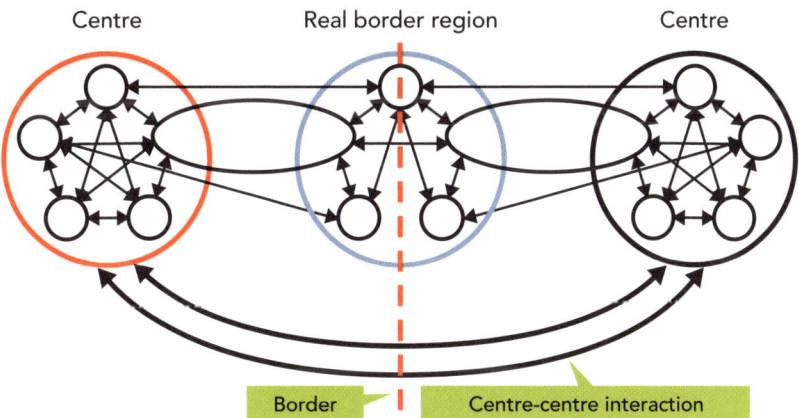

competition between major cities. Moreover, the construction of the fixed Fehmarnbelt link will provide great opportunities for linking the Øresund City and the heavy Scandinavian centres to the network of the high-speed train network that is increasingly set to become the backbone of Europe's mass transport system. These opportunities are too good to miss and the Øresund City, which is basically an international service centre and networking city, will lose ground if this link to the transport system does not materialise. High-speed trains will also contribute to growth in and around the cities with stations.

Those areas (Lolland-Falster, the North Eastern part of Schleswig-Holstein) that border the future fixed link can expect job losses when the link opens and the ferry services cease operating. This is unavoidable, but it could mean that these areas mobilise or require new localisation of government assets. This was, for instance, the case with West Zealand's success in connection with the construction of the Storebælt Bridge where the Danish government was under pressure to move the Copenhagen naval station to Korsør, and did so. However, there are also other gains to be had. The property market will respond to more efficient transport connections and to the fact that access to major cities in the neighbouring country will be much faster and more convenient. The areas that border the fixed link will become "real" border regions with neighbours in another country within daily reach and commuting areas to the centres expanded.

Differences in property prices will not, to the same extent as has been seen around Øresund, promote border commuting although the new role as a hinterland for Copenhagen and Hamburg, Lübeck and Kiel will create new opportunities for what is today regarded as peripheral areas in Lolland Falster and in North-East Schleswig-Holstein. Similarly, the tourist market and the market for border localisation will react to the new-found accessibility. This also means significantly more realistic efforts within the EU's range of border regional policies.

REGIONAL BOUNDARY: THE FEHMARNBELT REGION

For the purpose of this report, we have used different borders of the region based on the themes we are aiming to clarify. The boundary used when we present statistical facts corresponds to the STRING partnership's Fehmarnbelt Region plus the North-Western part of Mecklenburg Vorpommern, which will also be directly affected by the fixed link; see Figure 4. In other parts of the book, the Zealandic archipelago, Bornholm, Scania, Schleswig-Holstein and Hamburg are included. In the analysis of major cities, we have employed a more comprehensive perspective; by analysing local interaction near the future fixed link, we have only looked at those parts of the region that will be directly affected.

FIGURE 4.
MUNICIPALITIES (DENMARK AND SWEDEN) AND DISTRICTS (GERMANY)

The Fehmarnbelt Region extends across three länder in Northern Germany, the eastern part of Denmark and Scania in Southern Sweden. The region can be defined on the basis of several sub-regional levels. First, the three countries, which form part of the region, can be compared followed by the regions in Denmark and Sweden and the länder in Germany. The regions and the länder can further be divided into municipalities in Denmark and Sweden and districts (Kreise) in Germany.

FACTS ABOUT THE REGION

The overall Fehmarnbelt Region covers many differences both between the three countries, of which the region is part, and between the different provinces within the borders of the three countries.

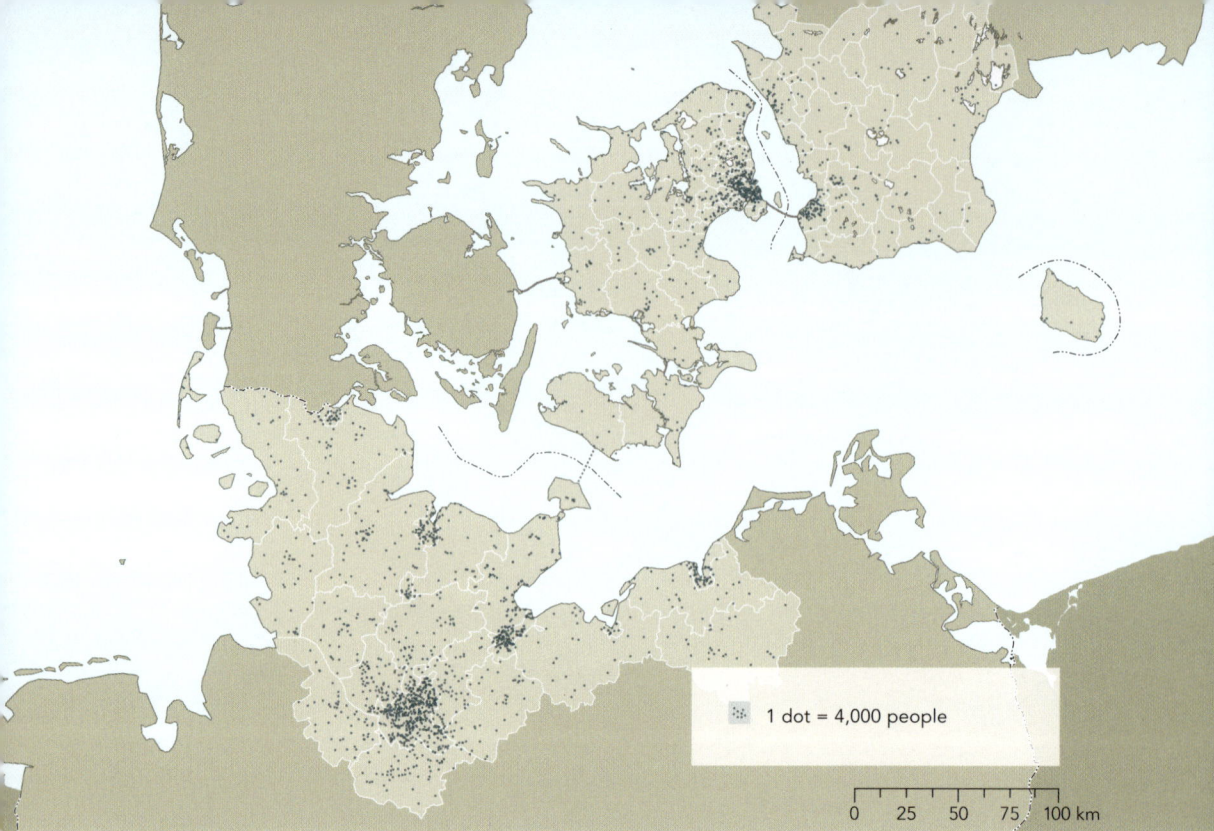

FIGURE 5.
POPULATION OF THE FEHMARNBELT REGION (2008)

Source: Danmarks Statistik, Statistiska Centralbyrån and Statistisches Bundesamt Deutschland

The region comprises 9.3 million people with 1.2 million in the Swedish part, 2.5 million in the Danish part and 5.6 million in the German part. In the Danish and Swedish parts of the region, the younger age groups constitute a larger proportion of the population compared to the German part. According to population forecasts, this trend will become stronger in the future whereas the German population will age.

Measured in gross product, there are differences between the national areas. The average figures are for Scania: EUR 72,000 per person employed (active daytime population) within the region's border, for the Zealand archipelago: EUR 85,000 and for the North German area: EUR 75,000. There are also large differences within the areas. Characteristic for all three regions is that the major city areas and their hinterlands have the highest gross

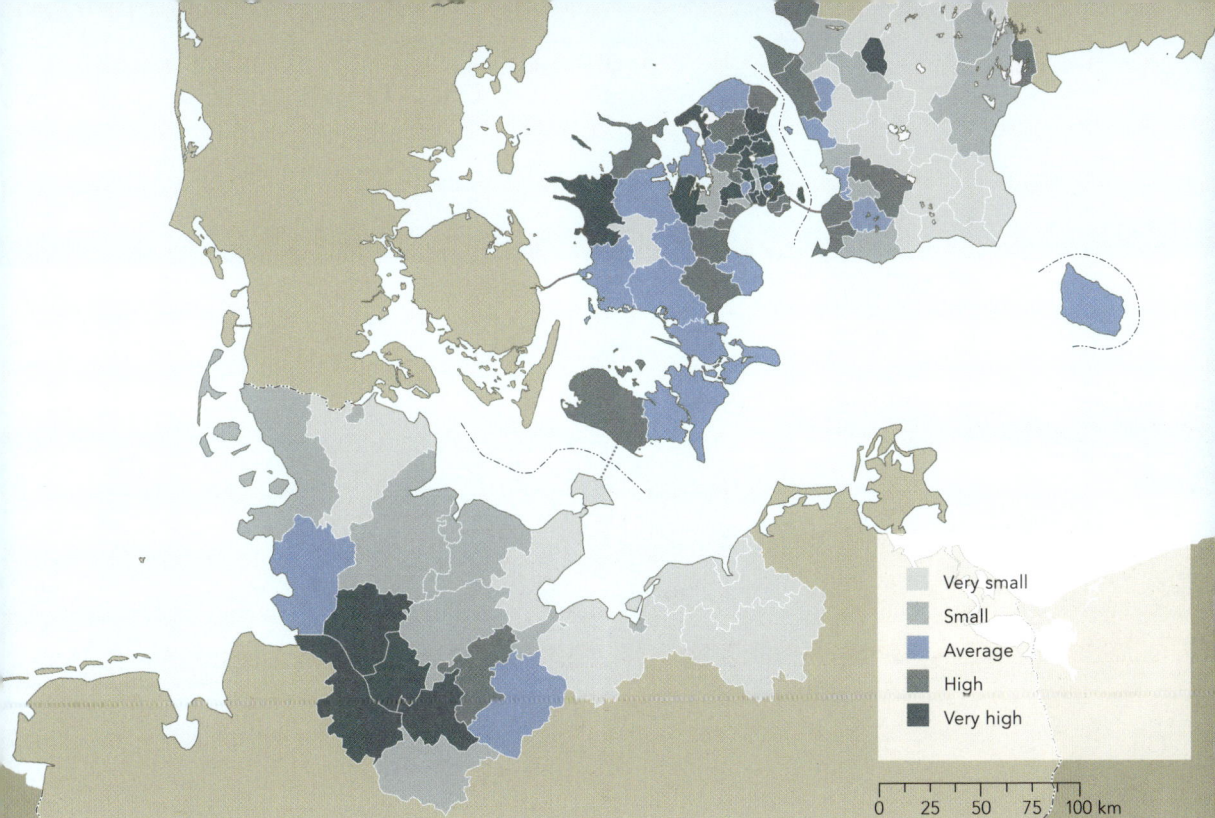

FIGURE 6.
GROSS PRODUCT PER EMPLOYEE. ACTIVE DAYTIME POPULATION (2007)

Source: Danmarks Statistik, Statistiska Centralbyrån, Eurostat

national product per person employed (active daytime population). This applies particularly to Hamburg and Copenhagen. The more rural areas of Northern Germany and Scania have the lowest gross national product per person employed (active daytime population). The opposite trend applies in terms of the unemployment figures. Here, the major cities and their surrounding areas have the lowest unemployment. In addition, there are differences between the three countries. In the Danish part of the region, unemployment is generally very low compared to the German and Swedish parts.

By far the majority of the region's inhabitants are employed within the service and information sectors, with only a small proportion working in agriculture or the manufacturing sectors. Employment within the manufacturing sector has been declining since 1996 in

largely all provinces in the region. Hamburg and Copenhagen are the two financial centres in the Fehmarnbelt Region. In these two cities, the largest proportion of the workforce is employed within the financial and business service-oriented sectors. Also, in other larger cities in the region such as Kiel, Lübeck, Rostock and Malmö, a significant number of people are employed in the financial sector compared to the rest of the region.

Tourism is economically important for the Fehmarnbelt Region and is especially concentrated around the coastal areas in Northern Germany. In 2008, there were 24.8 million overnight stays in the coastal areas of Northern Germany. With regard to the Danish and Swedish parts of the region, the number of overnight stays was somewhat lower. In the Danish part of the region, overnight stays are mainly centred in and around Copenhagen. In Lolland, however, there are also a relatively large number of overnight stays compared to the rest of the Zealand archipelago. In Scania, tourists mainly choose to overnight in Malmö and Helsingborg.

Commuting statistics reveal that the region's workforce is mobile. This is especially the case in the major cities which attract commuters from the surrounding areas. 105,601 individuals commute to Hamburg and its vicinity from areas in Northern Germany. By far the majority, 40 per cent, come from the Lübeck area in Schleswig-Holstein. In the Danish and Swedish parts of the region, Copenhagen and adjoining areas attract most of the commuting from the surrounding areas, i.e. 66,500 commuters. 74 per cent of regional commuters into the metropolitan area of Copenhagen come from Region Zealand, with 26 per cent from Scania. The many commuters from Scania to Copenhagen are largely a result of the increased integration between Denmark and Sweden that followed in the wake of the opening of the Øresund Bridge in 2000.

LOGISTICS AND INFRASTRUCTURE

In the Fehmarnbelt Region, there are two borders that act as system separators and localisation factors for infrastructure, transport and logistics. Compared to the domestic regional traffic, traffic across Fehmarnbelt is weak and cross-border infrastructure consists of ferry services. Although there are also ferries across Øresund, the Øresund Bridge constitutes the significant link. In terms of logistics, the Øresund Bridge has changed Southern Scandinavian systematics. At the same time, the ferry terminals and the bridge are crucial focal points for the entire area's overall infrastructure concept.

Copenhagen Airport is the leading air traffic centre for Denmark and large parts of Northern Europe – and since the opening of the Øresund Bridge, Southern Sweden is part of the local hinterland too. Traffic across the Øresund Bridge reflects the increasing integration of Greater Copenhagen-Malmö-Lund. Due to the short and frequent ferry services between Helsingborg and Elsinore, this border-area is also displaying some signs of integration. The Fehmarnbelt currently shows no evidence of developing cross-border systems except within some retail areas driven by price differences.

The network position of the two major conurbations within the Fehmarnbelt Region – Copenhagen and Hamburg – has been subject to an analysis in relation to two important, international networks. International air transport indicates the potential accessibility for the flow of people and the handling of high value cargo and the internet indicates potential non-physical accessibility for the cities in question. The question is how the metropolises in the Fehmarnbelt Region present themselves as strong centres in the dominating flows of the modern world. Copenhagen is an important centre with flight connections to cities on four continents and a strong European network while Hamburg is served by relatively few international flights and has a modest European network. Compared to other European cities, Copenhagen performs well within key areas in the internet network. Hamburg is also a central hub, but not as important as Copenhagen.

The Fehmarnbelt link and the Øresund Bridge will bring Schleswig-Holstein and Hamburg closer to the Øresund regional market. Perhaps even more importantly, they will create a direct portal for the entire Scandinavian market of almost 20 million inhabitants (Sweden, Denmark and Norway). This will result in a strengthening of the logistical centre of gravity in Northern Germany.

Hamburg is already a strong European logistics region and there is no risk that the city will lose this position to the Øresund Region. By contrast, direct accessibility to the Øresund Region and the Scandinavian market may contribute to Hamburg strengthening its position vis-à-vis competing regions and a certain shift from, for instance, Luxembourg, Belgium and Holland upwards towards Hamburg may occur.

In the same way, the fixed link across Fehmarnbelt will mean that the Øresund Region will strengthen its position as a Scandinavian hub for logistics activities. Direct accessibility to the German market will mean that within a transport radius of three hours, a market of more than 10 million people can be reached. This will be a position of strength for the Øresund Region which may attract more companies from, for instance, Central Sweden.

As a consequence, the Fehmarnbelt link will, first and foremost, mean that Hamburg and the Øresund Region will strengthen their position in each their own way. As a result, we will not immediately see the direct transfer of logistics activities across the Fehmarnbelt. Instead, logistics companies will be able to benefit from the opportunities offered by the link. In the longer-term, differences in transport prices, accessibility in infrastructure, bottlenecks and labour costs may mean that we will see a transfer of activities from one side of Fehmarnbelt to the other.

By stimulating developments in various ways, including through co-ordinated communication and marketing across national borders, the Øresund Region and Hamburg will quickly gain advantages after the opening of the link.

As logistics services become ever more advanced, this sector will also become increasingly knowledge heavy. With increased focus on e.g. traceability, improved security, "green" logistics solutions and postponement activities, the companies' interest in establishing close partnerships with universities and scientific institutions will grow. Access to well-qualified employees will thus become important for creating a competitive logistics concept for the future. In Hamburg, Schleswig-Holstein and the surrounding German regions, there are several research and educational institutions which work with logistics-related issues. Since the late 1990s, the Øresund Region has benefited from crossborder partnerships between the region's universities. There are currently logistics-related training programmes and research at five universities. Together with Schleswig-Holstein and the Hamburg region, the Øresund Region can create a large knowledge centre for the research and development of logistics systems of the future. A knowledge centre which could become an internationally leading institution while at the same time supporting the region's logistics chains.

A NEW EUROPEAN METROPOLITAN REGION ON THE DRAWING BOARD

The Fehmarnbelt Region's urban system is structured with a number of large heavy centres within and outside the region as important nodes (co-ordinating network centres). The Øresund City and Hamburg are crucial for the region's function, activity level, prosperity and future prospects. Without these cities, the region would not have an international format. These two cities, however, are not alone as high level centres. Berlin, Frankfurt and Stockholm also play significant roles in the region, Berlin as Germany's capital and a so far failed bid to establish itself in the elite of world cities. Frankfurt and Stockholm are in a class that Berlin aspires to. Frankfurt has a dominating role within Europe's financial world, which in other major nations is located in the capital. In addition, the city is one of the world's large intercontinental airport centres. Stockholm occupies a significant role in terms of large international business groups as well as being Sweden's capital, but is nevertheless more isolated in respect of global integration than the other heavy centres.

Within a European perspective, the Øresund City is small measured in terms of population, but large in economic strength, access to international networks and scientific output. Hamburg is also relatively small measured in terms of population, but has significant economic strength. The city is in a strong position in terms of access to international networks (except air transport), but is not on the same level as the other three metropolises in terms of scientific output. Berlin is different, i.e. with a larger population, but with weaker economic impact and poor links to international air transport networks. By contrast, the city has a strong position with regard to scientific production. Finally, Stockholm has a relatively small population and significant economic strength while having relatively poorer access to international air transport network compared to the Øresund City. Stockholm, however, is strong in terms of scientific output. The four metropolises each dominate their hinterland and compete directly with each other in respect of customer-related service businesses, cultural offerings, access to terminals and use of business-to-business services.

The way in which the general international business to business service networks function shows notable patterns. We have used the Taylor group's analysis of the cities' roles, see Figure 7. The strongest role is that of London, which is the real world city of Europe. Further down in the city hierarchy is Paris, Amsterdam, Brussels and Frankfurt. The cities interact in bands, cliques or families where they have strong mutual interaction patterns and interaction patterns with the rest of the world, which are uniform. The individual city may participate in several bands. Between them, the Danish, Swedish and German cities do not demonstrate any particular degree of mutual cohesion but are part of different

FIGURE 7.
EUROPEAN GROUPINGS OF INTERACTING CITIES AT HIERARCHICALLY DEFINED LEVELS

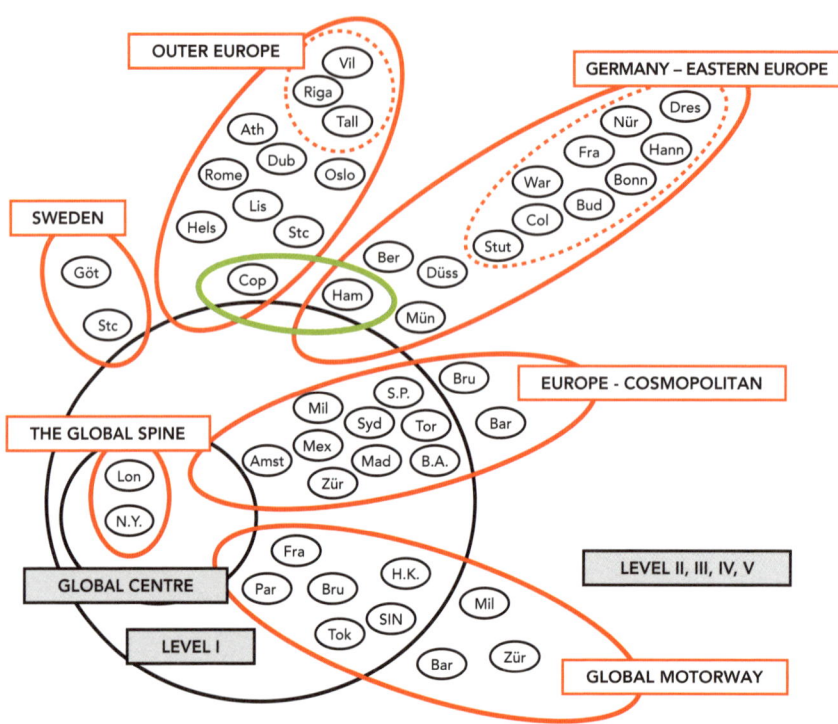

The complex figure comprises the Taylor group's analysis, see Chapter 4. Circles denote levels, ovals indicate groupings (bands, families, cliques), and dotted ovals indicate groupings of smaller cities that interact with the dominating city groupings. Note that the individual city can be part of more than one grouping. The potential new interaction is indicated by a green signature.

FIGURE 8.
CITIES LOCATED CLOSER TO THE FUTURE FIXED FEHMARNBELT LINK'S MID-POINT THAN 300 KM

bands of cities, some of them together, others on their own. In the outer Europe grouping, Copenhagen plays a leading role. However, Stockholm and a number of other cities also contribute. Another grouping is Germany – Eastern Europe, and here you find Berlin and Hamburg (together with Dusseldorf and Munich) on the main list. Moreover, it is interesting to note that, with the exception of Frankfurt, no cities from Denmark, Sweden or Germany rank among the hierarchy's two upper levels.

Interaction is always an expression of added value. As a result, it makes sense to examine new opportunities and what these analyses can be used for. The view is that if stronger links, first between Copenhagen and Hamburg, and second with Stockholm and Berlin could be created, a North European band could result, i.e. a network of mutually strongly linked cities with uniform partnership relations with the rest of the world. Such a band could claim a position at a higher level within the continent's urban hierarchy and thus contribute to development, growth and wealth.

The urban system within and close to the Fehmarnbelt Region includes a number of other centres. There are other large cities of which some with larger or smaller justification claim metropolis status. Three large German cities are found on a somewhat lower level in the city hierarchy than the Øresund City, Hamburg and Berlin. They consist of the specialised centres Braunschweig–Wolfsburg, Hanover and Bremen and are overshadowed by Hamburg but nevertheless play strong independent roles as industrial centres, meeting places and gateway cities.

The region's urban system is also structured by a number of other major cities that play a role as regional centres with a strong concentration of hinterland-oriented public service activities. Most of these cities have a university, some have gateway function and all have considerable industrial niches. As part of the picture, there are a series of medium-sized cities in the Fehmarnbelt Region whose roles are mainly local although a few, like some of the major centres, also function as a supplement to, and interact with, the larger gateway cities.

THE LABOUR MARKET: POTENTIAL INTEGRATION

The benefits of a cross-border region with significant labour mobility between the two sides stem from the fact that commuters themselves contribute to reducing border barriers and promoting social cohesion across the whole of the region. Moreover, such a new cross-border region profits from the economic benefits of a large and diverse labour market.

Barriers to mobility in cross-border regions are created by geographical distance and other impediments to travel between two countries: administrative barriers, different labour market conditions, qualification barriers and other barriers in the daily lives of the populations of these regions. Furthermore, information about the conditions on the other side is often fragmented. Strategies and initiatives aimed at reducing border barriers are based upon two principles: (a) problem solving, such as harmonisation of regulations through bilateral agreements, and (b) information and consultancy. Strategic success also depends on the learning process of the labour force and of the consultants.

Cross-border labour mobility comes from differences between the two border regions. These provide an incentive for people to move to the neighbouring region. If the conditions on both sides were more or less the same, there would be no incentive to cross the border. However, if the differences are sufficiently strong, the barriers can be overcome. So, there is a tension between barriers and incentives. The third component is the market's level of information concerning these two factors. On the one hand, the right level of information will raise awareness of the benefits of labour mobility and on the other, it reduces the constraints on cross-border mobility.

For most of the mobility barriers, an ongoing process of reduction is likely, either through agreements and regulations, sharing experiences, learning processes or by information and consultancy services. However, reduction proceeds at different speeds for different barriers. In the long-run, the most important challenges will be language barriers, acceptance of qualifications and some psychological barriers.

For some established cross-border regions with a long tradition for cooperation and often substantial numbers of commuters, we have analysed current cross-border mobility, barriers and incentives as well as the information and advice provided to the labour force in relation to their relevance to the future of the Fehmarnbelt Region. Within the selected regions, the consultancy structure of authorities, consultants and internet services frequently consists of an information centre, which helps to overcome the many barriers, complemented by institutions responsible for dealing with specific problems. In addition, EURES offices specialise in labour market consultancy.

The number of commuters from south to north across the Danish-German land border has grown significantly over recent years whereas the flow in the opposite direction has stagnated at a low level. This asymmetric trend developed during the 1990s when labour market conditions on the Danish side improved considerably and unemployment rates began to fall below those of Germany. Particularly in recent years, the incentives inherent in the Danish labour market have been the main driver for cross-border mobility. In keeping with increasing cross-border commuting, a broad consultancy structure for the mobile labour force has been established around the information centre in Padborg. With its qualities and experience, but with some deficiencies, too, the consultancy structure can be a prototype upon which similar structures at Fehmarnbelt could be established. Some additional elements would, however, have to be organised or located differently.

For the region around the Fehmarnbelt, the Øresund Region is not especially relevant as a prototype. First, the spatial structure differs between the two regions, especially around the border areas. Furthermore, the incentives for cross-border mobility in Øresund has been driven by price differences for properties and homes, which are a strong factor in commuting from the Swedish to the Danish side of the Øresund. According to our 2010 analysis, these incentives do not exist around the Fehmarnbelt. Moreover, the attractiveness of a large and diverse labour market close to the border (which is part of the Øresund Region's character), does not exist around the Fehmarnbelt either. At the same time, the information and consultancy structure around Øresund provides a large number of examples for building similar structures around Fehmarnbelt. In particular, the information service "Øresunddirekt" (website and information centre) that serves as a platform for knowledge about the labour market on both sides of Øresund could serve as a model.

Despite the strong incentives for labour mobility to the north of Zealand, the minor language barriers and a good consultancy structure, the number of commuters crossing Øresund from Sweden lags significantly behind those heading towards Denmark's capital from the Danish hinterland. This also applies to the prototype for all European border regions, the German-Dutch EUREGIO, although the consultancy and strategies aimed at removing barriers have existed for many years. Even EUREGIO, therefore, is far from being a fully integrated labour market with strong bi-directional mobility.

In the region surrounding Fehmarnbelt, the labour markets are presently almost completely separate. There are no sufficiently strong preconditions for achieving the level of cross-border commuting comparable to the levels at the German Danish land border or in the Øresund Region. On the one hand, a clear incentive for German commuters is provided by the favourable labour market conditions in Denmark. On the other hand, even with a fixed link, commuting distances between the large population and job centres will remain so great that mobility is likely to be largely limited to weekend commuters. If we apply today's perspectives, we expect no strong incentives for an increase in commuter activity because of regional differences in living costs, property prices, salaries and wages. Regional differences, which in other cross-border regions have led to considerable commuting, have not yet come into play.

We expect a strong development of information and consulting infrastructure and further progress in the removal of the border barriers to take place simultaneously with the construction of the fixed link. An increase in the number of commuters can be expected as a result of interaction of these impulses. We quantify this impact using the scenarios of commuter mobility.

MOBILITY: NEW COMMUTER FLOWS

The German and Danish labour markets, particularly in the Fehmarnbelt Region, are largely distinct from each other – as is common with many other border regions in Europe. Cross-border commuting between the two countries is characterised by significant differences in the flows between north-south and south-north directions. This is owing to the current market situation where the Danish side offers a greater incentive for cross-border employment. The absence of systematic, statistical information about cross-border commuters in

the Fehmarnbelt Region severely limits the scope of our analysis. In total, we estimate that some 11,600 individuals work in Denmark and live in Germany while 1,600 individuals work in Germany and live in Denmark (2008).

Compared to the German-Danish land border, the Fehmarnbelt connection has roughly six times fewer commuters in both directions. We believe that the longer commuting distance is an important factor behind commuting in a south-north direction. The flow, therefore, would be significantly affected by the construction of the fixed link. For commuters in the opposite direction, however, travel patterns seem to depend much less on physical distance, but more on opportunities for cross-border employment (e.g. as in the German metropolitan regions).

Price levels at the fixed link will be an important factor in the development of future commuting patterns. Assuming a special fare of, e.g. EUR 20 per passage for commuters on the new link, the immediate effect on the German metropolitan regions numbers from Germany to Denmark would be in the order of a 50 per cent increase.

We believe that physical proximity does not currently play a decisive role for Danish commuters to Germany as the majority work some distance from the border. This commuter category will, therefore, not be seriously affected by the fixed link in itself. However, we believe that steps towards the integration of the labour markets (e.g. reducing administrative barriers) would have a strong effect on such commuters. In particular, we wish to emphasise the importance of inter-regional co-operation agreements that will become much easier to achieve than agreements at governmental level and are significantly more efficient.

The role of the Fehmarnbelt fixed link in a new cross-border labour market will be substantial. Nevertheless, forecasts based on the experience from the labour markets at the Danish-German land border and in the Øresund Region are unrealistic in the short-term. Long distances will remain an important factor in limiting cross-border labour mobility in the area. Hopes for greater economic co-operation in general and cross-border commuting in particular are based on the creation of a new transport hub near Fehmarnbelt, which would attract investment and generate employment in the region. The possible effects hereof can be inferred from our integration scenarios of which the most favourable predicts a doubling of current commuter numbers.

The model team has presented a new assessment of the commuting potential across the Fehmarnbelt once the fixed link is commissioned and the necessary policy steps taken to reduce the mental distance between the German and Danish regions separated by the Fehmarnbelt. The team presents a status quo scenario, which is an update from the 2008 assessment for 2020 as well as four cross-border commuting scenarios:

1) implementation of the fixed link
2) implementation of the fixed link + moderate integration of the labour market
3) implementation of the fixed link + high integration of the labour market
4) implementation of the fixed link + high integration of the labour market
   + Hamburg-Copenhagen axis integration

Figure 9 summarises the weekly commuter flow across the Fehmarnbelt as envisaged in the various scenarios.

One part of the mobile labour force, namely those who – generally once a week – commute between the metropolises and usually use trains or fly, are in a special position. This group specialises in particular jobs in the cities, mainly in highly-skilled activities in the

FIGURE 9.
COMMUTING ACROSS THE FEHMARNBELT 2020 – ALTERNATIVE SCENARIOS

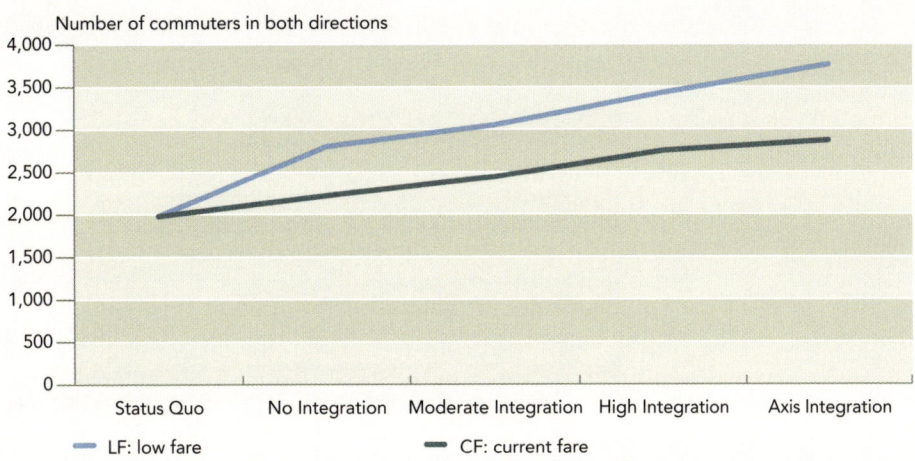

service sector usually within management, finance and business services, culture and media, research and development and higher education. Since they have specific personal characteristics (age, education, skills, etc.) which differ from those of the average commuter, they show different mobility patterns, for instance in the form of a greater willingness to commute over long distances. In Germany, fairly large numbers of commuters travel between the major cities so we have made further calculations specifically for this group. The actual flows are very small. Fewer than 100 individuals commute from Hamburg to Copenhagen and even fewer from Copenhagen to Hamburg. In Figure 10, we have calculated the potential flows between the two metropolises with increased train speed and cost structures and we have used the application of the high integration model.

In the event of a strong barrier reduction following the opening of the Fehmarnbelt link, for which we have used the high integration scenario, and in the event of symmetric incentives, we can expect commuter figures of about 1,000 to Copenhagen and nearly

FIGURE 10.
ESTIMATES FOR WEEKLY TRAIN COMMUTERS BETWEEN HAMBURG AND COPENHAGEN (2020)
HIGH INTEGRATION

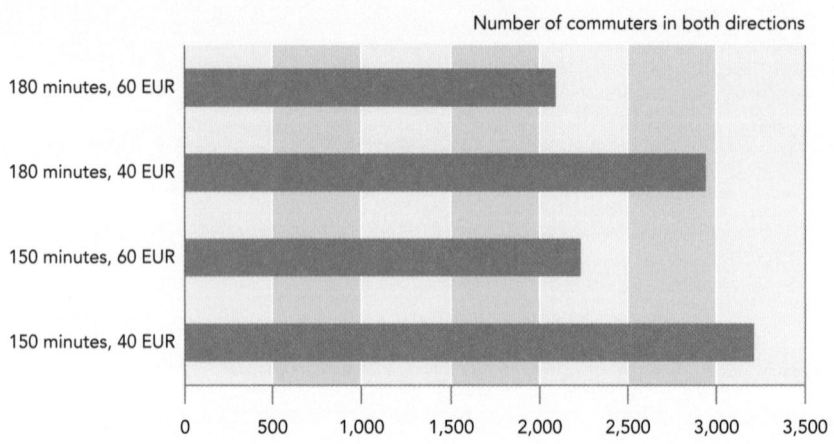

1,300 to Hamburg for the 150 minute journey and EUR 60 fare (2,300 per week). For the EUR 40 fare, the result will be 1,400 and 1,800 respectively for the 150 minute journey (3,200 per week).

The links between the labour markets in the metropolitan regions, Hamburg and Copenhagen, are currently very weak with current travelling times being 280 minutes with fares of EUR 60. In addition to the dramatically shorter train travelling times generated by the Fehmarnbelt link, significant efforts to diminish border barriers are needed to achieve the numbers projected by our study of long-distance rail commuting.

STRONG BUSINESS CLUSTERS: OPPORTUNITIES FOR PARTNERSHIPS

Scania, Zealand, Bornholm, Schleswig-Holstein, Hamburg and Mecklenburg-Vorpommern each have their own industrial profiles, focusing on specific clusters and their development. While these regions differ, they also operate clusters of similar structure and focus. The object of the cluster analysis in this report is to identify clusters for potential cooperation. The immediate strategy is based on the fact that life sciences and health are important business sectors in most parts of the Fehmarnbelt Region. This research focus of many universities is reflected in the cluster policy of the respective organisations. Also, the business sectors of food and information technology (including the media) are widely represented in the Fehmarnbelt Region where they have important roles in the regional economies and are the target of cluster development efforts. A fourth area with potential for regional partnerships is logistics, focusing on shipping. A fifth is wind energy/green technology and a sixth is tourism (including business tourism). There are other strong sectors although these only cover parts of the region. Maritime industries play an important role in all North German regions, nanotechnology in Schleswig-Holstein and Scania, the financial sector (with business-to-business services) is important in Copenhagen and Hamburg as, indeed, are the cultural sector and airport-related activities. Aviation is strong in Hamburg, but we have been unable to discover information from other parts of the Fehmarnbelt Region although we would like to do so in view of the central role of the industry.

Life sciences/health is mentioned as a cluster by all regions. External relations with life sciences/health clusters in Schleswig-Holstein are directed towards neighbours in the Baltic area, in particular towards the life sciences' network in Mecklenburg-Vorpommern (BioCon-Valley). Based on participation in the ScanBalt network (life sciences meta clusters in the Baltic region), the BioCon Valley has connections to one of the strongest life sciences clusters in Europe, the Medicon Valley in the Øresund Region. With an expansion of these links, not least inspired by the upgrading of the transport corridor between Hamburg-Lübeck and Copenhagen-Malmö, and promoted by different and complementary priorities of the two networks, a "twin" life sciences cluster in the Fehmarnbelt Region would achieve an undisputed top position in Europe.

Food networks and clusters across the Fehmarnbelt Region are partners here as well, particularly between North Germany and Øresund Food together with the Scania Food Innovation Network. Objectives and recommendations for the future include the establishment of joint cluster management for the Schleswig-Holstein region and the metropolitan region of Hamburg and closer relations with the Øresund Food Network for which a fixed Fehmarnbelt link would serve as a catalyst.

The information technology (IT) and media cluster should focus on cooperation between Hamburg and Copenhagen, especially within the media sector, since Hamburg and Copenhagen are the two dominant media locations in the western Baltic. Despite the language barrier which is especially relevant here, there is considerable potential for further cooperation as a result of a fixed Fehmarnbelt link.

Links to the logistics networks in the Baltic region are supported by the LogOnBaltic network. In connection with the future upgrading of the Fehmarnbelt route, cooperation between the logistics clusters of Northern Germany and the Øresund Region could help to promote and coordinate the logistics industry, especially along the Fehmarnbelt corridor. Eventually, a "Fehmarnbelt logistics cluster" could be created connecting the two gravity centres of Hamburg/Lübeck and Copenhagen/Malmö.

FIGURE 11
SUMMARY DIAGRAM: CLUSTERS IN ALL OR IN SOME REGIONS OF THE FEHMARNBELT REGION

Present in all regions:
- Life science/health
- Food
- Information technology (plus the media)
- Logistics (with focus on maritime)
- Wind energy/green technology
- Tourism (inclusive of business tourism)

Present in some regions:
- Financial sector (with business services)
- Cultural sector (media)
- Airport related activities, civil aviation
- Nanotechnology
- Maritime industries

The generation and use of renewable energy (wind) is a growing part of the economy. International competition has intensified significantly in recent years, especially based on competitive Danish, Dutch and German (Lower Saxony, Mecklenburg-Vorpommern) industries. This makes cluster co-operation particularly important. Currently, there are links between Northern Germany and Southern Denmark as a result of the presence of important companies in the region as well as between the University of Flensburg and the University of Southern Denmark (together with regional development agencies) within the "FURGY" project ("Future Renewable Energy"). This could be a model for cooperation between the German and Danish parts of the Fehmarnbelt Region and could comprise research institutions in Nakskov and in the rest of the Region Zealand.

Although important for the regional economies, tourism is an area in which the regions see each other as competitors. Hamburg and Copenhagen compete for metropolitan tourism, including business tourism (meetings, incentives, conferences, events). The two metropolises also compete for cultural tourists and families looking for a city product. The many fine beaches around the Fehmarnbelt Region are also attractive destinations, especially for families and for water sport enthusiasts. Although competition is strong, opportunities for partnerships should be explored and joint cluster development should be placed on the agenda.

Current nanotechnology cluster relations between Germany and Denmark are mainly linked to the University of Southern Denmark in Sønderborg. Given the strong competition between the microtechnology clusters in Germany, e.g. in Saxony, building partnerships with other networks makes sense. There is actual set a great pressure to establish cooperation on material technology/nanotechnology in relation to existing and planned mega format research facilities. Future changes in the Fehmarnbelt Region will create opportunities for cooperation between the Øresund Region and Hamburg (c.f. the following section).

We also believe that the potential for co-operation between Copenhagen and Hamburg should be explored in terms of financial and related services as well as for the cultural sector. The cultural sector effort could be linked to the media industry. Airport related activities should also be explored with a view to cooperation.

THE WORLD OF SCIENCE: NEW AXIS BASED ON POSITIONS OF STRENGTH

The Fehmarnbelt Region comprises five scientific centres. The Øresund City belongs among the group of Europe's scientific metropolises; Hamburg and Kiel are research cities at a slightly lower level while Rostock and Lübeck belong to the group of regional research centres.

Denmark, Sweden and Germany are international heavyweights in the world of science. The same applies to a number of metropolises of which three German urban regions (Berlin, Munich, Dortmund-Düsseldorf-Cologne), one Swedish (Stockholm-Uppsala) and one Danish-Swedish (The Øresund City) feature on the international top 40 list. None of these cities, however, has a place among the world cities' global top level, but are considered second level centres. It is also notable that in terms of growth these cities are not doing particularly well. Asian and South European cities are overtaking our centres and racing to the upper global levels. However, in terms of the networks, characterised by partnerships with researchers from other top 40 cities, they have a strong position and, in this respect, Danish, Swedish and German metropolises are not losing ground.

Research partnerships between scientific environments in different large cities will accelerate, with international cooperation showing particularly high rates of increase. Analysis of the global level shows that cities with international profiles in the form of bilingualism (Montreal, the Øresund City, Aachen-Liege-Maastricht) have an advantage in so far as international collaboration is concerned. They have primary contact with more than one network.

Three European cities have leading positions in the global networks: London, Paris and the Amsterdam Region are the continent's world cities. The largest centres in the expanded Fehmarnbelt Region (Berlin, the Øresund City, Stockholm-Uppsala, Hamburg) are well linked to the leading trio and each account for consistent international partnership profiles. The links between the four major centres is such that Berlin and Hamburg are each other's largest partners on a global level, and the same is the case for the Øresund City and Stockholm-Uppsala, In addition, there are moderately strong co-operation axes between the Øresund City and Hamburg and between the Øresund City and Berlin, but not between Stockholm-Uppsala and the two German cities.

The two main axes, the Scandinavian and North German, can and should be supplemented by a third main axis which would strengthen the moderately strong axis between Hamburg and the Øresund City. This means that the two centres can further strengthen the links to their already well-established networks, which in turn, will offer supplementary as well as complementary opportunities. Potentially, a strengthening of the link between Hamburg and the Øresund City will mean that these two centres together will raise themselves to a research dominating level which is actually drawn by Europe's main centres. This, however, will require some effort, but it is an inspiring challenge to develop just as strong a link between Hamburg and the Øresund City as currently exists between Hamburg and Berlin and between the Øresund City and Stockholm-Uppsala. We recommend that the three regional North German centres, Kiel, Rostock and Lübeck, become part of such efforts.

The five research centres have different profiles, but also share some common features. The Øresund City's position of strength is primarily based on health research, geosciences and the natural environment. In Hamburg, focus is on health together with traditional natural science. Kiel's strength is centred on geo-disciplines and on marine science. Rostock also focuses on marine science while Lübeck has a specialisation profile, which exclusively focuses on health.

We have analysed the opportunities for partnerships by isolating those disciplines with potential for developing new links and which can partly supplement, partly complement, each other. We have also pointed to obvious opportunities for strengthening the interaction between the centres in order to achieve gains. On the basis of positions of strength, north as well as south of the Fehmarnbelt, a number of marine disciplines (oceanography, marine biology, limnology) health-science fields (anaesthesiology, endocrinology & metabolism, immunology, research into infectious diseases, rheumatology, haematology) the geoscience areas (soil science, meteorology and atmospheric science, multidisciplinary geosciences) and two traditional natural science disciplines (physics: particles and fields; mathematical biology) would be able to supplement each other at a high level.

Similarly, it should be recommended that disciplines that are strong on one side of the Baltic Sea and medium strong on the other, aim for complementary interaction. This is the case with a range of health-science disciplines where neuroimaging, virology, radiology, nuclear medicine, chemical medicine, oncology, dermatology, otorhinolaryngology, biophysics, orthopaedics and spectroscopy are strong in the south and medium-strong in the north while allergy research, nutrition & dietetics, research into public health, the environment, and parasitology are strong in the north and medium-strong in the south. This also applies to some geosciences disciplines where the south is strong within geochemistry and geophysics, while the north is strong within palaeontology, geology and mineralogy. Finally, there are development opportunities for complementary disciplines for some of the traditional natural science disciplines where astronomy and astrophysics are strong in the south while the north is strong within the disciplines of evolutionary biology, ecology, biodiversity and environmental research.

With regard to partnership relations, it should be noted that these are currently at a low level between the northern and southern parts of the Fehmarnbelt Region. Of the five cities' combined output of 60,181 papers in 2006-2008, 391 have authors from both the northern and southern part of the Fehmarnbelt Region, largely between the Øresund City and Hamburg. However, it should also be pointed out that there are opportunities for mobilising partnerships based on uniform positions of strength and that; in addition, there are strong grounds for focusing on a range of scientific disciplines where one part of the region has a strong position while the other has only medium strength. There are reasons for optimism, but a serious effort is needed. Such efforts comprise focus on the development of more partnership-oriented frameworks and on information about each other's respective advantages. We also recommend further analysis of existing partnership relations.

It is clear that a series of initiatives is currently under way to strengthen research within material science and nanotechnology. No fewer than four new scientific avantgarde-facilities in the form of gigantic research laboratories are under establishment. Two of these are located in Hamburg, European XFEL (an experimental facility which generates extremely fast x-ray flashes) and PETRA (synchrotron x-ray facility) and two in the Øresund City, the European Spallation Source (European experimental facility based on the world's strongest neutron source) and MAX IV (synchrotron radiation facility). Accounting for investments running billions of euro, these projects will also establish new contacts and new partnership relations with the business community. The perspectives for research into material technology and life science research are significant and are monitored with great interest by those commercial sectors that have the potential to participate in, and exploit, the planned research activities. It should be noted, however, that efforts within the field of nano-science and nano-technology are based on current productive forces on a level below the top-level. The Danish-Swedish-German environment with a demonstrated top level is Berlin, which plays a leading role within the discipline's network. We recommend that Berlin be included in these efforts.

THE PROPERTY MARKET: THE NEAR AREAS

As part of the project, we have estimated the impact of accessibility on house prices. Our estimates confirm that a fixed link will have a substantial and statistically significant, positive impact on house prices. These estimates do not take other future dynamic changes into account, such as new property developments or new commuting preferences. An 8 per cent increase in the price of the average house on the German side corresponds to an absolute increase in 2009 prices of EUR 16,000. The estimates for the Danish side are somewhat more uncertain, but can be expected to fall within the same range. Data from housing markets in other areas with high-speed train links show an overall increase in residential property values of EUR 1.6 billion on the German side of the Fehmarnbelt. The total increase for the local housing markets on the Danish side would amount to at least EUR 1.4 billion. The total minimum increase – assuming high-speed rail service links – thus amounts to EUR 3 billion in 2009 prices (providing the economic structure in Denmark and Germany remains unchanged). We assume, therefore, that the improved infrastructure in the areas near the fixed Fehmarnbelt link will result in relocations from Greater Copenhagen to the Danish areas near the link and similarly, relocations from Hamburg to the North German areas near the link.

THE CULTURAL SECTOR: INTERACTION PERSPECTIVES

Culture is a location factor and a factor behind change and challenges for the Fehmarnbelt Region. In order to gather different experiences and ideas regarding the cultural potential of the region, in-depth interviews were carried out with professionals on a range of issues:

- Personal links to the Fehmarnbelt Region
- The role of culture within a national and international framework
- The role of culture in rural and urban environments
- The role of cultural identities in regional projects
- Cultural cooperation across national borders
- Cultural potential and challenges for the Fehmarnbelt Region
- Recommendations for improving cultural life within the region

The main results of the interviews are that relationships with – and the definition of – the Fehmarnbelt Region differ significantly, that only a minority of the interviewees are familiar with the official extent of the region, and that the majority of interviewees did not include Scania in the Fehmarnbelt Region. Since the Fehmarnbelt Region is not yet a well-known (cultural) region, communication about the region is seen as vital. Several interviewees emphasised the importance of verbal communication and a visual profile of the region while also pointing out the risk of empty rhetoric and pure marketing.

With regard to the cultural potential and challenges for the Fehmarnbelt Region, many interviewees pointed to the weaknesses of existing cultural life within the region, particularly in relation to quantity (except for the cities). This weakness was explained by the low population density outside the centres, and also by the general structural problems in the region's rural areas. However, some important cultural projects ought to be mentioned, such as the well-established Schleswig-Holstein Music Festival, the Festival JazzBaltica and the recent initiative on the part of the Royal Danish Embassy "Kulturbrücke Fehmarn Belt". Several interviewees emphasised that political involvement in the cultural sector is essential for the success of the region.

The Øresund Region is a source of inspiration, but also provides a salutary lesson. Some interviewees mentioned that cultural cooperation across national borders has only existed at times when EU funding was available. Also, against the background of the experiences from the Øresund Region, "regional identity" is treated as a rather delicate issue. The focus on a "common identity" within the Fehmarnbelt Region is seen as rather dangerous and unnecessary.

With regard to recommendations for improving cultural life within the region, several interviewees suggested establishing artists' residencies in the region's rural areas. Closely connected to this is the idea of supporting joint exhibitions or events across national borders. To secure a high level of professionalism and ambition, working scholarships and the co-funding of concerts, exhibitions and workshops are seen as important. Concerning existing cultural offerings, there is general agreement that events for young people should be substantially improved. And "everything should be linked to good transport services", as one of the interviewees said. In this context, the importance of local public transport was stressed several times.

Mobility is seen as one of the basic requirements for cultural participation. Mobility is not only defined as public or private transport, but also as a financial and intellectual capacity. However in the view of several interviewees, the main challenges for the future cultural life of the region lie in the cost of crossing the link and the access to cultural institutions and events, both in the cities and in the region's rural areas. Another frequently raised and important issue is improved access to relevant, up-to-date information about cultural issues and events within the region.

There is no doubt about the important role of culture in the lives of local people as well as in terms of the region's development. Culture can be seen as the glue in the growth process, but should not be exploited for the political project "the region".

YOUTH: SAME VALUES BUT IGNORANCE ABOUT NEIGHBOURING COUNTRIES

In order to obtain a "baseline study" of the attitudes in the three countries involved in the new geography around the fixed link across the Fehmarnbelt, a survey was carried out in late 2009/early 2010 among students in the final year of their high school level education (aged 18-20) in the Fehmarnbelt Region. The survey reveals a great deal of asymmetry in terms of knowledge about the neighbouring countries. Despite this, interest in studying, working or living permanently elsewhere in the region is fairly high among young people (except that young Danes and Swedes are not attracted by the idea of living or studying in the German part of the region).

An important focal point in the survey was the difference between young people in the three countries with regard to general values and attitudes towards the labour market, housing and culture, politics and environmental issues. In general, it appears that the main dividing line for these themes lies between the sexes and not so much between the countries. Young people of the region have more in common in respect of their general values and attitudes than there are differences that separate them.

The topics covered in the survey, which comprised 800 young people were:

– Values and attitudes in general
– Attitudes towards the labour market
– Future society and politics
– Environmental issues
– Housing and culture
– Interaction between the countries
– Consequences of a permanent Fehmarnbelt link

Young people from Germany and young Danish women have the highest rate of post-materialistic values while Swedish men are the most materialistic; Swedish women are neutral. An interesting finding is that young Swedes who are generally assumed to be among the most post-materialistic in Europe are much less post-materialistic than young people from the other two countries.

Important values "today" are much the same among young people in all three countries. Family relationships and relationships between boyfriend/girlfriend are very important, as is earning money among some sub-groups. A happy life with parties to go to and hobbies to enjoy are important to men in all three countries – but less so among women. Enjoying life has great appeal at this stage of life.

The list of priorities 15 years from now gives a very clear picture of "responsible breadwinners". Young people today expect to have started a family within 15 years, have good quality housing and an interesting job. To achieve these goals they need to be healthy. We also noticed that earning money has become considerably more important for the future than is the case today. When it comes to more general values like censorship, abortion, ethnic diversity and religion, the major differences are between countries rather than gender.

Traditional job characteristics are ranked almost in the same order by young people from all three countries: young Germans are a little more materialistic when it comes to working conditions, i.e. they want to earn money while young Swedes and Danes regard work as both a part of their social life and a necessity. Job security is very important to women from all three countries. Job security is only important to young men from Sweden. Young German and Danish men are fairly indifferent.

When it comes to career, answers clearly demonstrate the gender gap. Men in general opt for technical and computer-related jobs while women prefer jobs that are people-oriented. The list of selected jobs is similar in the three countries, with only a few exceptions. A teacher at "gymnasium" level is much more highly rated in Denmark among both men and women than in Sweden.

There are distinct differences in political attitudes between men and women and these differences are most evident in the right of the spectrum. There are far more men among right extremists, while women tend to gravitate towards the centre or the left. It can be concluded that political interest is much higher among young Danes and Germans than among young Swedes – now and in the future.

When asked about their ideal future society, the more materialistic attitudes among Swedish men are reflected in their strong interest in an industrial society. By contrast, a knowledge society seems to be the preferred choice for all other sub-groups – around 50 per cent of all young people (two thirds of young Danes) opt for this type of society.

Another important issue relating to the future is how to solve our current environmental problems. We have found a striking difference between the countries in respect of alternatives: young Swedes are in favour of market solutions, young Germans prefer legislation and regulations while young Danes think that environmental issues are overrated.

With regard to future housing, there is complete unanimity. Eight out of 10 young people declare that they would prefer a detached house. After finishing school, however, the most important nearby amenities are friends, workplace, alternatively higher education and public transport. Within a 15-year perspective, most young people expect to have started a family, which makes a child-friendly environment important as well.

One of the main issues addressed in this survey is a possible asymmetry in knowledge about the respective neighbouring countries. The results from the survey clearly demonstrate the existence of such asymmetry. Contact with – and knowledge of – the German part of the region is rather limited. Contact between the three countries is mainly in the form of visits by young Danes and Swedes to Germany (possibly on their way to skiing holidays) seldom the other way round. The Danish part of the region, including Copenhagen,

FIGURE 12.
OVERVIEW OF THE THREE SUB-REGIONS' ATTRACTION FORCE TO YOUNG PEOPLE IN THE NEIGHBOURING COUNTRIES

Do you want to:	Work in Denmark	Live in Denmark	Study in Denmark
Young Germans	Yes	Yes	Yes
Young Swedes	Yes	Yes	Yes
	Work in Germany	**Live in Germany**	**Study in Germany**
Young Danes	Yes	No	No
Young Swedes	Yes	50/50	50/50
	Work in Sweden	**Live in Sweden**	**Study in Sweden**
Young Danes	Yes	No	No
Young Germans	Yes	Yes	Yes

is very well known to young people from both Sweden and Germany while young Danes and Swedes know almost nothing about Hamburg. Only a few young people from the two countries are able to mention tourist attractions in Hamburg. Young Germans' knowledge of Malmö is equally limited.

When it comes to studying, working or living in the neighbouring countries, contact between Denmark and Sweden is well established and interest is quite high. In relation to Germany, interest among young Germans in the other two countries is much higher than the other way around. Young Danes and Swedes are not interested in living or studying in Germany, but see working there as an interesting possibility. Young Germans, on the other hand, are interested in studying and living and, to an even greater extent, working in one of the two other countries

CHAPTER 2
MAPS AND FIGURES

PETRA AULIN, JACEK ROKICKI & SIGNE SCHILLING

The Fehmarnbelt Region comprises parts of Northern Germany, the eastern part of Denmark and parts of Southern Sweden. The region can be defined on the basis of three sub-regional levels. First on country level, i.e. the three countries comprised by the region, and secondly, on regional/länder level in Denmark, Sweden and Germany. Finally, the regions/länder can be divided into municipalities in Denmark and Sweden and into districts (kreise) in Germany.

The overall Fehmarnbelt Region covers many differences between the three countries, of which the region is part, as well as between the different provinces within the borders of the three countries.

The region comprises 9.3 million people with 1.2 million in the Swedish part, 2.5 million in the Danish part and 5.6 million in the German part. In the Danish and Swedish parts of the region, the youngest age groups constitute a larger proportion of the population compared to the German part. According to population forecasts, this trend will become stronger in the future, particularly in respect of the German population.

There are several universities and institutions of higher education in the Fehmarnbelt Region. The majority of students are concentrated in and around the university cities, primarily Hamburg, Copenhagen and Malmö/Lund.

Economically, three are major differences within the region's borders. Characteristic for all three regions is that the major city areas and their hinterlands have the highest gross product per (active) daytime population. This applies particularly to Hamburg and Copenhagen. The more rural areas of Northern Germany and Scania have the lowest gross product per (active) daytime population. The opposite trend applies in terms of the unemployment figures. Here the major cities and their surrounding areas have the lowest unemployment. However, there are differences between the three countries. In the Danish part of the region, unemployment is generally very low compared to the German and Swedish parts.

By far the majority of the region's inhabitants are employed in the service and information sectors with only a small proportion working in agriculture or the manufacturing sectors. Employment within the manufacturing sector has been declining since 1996 in largely all provinces in the region. Hamburg and Copenhagen are the two financial centres in the Fehmarnbelt Region. In these two cities, the largest proportion of the workforce is employed within the financial and business service sectors and within trade, hospitality and transport. Other larger cities in the region such as Kiel, Lübeck, Rostock and Malmö have a significant number of people employed in the financial and business service sectors compared to the rest of the region.

Tourism is economically important for the Fehmarnbelt Region and is especially concentrated around Northern Germany. In 2008, there were 24.8 million overnight stays in hotels, inns and other accommodation in the coastal areas of Northern Germany. With regard to the Danish and Swedish parts of the region, the number of overnight stays was somewhat lower. In the Danish part of the region, overnight stays are mainly centred in and around Copenhagen. In Lolland, however, there are also a relatively large number of overnight stays compared to the rest of the Zealandian archipelago. In Scania, tourists mainly choose to overnight in Malmö and Helsingborg.

Commuting statistics reveal that the region's workforce is mobile. This is especially the case for the major cities that attract commuters from surrounding areas. 105,601 individuals commute to Hamburg and its vicinity from surrounding areas in Northern Germany. By far the majority, 40 per cent, come from the Lübeck area in Schleswig-Holstein. In the Danish and Swedish parts of the region, Copenhagen attracts most of the commuting from surrounding areas, i.e. 66,500 commuters. 74 per cent of regional commuters to Copenhagen come from Region Zealand and 26 per cent from Scania. The many commuters from Scania to Copenhagen are largely a result of the increased integration between Denmark and Sweden that followed in the wake of the opening of the Øresund Bridge in 2000.

THE EXTENT OF THE FEHMARNBELT REGION

The decision to plan and construct a fixed link across the Fehmarnbelt also marked the starting point for building a region encompassing both sides of the belt. Suddenly, the concept of a "Fehmarnbelt Region" began to take shape in the minds of politicians and local stakeholders. In this chapter, we define this new region geographically in terms of the STRING Region (a political co-operation between Hamburg and Schleswig-Holstein in Northern Germany, Region Zealand and the Capital Region in Eastern Denmark and Region Scania in Southern Sweden). In Germany, the Fehmarnbelt Region also encompasses two districts south of Hamburg, i.e. Stade and Harburg, and the adjacent districts east of Lubeck in Mecklenburg-Vorpommern as well as Nordwestmecklenburg, Wismar, Bad Doberan, Güstrow and Rostock[i].

FIGURE 1.
THE FEHMARNBELT REGION

The statistics are presented at different levels depending on the topic. The general level (Figure 1) comprises Region Zealand, the Capital Region in Denmark and Region Scania in Sweden and the German Länder, Schleswig-Holstein, Hamburg and Mecklenburg-Vorpommern. The more detailed level (Figure 2) includes the municipalities in Scania and Zealand as well as the districts in Northern Germany. This level also comprises the two districts Stade and Harburg in Lower Saxony.

FIGURE 2.
MUNICIPALITY LEVEL (DENMARK AND SWEDEN) AND DISTRICT LEVEL (GERMANY)

In addition, the city level (Figure 3) covers the main cities in the region and their surrounding areas. At this level, there is: Greater Hamburg[ii], Greater Kiel[iii], Greater Lübeck[iv], Greater Rostock[v], Greater Copenhagen[vi], Greater Malmö[vii] and Greater Helsingborg[viii].

**FIGURE 3.
GREATER URBAN LEVEL**

POPULATION

With regard to population distribution, the Fehmarnbelt Region divides into two segments. On the one hand, there are densely populated areas especially around the main cities (Figures 4 and 5) and on the other hand, many areas are sparsely populated, especially within the periphery.

FIGURE 4.
THE POPULATION OF THE FEHMARNBELT REGION (2008)

Source: Danmarks Statistik, Statistiska Centralbyrån, Statistisches Bundesamt Deutschland

With close to 3.2 million inhabitants, Greater Hamburg accounts for one third of the region's population and is the Fehmarnbelt Region's largest urban region. The Øresund City (Greater Copenhagen, Greater Malmö and Greater Helsingborg) has a population of 2.6 million, of which 1.8 million in Greater Copenhagen.

FIGURE 5.
POPULATION FIGURES (2009)

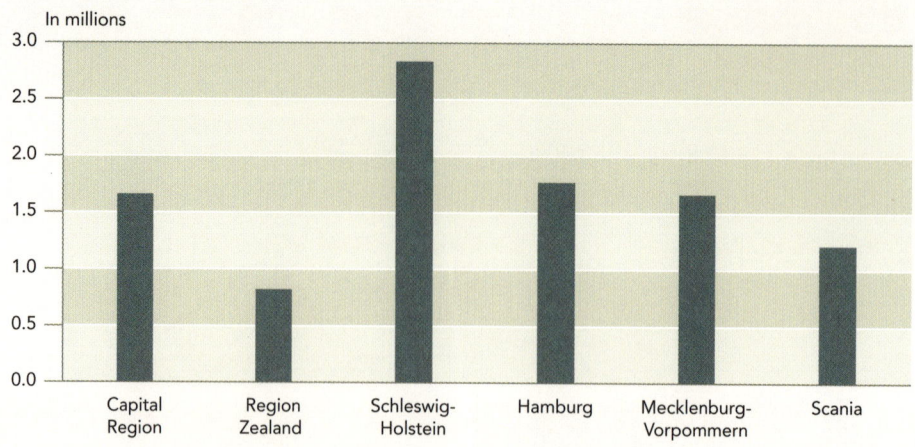

Source: Danmarks Statistik, Statistiska Centralbyrån, Statistisches Bundesamt Deutschland

Greater Kiel, with slightly more than 720,000 people and Greater Malmö with 600,000 residents represent the region's third and fourth largest conurbations. These are closely followed by Greater Lübeck with 580,000 inhabitants, Greater Rostock with slightly more than 420,000 inhabitants and Greater Helsingborg with almost 300,000 inhabitants.

Age distribution varies between the different parts of the region. In the German part, the population is generally older than in the Danish and Swedish parts although the inhabitants in the peripheral areas of Scania and Zealand also tend to be older compared to the more central areas.

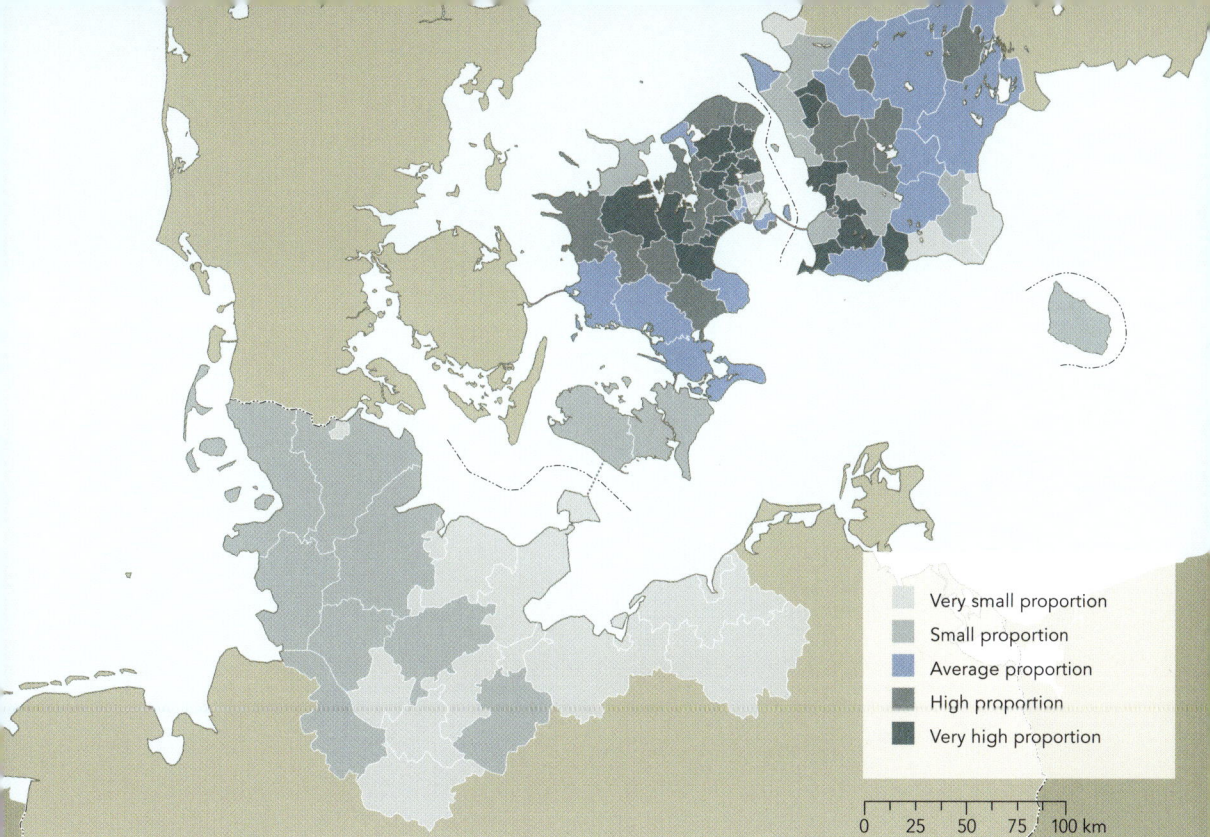

FIGURE 6.
THE 0-19 AGE GROUP OF PERCENTAGE OF THE POPULATION (2008)

Source: Danmarks Statistik, Statistiska Centralbyrån, Statistisches Bundesamt Deutschland
Note: The 102 municipalities/districts are divided into five groups with 20 to 21 municipalities/districts in each

The Scandinavian part of the Fehmarnbelt Region has a notably larger percentage of younger people (aged 0-19) compared to the German part (see Figure 6). On the outskirts of the larger cities, this group represents up to nearly 30 per cent of the city's population. Even in areas within comfortable commuting distances to larger cities, the proportion of the 0-19 age group is much higher than in the city itself. In inner cities such as Hamburg and Copenhagen, the percentage of the youngest group is low compared to the surrounding areas; one of the explanations is that people tend to move out of cities when they have children.

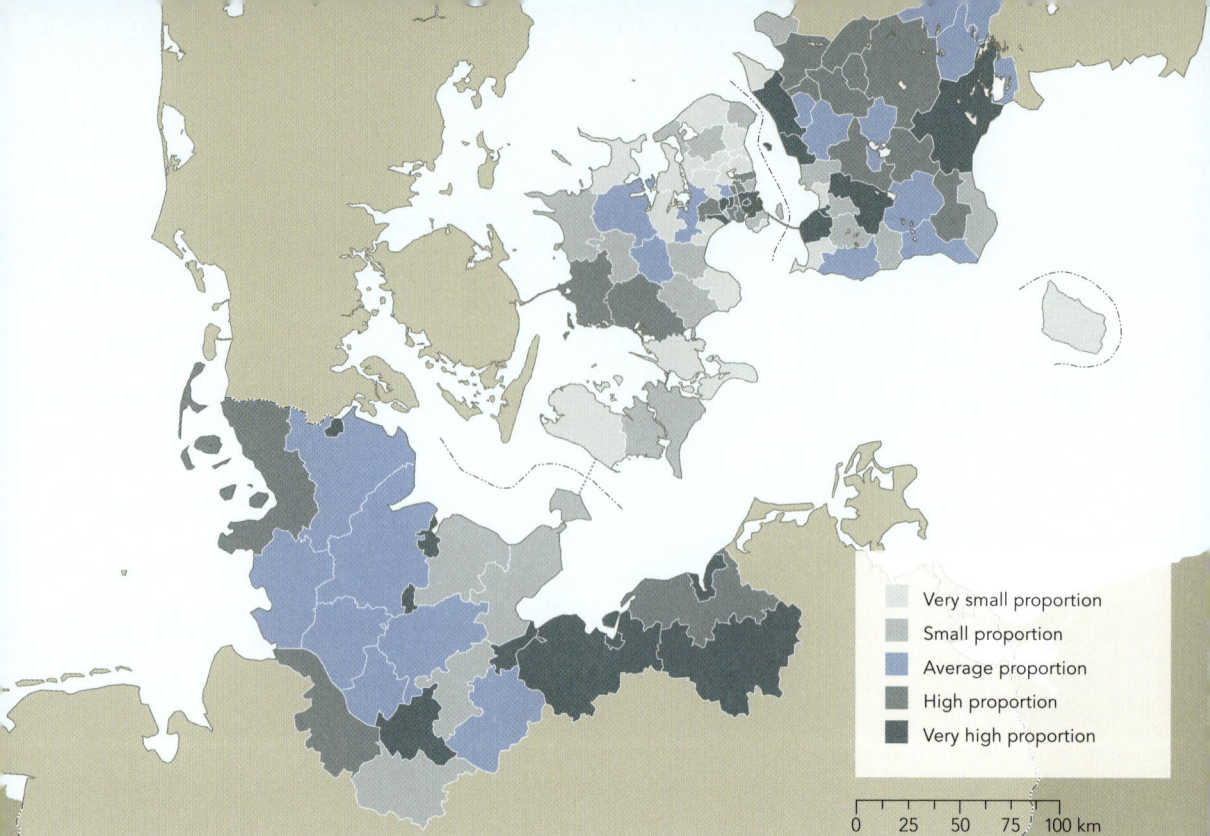

FIGURE 7.
THE 20-29 AGE GROUP IN PERCENTAGE OF THE POPULATION (2008)

Source: Danmarks Statistik, Statistiska Centralbyrån, Statistisches Bundesamt Deutschland

Figure 7 shows the percentage of 20 to 29 year olds, the age group comprising the largest number of university students. This segment is mainly located in the larger cities like Lund and Copenhagen with their many universities and institutions of higher education. In the German part, the 20-29 year group is largely located in Flensburg, Kiel, Lübeck and Rostock, which also have a number of institutions of higher education.

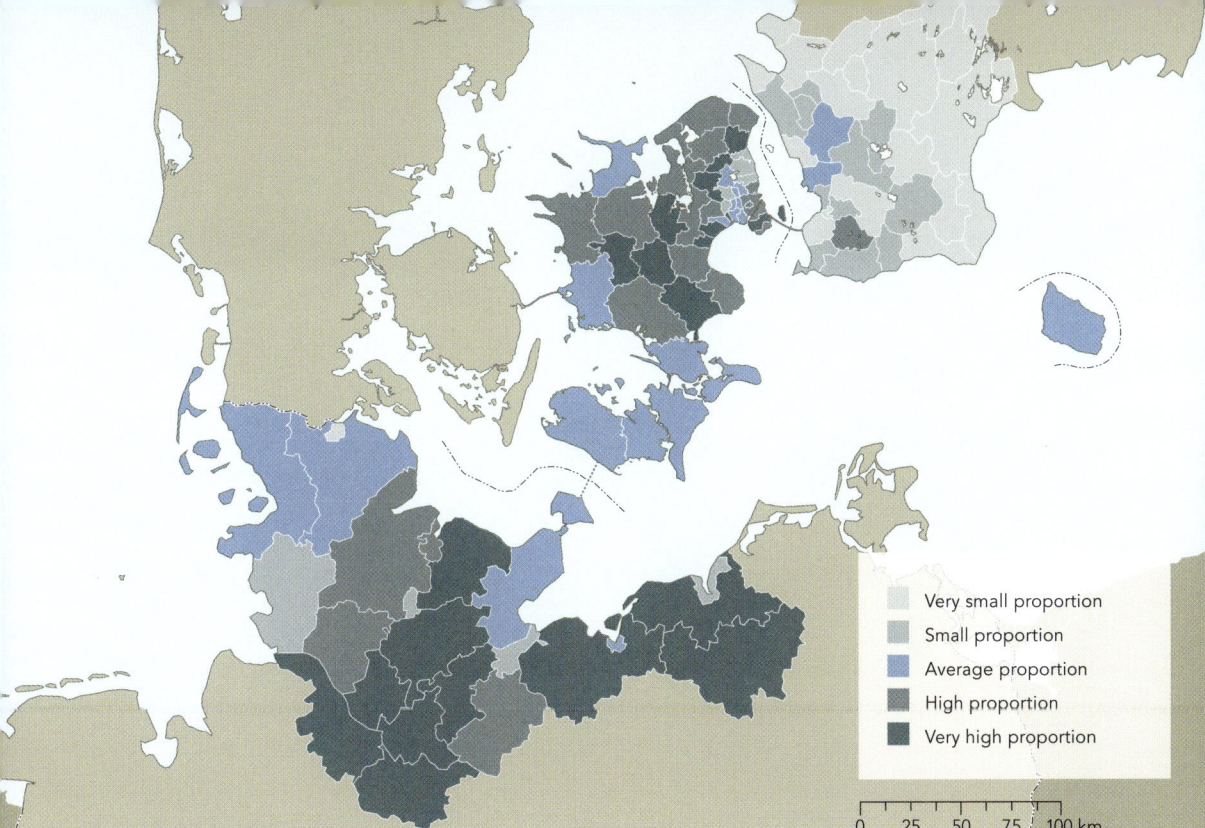

FIGURE 8.
THE 30-59 AGE GROUP IN PERCENTAGE OF THE POPULATION (2008)

Source: Danmarks Statistik, Statistiska Centralbyrån, Statistisches Bundesamt Deutschland

The majority of the 30-59 year age group (Figure 8) comprises the main working population (frequently with children) in the areas around the region's strongest concentrations of jobs. The largest proportion lives in reach of larger cities and central areas. In the North-Western part of Mecklenburg-Vorpommern, there is also just as large a proportion of 30-59 year-olds as there are in the Hamburg-Kiel corridor and on the outskirts of Copenhagen. Compared to these regions, Scania has the lowest proportion of 30 to 59 year-olds, particularly in the north eastern part.

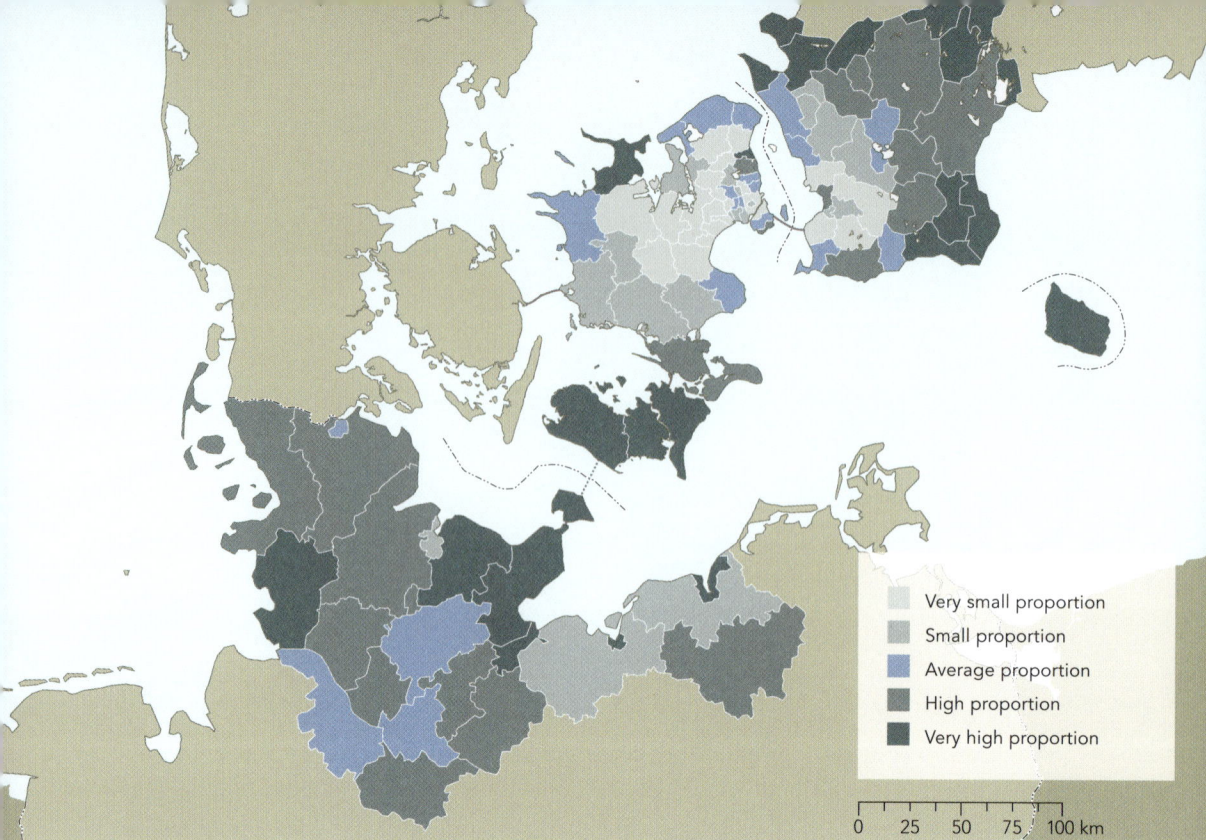

FIGURE 9.
THE 60 YEAR-OLD+ AGE GROUP IN PERCENTAGE OF THE POPULATION (2008)

Source: Danmarks Statistik, Statistiska Centralbyrån, Statistisches Bundesamt Deutschland

The "60 year-olds and above" group is mainly concentrated in the peripheral and coastal areas. Particularly in the areas surrounding the future Fehmarnbelt link, there is a high proportion of 60 year-olds and above (Figure 9).

The Danish and Swedish parts of the Fehmarnbelt Region also have a higher percentage of younger population groups (0-19, 20-29) compared to the German parts. By contrast, the German part has a higher proportion of 30-59 year-olds.

FIGURE 10.
AGE DISTRIBUTION

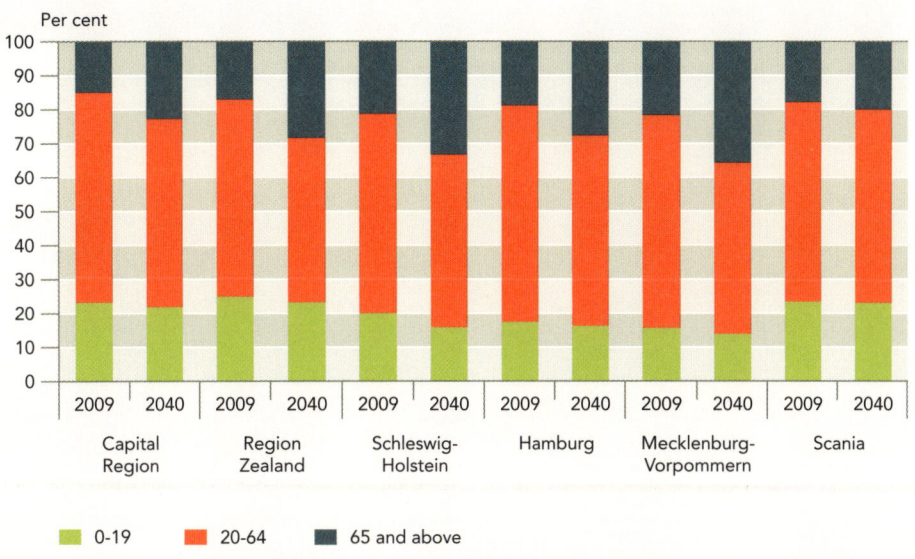

Source: Danmarks Statistik, Statistiska Centralbyrån, Region Skåne, Statistisches Bundesamt Deutschland

FUTURE POPULATION TRENDS

Forecasts for the Fehmarnbelt Region's future population trends show that the population is ageing, particularly in the Danish and German parts of the region (Figure 10). This gives rise to some concern. Economically, the 20-64 year age group is the most important segment because of its relevance to the labour market. In the event of a significant decrease in this group, there could be a risk of an economic slowdown which would impact on the social security system and increase benefit payments

The population issue varies across the different parts of the region. According to the forecast for 2040, the 20 to 64 age group in Region Zealand will decrease by 10 percentage points and in Mecklenburg-Vorpommern by 12 percentage points.

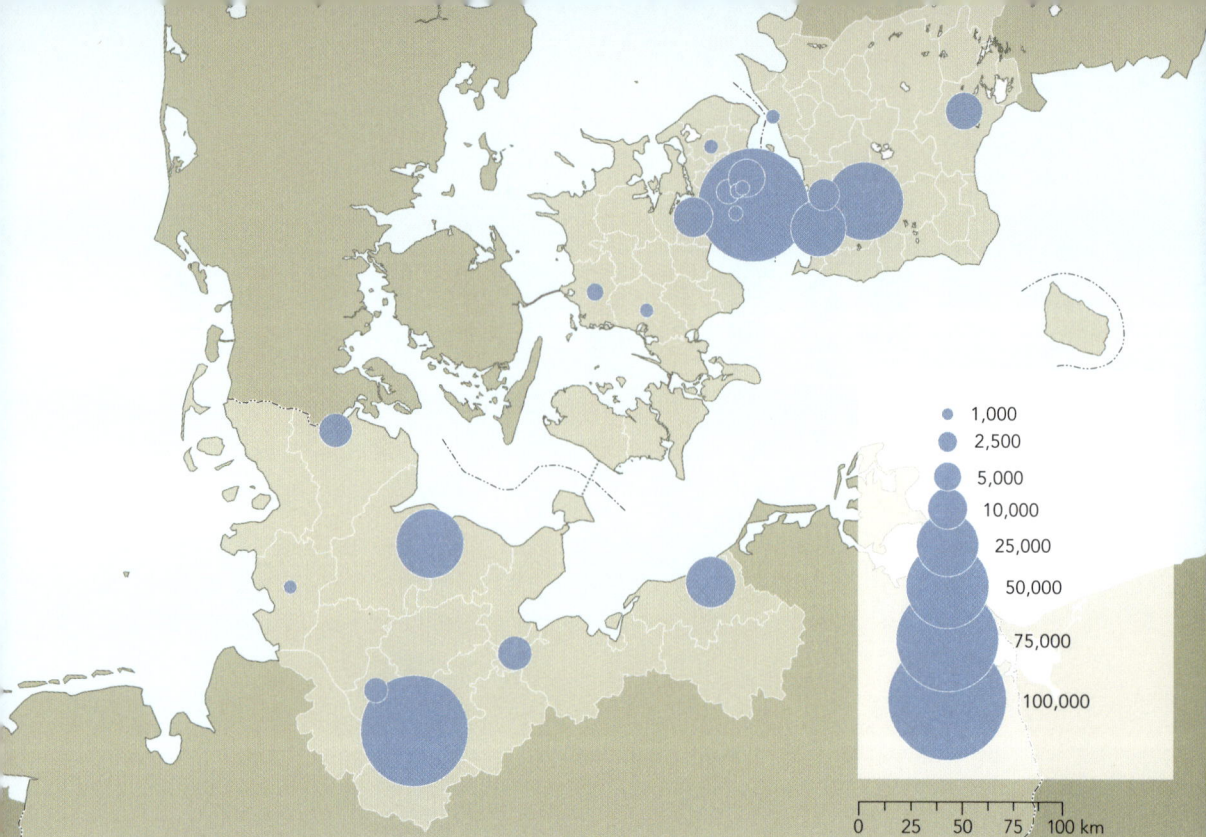

FIGURE 11.
STUDENTS ATTENDING HIGHER EDUCATION (2008/2009)

Source: Danmarks Statistik, Statistiska Centralbyrån, Statistisches Amt Mecklenburg-Vorpommern, Statistisches Amt für Hamburg und Schleswig-Holstein
Note: The data was collected in different parts of the region on different days. Only areas with more than 1,000 students are included.

UNIVERSITIES

The universities in the Fehmarnbelt Region are the key to further regional development and economic prosperity. Universities generate new knowledge and ideas, which have potential in the form of product development and entrepreneurship. They also represent further education and are, therefore, a source of new, highly educated employees.

The highest numbers of students are concentrated in or near cities (Figure 11). For Copenhagen this is, in part, due to the city's status as a capital and, in part, to the high

concentration of businesses needing highly qualified people. In Sweden, Malmö, Sweden's third city, has a substantial number of students. Close by is the university city of Lund with even more students. A similar picture can be found in Germany where the large universities are located in the larger cities. Hamburg has an almost comparable role to that of Copenhagen although it is not Germany's capital. The smaller universities in Kiel or Lübeck are also shown on the map.

FIGURE 12.
GROSS PRODUCT (2007)

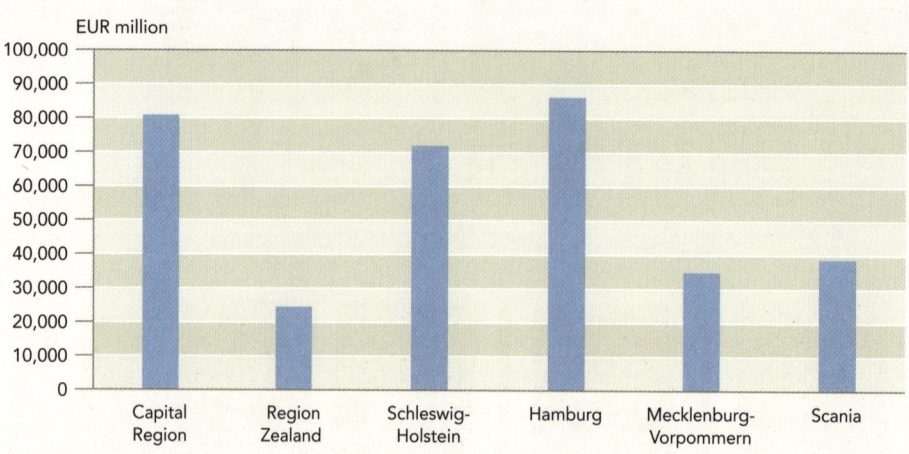

Source: Danmarks Statistik, Statistiska Centralbyrån, Eurostat

ECONOMY AND LABOUR MARKET

The economic situation varies between the different parts of the region. Whereas the areas with the larger cities, e.g. Copenhagen and Hamburg, have the highest gross product (Figure 12), Mecklenburg-Vorpommern and Region Zealand have the lowest. Scania, too, has a low gross product compared to Hamburg and the Capital Region.

In economic terms, there are differences between the national areas. Scania: EUR 72,000 per employee within the region's borders, the Zealand archipelago: EUR 85,000

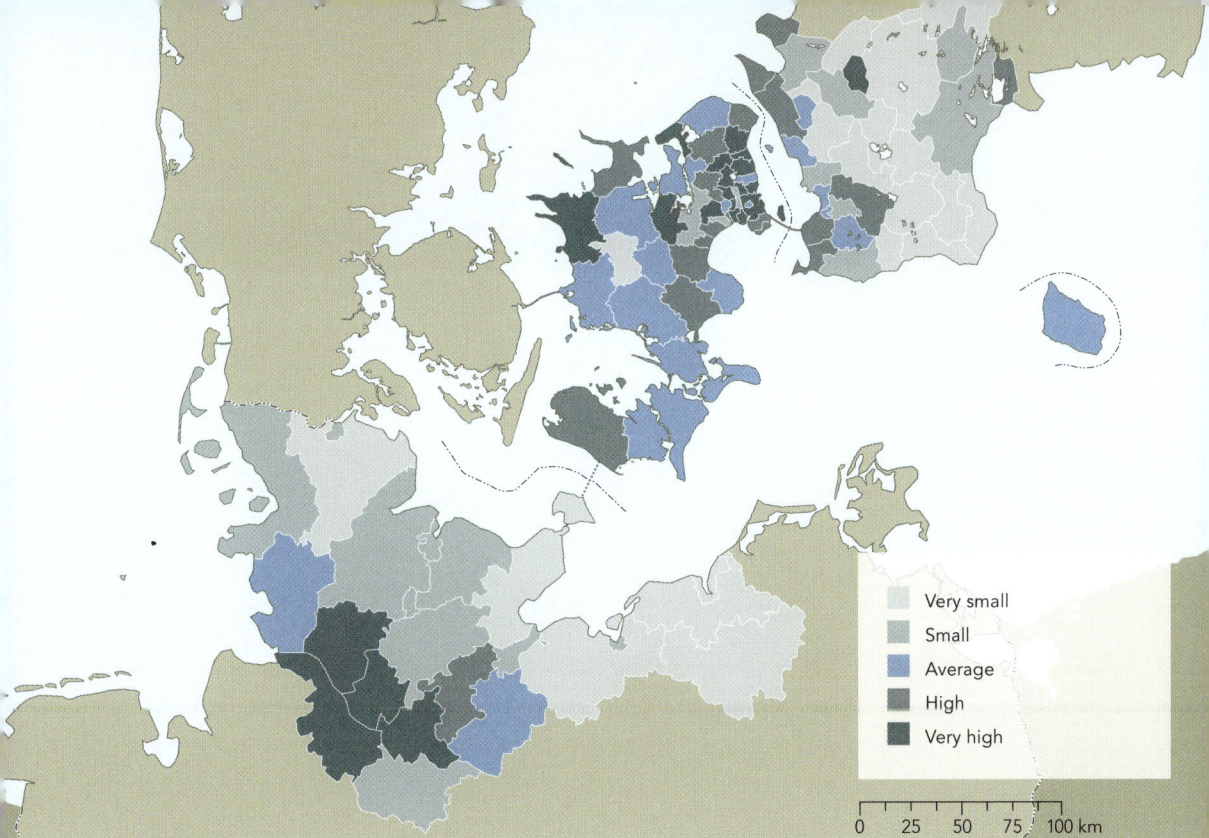

FIGURE 13.
GROSS PRODUCT PER (ACTIVE) DAYTIME POPULATION PER MUNICIPALITY/DISTRICT (2007)

Source: Danmarks Statistik, Statistiska Centralbyrån, Eurostat

and the North German area EUR 77,500. There are also major differences within the areas. It is characteristic for all regions that the major urban areas and their hinterlands have the highest gross product (active) daytime population. This applies particularly to Hamburg and Copenhagen. Some rural areas in North Germany and Scania have the lowest gross product (active) daytime population in the region. There are deviations from the expected centre-peripheral picture. This concerns areas with high gross product figures, Kalundborg, Perstorp, Lolland and Bromölla whose figures are somewhat above the average.

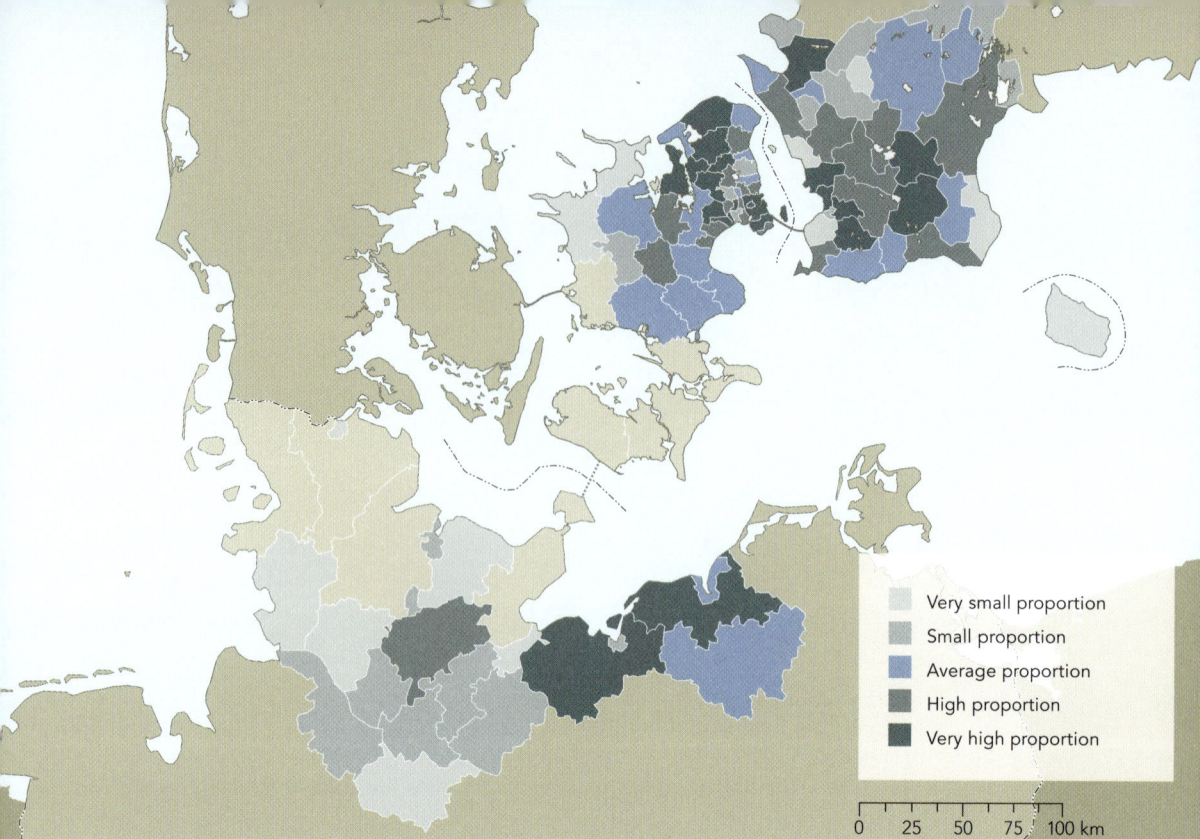

FIGURE 14.
WORKFORCE 2008 IN PERCENTAGE OF THE TOTAL POPULATION (2008)

Source: Eurostat
Note: Due to lack of data at municipal level in Denmark and Sweden, employed and unemployed at municipality level in Denmark and Sweden have been estimated. The estimates have been made by using the register-based workforce statistics (Danmarks Statistik) and the register-based workforce statistics (Statistiska Centralbyrån) to calculate the proportion of employed and unemployed people in the municipalities in the year the regional data was collected. Differences between the starting ages of the workforce have been ignored. (Denmark and Germany: 15+, Sweden: 16+).

FIGURE 15.
NUMBER OF PEOPLE IN THE WORKFORCE (2008)

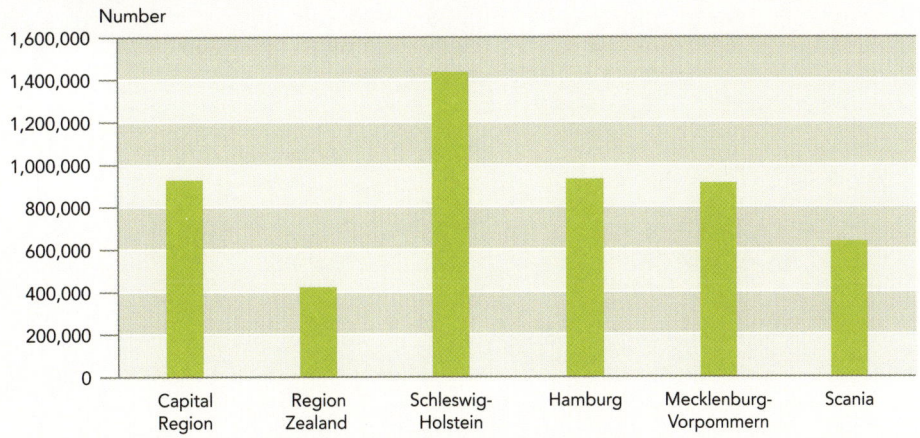

Source: Eurostat

The workforce within the Fehmarnbelt Region (Figure 14) comprises both the employed and unemployed. One aspect common for all three national components of the region is the fact that the proportion of the workforce in relation to the general population is highest around the major cities.

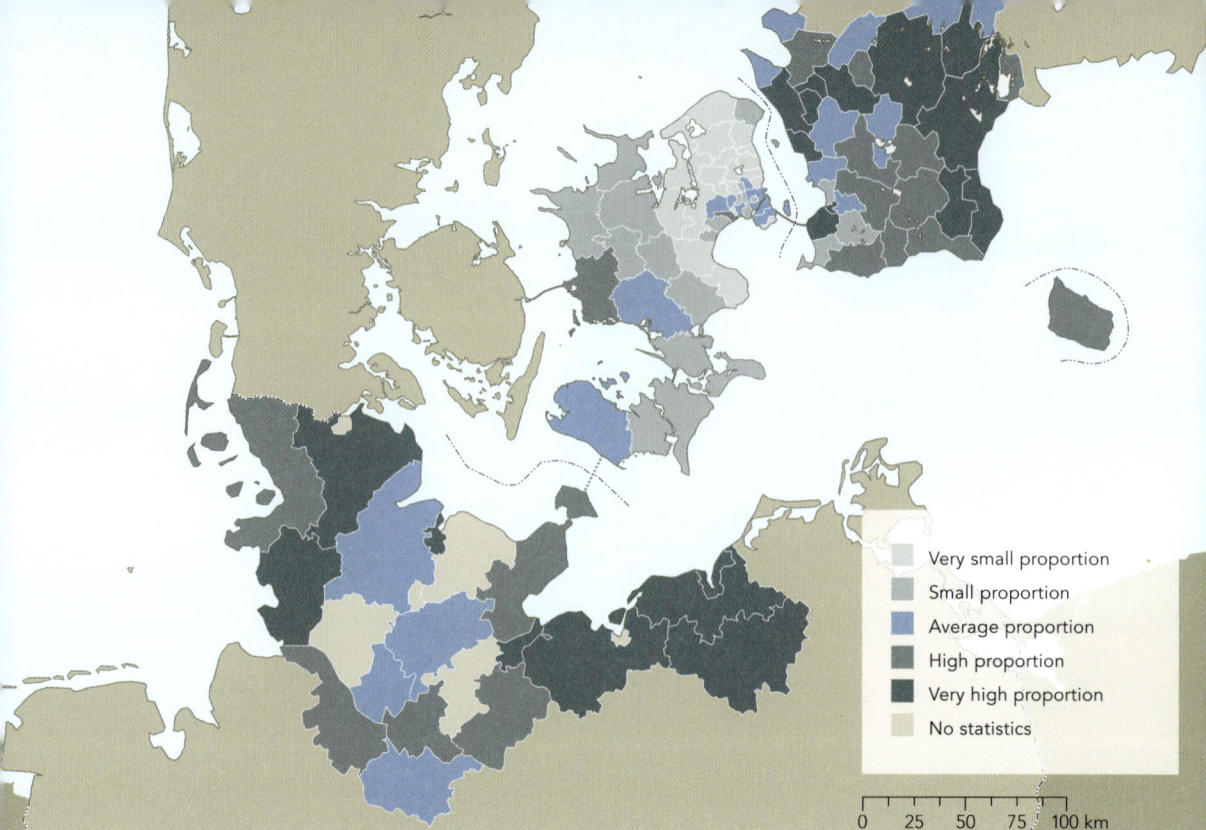

FIGURE 16.
UNEMPLOYMENT IN PERCENTAGE OF WORKFORCE (2008)

Source: Eurostat
Note: Due to a lack of statistical material, three districts have been excluded from the map. See also note for Figure 14.

Unemployment figures in the Fehmarnbelt Region vary significantly (Figure 16). Denmark has a low percentage of unemployed, while the percentage is higher in Sweden and Germany. In the Danish part, the lowest unemployment percentages are found within commuting distance of Copenhagen while the central municipalities have higher unemployment compared to their surroundings. In the Danish part, the highest unemployment percentages are found in the South Western part of Zealand and in Lolland. The lowest unemployment figures in Scania equate to the highest unemployment figures in the Danish part. The lowest percentages of unemployed in Scania are found around Malmö and the greater the distance from Malmö, the higher the unemployment. This is especially the case

in a corridor from Helsingborg to Hässleholm in the north of Scania and from Kristianstad to Tomelilla in the east. In the German areas, there are clear differences between west and east. While the western part, Schleswig-Holstein and Hamburg, has relatively low unemployment (similar to Scania), unemployment figures (up to 16.4 per cent) in the northern districts in Mecklenburg-Vorpommern are the highest in the Fehmarnbelt Region. One explanation is that the reunification of the former GDR with the Federal Republic in effect merged the economies of the two Germanys, in the course of which many people lost their jobs (Focus Money Online, 2007).

FIGURE 17.
INDUSTRY BREAKDOWN

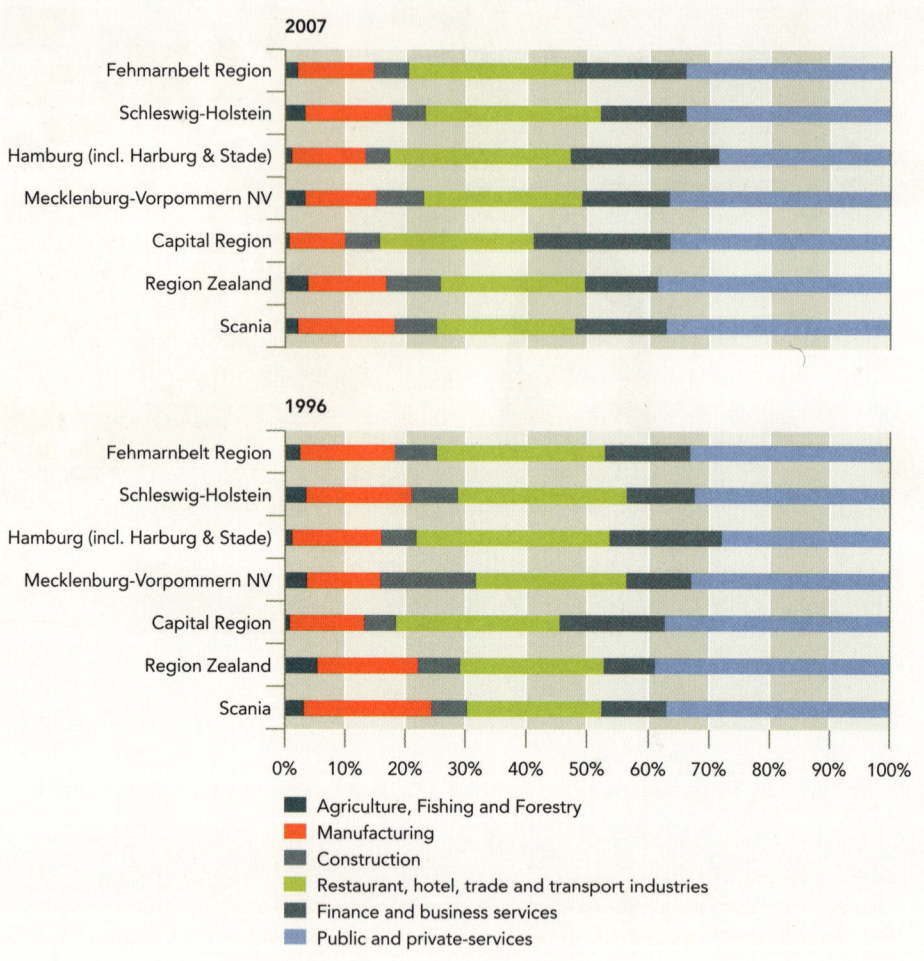

Source: Ørestat, Statistisches Bundesamt Deutschland

FIGURE 18.
NUMBER OF PEOPLE EMPLOYED WITHIN INDUSTRIAL SECTORS

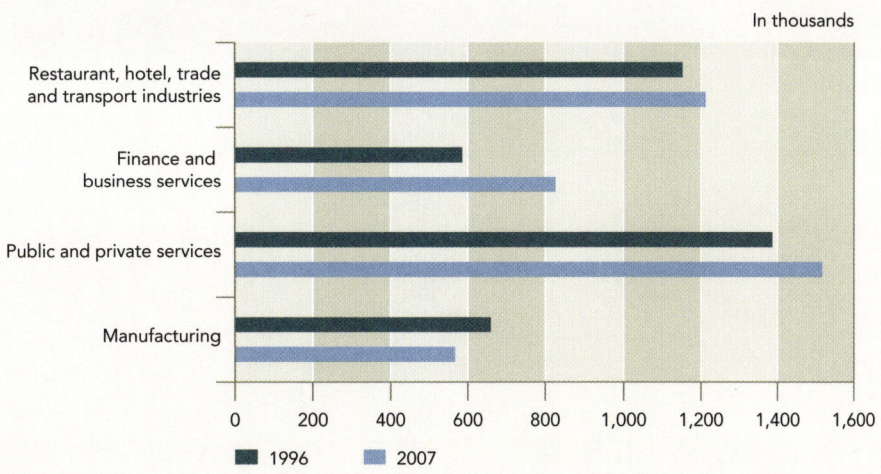

Source: Ørestat, Statistisches Bundesamt Deutschland

INDUSTRIES

The Fehmarnbelt Region is characterised by the fact that most of its workforce is employed in the service sector while industry, agriculture, horticulture and forestry are less prevalent. The largest group, 34 per cent of all employees, work within the public and private services such as education, health, public administration, defence and administration. A significant 27 per cent are employed in the trade, hospitality and transport sectors (Figure 17). These figures cover inter-regional differences. 39 per cent of people employed in Region Zealand work in public and private service industries whereas only 29 per cent in Hamburg work in this segment. With around 20 per cent each of the workforce within finance and business services, Hamburg and the Danish Capital Region have a notably higher percentage of these categories than other places in the Fehmarnbelt Region. In Region Zealand this group only accounts for 12 per cent.

Figure 17 demonstrates the changes to employment figures for different industries between 1996 and 2007, a period during which the percentage of people employed in manufacturing, building and construction in the Fehmarnbelt Region decreased. The

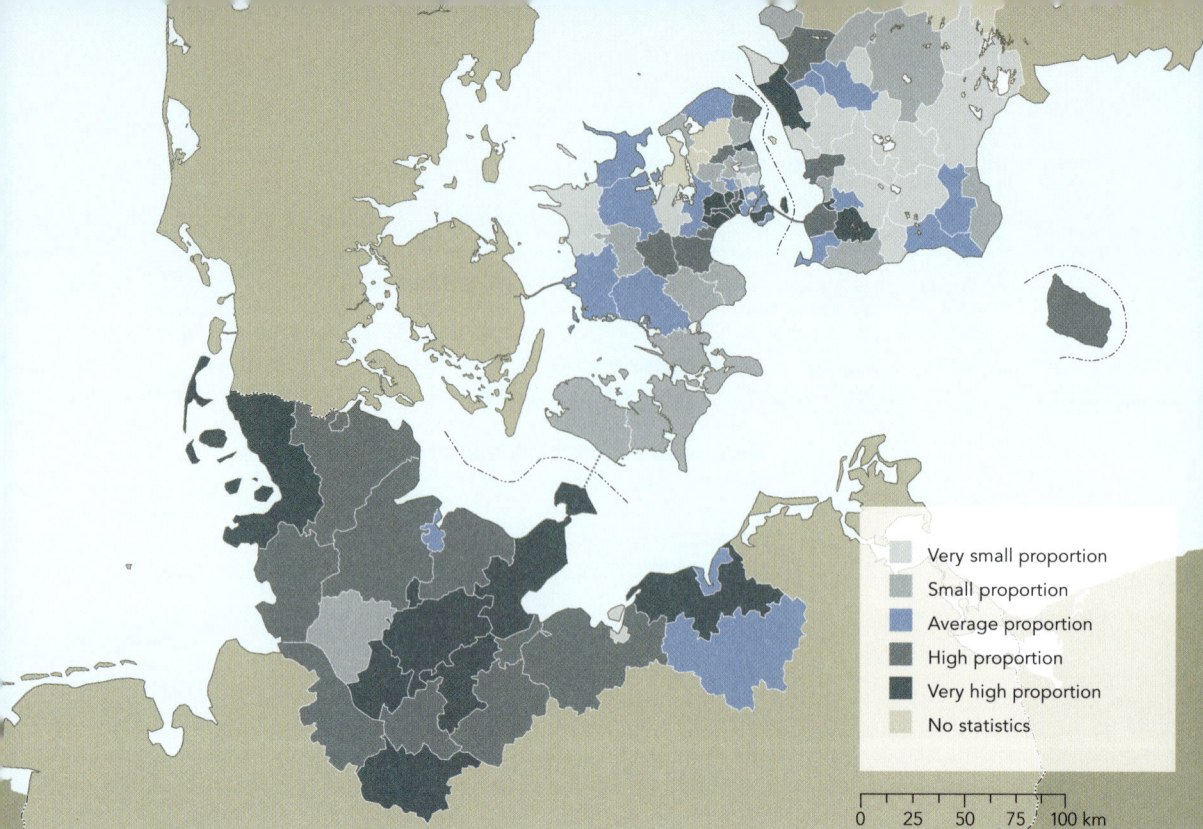

FIGURE 19.
PERCENTAGE OF EMPLOYEES WITHIN TRADE, HOSPITALITY AND TRANSPORT (2007)
ACTIVE DAYTIME POPULATION

Source: Ørestat, Statistisches Bundesamt Deutschland

percentage of people within the manufacturing industry declined by 3 percentage points and in the building and construction industry by 1 percentage point. At the same time, the percentage of people in the finance and business service sectors is higher than in 1996 (4 percentage points) and in public and private services (1 percentage points).[ix]

From 1996-2007, the individual business groupings underwent significant change as municipalities and districts developed in different directions. To illustrate this, we first show the distribution patterns for the individual categories 2007 and then we use the shift-term concept which shows how one municipality or district has changed (the growth rate) in the number of employees in one industry group compared to the average change in the same

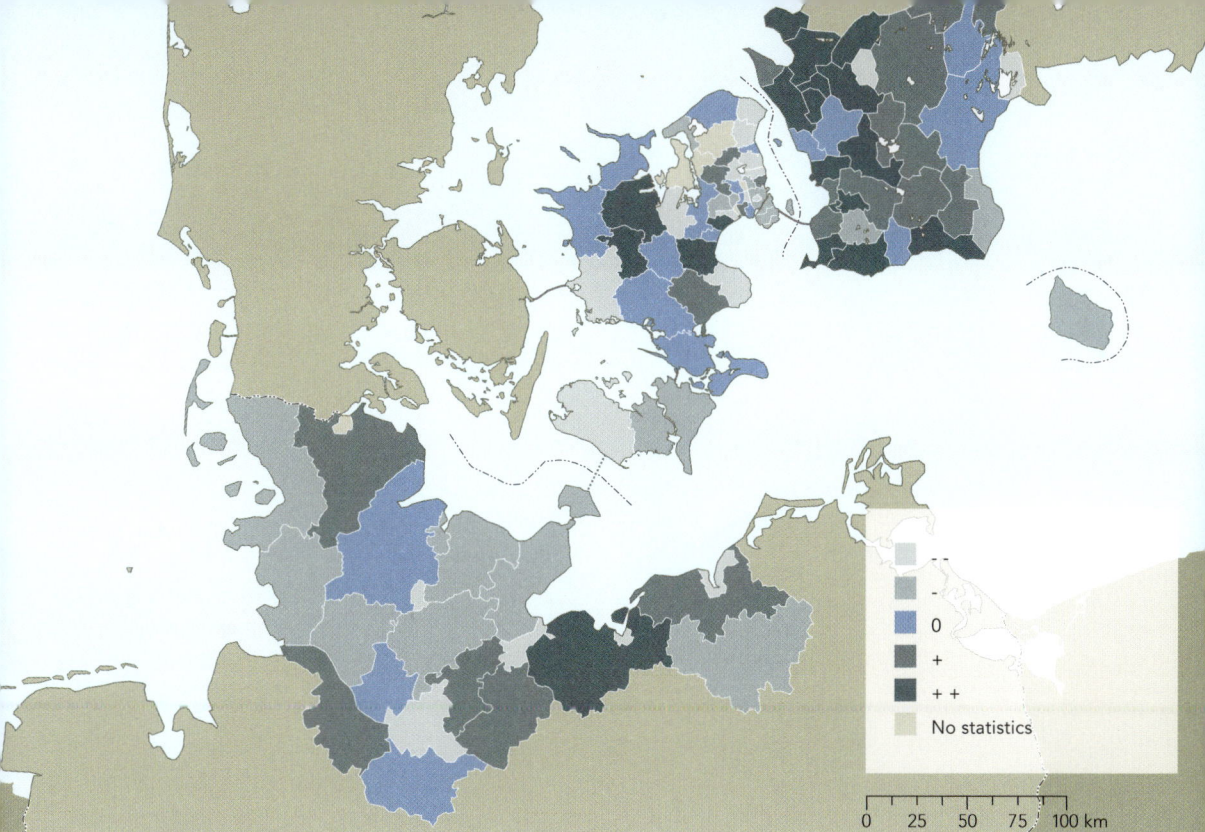

FIGURE 20.
SHIFT-TERM MAP FOR TRADE, HOSPITALITY AND TRANSPORT (1996-2007)
ACTIVE DAYTIME POPULATION

Source: Ørestat, Statistisches Bundesamt Deutschland [xi]
Note: --: 20 percent of observations with highest decline; -: 20 percent of observations with high decline;
0: 20 percent of observations with average change; +: 20 percent of observations with increase;
++: 20 percent of observations with high increase.

industry group in the whole of the Fehmarnbelt Region. The shift-term maps provide a picture of whether a municipality/district has strengthened or weakened in a particular industry compared to the average for the Fehmarnbelt Region and demonstrate the concentration processes.

TRADE, HOSPITALITY AND TRANSPORT

The absolute figures (Figure 18) show that the trade, hospitality and transport sectors have seen relatively marginal growth in the number of employed from 1996 to 2007. This, in fact, is the case across the whole of the Fehmarnbelt Region with the exception of Hamburg

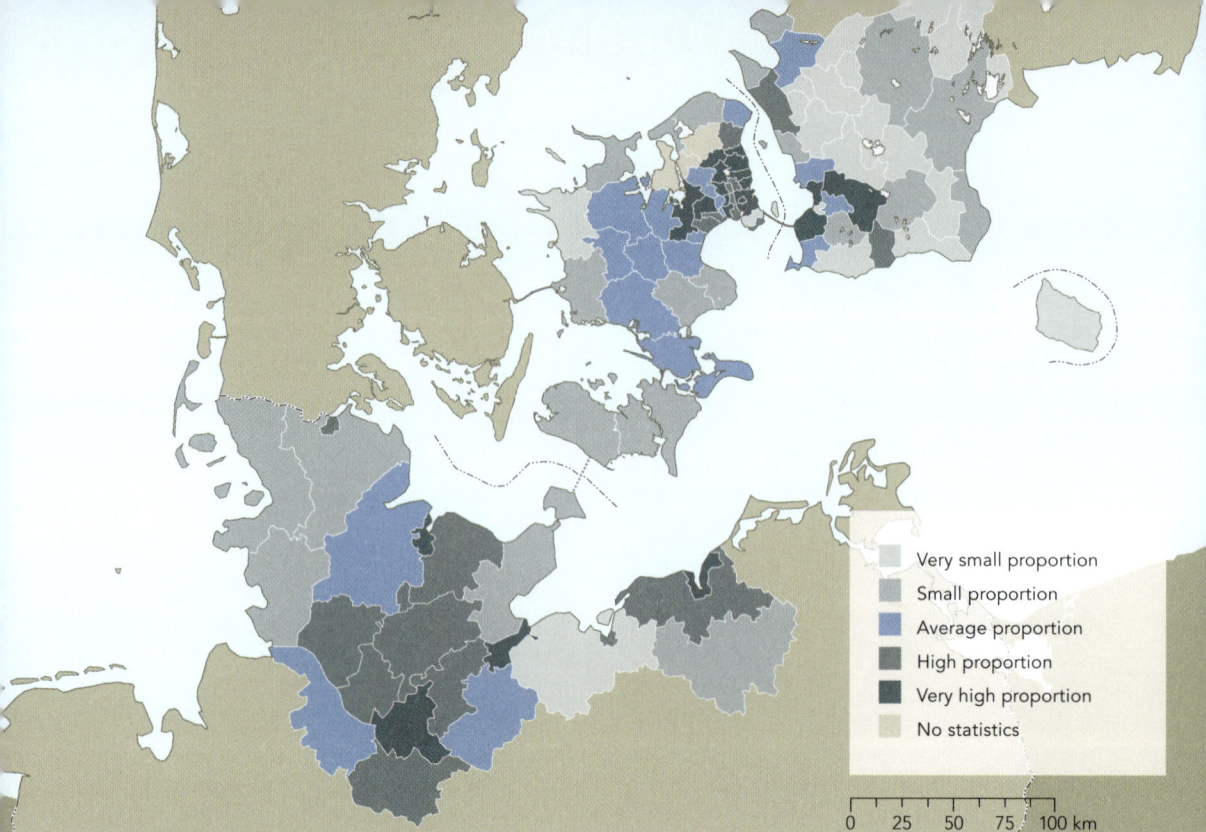

FIGURE 21.
PERCENTAGE OF EMPLOYEES WITHIN THE FINANCE AND BUSINESS SERVICES (2007) ACTIVE DAYTIME POPULATION

Source: Ørestat, Statistisches Bundesamt Deutschland

where there was modest growth. Figure 19 shows the percentage of the labour force active in these sectors in the Fehmarnbelt Region's districts/municipalities. That the highest concentration of the workforce is found in this category applies to many districts in Germany.

The shift-term maps of trade, hospitality and transport demonstrate a relative dispersion process. There is also above average growth for Malmö, Lund and Helsingborg as well as for most of Scania's municipalities (Figure 20). In the German part of the region, the picture is twofold. There is above average growth in many areas although growth rates are below average in most of the larger cities such as Hamburg, Lübeck, Neumünster and Rostock. In Denmark, the shift-term span is bigger than in Germany and Sweden, including

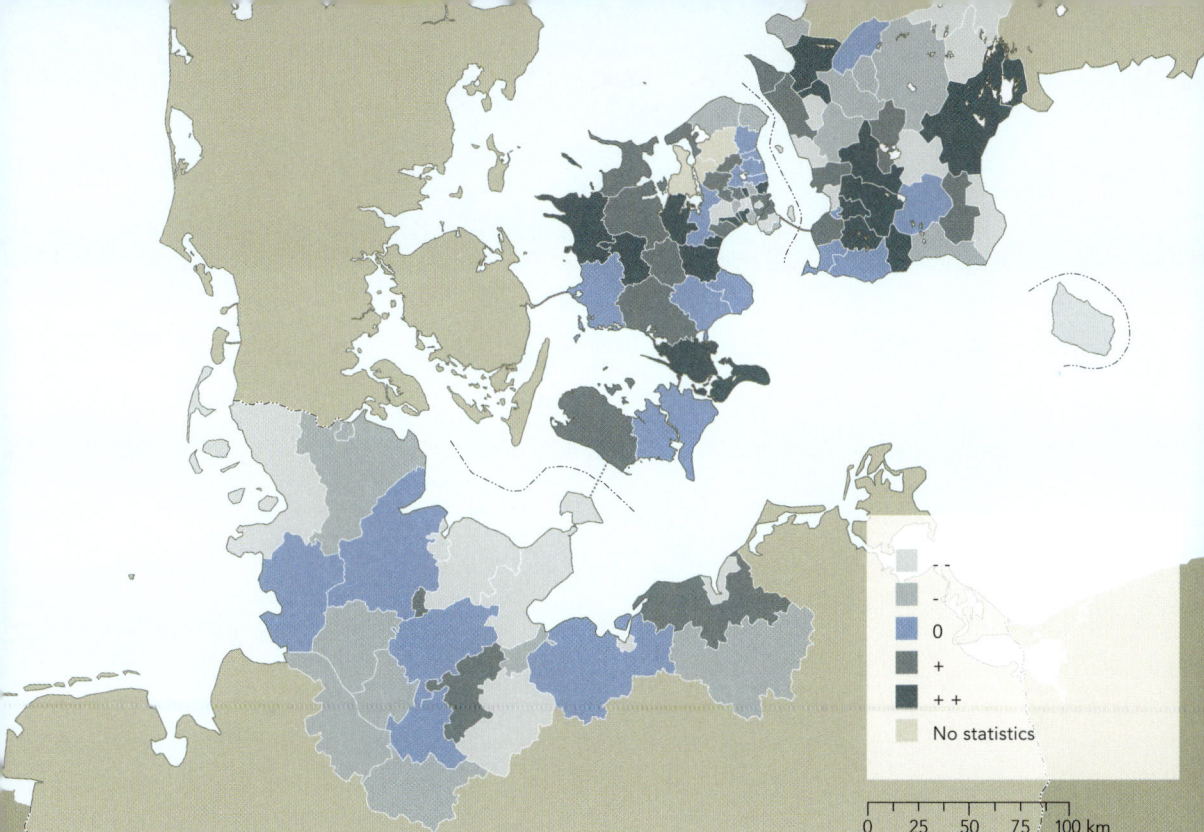

FIGURE 22.
SHIFT-TERM-MAP FOR THE FINANCE AND BUSINESS SERVICE SECTORS (1996-2007)
ACTIVE DAYTIME POPULATION

Source: Ørestat, Statistisches Bundesamt Deutschland
Note: --: 20 percent of observations with highest decline; -: 20 percent of observations with high decline;
0: 20 percent of observations with average change; +: 20 percent of observations with increase;
++: 20 percent of observations with high increase.

the two municipalities at the extreme ends of the spectrum. The municipality with the lowest growth rates within these industries compared to the average for the whole of the Fehmarnbelt Region is Lolland municipality, while the highest growth rates are found in Vallensbæk municipality in Greater Copenhagen. In Copenhagen and Frederiksberg municipalities, the growth rates are below average compared to the Fehmarnbelt Region.

FINANCE AND BUSINESS SERVICES

The (active) daytime population within the financial and business service sectors grew throughout the Fehmarnbelt Region from 1996 to 2007 (Figure 18). In total, there were

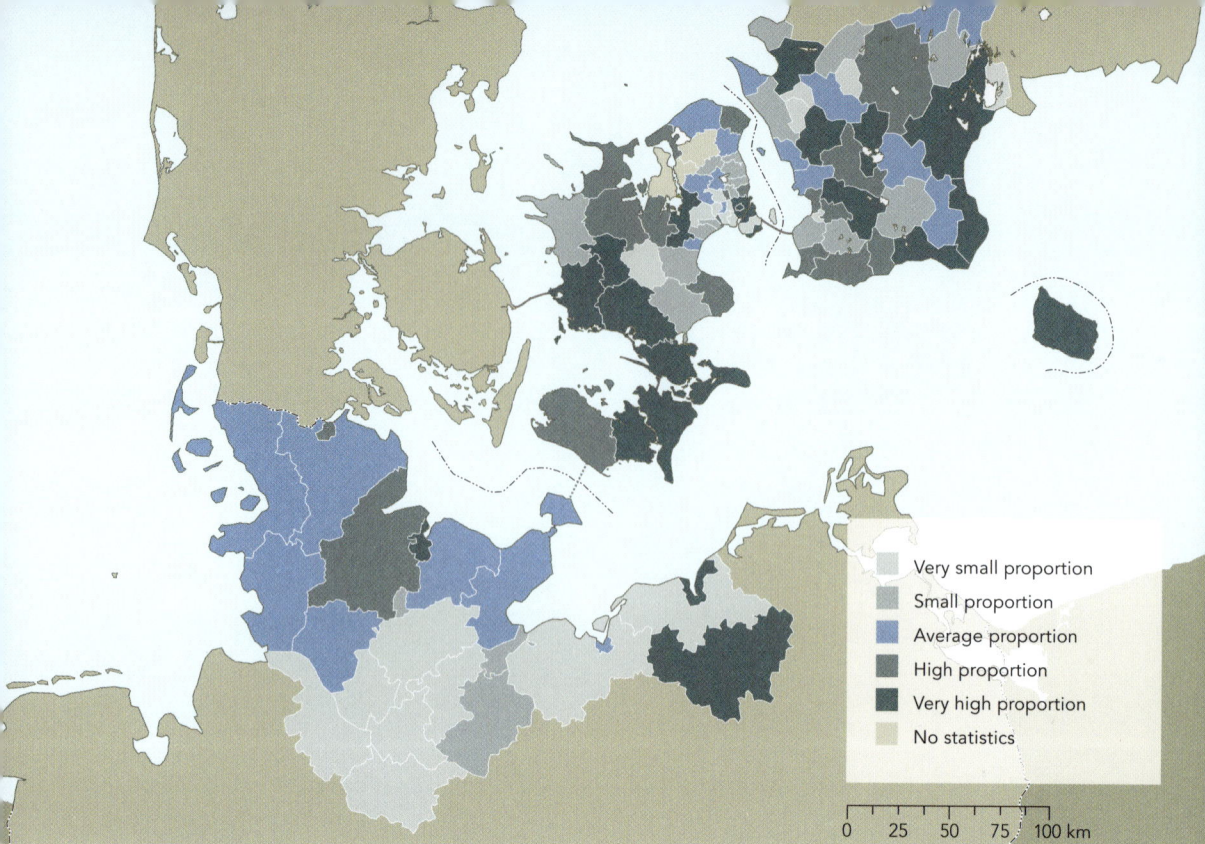

FIGURE 23.
PERCENTAGE OF EMPLOYEES WITHIN THE PUBLIC AND PRIVATE SERVICES (2007)
ACTIVE DAYTIME POPULATION

Source: Ørestat, Statistisches Bundesamt Deutschland

around 240,000 more people employed in these sectors in 2007 than in 1996. Figure 21 shows that the municipalities/districts with the highest percentage of the workforce within the financial and business services sector is dominated by major cities such as Hamburg, Kiel, Lübeck, Rostock, Copenhagen and Malmö.

The shift-term map (Figure 22) shows that the concentration pattern is maintained almost unchanged in Germany whereas a dispersion occurred in the Scandinavian parts of the Fehmarnbelt Region. The categories are spread across the whole of the Fehmarnbelt Region without any particular clear patterns. Skurup in Scania has the highest growth rates within the financial and business service sectors while Östra Göinge in Scania has the lowest. In terms of the major cities in the region, where the largest concentration of

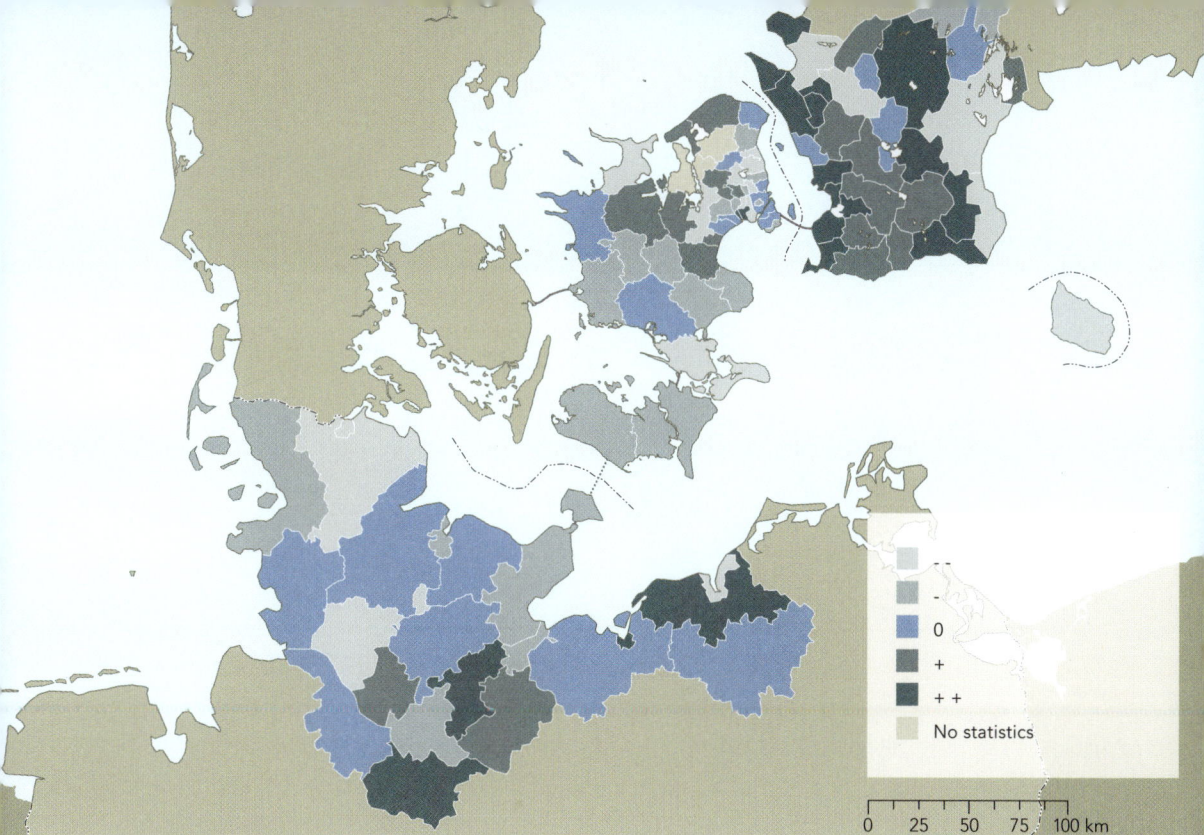

FIGURE 24.
SHIFT-TERM MAP FOR PUBLIC AND PRIVATE SERVICES (1996-2007)
ACTIVE DAYTIME POPULATION

Source: Ørestat, Statistisches Bundesamt Deutschland
Note: --: 20 percent of observations with highest decline; -: 20 percent of observations with high decline;
0: 20 percent of observations with average change; +: 20 percent of observations with increase;
++: 20 percent of observations with high increase.

individuals are employed in these sectors, Copenhagen and Malmö have higher growth rates for employees in the financial and business service sectors than the average for the Fehmarnbelt Region while the major cities in Germany – Hamburg, Kiel, Rostock, Copenhagen and Malmö – have growth rates at or below average.

PUBLIC AND PRIVATE SERVICES

Public and private services have experienced growth in absolute employment figures across the whole of the Fehmarnbelt Region (see Figure 18). Figure 23 shows that municipalities/districts with the largest number of employees in these sectors are predominantly concentrated in Denmark and Sweden, but there are no clear patterns.

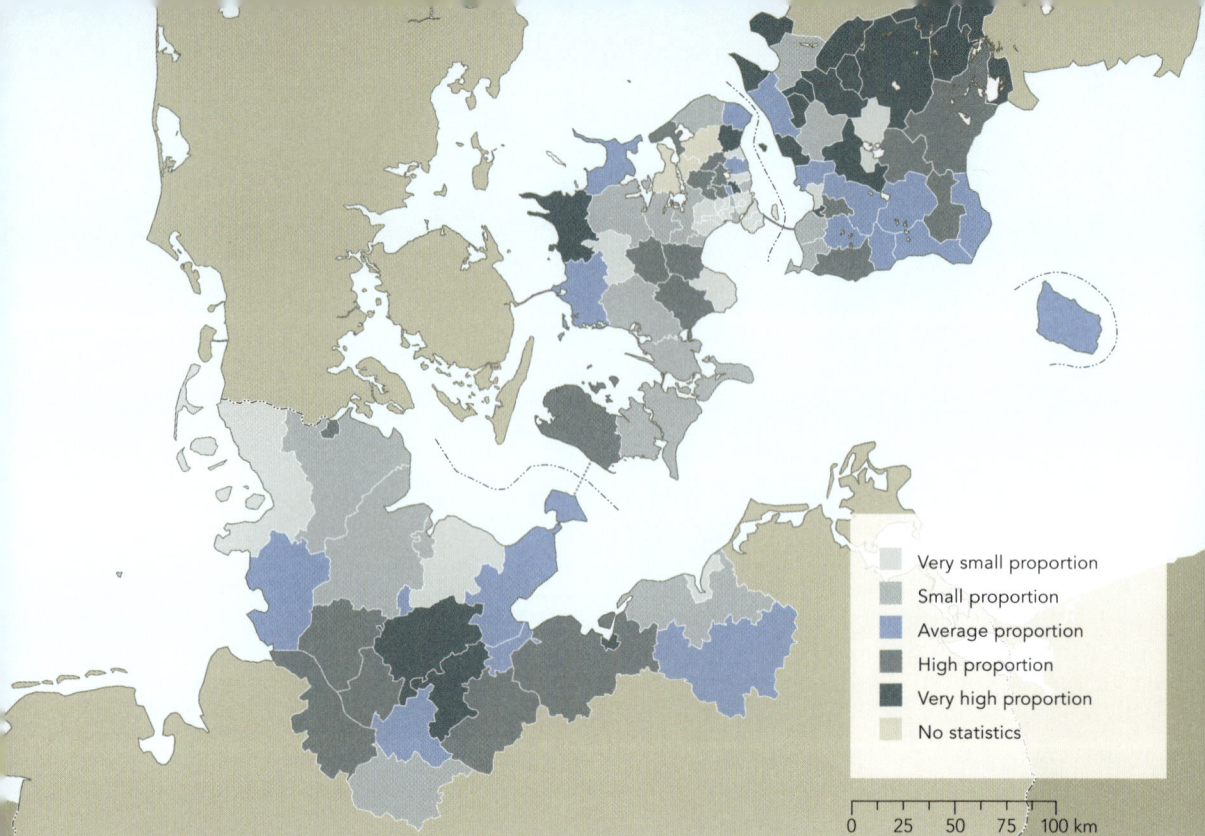

FIGURE 25.
PERCENTAGE OF EMPLOYEES WITHIN MANUFACTURING (2007)
ACTIVE DAYTIME POPULATION

Source: Ørestat, Statistisches Bundesamt Deutschland

The shift-term map shows that the majority of municipalities in the Swedish part of the region have above average growth rates for this sector compared to the Fehmarnbelt Region as a whole (Figure 24). In Germany and Denmark, the growth picture is more evenly divided. With the exception of the municipalities of Malmö and Helsingborg, all major cities in the region have experienced below average growth rates for the Fehmarnbelt Region as a whole.

MANUFACTURING (INCLUDING ENERGY AND WATER SUPPLY)

Manufacturing has seen negative growth in the number of employees throughout the Fehmarnbelt Region (Figure 18). In absolute figures, largely all municipalities/districts

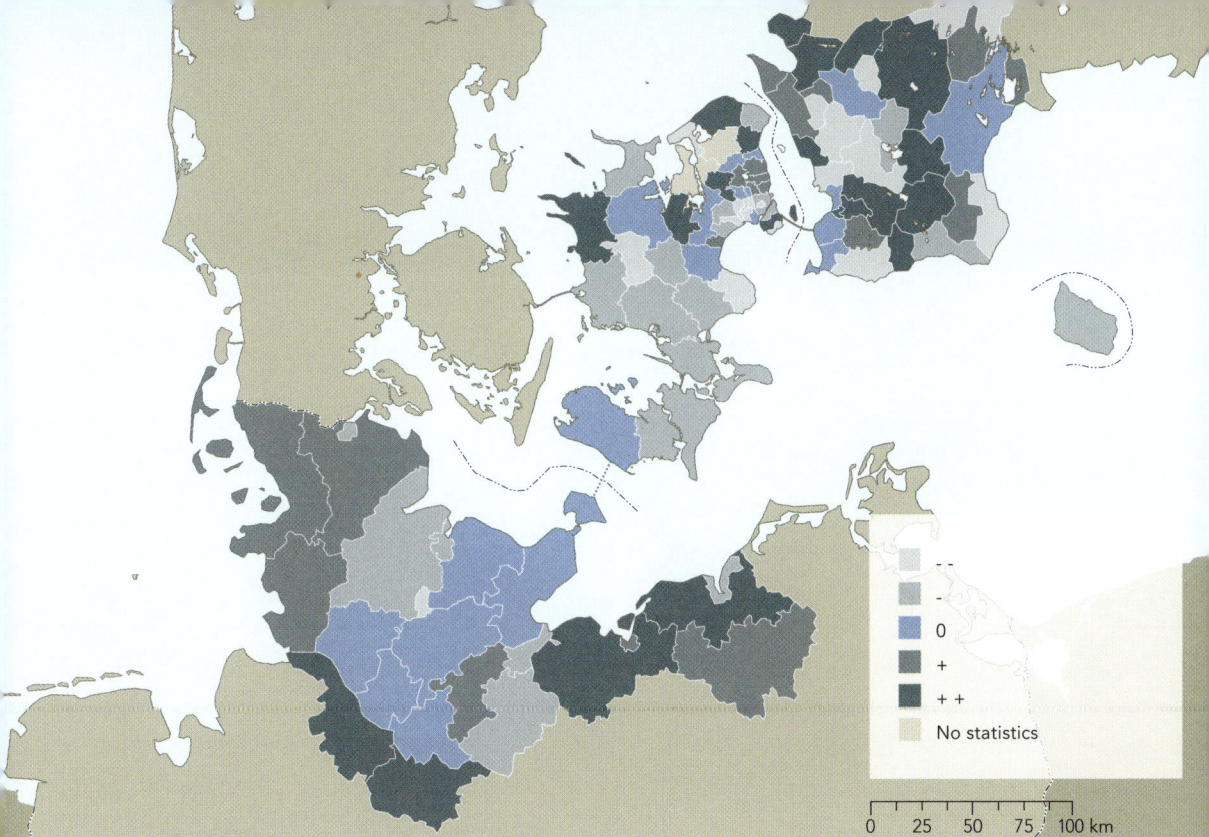

**FIGURE 26.
SHIFT-TERM MAP FOR MANUFACTURING (1996-2007)
ACTIVE DAYTIME POPULATION**

Source: Ørestat, Statistisches Bundesamt Deutschland
Note: --: 20 percent of observations with highest decline; -: 20 percent of observations with high decline;
0: 20 percent of observations with average change; +: 20 percent of observations with increase;
++: 20 percent of observations with high increase.

experienced a decline from 1996 to 2007. Only 19 of the 100 municipalities/districts recorded growth in the number of employees in the manufacturing sector. Figure 25 shows that municipalities in the northern part of Scania have a larger percentage of individuals employed in the manufacturing sector compared to the rest of the region.

The shift-term map (Figure 26) shows a slightly diffused image of concentration versus distribution, but forms a deconcentration picture. The Danish part of the region mainly shows growth rates close to, or, below average. The municipalities of Fredensborg, Kalundborg, Lejre and Tårnby are exceptions where growth rates are significantly above average. With regard to Scania, manufacturing is maintained in the highest industrialised areas where relative growth can be observed. The north eastern part of Schleswig-Holstein

FIGURE 27.
HOTELS AND OTHER OVERNIGHT STAYS IN THE FEHMARNBELT REGION (2007/2008)

Source: Danmarks Statistik, Statistiska centralbyrån 2007, Statistisches Bundesamt Deutschland
Note: It can be difficult to compare the statistics between the three countries because of different collection methods. In Denmark, statistics are only collected for hotels and other accommodation with more than 40 beds, and in Germany and Sweden for nine or more beds. A survey by Danmarks Statistik (2006) shows that the number of hotels and other accommodation with 10-40 beds in Region Zealand and the Capital Region was 108. These are not included in the statistics because the statistics relate to municipality level. Due to a lack of data for the lowest regional level, there are only statistics available at regional level for Sweden. Moreover, information from a number of Danish municipalities is missing.

and most of the districts in Mecklenburg-Vorpommern show above average growth rates. Nordwestmecklenburg in Mecklenburg-Vorpommern shows an increase in the number of employed in this sector – not only in comparison with the average for the Fehmarnbelt Region, but also in absolute figures.

FIGURE 28.
OVERNIGHT STAYS IN HOTELS AND RESORTS (2008)

Source: Danmarks Statistik, Region Skåne 2008, Statistisches Bundesamt Deutschland
Note: The difference in collection methods corresponds to the differences in the data for the number of hotels and other accommodation, see note to Figure 27. The survey undertaken by Danmarks Statistik (Danmarks Statistik 2006) showed that the number of overnight stays at hotels and other accommodation with 10-40 beds in 2006 accounted for 4.8 per cent of the total number of overnight stays. Data for the Danish municipalities have, therefore, been recalculated using this percentage so as to include small hotels. In some Swedish municipalities, an estimate of the number of overnight stays in holiday villages has been undertaken. These, therefore, have not been included in the statistics. Due to a lack of data, many of the Danish and Swedish municipalities are excluded. Area of circles proportional to number of overnight stays.

TOURISM

Economically important to the Fehmarnbelt Region, tourism is predominantly centred on the coastal areas in the German part. In 2008, visits to the German coastal areas constituted 24.8 million overnight stays[xii] out of a total of 36.6 million overnight stays in the region. The Baltic Sea area alone accounted for almost 17 million overnight stays (Statistisches Bundesamt Deutschland).

FIGURE 29.
NUMBER OF OVERNIGHT STAYS AT HOTELS AND RESORTS (2008)

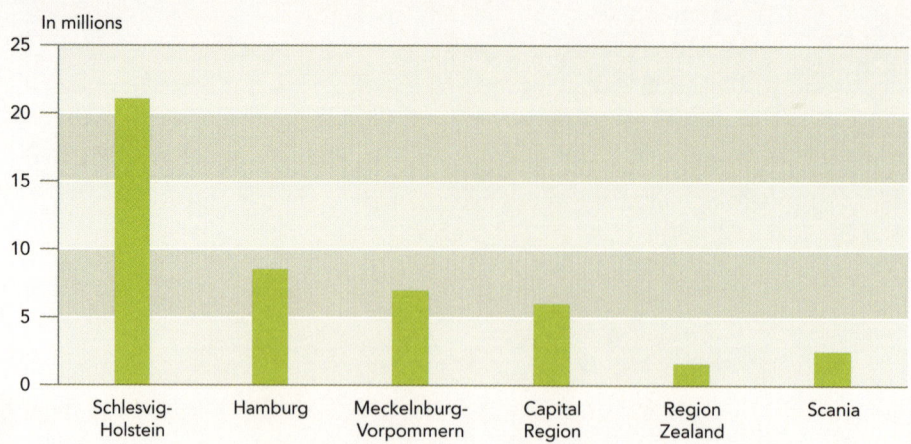

Source: Danmarks Statistik, Region Skåne (2008), Statistisches Bundesamt Deutschland
Note: See notes for Figures 27 and 28.

The map (Figure 27) shows existing hotels and resorts in the Fehmarnbelt Region. The German part of the Fehmarnbelt Region offers extensive hotel facilities situated along the coast.

In Denmark and Sweden the figures are lower. The City of Copenhagen has 70 hotels and resorts, which is the largest concentration in Denmark. Moreover, the number of overnight stays is significantly higher in the City of Copenhagen than in the rest of the Danish part of the Fehmarnbelt Region (Figure 28). The areas outside the capital have a low number of hotels and resorts apart from Lolland, which has a relatively high number of overnight stays compared to the rest of Denmark.

Figure 29 shows the number of overnight stays in the Fehmarnbelt Region. The figures for the German part of the region are considerably higher than for the Danish and Swedish parts.

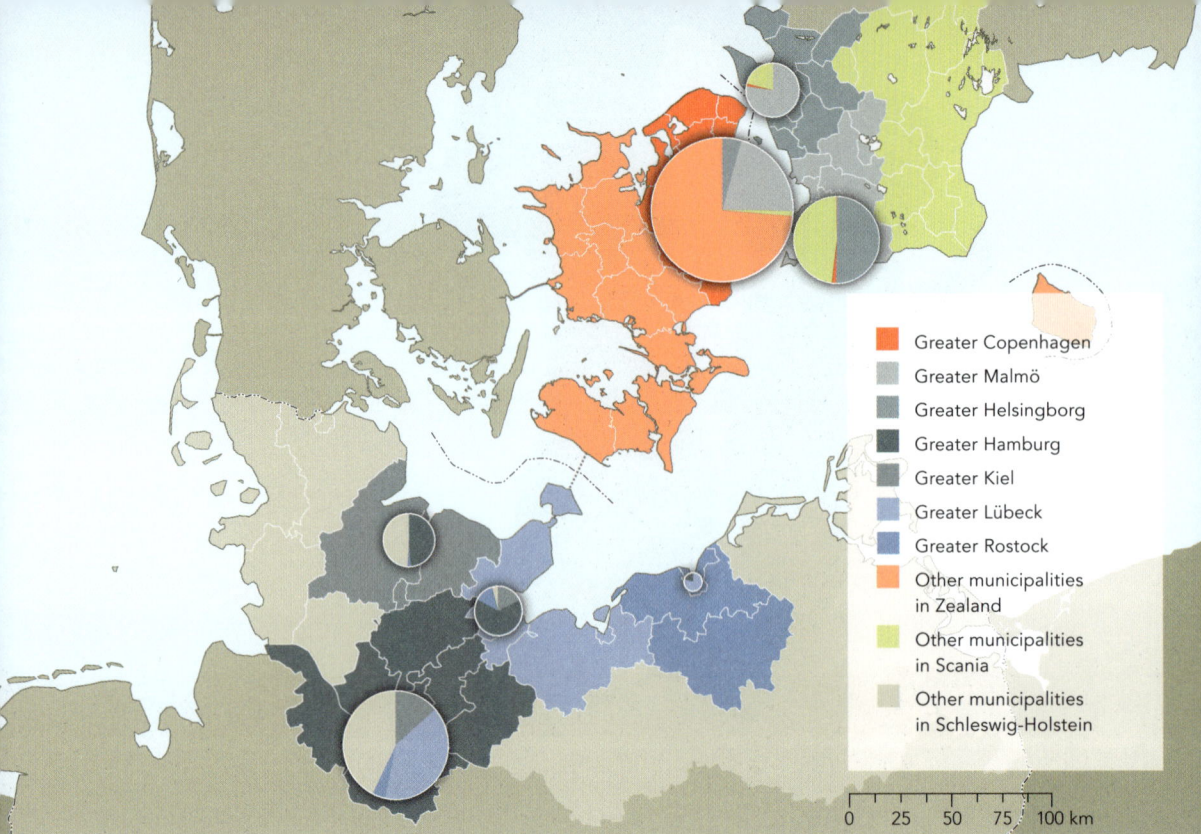

FIGURE 30.
INTER-REGIONAL COMMUTING TO MAJOR CITY REGIONS[xiii] (2007/2008)

Source: Ørestat, Statistisches Bundesamt Deutschland
Note: The German statistics only show commuters who pay social security contributions. (Sozialversicherungspflichtig Beschäftigte) and, therefore, do not represent the whole workforce. The statistics for the Swedish and Danish parts are from 2007 while the German statistics were taken from one day in 2008.

COMMUTING

The greater urban regions[xiv] have been given their own particular colour (Figure 30) (all municipalities/districts within it included). The pie chart shows the number of people commuting into one urban region from another. All commuters from one city to another are depicted in their 'home city colour' on the map. Those, for example, living in one of the municipalities in Greater Helsingborg and commuting to one of the municipalities in Greater Copenhagen are represented by a green stripe in the pie chart placed over Copenhagen on the map. This division shows the most attractive regions in which to work.

FIGURE 31.
THE NUMBER OF COMMUTERS FROM REGIONAL PARTS TO MAJOR CITY REGIONS (2007/2008)

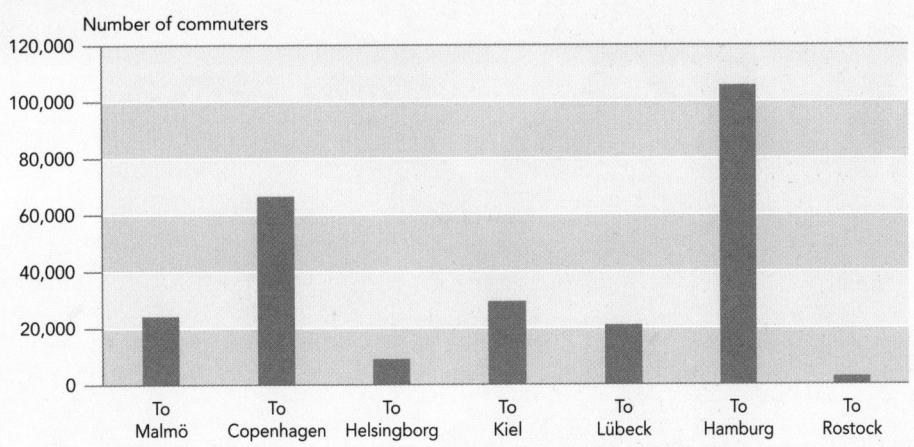

Source: Ørestat, Bundesagentur für Arbeit
Note: The figure shows the number of commuters to Greater Malmö, Greater Copenhagen and Greater Helsingborg from the Danish and Swedish parts of the region as well as commuters to Greater Kiel, Greater Lübeck, Greater Hamburg and Greater Rostock from the German parts of the region.

In the German part of the region, Greater Hamburg attracts the largest number of commuters (Figure 31) owing to the city's stronger economic position in the region. This is not only because of the city's large port, but also because of the large variety of attractive companies, research institutions and administrative bodies located in the greater urban region. 105,601 individuals commute into Greater Hamburg from other city areas and districts in the German part of the region. 40 per cent come from Greater Lübeck, 14 per cent from Greater Kiel, 4 per cent from Greater Rostock and 42 per cent from the other districts in Schleswig-Holstein.

Greater Lübeck and Greater Kiel also attract a significant number of commuters from the surrounding areas. Greater Kiel has around 29,000 commuters from other parts of the North German part of the Fehmarnbelt Region and Greater Lübeck has 21,000. With regard to both cities, most commuters come from Greater Hamburg. With just under 3,000 incoming commuters, including 77 per cent from Greater Lübeck[xv], Greater Rostock is more isolated than the other three urban regions in Germany.

In the Danish and Swedish parts of the region, Greater Copenhagen is the urban region that attracts most commuters from both Scania and Zealand compared to the two other urban regions in the area. The greater city region Copenhagen comprises the whole Capital Region. 66,500 individuals commute to Greater Copenhagen from the Danish and Swedish parts of the region. 74 per cent of these come from Region Zealand and 26 per cent from the Swedish part of the Fehmarnbelt Region, including 21 per cent from Greater Malmö. By comparison, only around 4,000 people from Greater Copenhagen commute to the Swedish part of the region. Greater Malmö also attracts a significant number of commuters from the surrounding areas. Slightly over 24,000 individuals commute to Greater Malmö, including 50 per cent from Greater Helsingborg.

REFERENCES

Bundesagentur für Arbeit, www.arbeitsagentur.de

Danmarks Statistik, www.dst.dk

Danmarks Statistik, 'Overnatninger på små hoteller og campingpladser 2006', 'Statistiske efterretninger, serviceerhverv 2007', 2007, 34

Die Regionaldatenbank Deutschland, www.regionalstatistik.de

Eurostat, http://epp.eurostat.ec.europa.eu

Focus Money Online, 'Wiedervereiningung prägt die Wirtschaft', 2007, www.focus.de/finanzen/news/deutschland_aid_51103.html

Region Skåne, 'Indkvarteringsstatistik December 2008', 2008, statistics, www.skane.com

Statistisches Amt für Hamborg und Schleswig-Holstein, www.statistik-nord.de

Statistisches Amt Mecklenburg-Vorpommern, www.statistik-mv.de

Statistiska Centralbyrån, 'Inkvarteringsstatistik för Sverige 2007, Totalundersökning av Sveriges hotell, stugor, vandrarhem och campingplatser', 2007, statistical reports, NV 41 SM 0805

Statistiska Centralbyrån, www.scb.se

Statistisches Bundesamt Deutschland, www.destatis.de

Ørestat, www.orestat.scb.se

Øresundsbro Konsortiet, 'Derfor rejser vi over Øresund', Øresundsbro Konsortiet, 2010, analysis, www.oresundsbron.com

NOTES

i Denmark, Sweden and Germany collect data in different ways. In Denmark and Sweden, the three levels of governance are represented in the statistics. The first level is the state, the second level is the regions in Denmark and regions/län in Sweden (referred to as regions in this chapter). The third level in Denmark and Sweden is the municipalities. In Germany, the three levels of governance are also represented in the statistics. The first level is the Bundesrepublik Deutschland (referred to as the state in this chapter), the second level comprises the Bundesländer (referred to by their names Hamburg, Schleswig-Holstein and Mecklenburg-Vorpommern, the third level comprises the Kresie and Kresifreie Städte, known as districts.

ii Greater Hamburg comprises Bundesland Hamburg and the surrounding districts Pinneberg, Segeberg, Storman, Herzogtum Lauenburg (located in Schleswig-Holstein) and the two districts Harburg and Stade in Lower Saxony.

iii Greater Kiel comprises the two major districts on both sides of the city as well as Kiel.

iv Greater Lübeck comprises East Holstein and has been extended by the district Nordwestmecklenburg and Wismar in Mecklenburg-Vorpommern.

v Greater Rostock comprises Bad Doberan and Gustrow.

vi Greater Copenhagen comprises the Danish capital and the surrounding municipalities in the Capital Region (minus Bornholm), as well as the municipalities in the former Roskilde County, the most south eastern municipalities.

vii Greater Malmö comprises the municipality of Malmö and its 11 neighbouring municipalities.

viii Greater Helsingborg comprises Helsingborg and the 10 municipalities in the north western part of Scania.

ix The figure does not show the total number employees in individual industries, but only the percentage of the total number of employees in a given company.

x It should be noted that one municipality can have a fall in the total number of people that work in a given industry but still show above average growth for the whole Fehmarnbelt Region – and vice versa.

xi Shift-term: growth rate for the industry 1996-2007 in municipalities/districts drawn from the growth rate for the same industry 1996-2007 in the whole Fehmarnbelt Region.

xii The number of overnight stays at hotels etc.

xiii See notes ii, iii, iv, v, vi, vii, and viii

xiv See notes ii, iii, iv, v, vi, vii, and viii

xv The Fehmarnbelt Region does not comprise the eastern part of Mecklenburg-Vorpommern, and this part is, therefore, not represented in the statistics.

CHAPTER 3
INFRASTRUCTURE, TRANSPORT AND LOGISTICS

PETRA AULIN, JACEK ROKICKI, PATRIK RYDEN, SIGNE SCHILLING,
LARS ROSTGAARD TOFT, EMMANOUIL TRANOS & MORTEN VEDBY

The Fehmarnbelt Region is divided by two borderlines, both of which are national borders and separated by waterways. These borderlines act as barriers and localisation factors with regard to infrastructure, transport and logistics. Compared to national traffic within the region, traffic across the Fehmarnbelt is modest and regional cross-border traffic within the Femernbelt Region is mainly handled by ferries, although with one exception, the Øresund Bridge.

The ferry terminals and the bridge are important focal points for the area's infrastructure. The Øresund Bridge has changed the logistics of Southern Scandinavia very considerably and since the opening of the bridge, Copenhagen Airport has become the main international centre not only for Denmark but also for Scania. The land based cross-Øresund traffic reflects the growing integration of Greater Copenhagen and Malmö-Lund while the short and frequent ferry crossings between Elsinore and Helsingborg also serve this border area's growing integration within specific sectors. With the exception of price-driven border trade, Fehmarnbelt does not present any particular cross-border systems.

This chapter is intended to analyse infrastructure, transport and logistics by examining some representative sectors. Moreover, the maps and diagrams will provide a picture of the Fehmarnbelt Region's international focus and its excellent infrastructure in the form

FIGURE 1.
ROAD AND RAIL LINES IN THE FEHMARNBELT REGION

Map by Femern A/S (2010)

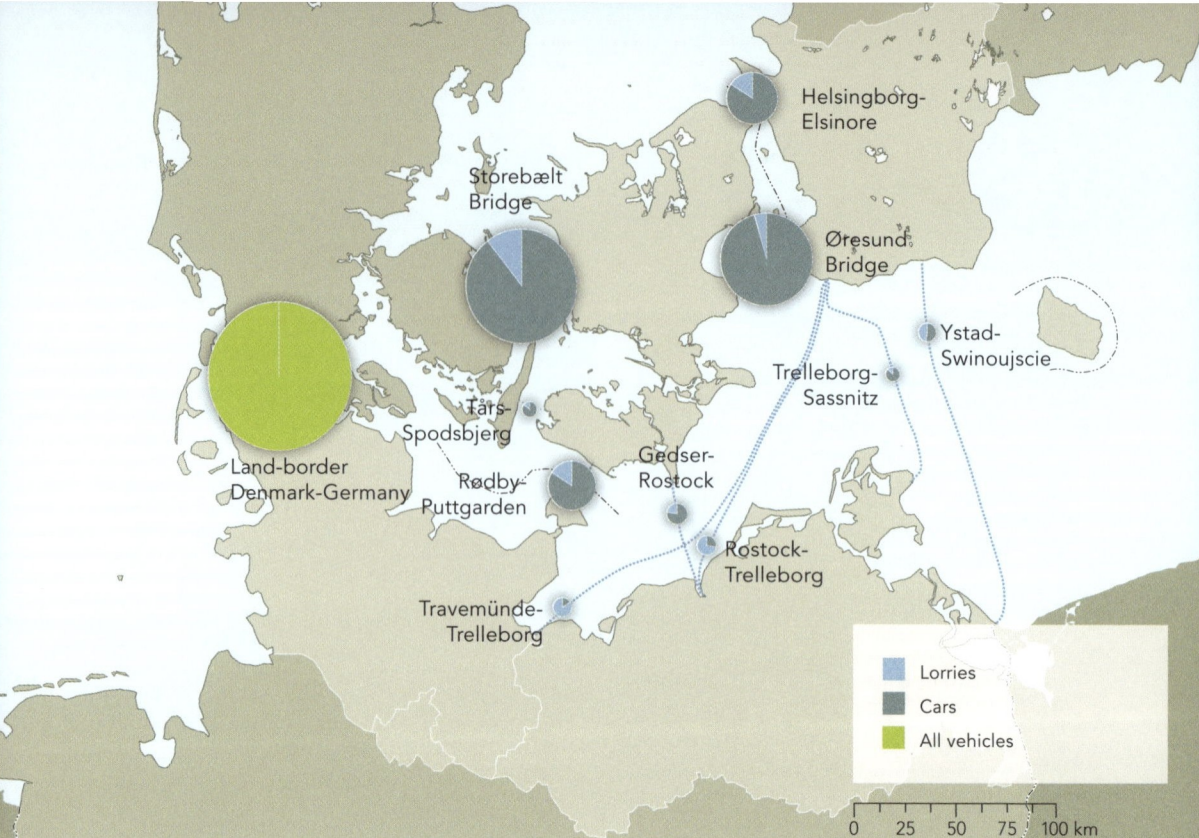

FIGURE 2.
AVERAGE DAILY TRAFFIC (2009)

Source: Shippax (2009) and Vejdiretoratet (the Danish Road Directorate) (2009)
Note: No statistical distinction has been made between cars and lorries at land-border connections

of motorways, ferry routes and railways. Sweden is linked to the European continent via direct ferry routes and via the Øresund Bridge and the Rødby and Gedser ferries to Puttgarden and Rostock. In addition, the European road network also links Zealand with Jutland via the Storebælt Bridge and the island of Funen before continuing to Flensburg in Germany. The establishment of a fixed link across the Fehmarnbelt will result in improvements to the region's infrastructure (Figure 1). This chapter will also look at international air transport and the internet's backbone structure. We will then consider logistics and give a brief overview of the logistical pre-conditions around the Fehmarnbelt as seen from a geographical perspective. The chapter will close with a general map of the Fehmarnbelt's near area.

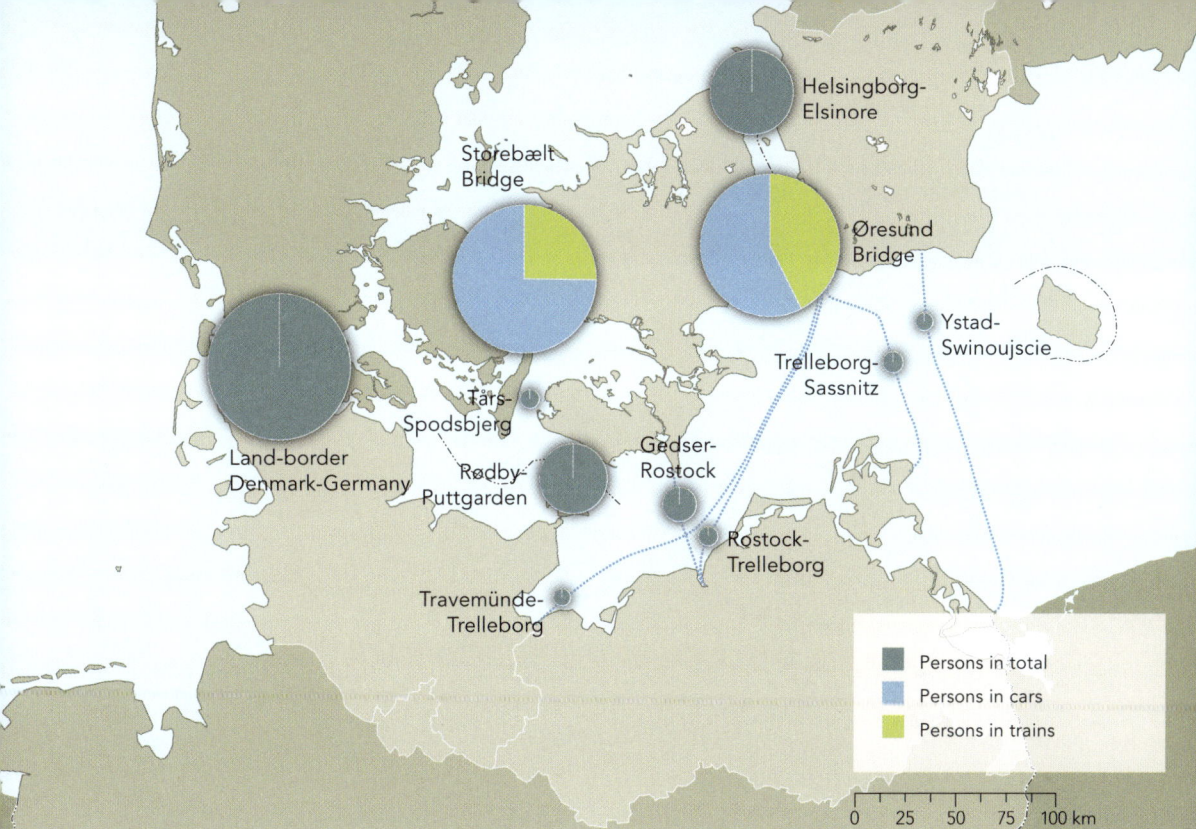

FIGURE 3.
AVERAGE NUMBER OF PERSONS (2009)

Source: Shippax, DSB and Storebælt
Note: The number of car passengers has been estimated by Øresundsbro Konsortiet

The Fehmarnbelt Region's average traffic illustrates its importance as a transport hub between the Scandinavian peninsula and continental Europe.

Figures 2 and 3 illustrate how the two major bridges, the Øresund Bridge and the Storebælt Bridge, together with the land border between Denmark and Germany, are the region's most important traffic corridors. The ferries between Helsingborg in Sweden and Elsinore in Denmark rank fourth, followed by the Rødby-Puttgarden ferries.

Figure 4 shows the general increase in the ferry services between Denmark, Germany and Sweden since the early 1980s. Over the period, the ferry service between Rødby and Puttgarden – i.e. where the Fehmarnbelt link will be built – has experienced average growth of 3 per cent.

FIGURE 4.
AVERAGE NUMBER OF VEHICLES PER DAY ON FERRIES IN DENMARK, GERMANY AND SWEDEN

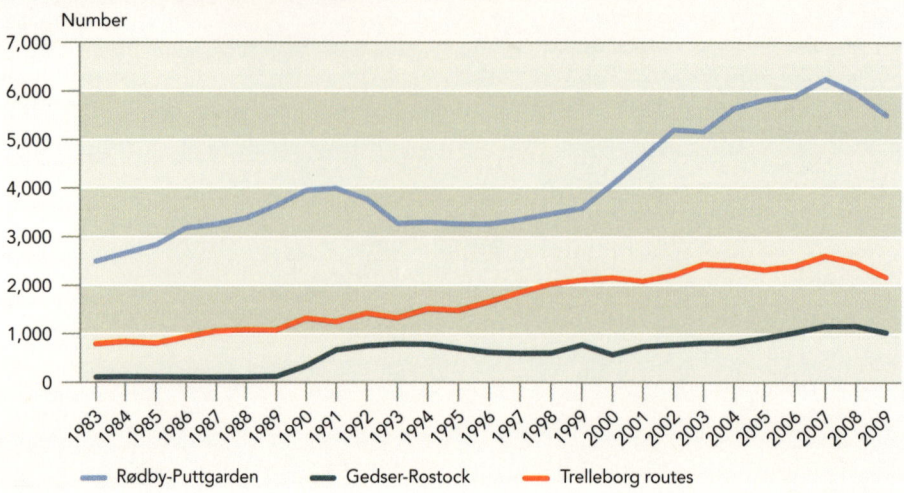

Source: Shippax (2009)

In general, the ferries between Sweden and Germany/Poland carry more lorries than cars (Figure 2). By contrast, the ferries between Denmark and Germany carry more passenger cars than lorries. In 2009, 64 per cent of the ferry traffic between Trelleborg and Germany consisted of lorries while lorries only accounted for 16 per cent of the traffic on the ferries between Rødby and Puttgarden.

Car traffic across the Øresund Bridge between Copenhagen and Malmö consists mainly of inter-regional traffic between Denmark and Sweden. Commuters, most of whom live in Sweden and work in Denmark, account for approximately 41 per cent of the traffic on the Øresund Bridge. Car traffic across the Storebælt Bridge consists mostly of traffic between the different parts of Denmark. Compared to the Øresund Bridge, commuters only account for 5 per cent of all cars on the Storebælt Bridge.

The number of air passengers illustrates the international focus of the main airports, Copenhagen and Hamburg (Figure 5). With around 21 million passengers per year, Copenhagen Airport is the region's largest airport followed by Hamburg with slightly less than 13

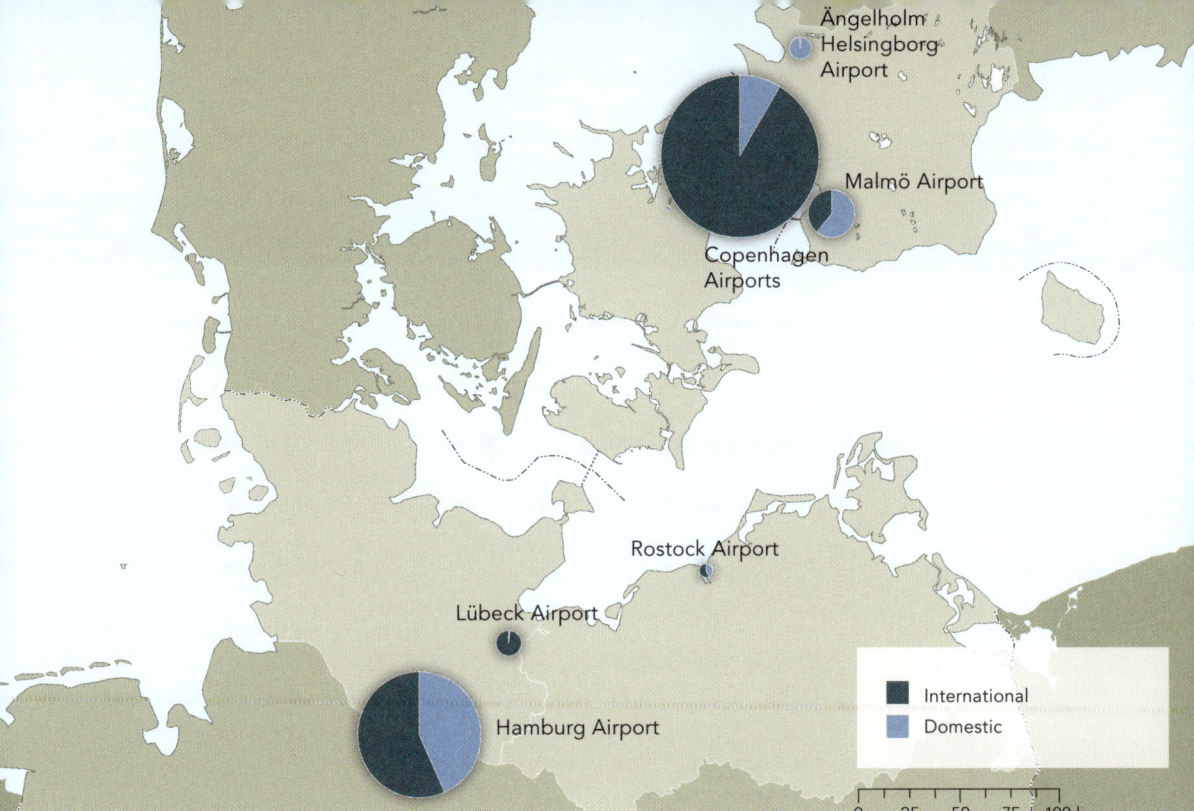

FIGURE 5.
AIR PASSENGERS TRAVELLING FROM AIRPORTS IN THE REGION (2008)

Source: Eurostat

million passengers annually (Figure 6). In the next section, we will look at Copenhagen and Hamburg airports and their international connections.

COPENHAGEN AND HAMBURG: INTERNATIONAL NETWORKS

We have chosen to analyse the position of the Fehmarnbelt Region's two metropolises in respect of two important international networks, i.e. international air traffic and the internet. International air traffic demonstrates the potential accessibility of people and high value freight to an area. Likewise, the internet backbone in the form of high capacity broadband indicates potential non-physical accessibility. The question is whether the Fehmarnbelt Region's major cities represent strong centres within these global networks.

FIGURE 6.
NATIONAL AND INTERNATIONAL FLIGHT DEPARTURES MEASURED IN PASSENGERS (2008)

Airport	Number of domestic flights	Number of international flights	Total
Copenhagen	1,885,054	19,614,822	21,499,876
Roskilde	9,809	4,670	14,479
Malmö	1,126,893	711,831	1,838,724
Ängelholm - Helsingborg	387,061	5,333	392,394
Hamburg	5,602,491	7,267,286	12,869,777
Lübeck	12,394	517,123	529,517
Rostock	68,232	91,208	159,440

Source: Eurostat

The analysis has been carried out by Lars Rostgaard Toft and Morten Vedby in respect of air traffic and by Immanouil Tranos with regard to the internet's backbone network. The analysis can be read in full at www.femern.com under "publications".

International air traffic demonstrates a city's potential accessibility regardless of whether the traffic is destined for the city itself or is transit traffic. The overall traffic shows the number of routes and frequency. The respective positions in the network for Copenhagen and Hamburg are calculated on the basis of week 11, 2010, as given at the airports' websites. Only routes with more than ten weekly departures have been included. The width of the route lines is proportional to the number of departures. Air traffic is addressed further on page 114.

Copenhagen is a key centre with an extensive European network and flight connections to cities in all four continents. Hamburg has few international routes and a modest European network.

The internet's international network (internet protocol links) is the backbone structure that links destinations over long distances and is responsible for the global dimension of the internet. The aim of the analysis is to explore the extent of the metropolises' links within the network and the role the cities play within the network. Such networks are structurally influenced by the shape of the network for the world's cities. As the telecommunications industry primarily consists of private providers, the infrastructure network has typically developed in accordance with demand. The need for communications between the world's metropolises and their surrounding areas is currently larger than ever and providers have a financial interest in investing in networks in areas with the greatest demand. This has led

FIGURE 7.
COPENHAGEN. AIR TRANSPORT'S INTERNATIONAL NETWORK (2010)
THICKNESS OF LINES PROPORTIONAL TO NUMBER OF DEPARTURES

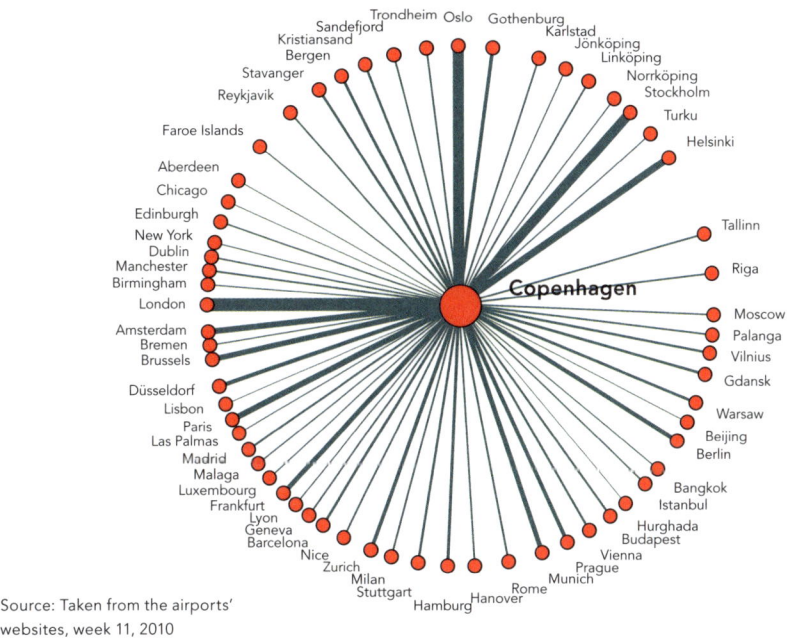

Source: Taken from the airports' websites, week 11, 2010

FIGURE 8.
HAMBURG. AIR TRANSPORT'S INTERNATIONAL NETWORK (2010)

Source: Taken from the airports' websites, week 11, 2010

**THE INTERNET BACKBONE STRUCTURE'S CENTRALISATION VALUES
(MAXIMUM VALUE = 100) AND RANKING IN EUROPE (2007)**

	Number of international broadband links		Total international broadband capacity		Links that pass through the city	
London	100	1	100	1	100	1
Paris	66	2	49	3	35	3
Frankfurt	58	3	70	2	64	2
Amsterdam	50	4	32	4	13	5
Stockholm	20	5	19	7	2	19
Copenhagen	18	6	17	9	8	8
Madrid	16	7	15	12	4	13
Vienna	14	8	28	5	14	4
Milan	13	9	25	6	12	6
Hamburg	13	10	12	14	3	14
Berlin	0	43	1	43	0	39

to the establishment of a number of global communication centres. Despite their global reach, however, the internet's backbone networks are highly selective with regard to the urban networks they interconnect with – not least in terms of the quality of the connection.

The data used for this analysis represent the international intercity internet backbone links and derive from Telegeography (2007), which is the only provider of data on the internet backbone network. The centralised nature of the binary (no weighting of the network links) and the weighted network (links are weighted in accordance with bandwidth capacity) are shown.

Compared to other major cities in Europe, Copenhagen performs well in terms of the internet backbone network. Copenhagen ranks sixth on the list with regard to the number of international broadband links and ninth in terms of international bandwidth capacity. The Danish capital ranks eighth with regard to the number of intercity links passing through the city.

FIGURE 9.
COPENHAGEN IN THE INTERNET'S BACKBONE (2007)
THICKNESS OF LINES PROPORTIONAL TO BROADBAND CAPACITY

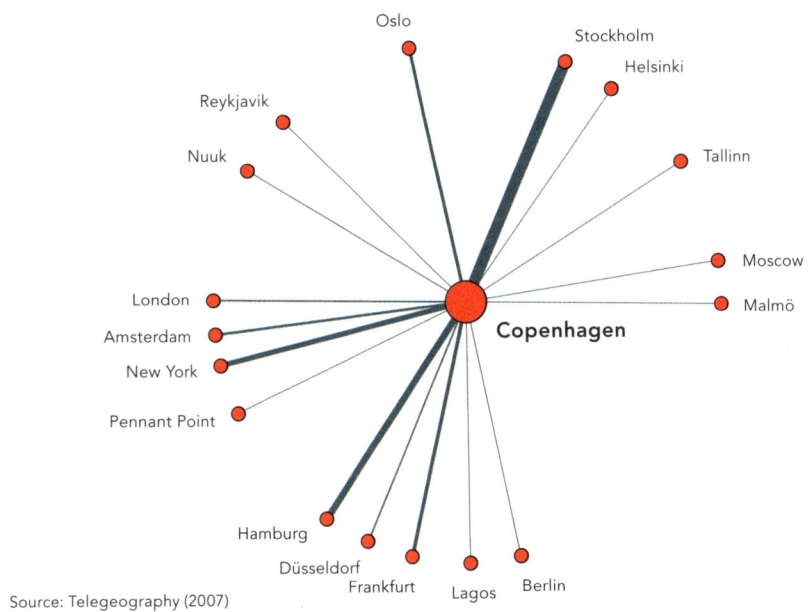

Source: Telegeography (2007)

FIGURE 10.
HAMBURG IN THE INTERNET'S BACKBONE NETWORK (2007)

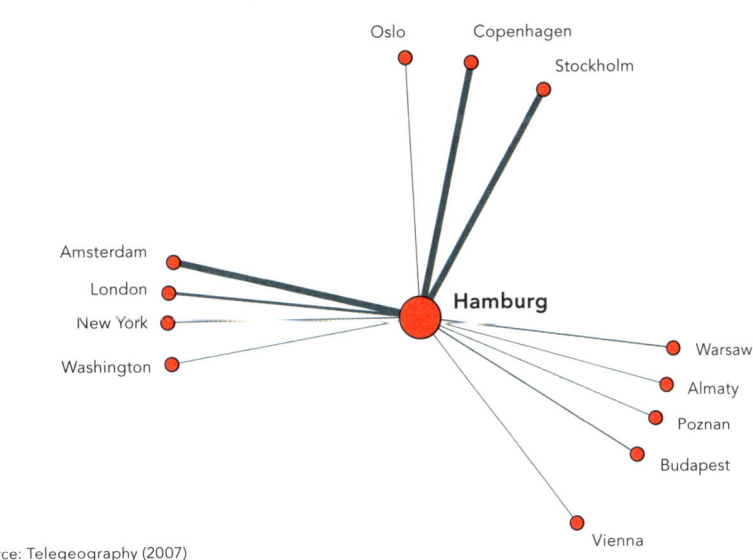

Source: Telegeography (2007)

Hamburg is also a central hub, albeit less important than Copenhagen. Hamburg ranks 10th in Europe with regard to the number of international broadband links and 14th in terms of international broadband capacity and the number of links between other major cities that pass through the city.

The position of the two cities within the network is, at one and the same time, identical and different. Both have strong positions in the network and both are well connected to Stockholm and to each other. Copenhagen has strong links to New York and Oslo and Hamburg is well connected to Amsterdam and London.

LOGISTICS AND FREIGHT TRANSPORT

The opening of the Øresund Bridge provided a unique opportunity for studying the impact of new fixed links. The Øresund Bridge generated new distribution structures and more efficient goods chains with fewer links in the logistics chain feeding the Scandinavian market. The Øresund Region's potential for strengthening its position as Scandinavia's leading logistics centre is underpinned by four main trends:

- Greater globalisation: increased global trade has meant that logistics is becoming ever more important as a competitive parameter. Today companies buy and sell products in the global market with the result that the price of goods is under pressure while the proportion of the logistics costs of the product price is increasing. With increased logistics costs, it becomes more important for companies to reduce such costs. (Söderström 2002).

- Centralisation: the cost of transport relating to goods distribution comprises two major aspects, i.e. transport from production to the warehouse and transport from the warehouse to the customer. This, however, is not the only way in which transport impacts on the overall logistics costs. The number of warehouse points also plays an important role. Changes to the number of distribution centres, therefore, affect a company's overall distribution costs. With the exception of transport costs, all costs fall when the number of warehouse points is reduced. The largest savings from consolidating the number of warehouses are achieved through warehouse management and stock. In principle, this means a 50 per cent reduction in the number of warehouse points and that the volume of stock can be reduced by approximately 30 per cent overall. (Abrahamsson & Aronsson 1999).

- Innovative logistics: logistics companies in Western Europe are currently subject to tough competition within transport and forwarding and many have lost out in favour of Eastern European companies. Those companies that have coped better with the intensive competition and have bigger margins are those that offer more than just transport solutions. Extended services such as third party logistics, fourth party logistics, postponement activities and other added value services create the preconditions for increased margins for individual businesses. (Olsson & Sevandersson, 2005).

– Concentration trends: in view of increasing global trade it is crucial that individual businesses exploit the savings potential within logistics. One way of achieving this is a so-called late customer adjustment (postponement). The concept means that the products are customised as late as possible in the value chain; in some cases not until a customer order is received. The method is in stark contrast to situations where a company has substantial stocks of finished products. Through deferred customisation, both warehousing levels and more flexibility in response to rapid changes in demand are assured. This will achieve cost savings that can be important for many companies. At the same time, the method requires that the product offer is standardised and module adapted.

For companies taking up this concept, the result is that the distribution systems can be compared to "mini factories" where assembly, packaging, labelling etc. are carried out within the framework of the distribution system, Schary 2001. With a larger market, a strong logistics centre and a strong sector within high tech products, the concept, which includes value adding activities, becomes increasingly interesting for all regions in the near area, i.e. Schleswig-Holstein, Hamburg and the Øresund Region.

The same factors mean that the Øresund and Hamburg Regions together will strengthen their positions as the most important logistics hub in Northern Europe once the Fehmarnbelt link is completed. Both the Øresund and Hamburg Regions are currently extremely strong logistics regions. In the Øresund Region, for instance, the logistics sector employs around 77,000 people while in the Hamburg Region, more than 170,000 individuals work within this sector. Hansen (2006). When the regions are connected by a fixed link, all indications are that both regions will strengthen their positions as leading logistics hubs in Northern Europe and as trading platforms for the Baltic area. In the following, we shall analyse logistics from a geographical perspective.

Helsingborg in North-Western Scania has a strong tradition as a trading centre, especially in respect of road and sea transport. Despite the opening of the Øresund Bridge in 2000, the ferries operating between Helsingborg and Elsinore have maintained their position. With respect to transport in the north-south direction, the Helsingborg/Elsinore ferry services offer a 50 km shorter distance as well as a break on the ferries and, therefore, represent an alternative to the Øresund Bridge. Besides the ferry link across Øresund,

Helsingborg's port also has feeder traffic to e.g. Hamburg, Bremerhaven, Rotterdam, St Petersburg and Tallinn. Helsingborg's strongest sectors are food, logistics and, to a certain extent, pharmaceuticals. The town's major companies include DSV, Bring, Frigoscandia and Unilever.

Hässleholm in North-Eastern Scania was previously a significant centre for transport and logistics and the transport sector remains an important part of its commercial activities. Hässleholm's geographical location, together with the town's position as a rail hub, is still attractive to many companies and plans are underway to establish Hässleholm as an intermodal hub. Currently, Hässleholm has one of Sweden's largest concentration of food companies, especially with regard to agricultural products and meat. (Magnusson 2002).

In South-Western Scania, the logistics industry is dominated by the activities in and around Malmö and Trelleborg. Trelleborg's port is Sweden's second largest after Gothenburg in terms of turnover of goods and has ferry services for ro-ro traffic to Travemünde, Rostock, Sassnitz and Swinoujscie. Trelleborg's commercial life is dominated by manufacturing companies such as Pergo AB and Trelleborg AB. The port of Trelleborg

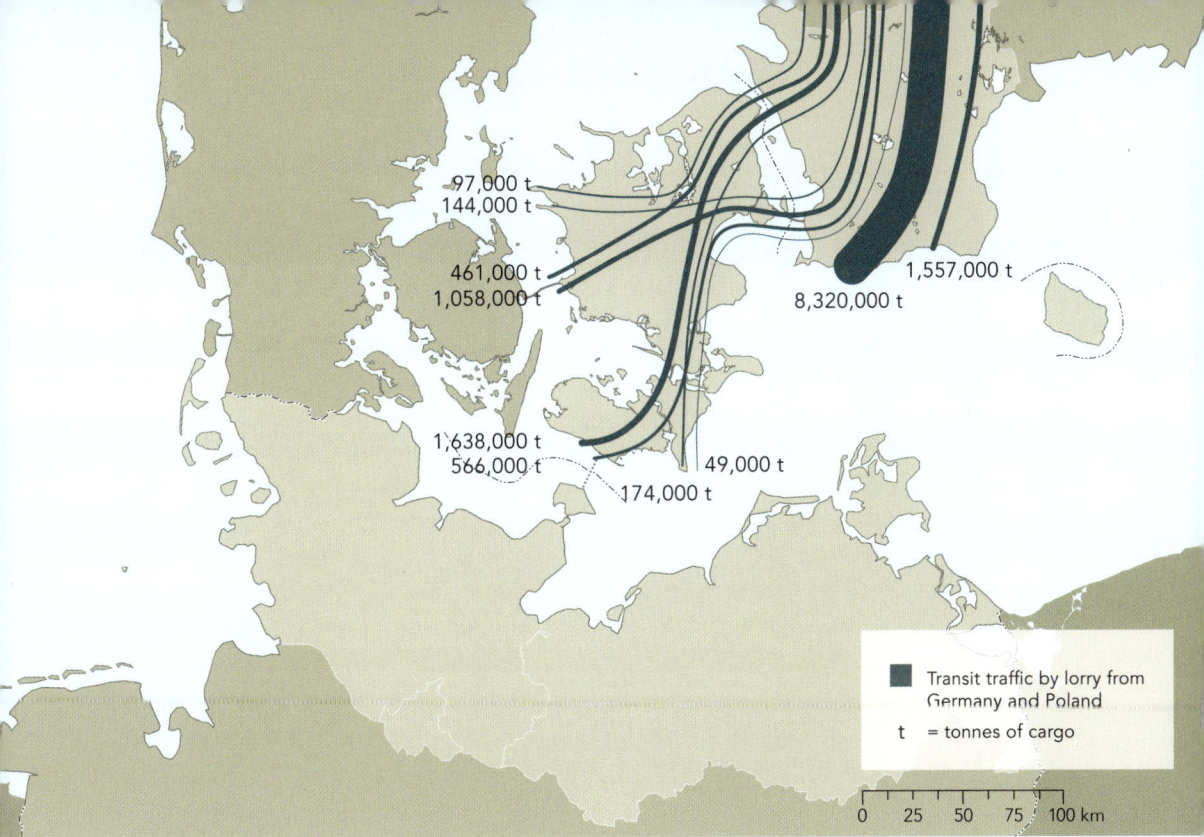

FIGURE 11.
TRANSIT TRAFFIC BY LORRY FROM GERMANY AND POLAND THROUGH THE ØRESUND REGION

Source: IBU Øresund (2009)
Note: Trelleborg has ferry links with Travemünde, Rostock, Sassnitz and Swinoujscie. From Denmark, there are links between Rødby-Puttgarden and Gedser-Rostock

also has a strong position in terms of Sweden's links to the European continent. This is particularly emphasised by the IBU Øresund project's report from 2009 (see also Figure 11).

The port of Malmö's current freight turnover is, in principle, equal to that of Trelleborg. In 2008, Malmö's freight turnover amounted to approximately 11 million tonnes. There is feeder traffic to e.g. Hamburg, Bremerhaven, Tallinn and Riga. The merger of the ports of Malmö and Copenhagen has proved highly successful. Strong sectors in Malmö include logistics, retail and wholesale trade as well as construction and property. Among the companies located here are DSV Transport, Pågen AB and Skanska. Sturup Airport is located in South-Western Scania.

Logistics activities in South-Eastern Scania are centred around the port of Ystad, a bulk, ferry and industrial port where, among others, Schenker and DSV are active. The area around Ystad has some chemical production of plastic and paint products. Among the larger companies in South-Eastern Scania are Polykemi, Superfos Packaging and Swedish Rail System (www.transportgruppen.se).

The entire Danish metropolitan region can be regarded as a freight transport hub. In general, however, industrial companies (including warehousing and distribution companies) have settled outside the centres of the major cities, including Copenhagen. Companies are centred on the outskirts of the capital, especially in the southern and south western suburbs. In Taastrup, Hvidovre and Brøndby, there is access to both road and rail transport and these locations are important hubs for freight transport on Zealand. DSV, DHL and Schenker operate only a few kilometres from each other. Besides logistics companies, there is a high concentration of high-tech companies within the area. With its annual freight turnover of approximately 7 million tonnes, the Port of Copenhagen is one of Denmark's largest. The majority of the incoming freight to the Port of Copenhagen is used in the capital. Copenhagen Airport is Scandinavia's largest and is of significant strategic importance for company set-ups in the Øresund Region. Høje-Taastrup and Elsinore are the most prominent logistics areas in the metropolitan region. The port of Elsinore has a freight turnover of around 4.5 million tonnes annually (Olsson & Sevandersson, 2005).

Within Region Zealand, Roskilde, in certain aspects, provides an interesting alternative to Taastrup and Hvidovre. In general, there are also many logistics activities around Køge. With just 10 per cent of the Port of Copenhagen's freight turnover, Køge is one of Denmark's smaller ports. It does, however, have the capacity to receive ro-ro transport as well as dry and liquid commodity products and the area's geographical position means that it is well suited for distribution activities in Zealand, including Copenhagen. As part of this, Skandinavisk Transport Centre Køge (STC) has been established west of the E20 motorway and there are plans for extending a rail link to the centre. Netto and DBK Book Distribution are some of the companies that distribute their products across Denmark from the centre in Køge. In the north western corner of Zealand, Kalundborg is another transport hub. Kalundborg Port has an annual freight turnover of approximately 4 million tonnes with regular ro-ro traffic to Århus etc. In Lolland and Falster, Rødby and Gedser are the most important freight hubs due to their proximity to Germany. Today, there are links to Germany via Rødby-Puttgarden and Gedser-Rostock. Rødby port, which has an annual goods turnover of 6 million tonnes, is around three times larger than Gedser port (www.danske-havn.dk).

Hamburg is one of the German cities that, due to increased globalization, has been most successful. Hamburg functions as a global hub for Central Europe and, in certain instances, also for Eastern Europe and the Baltic area. Many of the logistics activities are centred around the port, which is one of Europe's largest. Opened in 2001, HHLA Altenwerder container terminal remains one of the world's most modern. In general, all port activities are fully automatised.

Despite the very substantial investments in port facilities in and around Hamburg, the port was hit by capacity problems in 2008. The economic crisis, which subsequently impacted on the global market, alleviated the port's capacity problems, making its significance for Hamburg even more evident. Following some months of low volumes in 2008 and 2009, Hamburg has, however, focused significantly on how to recover the previous high volumes of 2006 and 2007 (www.hamburg-logsitics.com).

Large incoming freight volumes in Hamburg derive from China, Singapore, South Korea and Brazil. Most of the imports are subsequently channelled into the German market and to other Baltic markets, not least the Scandinavian countries. Its strong position as a global port also means that Hamburg is one of Europe's largest rail hubs. In addition, there are a number of strong intermodal hubs in the near area, Billwerder Moorfleet, Maschen, Meimersdorf and Stade-Brunshausen. Overall, Hamburg's dominant logistics sector employs more than 170,000 individuals (Magnusson & Rydén, 2002).

The dominant ports and, therefore, the logistics hubs in Schleswig-Holstein, comprise Lübeck, Kiel and Brunsbüttel although there are other ports in the region, more than 40 in all. Much of the regional transport consists of products to and from the Scandinavian market. Besides Lübeck, Kiel and Brunsbüttel, there are small areas under development in Schleswig-Holstein, e.g. Neumünster.

Kiel has ferry links, which handles hazardous goods to Gothenburg in Sweden. From Kiel there is also feeder traffic to Russia and the Baltic area and the port facilities include lo-lo as well as ro-ro activities. The Kiel port area also has rail terminals. Moreover, Kiel has a small airport although this is not particularly active.

Brunsbüttel enjoys a good geographical location between the Elba River and the Kiel channel which offers strong opportunities for maritime transport. Overall, the port facilities handle containers, hazardous goods, oil, paper, gas and components for the construction industry such as cement and timber. Brunsbüttel's main operations, however, relate to commodities although food and agricultural products are also shipped from Glückstadt port. Brunsbüttel port is closely linked to Hamburg port which has been important in terms of solving the problems caused by lack of capacity in and around Hamburg.

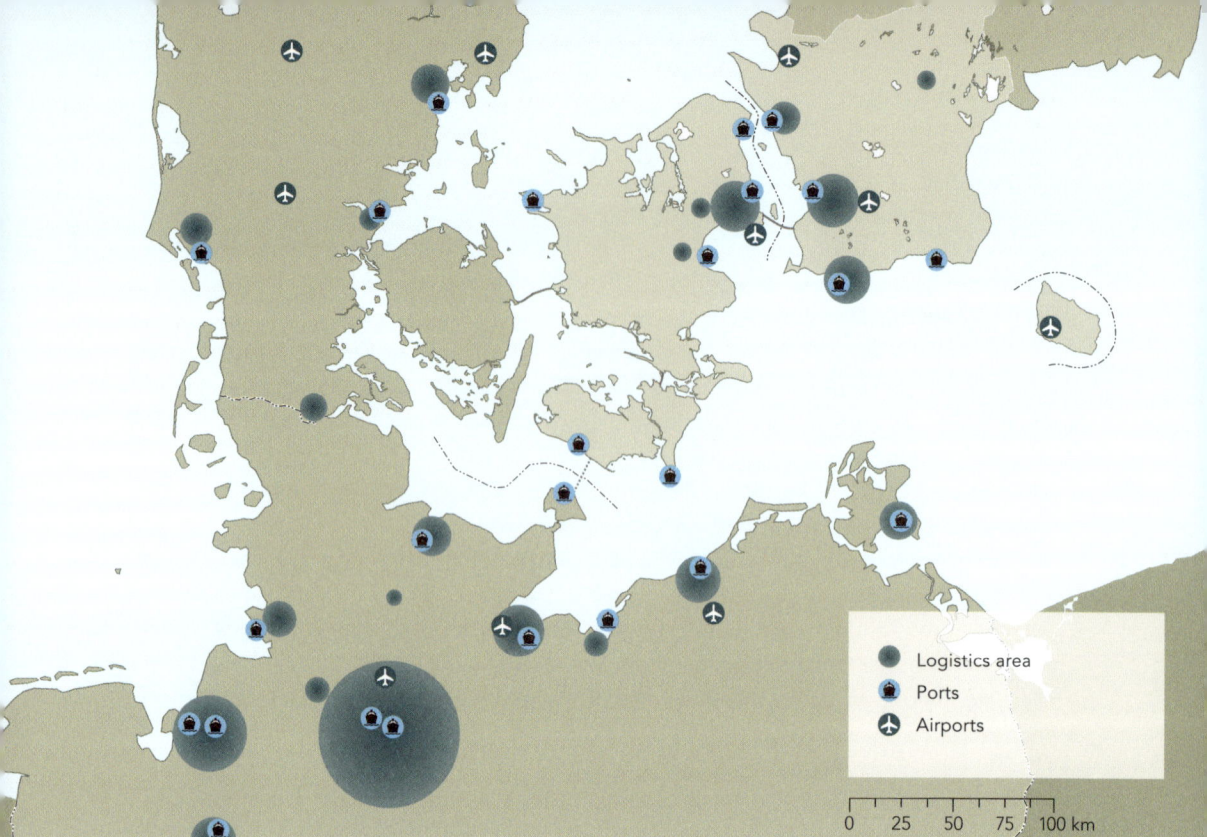

FIGURE 12.
AREAS WITH LARGE CONCENTRATIONS OF LOGISTICS COMPANIES AND EMPLOYEES IN LOGISTICS-RELATED JOBS AND PORTS AND AIRPORTS

Source: Metadata from Eurostat, http://epp.eurostat.ec.europa.eu, list of companies from the Hamburg Chamber of Commerce, Schleswig-Holstein, www.transportgruppen.se, www.danske-havne.dk and Hansen & Serin (2005)

Together with Puttgarden, Lübeck and Travemünde are important for transport between Germany and Scandinavia. Lübeck is also an important German hub for trade with other Baltic countries. Lübeck, for instance, has a PDI facility for reloading cars. 200,000 cars were expedited through Lübeck in one year. Food and timber are also loaded here. All in all, the logistics sector employs some 4000 people in Lübeck alone (www.luebeck.org). Lübeck Blankensee Airport is Schleswig-Holstein's largest although its route network is rather limited (Logistics Initiative Schleswig-Holstein).

FIGURE 13.
COMPILATION OF PORT STATISTICS, FREIGHT TURNOVER

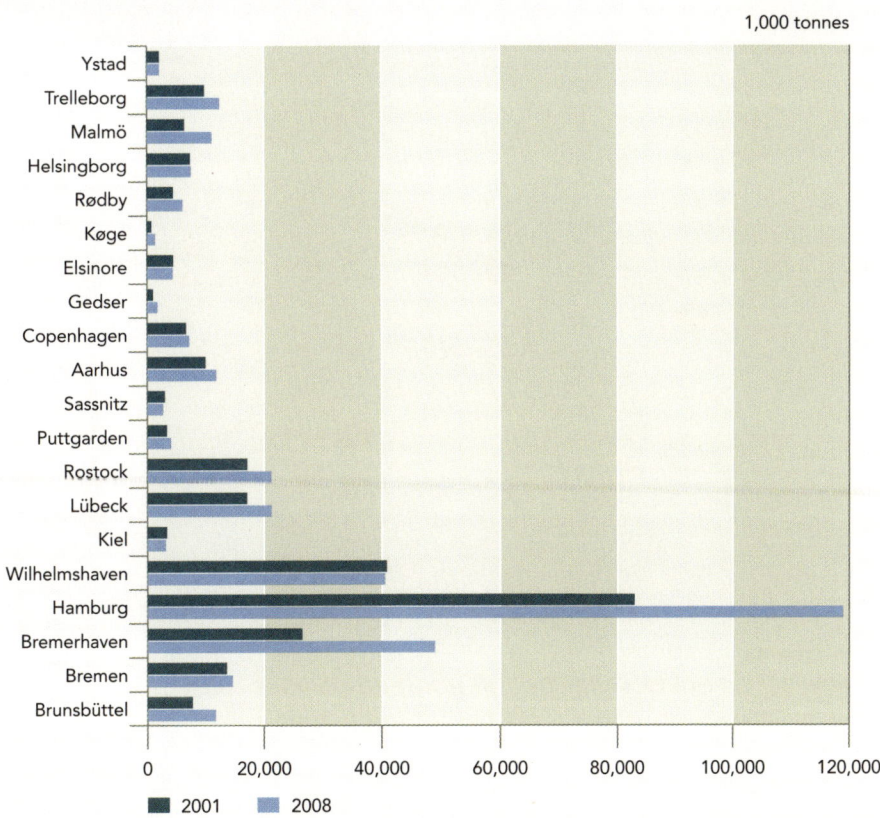

Source: Eurostat

The chart in Figure 13 shows the region's major ports.

The Øresund Region is one of the most attractive regions in Northern Europe in terms of air transport. Together with Sturup Airport, Copenhagen Airport provides excellent opportunities for companies involved in air freight.

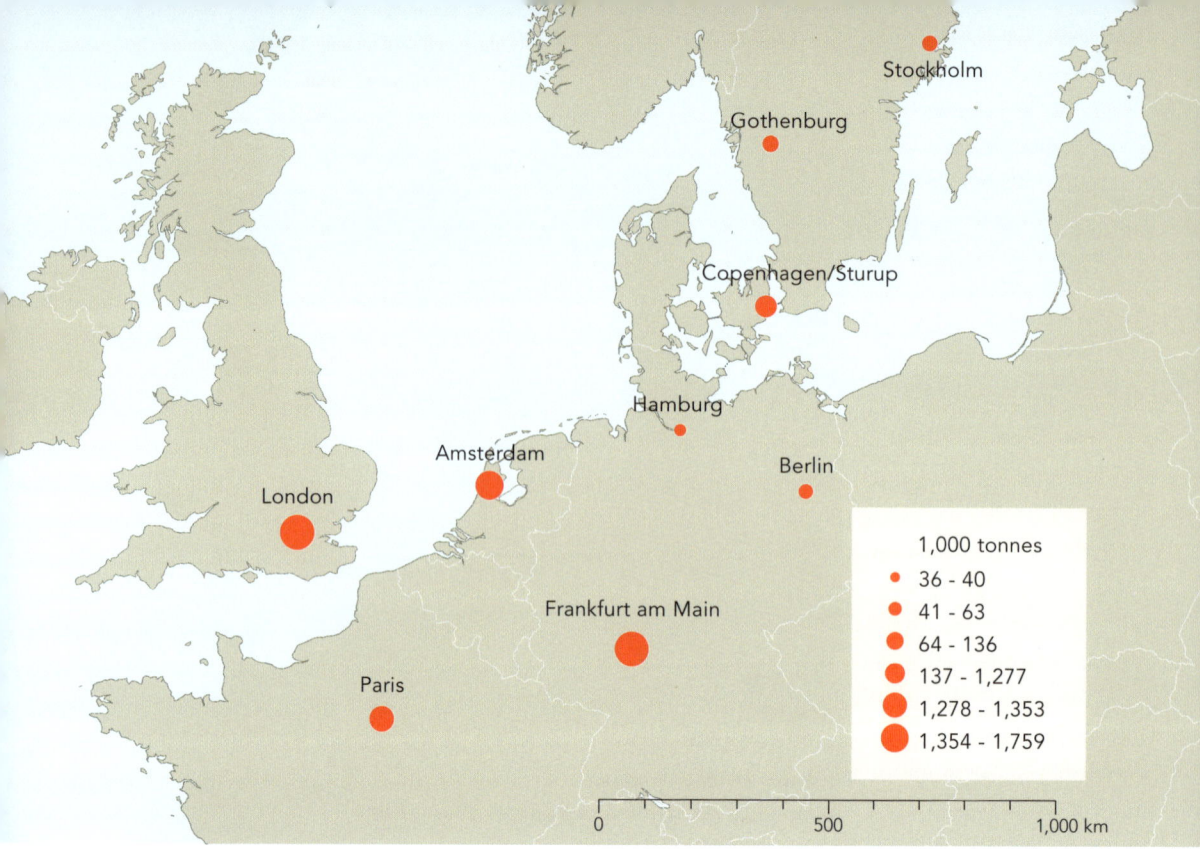

FIGURE 14.
FREIGHT TURNOVER AT AIRPORTS IN NORTHERN EUROPE

Source: Hansen & Serin (2005)

Although, in terms of volume, air freight accounts for a very small part of overall freight transport, the value of such freight is generally high. Proximity to international airports is strategically important for company formations. Companies that do not usually use air freight may, in certain situations, have a significant need for the lifeline offered by air freight (Magnusson 2002).

The section below gives a brief description of some of the logistical effects from a fixed link across Fehmernbelt.

Changes to distribution structures: The opening of the Øresund Bridge did not immediately lead to companies starting to consolidate their logistical structures across the Øresund waterway. A few years later, however, changes to their distribution structure were noticeable in a number of companies. The Øresund Bridge laid the groundwork for this process, driving innovative thinking within this field. There were also other drivers – e.g. early movers – that acted as inspiration for others. One such flagship was Toyota's localisation and centralisation at Malmö port.

Toyota's car terminal in Malmö was commissioned in 2003, i.e. three years after the opening of the Øresund Bridge. Toyota decided to set up a centralised distribution centre in Malmö port for the Nordic countries and the Baltic area which, to a certain extent, also supplies the Russian market. For the southern Swedish market, the cars are transported to dealers by lorry while rail is used for Northern Sweden and Norway. The Danish market is only supplied by lorries while cars for Finnish dealers are transported from Malmö by smaller vessels.

This is an example of the new distribution structure where distributors no longer operate national distribution terminals for national markets. Decisions whether to centralise and/or re-locate distribution terminals are often taken by the owner of the goods themselves.

The Fehmarnbelt link will create new distribution patterns for businesses in the same way as the Øresund Bridge tied two markets together and thus created the pre-conditions for innovative thinking with regard to which markets should be served from which distribution centres. Precisely as was the case with the Øresund Bridge, early movers can achieve short-term competitive advantage while, at the same time, provide inspiration for others.

The new fixed link across Fehmarnbelt will connect two of Northern Europe's biggest logistics clusters which between them will employ approximately 250,000 people. This will link the Øresund Region directly to some of Europe's largest container ports and increase competition between the Øresund Region's ports. In part, this will also create opportunities for launching new logistics concepts for the ports at Schleswig-Holstein or Hamburg and added value activities in the Øresund Region.

Part of the current feeder traffic between the ports in the Schleswig-Holstein area and Hamburg and ports in the Øresund Region may, in the longer term, be replaced by rail or road transport. This, however, assumes that track will be fully developed, including on the German side, and that capacity is sufficient. With regard to rail transport, there is a certain risk that the entire rail system may become more vulnerable after the link's completion. For instance, electricity problems in Hamburg may disrupt rail traffic in both Denmark and Sweden.

Another potential development area is air freight. Copenhagen Airport is not only Northern Europe's largest airport for freight, but also one of the most efficient. For companies in Hamburg, the proximity to Copenhagen Airport may be important, e.g. in respect of urgent transport. This means that Copenhagen Airport could be an interesting alternative or supplement to, for instance, Frankfurt or Amsterdam. There is also excellent potential for increased collaboration between air freight operators. According to the Institute for Transport Research (TFK 2001), air freight operators lag significantly behind their land-based competitors in respect of exploiting modern system solutions for logistics. The majority of freight operators rarely co-operate, neither within the air segment nor within other forms of transport.

Out of the total transport time, air freight only accounts for 10-15 per cent, which is an indication that there could be business opportunities in persuading logistics operators to rationalise their logistics concepts for air freight that does not "fly". (Magnusson 2002).

Moreover, there could be significant opportunities for increasing border regional partnerships within the future infrastructure planning. There is already some co-operation with regard to infrastructure issues in the form of the STRING partnership between Region Scania, The Capital Region of Denmark, Region Zealand, Schleswig-Holstein and Hamburg. More partnerships could, however, materialise. To take an example, the STRING partnership could be used to prepare future green corridors for freight transport in Europe. Green corridors is a European concept under which the structure consists of freight transport by rail supplemented by specially adjusted road transport.

DIVIDED SYSTEMS: INTEGRATION PERSPECTIVES FOR INFRASTRUCTURE, TRANSPORT AND LOGISTICS

Do the Fehmarnbelt Region's metropolises form strong centres within the dominating flows in a changing world? Copenhagen ranks highly in terms of flight connections to cities in four continents and with a strong European network. Hamburg has only a few international connections and a modest European network. Compared to other European cities, Copenhagen performs well with regard to central points in the internet backbone network. Hamburg is also a central hub although not as important as Copenhagen.

For Schleswig-Holstein and Hamburg, the Fehmarnbelt link and the Øresund Bridge create proximity to the Øresund regional market but also – and perhaps more importantly – provide direct access to the entire Scandinavian market, a prosperous market of close to 20 million people (Sweden, Denmark and Norway). As a result, the fixed link will strengthen the logistical pivot for Northern Germany.

Since Hamburg currently enjoys a strong logistics position in Europe, there is no risk that Hamburg's position will diminish in favour of the Øresund Region. By contrast, the proximity to the Øresund Region and the Scandinavian market will contribute to strengthening Hamburg and Schleswig-Holstein's position vis-a-vis competing regions and make it likely that a certain shift will occur away from e.g. Luxembourg, Belgium and the Netherlands towards Schleswig-Holstein and Hamburg. One pre-condition, however,

is that capacity problems do not impose limitations on the port of Hamburg or on the road and rail network around Hamburg.

In the same way, the fixed link across Fehmarnbelt will enhance the Øresund Region's position as Scandinavia's logistic hub. The proximity to the German market means that within three hours, a market of more than 10 million people will be accessible.

The Fehmarnbelt link will, therefore, primarily result in a strengthening of Schleswig-Holstein, Hamburg and the Øresund Region's positions. We do not expect to see a direct transfer of logistics activities across the Fehmarnbelt. However, logistics companies will benefit from the opportunities created from the opening of the link. In the longer term, differences in transport prices, accessibility to infrastructure, bottlenecks and labour costs will, however, result in the transfer of activities from one side of the Fehmarnbelt to another.

By stimulating developments in various ways, e.g. by co-ordinating communication and marketing across national borders, the Øresund Region, Schleswig-Holstein and Hamburg may achieve advantages in a relatively short time following the completion of the link.

As logistics services advance, the sector will also become dependent on the accumulation of knowledge. With increased focus on traceability, improved security, "green" logistics solutions and postponement activities, the interest in collaborative projects with universities and knowledge generating institutions will rise accordingly. Access to an educated workforce will, therefore, come to play a greater role in the effort to create competitive logistics concepts.

Several research and educational institutions working with logistics-related issues already exist in Hamburg, Schleswig-Holstein and the surrounding German regions. Hamburg University of Technology, Hamburg University of Applied Sciences), Helmut Schmidt University, Leuphana University in Lüneburg and Wismar University are some examples of institutions of higher education located near the link and which carry out research and education within supply change management, logistics etc. Since the late 1990s, the Øresund Region has seen cross-border regional partnerships between the region's universities. Of the region's universities, research and education relating to logistics can be found at the following five universities: Lund University, Copenhagen Business School, Denmark's Technical University in Lyngby, Malmö University and Roskilde University.

In addition, research and education take place within, for instance, packaging logistics at the Technological Institute in Denmark. Together with Schleswig-Holstein and the Hamburg Region, the Øresund Region is clearly capable of creating a major knowledge centre for the research and development of future logistics systems – an internationally leading node providing support for the region's logistics sector. Such a centre would also be a major driver in terms of research and innovation.

REFERENCES

M. Abrahamsson & H. Aronsson, '*Measuring Logistics Structure*', International Journal of Logistics: Research and Applications, artikel, 1999, vol. 2, no. 3

H. Aronsson, '*Logistikindikatorn - del 1 verktygsframtagning*', report, 2000

W. Björnsson m.fl. '*Öresundsförbindelse med ett hinder mindre*', report, 2002

Vejdirektoratet, '*Personer per bil*', Vejdirektoratet, report, 2002, no. 268

Vejdirektoratet, data, 2009, www.vejdirektoratet.dk

DSB, data provided by DSB, own database, 2009

Europa-Kommissionen, '*White Paper - European Transport Policy for 2010: time to decide*', report, 2001

Eurostat, '*Energy, transport and environment indicators*', report, 2009

P. A. Hansen & S. Göran, '*Godstransportsektorens udvikling i Øresundsregionen*', report 2006

IBU-Øresund, '*International godstransport i Øresundsregionen*', report 2009

A. Jensen, '*Lagerlokalisering og distributionseffekter*', 1991

Magnusson & Rydén, '*Lokalisering av logistikhub i Öresundsregionen. Norra hamnens möjligheter att utvecklas till ett konkurrenskraftigt trimodalt logistikcenter*', report, 2002

C. Olsson & H. Sevandersson, '*Benchmarking of the Øresund Region from a logistic perspective*', report, 2005

Schary & Skjøtt-Larsen, '*Managing the global supply chain*', Danmark, 2001, 2nd edition

Shippax, data provided by Shippax, Cruise and Ferry, own database, 2009

SIKA, '*Stråkanalyser för godstransporter*', rapport, 2001, vol.1

Sjöfartsverket, '*Sjöfarten och hamnarnas roll i transportsystemet*', report, 2002

Storebælt, data provided by A/S Storebælt, own database, 2009

Teleopgrapy, www.teleography.com, 2007

TFK, '*Luftfartsforskning – Trender och framtida behov*', report, 2001

Femern A/S, www.femern.com

Eurostat, http://epp.eurostat.ec.europa.eu

Danske Havne, www.danskehavne.dk

Logistik-Initiative Hamburg, www.Hamburg-logistik.com

Logistik Initiative Schleswig-Holstein, www.logistik-sh.de

Institutet för Transportforskning, www.tfk.se

Sveriges Hamnar, www.transportgruppen.se

CHAPTER 4
ROLES IN THE URBAN SYSTEM
– A GLOBAL PERSPECTIVE

CHRISTIAN WICHMANN MATTHIESSEN

The world's cities are growing at different rates with, in relative terms, winners and losers. In absolute figures there are also many examples of cities whose populations and activities have declined. Their growth is determined by their relative location and the combination of growth drivers. Their growth is also a result of the way in which their leaders deal with opportunities and challenges. This is not a question of a zero sum game even if some activities are a consequence of the individual city's and its hinterlands demand for city functions and even if hierarchical and territorial distribution mechanisms impact on the distribution of national, regional and local authority activities.

Companies, organisations and institutions divide their activities in time and space and their leaders make decisions about localisation which reflect the decision-makers' more or less sound assessments of what best serves the individual entity in the short as well as in the longer term. Cities build organisations aimed at promoting their growth and attract activity in the form of investment, tourists and a skilled labour force. It is, however, also about influencing the framework conditions for trade and industry so that the city's own companies enjoy better conditions than their competitors in other cities.

Cities create networks for the purpose of pooling their common interests – interests that range from obtaining information to influencing decisions through lobbying activities to taking investment decisions about physical networks, such as the establishment of air routes or linking up to high-speed rail networks. Companies and organisations also form networks internally or together with others. These activities are allocated on the basis of expediency criteria for the companies and organisations.

Analyses of cities and urban systems present a range of inherent problems regarding data accessibility and city demarcation. This is particularly the case in terms of comparisons across national borders. Data carrying entities differ from country to country and change over time. The data-carrying entity is often the municipality of which there are, for instance, 36,569 in France against only 98 in Denmark where the number of municipalities was reduced from 271 to the current 98 in 2007. Moreover, it is rare to see definitional consistency within the individual countries. Distinctions are often made between urban and rural municipalities councils and there are different criteria in different parts of a country. The city definition – and therefore the data-carrying entity – which analysts of urban systems prefer to use is the daily functional city, i.e. a city with a labour hinterland.

A city is a concentration of buildings, people, commerce and infrastructure. In order to use the word city, a certain – not very accurately defined – size must have been achieved. A city is made up of markets for work, housing, goods, public services, events and information. A city functions through flows of people, goods, energy, information and money. A city's structure comprises terminals, road networks, rail networks and other networks. A city has a cultural history and a name owned by its people, which can be used in a branding process.

Cities were usually formed as trading places and grew from their original modest size to their current size – some into grotesque and unmanageable concentrations (megacities).

Many cities grew exponentially during the industrialisation process where economies of scale were clear and undisputed, where shipping and rail transport favoured large scale operations and where consolidation benefits were strengthened by the finance and educational sector's location patterns. These consolidation benefits have slowly but surely broken down and today the city regions are being transformed into a post-industrial structure with rapid and finely ramified systems for telecommunication, people and freight transport and where most cities and regions are accessible to importers and exporters. The new processes, however, mean that new consolidation benefits are emerging, e.g. in the form of relatively stronger demand for face-to-face contact and in the form of links to knowledge environments. The changed consolidation picture is also a consequence of the increasingly easier access to information and ever cheaper transport. This has resulted in a much greater choice of localisation and concentration to centres that offer optimum living conditions for companies and people. As companies are dependent on labour – and vice versa – the end result is dependent on the changing combinations of preferences.

Metropolises are power centres as well as network centres. They attract quality production, not just in these sectors, but in a broad range of associated services and consumer-focused activities such as culture, events and retail trade. They are often characterised by relatively large high income groups (but also by low income groups within service sectors with low qualification requirements). There are several reasons why these metropolises are the hotspots of the knowledge economy.

Metropolises are characterised by having the strongest knowledge infrastructure in the form of institutions of higher education, universities and research institutions. This is partly for historical reasons, but also because local synergy effects play a part and, in general terms, provide a better result in larger rather than smaller centres. Quite simply, the number of contact opportunities with a rising number of entities is growing exponentially.

The populations of the metropolises are better educated than the average. Both in absolute and in relative terms, education levels are highest in these cities. Historically, metropolises have demanded highly educated people and their young people have traditionally been highly motivated towards higher education. Moreover, the latter has been easily accessible – students do not have to leave their environment to study if they live in a city with a university. The labour markets in metropolises have also attracted highly educated population groups from other areas. Local, regional, national and international brain drain processes have been and remain active.

Physical transport's quality terminals and the most important cross points are found in, or near, the major centres. In this respect, capitals often have a kind of primogeniture because it is here that contact to international levels and between the capital and the provinces was, and still is, at its strongest. It is no coincidence that Denmark's air transport centre is located in Copenhagen and that it is considerably larger than the other airports. Copenhagen Airport is simply in a class of its own compared to other Danish aviation centres and has an irreversible advantage in relation to these. The metropolises are well connected to the international economy and are, therefore, often – also because of their other qualities – key destinations for tourists (private or business). The metropolises are also conference centres which constitute an import function for knowledge and innovation.

With regard to intellectual infrastructure, the metropolises also offer benefits compared to other centres. Their commercial life is more sophisticated, their workforces have stronger skills and their access to physical networks is optimal. These factors justify a significant use of information technology and intellectual networks while, at the same time, the historical dimension (i.e. their advantage) is significant. The metropolises are the preferred choice of localisation for international companies. Trans-national companies can be particularly important importers of knowledge information and innovation if they are linked up to local networks.

Metropolises are also characterised by their size and attributes. Below are four examples of how Europe's metropolises can be characterised. We have defined the cities as functional regions and sought a spatial limitation where the city and its daily hinterland constitute one entity and where city regions with many nucleii – e.g. the Dutch urban region, Randstad

FIGURE 1.
EUROPE'S MAJOR CITY REGIONS MEASURED IN TERMS OF POPULATION
TOP 30

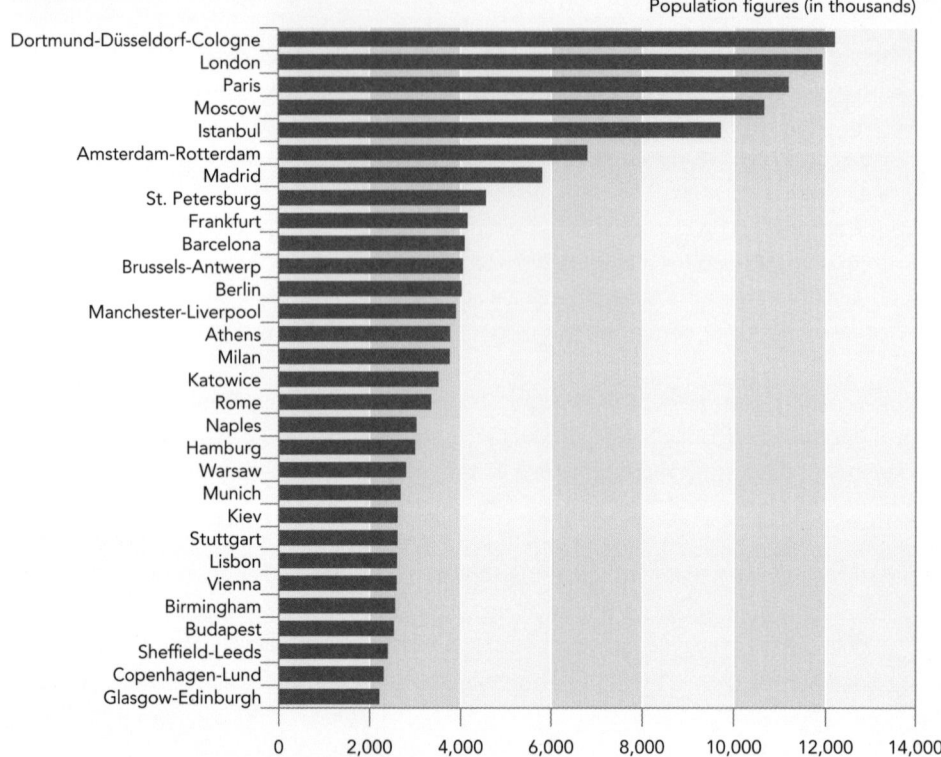

Source: www.citypopulation.de supplemented by other statistical sources (2010)

with Amsterdam, Rotterdam, Utrecht, Hague, Leiden, Delft and Harlem – are registered as one entity. The definition method has been used regardless of national borders.

The most common measurement for the size of cities is the population figure which also gives the activity level, see Figure 1. The continent comprises five giants, of which the largest population concentration is in the West German conurbation, Dortmund-Dusseldorf-Cologne (often named Rhine-Ruhr). Denmark, Sweden and Germany have five cities on the list. Berlin is 12th, Hamburg 19th and the Øresund City 29th. As 34th, Stockholm is not included in the list.

FIGURE 2.
EUROPE'S LARGE CITY REGIONS MEASURED IN GROSS PRODUCT
TOP 30

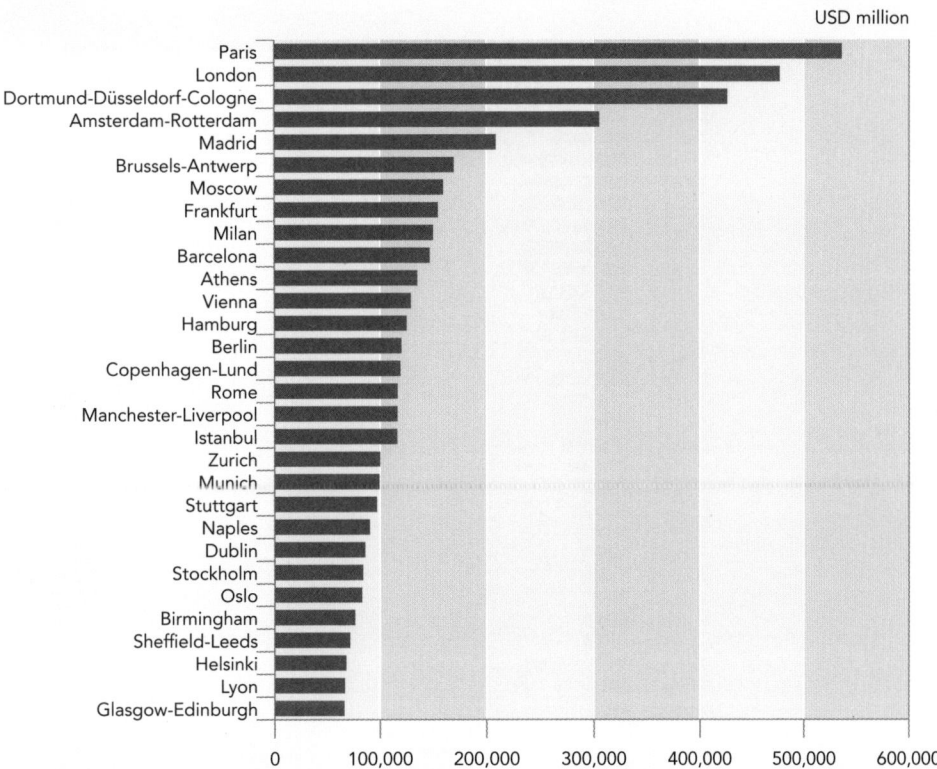

Source: ESPON supplemented by other statistical information

The gross product of major cities shows the added value in the production of goods and services and, therefore, indicates the economic forces for each city. Figure 2 shows an entirely different list than the one that shows the weight as measured by the size of the population. Whilst East European cities have a weaker position, capitals and financial centres are stronger. The list comprises four heavy centres at the European top and includes seven cities from Denmark, Sweden and Germany. Measured by population, Berlin is much larger than Hamburg, but measured by economy the two cities are almost equal. Thus the list illustrates a significant European structural feature, i.e. Berlin's position in a mediocre economy. Hamburg is 13th, Berlin 14th while the Øresund City is 15th. Stockholm is 24th.

FIGURE 3.
EUROPE'S MAJOR CITY REGIONS MEASURED BY INTERNATIONAL AIR TRANSPORT (2007) TOP 30

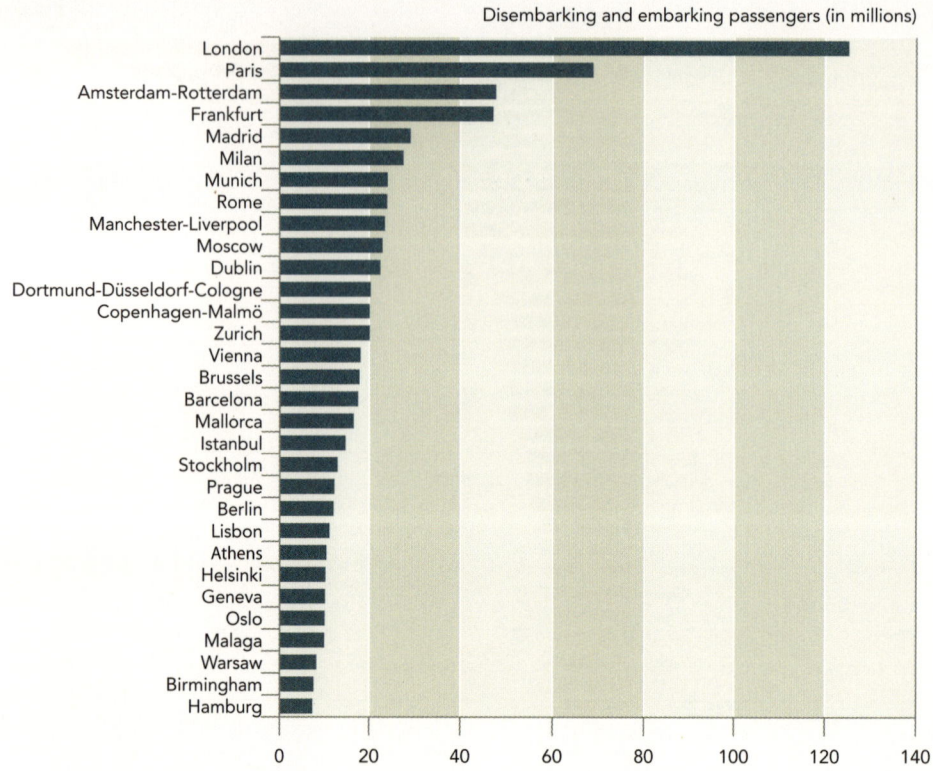

Source: Airport Council International (2009)

The figures for international air transport show the potential access to the most important network for decision-makers – even if there are many other categories of traveller than decision-makers. The calculation shows the traffic figure for the entire city regardless of the number of airports, see Figure 3. The figure comprises traffic to, from and through the city. This calculation method was chosen because the overall number of passengers determines the total number of routes and for a city, it is important to operate many routes in order to have a position as a strong potential meeting place. London is Europe's centre for international air traffic followed by Paris, Frankfurt and the Amsterdam region. There are seven centres in Denmark, Sweden and Germany on the list. The Øresund City is 13th, Stockholm 20th, Berlin 22nd and Hamburg 30th.

FIGURE 4.
EUROPE'S MAJOR CITY REGIONS MEASURED IN SCIENTIFIC OUTPUT
TOP 30

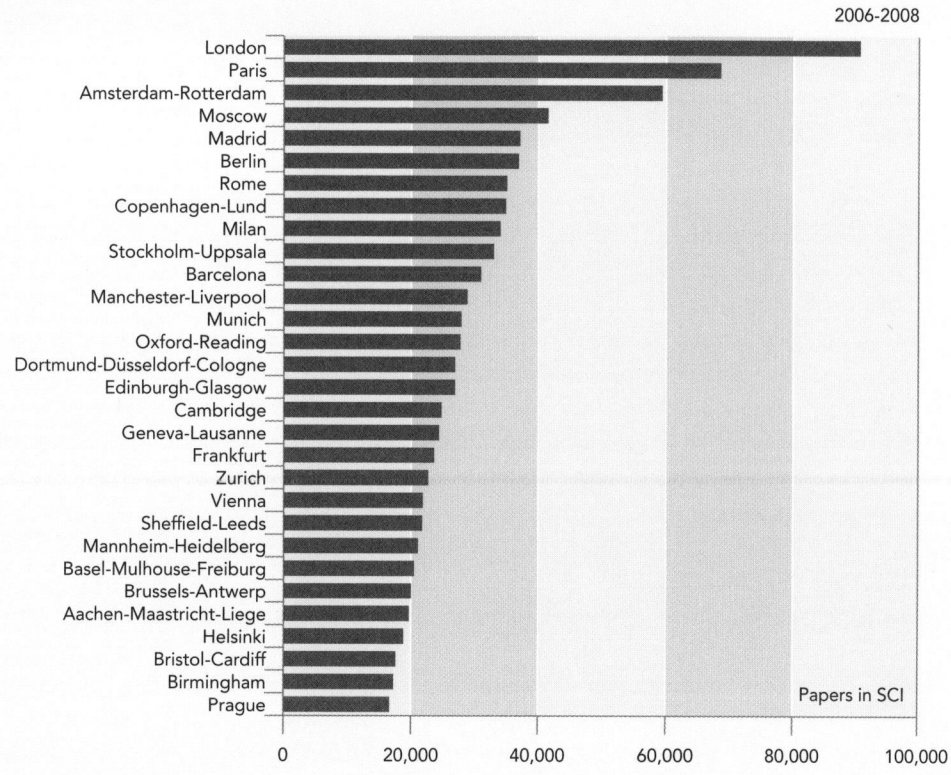

Scientific creativity is hard to gauge. We have chosen output as the parameter. Although you could also register patents, we have chosen publishing activities in the form of bibliographical papers within the approximately 6,700 most cited international scientific referee (quality rated) periodicals and a number of other scientific publications of high quality for "hard" sciences (engineering, natural science, medicine). The methodology is described in more detail in chapter 8. Figure 4 shows the top 30 list in which London is Europe's strongest scientific centre followed by Paris and the Amsterdam region. The list includes no fewer than nine centres from Denmark, Sweden and Germany (of which three are border regions). Several of the three countries' major cities (Hamburg is an exception) occupy prominent positions on the list. Berlin is 6th, the Øresund City 8th and Stockholm 10th. Hamburg is 37th.

The four attribute variables each demonstrate how to identify the European continent's heavy centres. London and Paris are among the top three measured by all parameters. Measured in terms of population, the Rhine-Ruhr region, Moscow and Istanbul are significant while the latter two are relatively small measured according to the other parameters. In terms of financial strength, access to international networks and scientific output, the Amsterdam region belongs at the absolute top while Frankfurt and Madrid have similar positions in respect of international air traffic.

In relative terms, it is clear that the Øresund City is small in terms of population, but large in terms of economic strength, access to international air transport networks and scientific output. Hamburg is small in terms of population, but has significant economic strength. By contrast, Hamburg does not have a particularly strong position in terms of access to international air transport networks and scientific output. Berlin is different, i.e. as a large population concentration with weak economic strength and poor links to international air transport networks. At the same time, the city has a strong position in terms of scientific production. Finally, Stockholm has a small population and ranks high in respect of economic strength although the city has relatively poor access to international air transport networks compared to the Øresund City. In terms of scientific output, however, Stockholm has a strong position.

URBAN SYSTEM THEORY

The basic theoretical work on the urban system's structure and function dates back to the 1930s and has since been developed and modified. The Central Place Theory – as the theory is called – views cities as service centres in relation to the surrounding hinterland which is defined on the basis of natural and human-created resources. The theory offers a simple explanation which can be understood by most people. Traditional Central Place Theory describes national urban systems as completely hierarchical. Cities at the top level dominated cities at the underlying level which again dominated cities at the next level down and so on. The hierarchy was completely dependent on the hinterland and each city dominated a number of towns, e.g. three on the next lower level within their geographical surrounding area. Customer behaviour was rational and dependent on distances which meant that services were demanded from the nearest supplier. All controlling interaction between cities and towns was determined by the hierarchy. The same was the case with flows of people, goods, information, energy and money. As part of this picture it should be mentioned that the composition of service functions reflected the city or town's place in the hierarchy. Cities on similar levels offer more or less the same spectrum of activities because rational customer behaviour favours the function with the broadest range and the smallest

FIGURE 5.
THE CENTRAL PLACE THEORY'S CITY SYSTEM

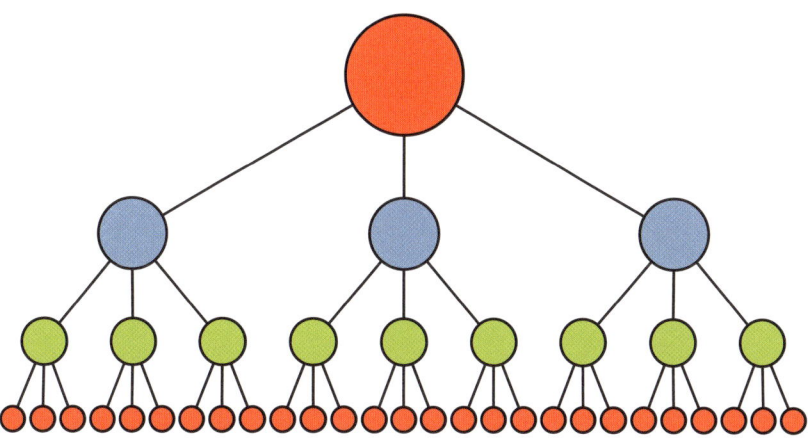

The figure indicates four levels of cities where each level comprises similar entities.
The links between the cities are on a vertical level. Each city at a higher level dominates
a number – here 3 – cities at the level below.

threshold customer base. A hinterland-focused centre structure is not a utopia and it is easy to identify patterns that are conditional on these. Figure 5 outlines the Central Place Theory's urban system.

The city system has, however, never only been structured as in the Central Place Theory's hierarchy. Trade and communication have taken place between towns and cities at different levels. A company in Aalborg does not need to send its product to Copenhagen in order to trade with a company in Aarhus. Customers are driven by many other factors than just the rational. Some hierarchical systems will be overtaken by new systems while others will become stronger. Direct links between cities supplement hierarchical systems. The spatial system has "always" been complex and new technologies have multiplied the complexity to multi-hierarchical and global networks of flows and control. In her book about "The Global City" (1991), Sassen formulates how international business partners require interaction with advanced financial and business services located in key city centres while the trading flow does not need such centre's services, but can follow totally different routes depending on the location of manufacturer and consumer and the transport sys-

FIGURE 6.
PLANNERS AND AUTHORITIES' CITY SYSTEM
AN EXAMPLE OF DANISH PLANNING

Inspired by The Danish Ministry of Environment (2006)

tems' structure which have their own in-built hierarchies. Cyberspace is not hierarchically structured, but functions as a combination of numerous networks with a floating and changing centre structure which nevertheless reflects the globalisation's urban hierarchy. Taylor (2004) points out that all cities are globalised. They operate in the present's spatial flows and they have global scope if this is to their advantage.

A few decades ago, literature on city systems was highly nationally focused and theories about closed national city systems were commonplace within national planning. Taylor even believes that this constitutes a paradigm and that national focused city system theories safeguarded against international thinking. Theorists described – and describe

– national urban patterns and urban systems where the systematics justified that national centres, provincial centres, regional centres, municipal and local centres are singled out. With regard to public services and infrastructure investments, the desire was to adjust the system and find justification in the centre–periphery theories and system theory. A few theorists even involved the international economy, but as a system with external impact on national urban systems.

The process that, over the past few centuries, developed powerful national states also nationalised cities and – Taylor believes – undermined their vitality. In his terminology, nationalisation is basically a territorial reorganisation where space is perceived as a mosaic of locations. The development of the national state favours territorial institutions rather than network institutions. Some cities have profited from the entrepreneurial spirit of national states, first and foremost the capitals, but also administrative centres at lower levels and, for instance, garrison towns have gained from national policies. Within an overall perspective, national states have, however, restricted the cities in their activities. What we have seen in recent years is an emerging liberation from the narrow ties imposed by the national states on urban development.

This paradigm shift becomes clear in Castells' theories on Social Space (1996). He believes that the use of localities is based on social practice and, therefore, historically determined. A given location offers social opportunities – e.g. a shopping centre offers buyers and sellers an opportunity to trade with each other. This example points towards the traditional use of space as a physical facilitator. However, says Castells, new information technology fundamentally changes the perception that the dominating form of space can be described through the expression "spaces of places". In the network society, the dominating form of space can be described much better through the expression, "spaces of flow". Locations do not disappear, but are defined on the basis of their position in relation to flows. Schein & Thierstein (2009) consider the two categories as linked together. The expression "spaces of flow" conceptualises the relational world of non-physical functionally merged networks while nodal functions (nodality means the ability to coordinate a system) in the form of terminals and control centres can be considered as "spaces of places".

Castells (1996) focuses on social practice in the form of economic, cultural and political functions, but regards the physical support as crucial. Pointing at three areas, he regards the first area as comprising infrastructural support ranging from the global internet to international air transport networks. The second area comprises centres for strategically important functions that link localities to general networks and places that coordinate interaction between the networks. Such privileged cities are central and general localities. The third area is the spatial organisation of the elite: technocratic, financial and managerial

that support their interests. All three functions have in-built hierarchical features. According to Castells, the term "the global city" comprises a continuum of cities of varying intensity and different scales in terms of integration into the global system. What defines a global city is its position in the processes that characterise the spatial system of advanced service activities.

The theories on the city system, therefore, indicate three ways of looking at cities:

– As service centres for a hinterland that also comprises the city itself. Their development potential is determined by the area's resources. Their relationships with other centres are determined by their position in the hierarchy.
– As spaces of places where their characteristics are determined by the city's qualities. The same goes for their development potential. Their relationships with other cities are determined by their position in the international division of labour.
– As spaces of flow where their position (management, cross-point) in the spatial flows drives the city's development and growth. Their relationships with other centres depend on how they are part of the globalised networks.

The individual city's conditions and growth potential are, in fact, a dynamic combination of these three views and it is clear that the network society's city system is far from simple, see Figure 7. City leaders must take their starting point in their own city's conditions and endeavour to achieve an ambitious but realistic development strategy.

THE EUROPEAN URBAN SYSTEM

The original work on the overall European urban system was published in 1989 (Brunet 1989). It was based on a multitude of well chosen data describing the individual cities. This data was gathered in groups of variables whereby each was individually used to describe a dimension of the cities' function. The cities were subsequently categorised within the individual groups according to their status, e.g. in the form of cultural function, international links or traffic. The general picture was then analysed and the conclusion was: The Blue Banana. The expression covers a picture of activity and production where Europe's centre can be described as a banana-shaped figure that forms a curve from Central England's cities to Milan via the Netherlands and Belgium's large cities, the Rhine Valley's heavy centres and Zurich to Milan, see Figure 8. The banana is blue because it was drawn in this colour when the work was first published. Describing the centre of Europe as "The Blue Banana"

FIGURE 7.
THE NETWORK SOCIETY'S CITY SYSTEM HIERARCHIES AND BANDS

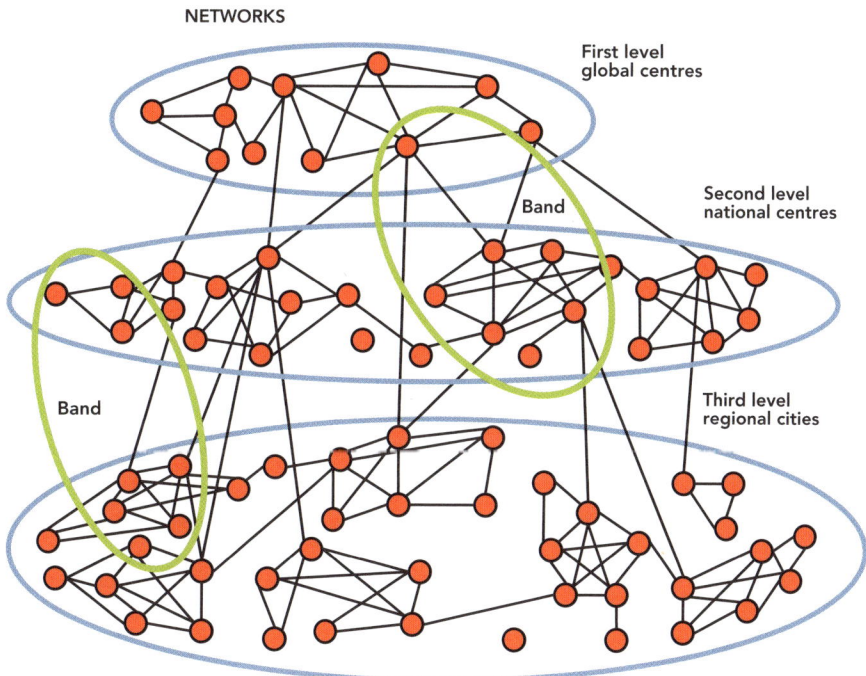

gradually turned into scientific jargon. Paris lies outside the banana, but is considered part of the centre. The European centre comprised a third of the continent's economic activities, 25 per cent of its population and covered 10 per cent of the then EU's area. The metropolises in the banana are deeply specialised and part of a division of labour. The metropolises outside the banana are not specialised to the same degree and their function is more a consequence of demand from their hinterland than is the case for the major cities within the banana.

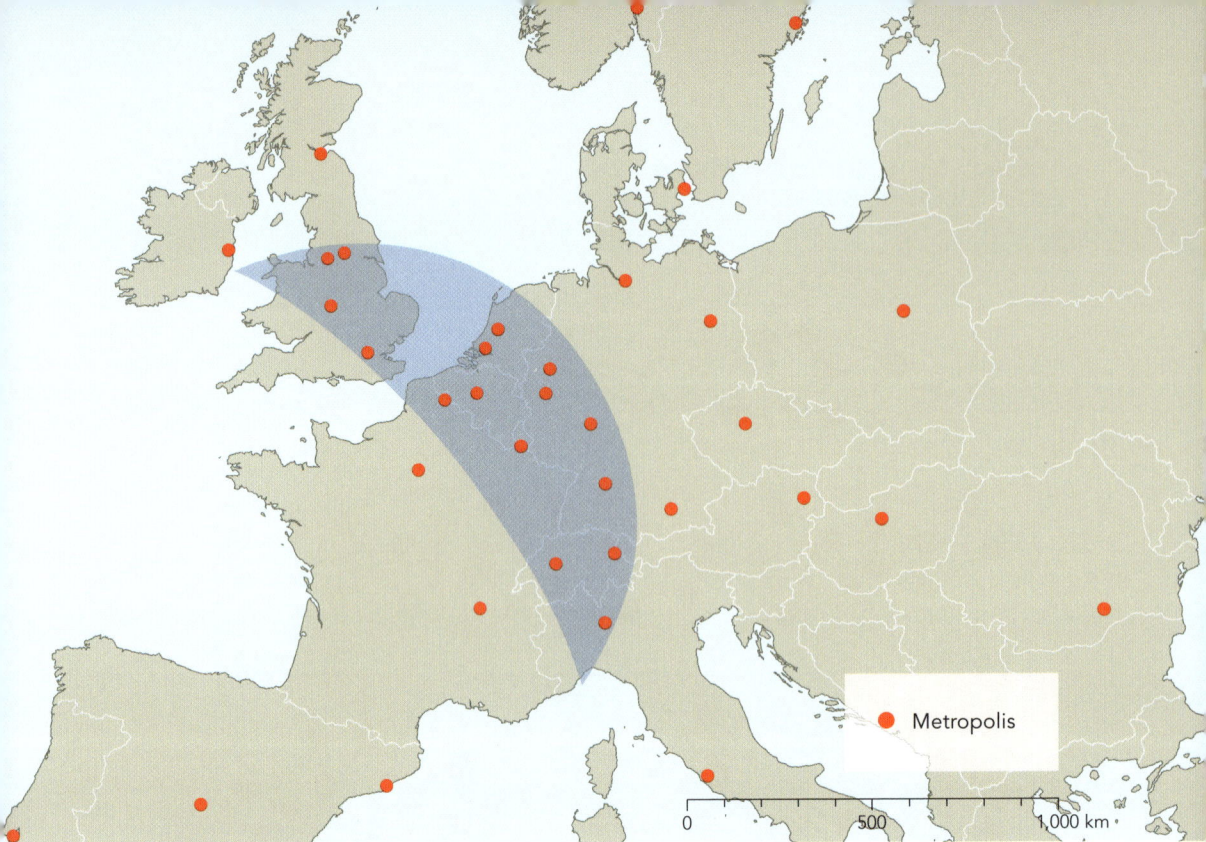

FIGURE 8.
THE BLUE BANANA

"The Blue Banana" publication was published in the year when the Iron Curtain began to crumble, when the Berlin Wall fell and when openness and market economy became part of the Soviet Union's agenda. A few years later, the world and Europe had undergone fundamental change. The market economy and democracy had prevailed, Germany was reunited, the Soviet Union was replaced by 15 new republics, Yugoslavia was in a state of dissolution and the EU grew from 12 member countries to 15 in 1995, and then to 25 in 2004. Today, it comprises 27 nations (since 2007). The Banana publication has, nevertheless, withstood the tests to which the changes in Europe have exposed it. Its way of describing Europe's urban system is enduring. Several later publications on the general European urban system have been published and the EU has established an analytical entity,

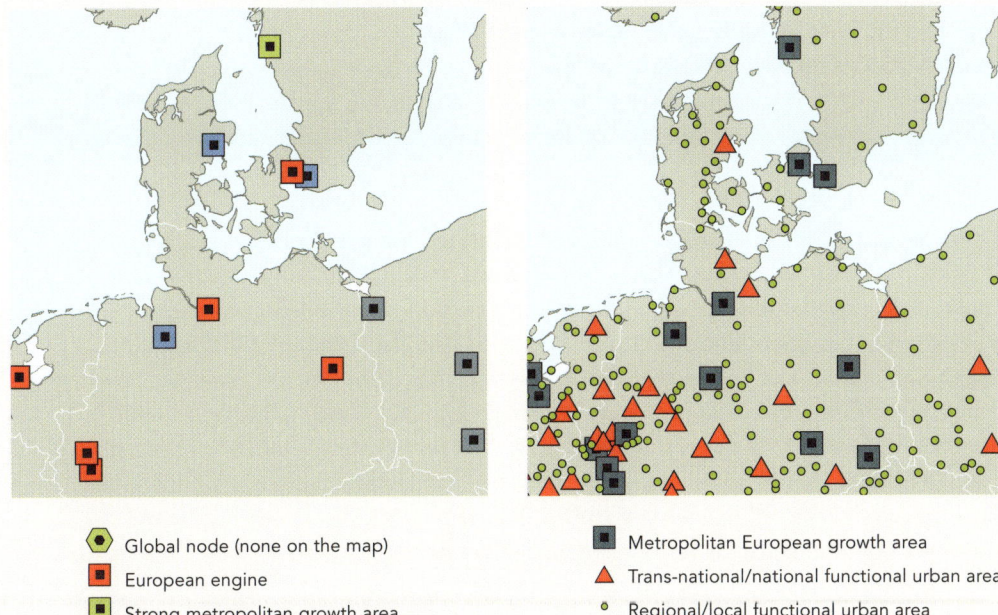

FIGURE 9.
ESPON

The ESPON institution works with Europe's spatial structure. The maps show how it will be viewed. The categorisation is based on facts combined with politically motivated assessments. The map to the left shows the basic perception of Europe's system of metropolises. The map to the right supplements the picture with cities below the level and changes the metropolis categorisation. The oldest map (to the left) - Aarhus, Szczecin-Swinoujscie, Poznan and Wroclav are shown as metropolises, but not Hanover, Leipzig and Dresden. The newer map (to the right) shows the reverse categorisation. Now neither Aarhus, Szczecin-Swinoujscie, Poznan and Wroclav are regarded as metropolises while Hanover, Leipzig and Dresden are categorised as such.
Source: ESPON

the European Spatial Planning Observation Network (ESPON), tasked with examining these issues and presenting policy proposals, see Figure 9. Concurrently, neutral scientific networks have been set up to continue the more objective tradition which was founded by the people behind the banana publication, e.g. Globalisation and World Cities Research Network (GaWC).

THE PETER TAYLOR GROUP'S NEW ANALYSES: GLOBALISATION AND WORLD CITIES

Peter Taylor (2004) does not merely analyse city attributes and transfer his observations into an assessment of their relational conditions. Under his leadership, the GaWC-Group has been responsible for original attempts to identify global hubs and furthermore, identify lower levels. So far, the group's research has been summarised by Olshov, Levring & Matthiessen (2004), but a newer analysis of the global network of major cities (Taylor et al., 2007) has subsequently been followed up (Taylor & Aranya, 2008, and Taylor et al., 2009). These analyses will be summarised in the following sections. Localisation strategies for 100 leading global service businesses in more than 315 cities (subsequently extended to 526) have been carried out and, within this framework, the cities' links to networks, their connections to the service sectors and their relations to the world's other urban regions have been assessed. The analysis represents the first systematic description of the backbone of the major urban system on which the current globalisation process is based. The Taylor group's longstanding analytical work with regard to the world's urban systems substantiates the selection of cities of economic importance, including 24 from Denmark, Sweden and Germany.

Taylor takes his starting point in the business service companies that export their products and identifies four types of drivers. Firstly, he establishes that trade in services usually requires face-to-face contact between producer and customer who often both belong to large multinational production and distribution companies. This means that the companies establish themselves close to the customers and (since 1980) that many service companies have become global in their localisation patterns. Companies could choose to follow their customers around the world – which many did – but an increasing number opt for their own global localisation strategy – in part to attract new customers. Their offices will almost invariably be located in cities and almost always in large – internationally-oriented – main centres i.e. metropolises. Secondly, he identifies local, formal and informal networks of interacting political and economic decision-makers as typical examples of drivers. Thirdly, a multitude of institutions and companies adjust and codify the frameworks for the companies' practices in one way or another. Finally, the fourth driver behind urban development is the national state with its economic policies, level of liberalisation and nationally fixed cultural patterns. Taylor believes that these four types of drivers – service companies, city management, service sector institutions and the national state – between them are responsible for current urban development and for designing the global network of cities. Companies and city leaderships represent an equal interaction while the national state and public service sector institutions represent a dominating force in relation to local companies and city leaderships.

Business service companies have, therefore, developed from following their clients to establishing their own localisation strategies. As a result, they are increasingly focused on their respective brands. Companies must ensure that customers know what they stand for and that the individual client can expect to receive the same product anywhere in the world. Information technological development means a strengthening of the organisation of products and controls, but also implies that expansive parts of the individual service company can be localised independent of customer contact. This makes the consolidation trends for the world's development centres even stronger. This, therefore, is how Schein & Thierstein (2009) describe major cities where universities, advanced business services and high-tech companies are concentrated and form an interactive knowledge economy.

The Taylor group has selected 100 service companies that are present in at least 15 of the 315 cities initially analysed and which must be represented in the three regions US-Canada, Western Europe and Asia-Pacific. The companies have been grouped under accountancy, advertising, banking and finance, insurance, law and management consultancy. If companies own each other, they are registered as one company. The information derives from a wide range of sources – the so-called scavenger method – with extensive use of websites, annual reports and internal registrations (directories). The presence or non-presence of all firms in all cities are registered and their presence has been weighted according to the number of professional employees or the number of office locations per city. The registration comprises customer relations and a categorisation of the function at the location (e.g. head office, development department, branch). On the basis of the very diverse information material from company to company, the Taylor group chose a scoring system where the head office results in five points and non-presence zero points. A company's service value can, therefore, be calculated for each city and the cities' service value for each individual company. Connectivity (an indication of flows in the system) between two cities for each company is calculated as the product of these two service values. The figures can be cross-summarised and indicate both the connectivity between cities as well as the connectivity within a company. Moreover, the data matrix can be categorised resulting in an identification of a series of patterns. The basic assumption is, therefore, that a company's office function in a city determines the connectivity with the company's office in another city – also measured by function.

The Taylor group's methodology is open to criticism in a number of ways. The cities are simply defined by their name, which means that more complex forms of cities, such as the Dutch urban region, appear as several independent cities (Amsterdam, Rotterdam, The Hague, Utrecht etc), even if such urban regions in terms of business service suppliers are often defined as one entity. The scoring system can be debated, as can indirect targets

for interaction and the use of websites whose source is uncertain. Such criticism, however, cannot conceal the fact that the Taylor group's analysis provides strong indicators as to how the world's urban systems are bolted together.

The aim of Taylor's analysis of the global urban system is to shift focus from attribute analysis to network analysis. His results combine well known features with new and surprising assessments. That London and New York are the world's leading centres is not surprising, but it is surprising how far above the cities at the next levels New York and London rank by virtue of their links to the other cities. The global system of dominating cities and cities with a function as command centres comprises well known features while the global system of network cities comprises a number of new start-ups from the world outside the three dominating macro regions together with a number of West European and Canadian centres, but without any special US representation. The system of "world cities" is summarised in the outline below, based on a number of the Taylor group's presentations.

PLACES OF FLOW
THE HIERARCHY'S HIGHEST LEVELS

Command centres	Dominating centres	Network centres	
London	London	Toronto	A
New York	New York	São Paulo	
		Madrid	
		Milan	
		Singapore	
		Hong Kong	
		Sydney	
Chicago	Hong Kong	Miami	B
Paris	Paris	Mexico City	
Tokyo	Tokyo	Buenos Aires	
	Frankfurt	Mumbai	
	Chicago	Taipei	
	Miami	Kuala Lumpur	
		Jakarta	
		Melbourne	
Boston	Toronto	Montreal	C
Washington	Los Angeles	Atlanta	
Amsterdam	Amsterdam	Dublin	
Brussels	Brussels	Lisbon	
Frankfurt	Madrid	Barcelona	
Zurich	Milan	Copenhagen	
	Singapore	Hamburg	
	Sydney	Vienna	
		Prague	
		Budapest	
		Warsaw	
		Moscow	
		Istanbul	
		Johannesburg	
		Beijing	
		Shanghai	
		Seoul	
		Manila	
		Auckland	
San Francisco	San Francisco		D
Los Angeles	Detroit		
Minneapolis	Indianapolis		
Dallas	Atlanta		
Cleveland	Boston		
Philadelphia	Washington		
Lyon	Lyon		
Düsseldorf	Copenhagen		
Munich	Stockholm		
Stockholm	Hamburg		
	Berlin		
	Düsseldorf		
	Munich		
	Mumbai		
	Taipei		
	Jakarta		
	São Paulo		
	Melbourne		

**FIGURE 10.
WORLD CITIES**

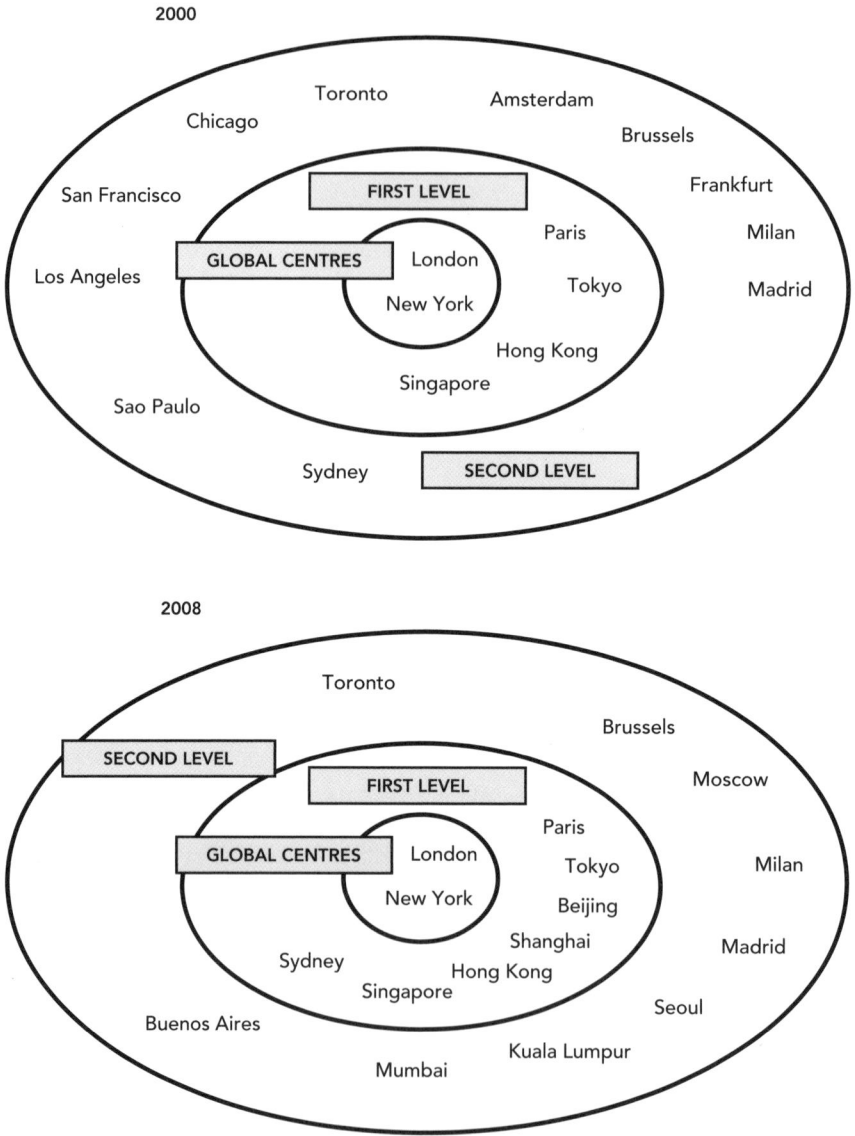

London and New York dominate the world scene in both periods. The second level comprised Paris, Tokyo, Hong Kong and Singapore in 2002 while the same four cities plus Beijing, Shanghai and Sydney were on the list in 2008. Sydney was at the third level in 2000, while the two Chinese cities got directly on to the second level in 2008. The third level comprises Milan, Madrid, Brussels and Toronto. San Francisco, Amsterdam and Frankfurt left the world scene after 2000. The same was the case with Chicago, Los Angeles and Sao Paulo while Buenos Aires, Mumbai, Kuala Lumpur, Seoul and Moscow arrived on the world scene in 2008.
Source: Taylor et al.

FIGURE 11.
THE FIVE UPPER LEVELS OF WORLD CITIES

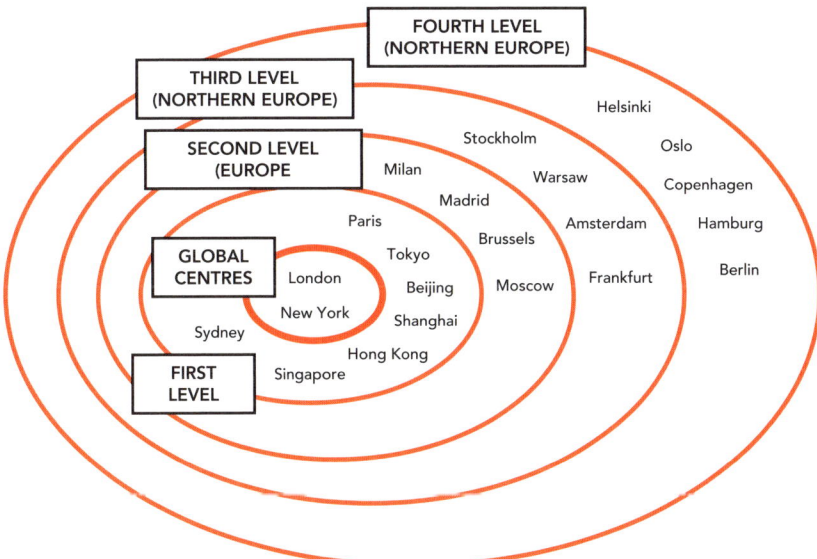

The diagram is an expanded version of Figure 10 on the opposite page: World cities 2008. With regard to cities in Denmark, Sweden and Germany it should be noted that Stockholm and Frankfurt have prominent positions while Copenhagen, Hamburg and Berlin have to accept that they are located at the level below.
Source: Taylor et al.

Six cities from Denmark, Sweden and Germany are included among the world cities. Frankfurt is at the third level among the command centres and on the second level on the list of dominant centres. Dusseldorf, Munich and Stockholm are on the fourth level among the command centres and together with Copenhagen, Hamburg and Berlin are on the fourth level in terms of the dominance function. Finally, only Copenhagen and Hamburg are on the list of network centres – at third level.

The Taylor group has presented an analysis of the development in the overall hierarchy of world cities 2000-2008. (Taylor et al., 2009) based on new data, see Figure 10. New York and London continue to be the centres of the world economy, but in 2008 Hong Kong started to approach this level and Taylor predicts that before long there will be a triad of world cities.

Taylor (2009) describes the development between 2000 and 2008 as a dramatic process. Once again, territories gained a growing importance for the world economy to the detriment of networks and flows. Relationships between cities and states have been adjusted in favour of the latter because the world's financial crisis has resulted in full or partial nationalisation of many financial service companies. In North America, only New York and Toronto have survived at the three upper levels and the European influence has diminished in that some of the major financial centres (Frankfurt and Amsterdam) have lost status. By contrast, some cities from "emerging markets" have achieved dominant positions. Taylor does not believe, however, that all the effects of the financial and economic crises have been alleviated.

The list of cities included in the analysis now comprises a total of 526 entities. One can be reasonably certain about the ranking of the top half of the list, but the further one goes down the list, the less certainty there is because the cities that should have been involved in the analysis are not included.

BANDS (FAMILIES, CLIQUES) OF CITIES

As for networks, general urban systems can be characterised as multifaceted and linked. At any given time, an individual city plays a role at a level in the global hierarchy and the role can be described in terms such as control, dominance and position in the network. It is also clear that the cities are linked in changing constellations determined by the quantity, quality and type of the links that connect them. A number of cities, for instance, are part of a Pan-European service area (Taylor, 2007) based on banking and finance, law and associated business-to-business service companies. This is centred around companies in Frankfurt and Munich and has London, Paris, Hamburg and Berlin as prominent participants. Dusseldorf, Cologne, Warsaw, Brussels, Milan and Budapest also belong to this group of cities, with strong interaction around these fields. Such constellations could also be called a band, a family or a clique. Another example is the London-centred band with regard to accounting, auditing and associated business-to-business service companies. Prominent participants here are the Anglo-American cities with a predominance of Commonwealth cities (Toronto, Montreal, Hamilton, Sydney). Paris and Copenhagen are also part of this clique at a high level. A third example is a Eurocentric band rooted in service companies relating to the media world where Berlin and Munich play central roles while Hamburg, Cologne and Los Angeles form the next layer. Dusseldorf, Frankfurt, London, Zurich and Milan are also present in the clique. A clique of media-related links constitute another band around London in which Manchester, Amsterdam, Toronto and Melbourne are important members. In the next layer are cities such as Boston, Lisbon, Madrid, Milan and Athens.

These cities, therefore, interact in a number of changing constellations determined by production focus for those business-to-business service companies that represent identifiable links. Together, the cities form complex networks that are cross-linked both vertically and horizontally. The individual band is characterised by strong internal flows of information and knowledge. Taylor (2004) has identified a strong hierarchical element. Cities at the same level in an urban system have a tendency to be classified together. He also finds a regional dimension where proximity plays a role in interaction just as he sees a context between the two factors because cities with low mutual connectivity are more regionally fixed than cities with high mutual connectivity. Finally, he finds that European cities are significantly more cosmopolitan than cities from other of the world's large regions. This is especially the case for cities on the two upper levels, but also for a number of cities from the level below, e.g. Copenhagen and Berlin.

FIGURE 12.
EUROPEAN BANDS OF INTERACTING CITIES AT HIERARCHICALLY DETERMINED LEVELS

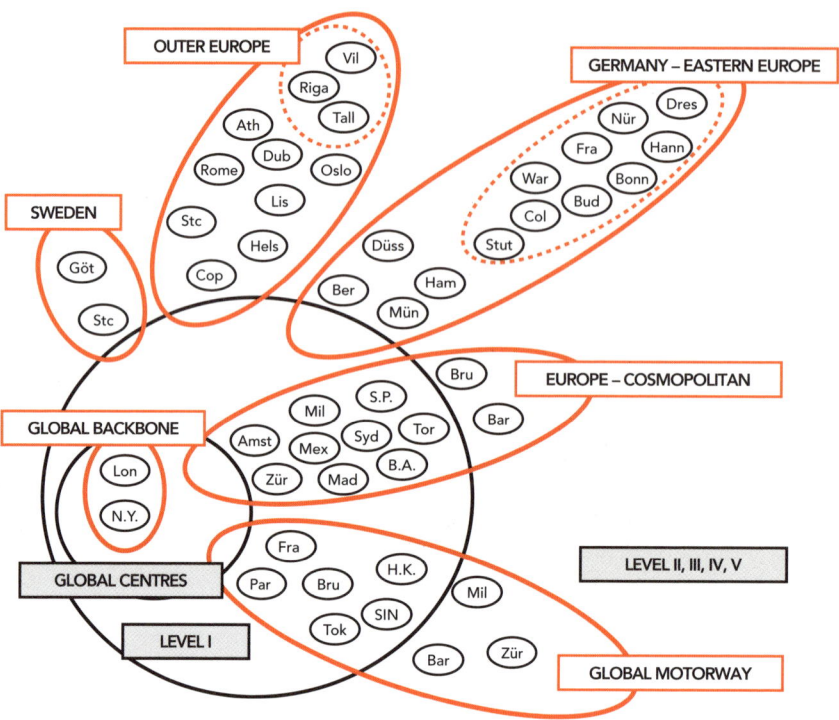

The complex diagram summarises the Taylor group's analysis. Circles indicate levels and ovals bands. The dotted ovals represent bands of smaller cities that are part of the dominant cities' bands. The stronger the role, the closer to the centre of the diagram. Note that individual cities may play a role in more than one band.
Souce: Derudder et al. (2003); Derudder et al. (2007), Taylor & Derudder (2004) and Taylor (2004)

The basis for the analysis of the world's city system is, therefore, a number of large international service companies' localisation patterns and the links within the individual companies indicated by this pattern. Companies with uniform production focus demonstrate uniform localisation patterns and, therefore, also represent links between cities where the networks comprise common features. The cities form bands that represent this type of network. If one studies the total localisation pattern and the total network, this also presents clear patterns where, once again, the term bands can be applied to cities that interact together and have uniform interaction profiles with all other cities. The overall pattern is set out in the diagrams above (Figures 10 and 11) where dominance and control issues explain the division into levels. Moreover, if the underlying patterns are isolated through a multivariate statistical method (see Taylor et al., 2002) there are five general bands: the British Commonwealth band, the US band, the Europe band, the Asia-Pacific band and an outer band. By further dissolving the material, it is possible to isolate bands of cities with particular interaction which also interact with the surrounding world's cities in a homogenous way. This grouping is presented in Figure 12 where the Eurocentric band has been sub-divided.

The way in which the overall international business-to-business service networks function reveals obvious patterns. In general, Danish, Swedish and German cities do not demonstrate any particular degree of mutual connectivity, but are part of different bands of cities, some of them together and others separately. Interaction is always an expression of added value. This is why it makes sense to examine new opportunities – i.e. what this analysis can be used for. Figure 12 shows a defined band called Outer Europe in which Copenhagen plays a leading role and in which Stockholm and a number of other cities form a part. A second band is named Germany-Eastern Europe, with Berlin (together with Dusseldorf and Munich) on the main role list while Hamburg, together with a number of other cities, have more subsidiary roles. Finally, it should be noted that Stockholm plays a key role within a Swedish band, which is somewhat isolated. It is also interesting to note that, with the exception of Frankfurt, no cities from Denmark, Sweden or Germany are part of the continent's strongest bands.

DENMARK, SWEDEN AND GERMANY

The broad spectrum of analytical endeavours to identify the roles of cities and thus determine how the urban system is structured implies a considerable lack of cohesion. This is hardly surprising considering the analysts' different starting points. Some see the roles of cities in relation to the surrounding area, others focus on their attributes and qualities, while others focus on the identification of nodes and links. Some analysts are interested in hierarchies, others in gateways and crosspoints and yet others in the reciprocity of the marketplace. Danish, Swedish and German government analyses – which is the basis for a number of planning-related dispositions – regard urban systems as national and only rarely extend across the country's or region's borders.

FIGURE 13.
THE INTEGRATION OF DANISH, SWEDISH AND GERMAN CITIES IN THE WORLD CITIES NETWORK

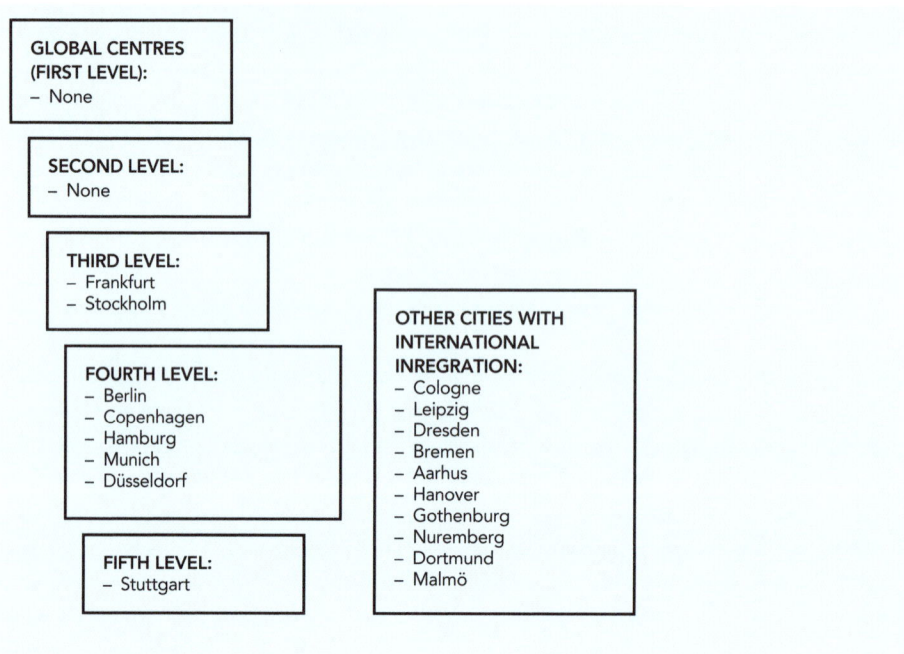

Taylor (2009) and GaWC database (2010)
Cities in Denmark, Sweden and Germany

Based on the Taylor group's analysis, Figure 13 shows Danish, Swedish and German cities' integration levels within the world cities' network. The urban system consists of a number of large, heavy centres within and outside the Fehmarnbelt Region as important nodes (co-ordinating network centres). The Øresund City and Hamburg are crucial to the region's function, activity level, prosperity and future prospects. Without these metropolises the region would be without international format. The two major cities are, however, not the only high level centres. Berlin, Frankfurt and Stockholm also have main roles. Berlin is Germany's capital and presents a so far failed attempt to join the world cities' upper levels. Frankfurt and Stockholm are in a class to which Berlin aspires. With its European dominance within the finance world and boasting one of the world's large inter-continental air transport centres, Frankfurt offers a marketplace which, in other powerful nations, is found in their capitals. Stockholm, Sweden's capital, occupies an important position in terms of large international (Swedish) business groups. Nevertheless, it is more isolated in terms of global integration than the other heavy centres. Stockholm continues to compete with Copenhagen, arguing that Stockholm is the capital of Scandinavia's largest economy while Copenhagen has a substantially larger part of the Scandinavian market within a shorter distance and is more internationally orientated than Stockholm. Stockholm's brand is "Stockholm - the capital of Scandinavia" while Copenhagen brands itself as a flexible and open city under the slogan "cOPENhagen-OPEN for you".

The Øresund City is the largest urban region in the Nordic countries. Hamburg is the gateway city par excellence, not just for the region, but for the whole of Germany apart from air transport. The city brands itself as "Hamburg - die Metropole am Wasser" and "Hamburg - das Tor zur Welt". Berlin's branding is "Be Berlin".

Among the Danish, Swedish and German cities, Munich and Düsseldorf rank on a par with Hamburg, Copenhagen and Berlin while Stuttgart has to accept a position at a lower level. The Taylor group's analysis also identifies a number of cities at a lower international integration level from the three countries. From the somewhat extended Fehmarnbelt area (cities closer than 300 km to the Fehmarnbelt centre) the list comprises Bremen, Hanover and Malmö.

THE FEHMARNBELT REGION: EU ANALYSIS OF THE CITY SYSTEM

The EU and its observation network (ESPON), with its focus on analysis of urban systems and other spatial and planning oriented factors, highlights cross-border city structures and city development processes and thus contributes to strengthening the analytical base because the current urban system is anything but border fixated.

Figure 14 was prepared on the basis of ESPON (2007) where the cities are classified. The observations are supplemented by other ESPON publications (www.espon.eu.) These include cities that lie closer to the future fixed Fehmarnbelt link than 300 km. The EU concept, MEGA (Metropolitan Growth Area) classifies cities within five categories. The top layer comprises only London and Paris. The level immediately below is named European Engines. This comprises four large cities close to the Fehmarnbelt. Moreover, a number of other large cities within the Fehmarnbelt Region are categorised as MEGAS on levels below the two top levels. As this classification is coloured by national input, the sub-division in figure 14 is according to size. Three large German cities, therefore, are found at a somewhat

FIGURE 14.
THE EU'S CITY CONCEPT
CITIES WITHIN A DISTANCE OF A MAXIMUM OF 300 KM FROM THE FUTURE FIXED FEHMARNBELT LINK'S CENTRE HAVE BEEN INCLUDED

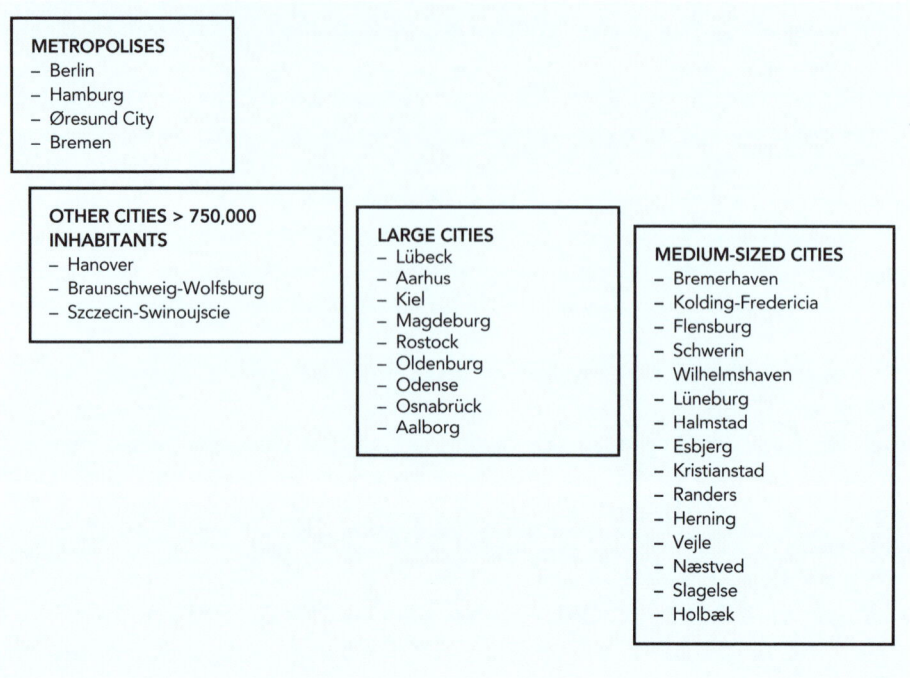

ESPON (2007) project 1.4.3 (Final report 2007): Study of Urban Function supplemented by other ESPON publications

lower level in the urban hierarchy. These are the specialised centres, Braunschweig-Wolfsburg, Hanover and Bremen, which are overshadowed by Hamburg, but which also play strong independent roles as industrial centres, meeting places and gateway cities. The same applies to the Polish metropolis Szczecin-Swinoujscie whose role within the Fehmarnbelt Region is unremarkable.

The region's city system is also structured by a number of large cities that play a role as regional centres with a strong concentration of hinterland-oriented public service activities. Most of these cities have a university, some have gateway functions and all of them have significant commercial niches. These include 15 medium-sized cities whose roles are largely local although a few – just like some of the large centres – function as a supplement to, and interact with, the major gateway cities. Figure 15 shows the cities near the future fixed Fehmarnbelt link.

SUMMARY

The Fehmarnbelt Region's urban system is structured according to a number of large, heavy centres within and outside the region as important nodes (co-ordinating network centres). The Øresund City and Hamburg are crucial to the region's function, activity level, prosperity and future prospects. Without these metropolises, the region would be without international format. The two major cities are, however, not the only high level centres of influence on the region. Berlin, Frankfurt and Stockholm also have main roles. Berlin is Germany's capital and presents a so far failed attempt to join the world cities' upper levels. Frankfurt and Stockholm are in a class to which Berlin aspires. With its European dominance within the finance world and boasting one of the world's large inter-continental air transport centres, Frankfurt offers a marketplace which, in other powerful nations, is found in their capitals. Stockholm, Sweden's capital, occupies an important position in terms of large international (Swedish) business groups. Nevertheless, it is more isolated in terms of global integration than the other heavy centres.

Frankfurt's role is somewhat remote in relation to the Fehmarnbelt regional problem. It is the four other metropolises that count in daily life. By top-end European standards, the Øresund City is small measured by population, but large measured in economic strength, access to international air transport networks and in scientific output. Hamburg has a rather small population, but significant economic strength. Hamburg, however, has no particular strength in respect of access to international air transport networks and scientific output. With its larger population, the situation for Berlin is different although its economic position is weak with poor links to international air transport networks. By contrast, the city is strong in terms of scientific production. Finally, Stockholm is small in terms of population and significant in respect of economic strength. The city has relatively poor access to the international air traffic network, but a strong position in respect of scientific output. The four metropolises dominate their hinterlands and compete directly with each other with regards to customer-related service companies, cultural offerings, access to terminals and use of business-to-business services.

Direct competition with regard to a hinterland for the metropolises' products has been supplemented by further dominance conditions where other cities than the four Fehmarnbelt–near metropolises play important roles. These roles depend on how the cities are part of globalised networks. To determine this we have used the Taylor group's analysis of business-to-business service networks. London, Europe's only genuine world city, plays the strongest role. Further down in the city hierarchy we find Paris, the Amsterdam region, Brussels and Frankfurt. Altogether six cities from Denmark, Sweden and Germany rank among "world cities". Frankfurt has a third position level among the command centres and

FIGURE 15.
CITIES CLOSER THAN 300 KM TO THE FUTURE FEHMARNBELT LINK

on the second level on the list of dominating centres. Dusseldorf, Munich and Stockholm are on the fourth level among the command centres and together with Copenhagen, Hamburg and Berlin also occupy a fourth level position in terms of dominance. Finally, only Copenhagen and Hamburg are included in the list of network centres where they occupy third level positions.

The way in which the overall international business-to-business service networks function reveals obvious patterns. The cities play together in bands with mutual interaction patterns and uniform interaction patterns with the rest of the world. The individual city can feature in several bands. Danish, Swedish and German cities do not show any particular degree of mutual connectivity but are part of different bands of cities, some of them together, others individual. In the Outer Europe band, Copenhagen plays a leading role, but Stockholm and a number of other cities also play a part. Another band is called Germany-Eastern Europe and includes Berlin (together with Dusseldorf and Munich) on the main list, while Hamburg, together with other cities, play more subsidiary roles. It is also interesting to see that, with the exception of Frankfurt, no cities from Denmark, Sweden or Germany have positions within the continent's strongest bands.

Interaction is always an expression of added value. Consequently, it makes sense to examine new opportunities and to see what this analysis can be used for. The belief is that if stronger links can be created between, first and foremost, Copenhagen/the Øresund City and Hamburg and, at the next level, also with Stockholm and Berlin, this could give rise to a Northern European band, i.e. a network of mutually strongly linked cities with homogenous partnership relations with the rest of the world. Such a band could acquire a position at a higher level within the continent's city hierarchy and, therefore, contribute to development, growth and prosperity.

The city system within the Fehmarnbelt Region also includes a range of other centres. There are other large cities, some of which with larger or smaller justification, claim metropolis status. Three German major cities can be found at a somewhat lower level in the urban hierarchy – specialised centres Braunschweig-Wolfsburg, Hanover and Bremen that are located within Hamburg's hinterland for major city product, but also occupy strong independent roles as industrial centres, conference centres and gateway cities. The region's urban system is also structured by a number of large cities that act as regional centres with strong concentrations of hinterland-oriented public service activities. Most of these cities have a university, some have gateway functions and all have commercially important niches. Finally, there are 14 medium-sized cities whose roles are primarily local although a few – like some of the large centres – function as a supplement to, and interact with, the major gateway cities.

REFERENCES

Airport Council International, 'Yearbook', 2009

R. Brunet, 'Les Villes "Européennes", la Documentation Francaise', 1989

M. Castells, 'The Information Age: Economy, Society and Culture' in 'The Rise of the Network Society', Oxford, Blackwell, 1996

B. Derudder, F. Witlox, P. J. Taylor & G. Catalano,'Fuzzy Classification in large Geographical Databases: Towards a Detailed Assessment of the World City Network', International Journal of Pattern Recognition and Artificial Intelligence, 2007, 21 (3), 439-462

B. Derudder, F. Witlox, P. J. Taylor & G. Catalano, 'Hierarchical Tendencies and Regional Patterns in the World City Network: A Global Urban Analysis of 234 Cities', regional studies, 2003, 37, 9:875-886

ESPON, 'ESPON 1.1.1. Potentials for polycentric development in Europe', project report, 2005, 118

ESPON, 'ESPON project 1.4.3. Study on Urban Functions', final report, 2007, 200

Miljøministeriet, 'Landsplanredegørelse 2006. Det nye danmarkskort – planlægning under nye vilkår', 2006

S. Sassen, 'The Global City', Princeton University Press, 1991

E. Schein & A. Thierstein, 'Urban Space of Emerging Cities in the Knowledge Economy Context', working document, American Association of Geographers, 2009

P. J. Taylor, 'World City Network', a global urban analysis, Routledge, London, 2004

P. J. Taylor & B. Derudder, 'Porous Europe: European Cities in Global Urban Arenas', Tijdschrift voor Economische en Sociale Geografie, 2004, 95:527-538

P. J. Taylor & B. Derudder, P. Saey & F. Witlox (ed.), 'Cities in Globalization', Routledge, 2007

P. J. Taylor & R. Aranya, 'A Global 'Urban Roller Coaster'? Connectivity Changes in the World City Network 2000-2004', regional studies, 2008, 42, 1:1-16

P. J. Taylor, G. Catalano & D.R.F. Walker, 'Explanatory analysis of the world city network', Urban Studies Journal, 2002, 39:2377-94

P. J. Taylor et al., 'Measuring the World City Network: New Developments and Results', GaWC research bulletin 300, 2009

CHAPTER 5
A LABOUR MARKET ACROSS NATIONAL BORDERS – BARRIERS AND OPPORTUNITIES

JOHANNES BRÖCKER, HAYO HERRMANN & ARTEM KORZHENEVYCH

The reason for analysing the labour market in the Fehmarnbelt Region is the long-term vision for the region as a business and residential area where people move freely across the borders, the Fehmarnbelt and the Øresund – not only at holiday time and for leisure, but also to work, to be educated, to conduct research, to shop and maintain social contacts.

Regardless of whether this vision is evaluated realistically or very critically, such an evaluation will always indicate that the vision is perhaps too ambitious. Similar visions have not yet been realised in other traditional border regions in Europe because of the barriers in the form of different languages and currencies as well as differences in national taxation and social systems, etc. These barriers impede interaction across the border. In the Fehmarnbelt Region, beyond the major impediment of the sea crossing, an additional barrier is the sparse settlement structure in the vicinity of the border.

In this and the following chapter on the labour market in the Fehmarnbelt Region, we will examine to what extent parts of the region have already been integrated and the perspectives that may open up ahead of the completion of the fixed link across the Fehmarnbelt and in the subsequent period. How have the special impediments in relation to the Danish/German border at Fehmarnbelt impacted so far, particularly in comparison

to other border areas such as the Danish/German land border or the Øresund Region which, in principle, have a stronger position in terms of population and labour density and because of the small distances between residential areas and workplaces. Are the hopes or expectations for an integrated labour market in the Fehmarnbelt Region possibly directed more towards the residential and labour market centres at both ends of the axis that will be upgraded with the fixed link – i.e. towards the areas around Lübeck and Hamburg and the Øresund City – and to a lesser extent towards the more thinly populated areas in between? Or will the distance between these two centres remain too large after the establishment of the fixed link?

A fixed link across Fehmarnbelt also raises the question of whether in the longer term, i.e. some years after commissioning, the link can achieve another important function in addition to its undisputed transit function as a corridor between Scandinavia and the European continent: as a bridge in the Fehmarnbelt Region with significant impetus for a common labour market and living space. In this way, the link could become a successful model similar to the bridges across Storebælt and Øresund.

Currently, there is a certain amount of scepticism with regard to the potential for creating a labour market across national borders – and not without reason. The border regions in large parts of the EU are – despite all attempts to achieve cohesion – still far from reaching the status of joint labour markets. The percentage of the EU's population that lives and works in a country other than their country of origin is only 1.5 per cent. Cross-border commuters are commuters who daily or at least once a week cross a national border to work[i]. The percentage of cross-border commuters among people in employment in the EU (EU-25) accounted for 0.6 per cent in 2005[ii]. The percentage of cross-border commuters to Germany from all neighbouring states is 0.4-0.5 per cent of those with a fixed workplace in Germany. This means that slightly more than 110,000 of 27 million employees are cross-border commuters. In Schleswig-Holstein there is, in fact, only 0.2 per cent, i.e. 1,500 commuters from outside Germany (Statistische Abteilung der Bundesagentur für Arbeit).

Despite this rather disillusioning background there are, however, also findings that provide grounds for optimism: in some regions near Germany's periphery there are signs of an emerging labour market across national borders which, however, is often limited to one direction, i.e. displays a strong asymmetry. Examples include Saarland and regions in Baden-Württemberg and Rheinland-Pfalz, which border France and Switzerland and have many commuters from France; or the Øresund Region with many commuters from Scania across Øresund to Greater Copenhagen. Moreover, the figures for cross-border commuters have increased considerably for some border regions over the past ten years. In the following, we will look at the rising number of commuters from Germany to Denmark at the Danish-German land border especially with regard to the question of to what extent this could be a likely scenario for the Fehmarnbelt Region.

BENEFITS OF BORDER REGIONS LINKED BY MOBILITY

The benefits of an increasing exchange within labour markets across national borders are two-directional: (a) on the one side, the integration of regions contributes to Europe's cohesion objective (b) and on the other, economic advantages deriving from large and multi-faceted regions can be documented in relation to the debate on agglomeration effects.

(a) Arguments for self-enhancing and sustainable integration of the labour market, business life and, not least, social networks across borders are quite obvious. Every time someone moves their work or life centre to the other side of the border there arise new experiences which make it easier for others to handle the many impediments for cross-border commuting presently still in place. It also becomes easier to identify and formulate such border impediments. And since most people find it natural to share and communicate knowledge, other potential cross-border commuters can draw on the experiences of the pioneers – either personally or through existing consultancy institutions. In regions with a low exchange of labour, cross-border commuters, therefore, assume a pioneering function for people who are about to take similar decisions. This can be clearly seen in connection with commuter mobility at the Danish/German land border which has risen considerably in recent years. A similar development in terms of mobility across the Fehmarnbelt can be expected when the exchange of labour across the border is increased, both after the construction phase and during the commissioning of the fixed link: commuters across national borders, therefore, contribute to reducing border impediments and, therefore, contribute to cohesion between European regions and peaceful co-existence between people in Europe – fully in accordance with Article 158 in the Treaty on European Union.

(b) Besides this societal benefit, there is one other benefit stemming from cross-border labour markets that are linked together by intensive workforce mobility. It is given by the economic value of a large and diverse market, as described by several different chains of reasoning in the New Economic Geography literature and, especially, in the theory of agglomeration effects. The benefits are owing to a better risk pooling in the event of fluctuations in demand for goods, better functioning of the regional labour markets as a consequence of more favourable matching conditions (matching of qualifications and workplace requirements) and sufficient exit opportunities in connection with the signing of contracts and, not least, a more intensive and easier transfer of knowledge. These factors are described briefly here through examples where we follow the explanation for agglomeration effects given by Duranton & Puga (2004).

Risk pooling: Risks relating to business cycles or fluctuations in demand in individual goods markets and consequently relating to fluctuations in employment do not affect all regions in the same way, especially not if they are part of different national economies and if their labour markets are organised differently or they specialise in different segments. When periodical fluctuations in labour demand in two neighbouring regions do not correlate positively, regions linked by intensive workforce mobility always have an economic advantage over separated regions. As a consequence, through mobility, risks can be distributed over time and across regions so that the overall economy in the two neighbouring regions will have a more favourable result than the sum of the two separate regional economies. This will be possible because the labour force in one region with low demand for labour will commute to the neighbouring region with greater demand for labour – as has been seen at the Danish/German land border in recent years. In addition, the income levels in a pooled labour market will, over time, diverge less in the event of fluctuations in demand for labour than is the case in an isolated market. For the risk averse employees, this is a further advantage. In terms of risk pooling, large or intensively linked neighbouring labour markets provide a kind of insurance against market fluctuations, especially when these correlate negatively between the regions.

Matching of qualifications: in the labour market, employees with different qualifications and skills face workplaces with different requirements. The qualifications that are required and that are offered must match as well as possible within a well functioning market. The advantages of matching in a large labour market with many employees and companies are that the average expected difference in terms of and requirements at a workplace is quite small. Correspondingly, the "mismatch – costs" that arise in connection with such differences in the costs of looking for specific qualifications are also small. For employees with their different skills, intensive mobility acts in the same direction thus creating a matching advantage over labour markets that are separated due to lacking mobility.

Exit opportunities and "hold-up problem": a disadvantage of small labour markets with a low number of workplaces with specific qualification requirements is that qualified employees at the time of the signing of their employment contracts do not have any, or only a few, exit opportunities in the region and that they have to bear the costs of a subsequent termination of the contract (e.g. purchase or rent of accommodation in the region). This means that from the point of view of both contracting parties there are barriers to entering into such contracts. This is why it is difficult for small isolated regions to keep or attract employees with specific qualifications. Large labour markets or labour markets that are linked together by mobility reduce this problem. They offer exit opportunities to their employees and thus secure reasonable employment contracts. To take one example, it is an advantage for Schleswig-Holstein's regions to see themselves and present themselves as part of the large labour market centred in Hamburg. For Hamburg/Lübeck and Copenhagen/Malmö, with a future more intensive link between the two labour markets, a similar effect could be achieved.

Transfer of knowledge: the advantages of large regions are obvious in connection with the generation and transfer of new knowledge. Large knowledge markets provide a wealth of ideas and even more knowledge. And knowledge is a network commodity: the larger the number of users, the lower the cost per user – yet another benefit of larger regions. The advantages of establishing sustainable, trust-based partnership networks for which geographical proximity is important owing to necessary personal contact are greater here than in small regions. Also in this case, the advantages that apply to a large region can be transferred to neighbouring – and closely linked – partner regions.

All arguments that demonstrate the social and economic benefits from closely linked border regions can also apply to a Fehmarnbelt Region without a fixed link. Within this context, efforts to intensify the labour markets links between Lübeck/Ostholstein and West and Southern Zealand and between the cities of Hamburg and Copenhagen/Malmö are also a promising strategy in connection with the current status and until construction begins. In consequence, these efforts should not be delayed until after 2020. On the other hand, the arguments and scenarios in this and the following chapter will be used in order to test the hypothesis of whether the fixed link across Fehmarnbelt together with the many diverse strategies aimed at reducing border barriers are a crucial incentive on the way towards a significantly integrated labour market located on the axis between Hamburg and the Øresund Region.

ANALYSIS OF THE LABOUR MARKET IN THE FEHMARNBELT REGION – AN OVERVIEW

In general, the analysis of spatial distribution follows the gravity concept according to which mobility between two regions is increased by mass (i.e. the size of the two regions) and is reduced by the distance between them. In this context, the distance consists of the geographical distance and a second component that comprises a number of impediments that do not depend on geography. The hypothesis is that this component is significantly larger between regions from different countries than between regions within the same country because it is decisively characterised by border barriers which, in particular, are linked to differences in institutional frameworks, language and culture. This means, for example, that labour mobility (mobility of commuters) between regions located in different countries is considerably lower than between the regions within the same country, ceteris paribus, i.e. when the regions are of the same size and are separated by the same geographical distance. The application of the gravity concept on labour mobility will then, in accordance with a simple gravity formula, result in largely symmetrical in the formula below:

$$I_{ij} = \gamma \cdot \frac{M_i^{\alpha_i} \cdot M_j^{\alpha_j}}{f(d_{ij})}$$

I_{ij} is the interaction between the regions i and j, M is the region's mass or size, d_{ij} is the distance between the regions, and γ, α_i and α_j are parameters. I_{ij} and I_{ji} acquire values that are very similar.

In reality, however, we often see asymmetrical mobility figures ($I_{ij} \neq I_{ji}$) between regions in two countries and occasionally with considerable differences. The reason for this observation are the incentives that lead to people being driven away from a region (push-factor) or attracted by a region (pull-factor). In other words, differences between working and living conditions in two neighbouring regions often lead to more intensive movement between them and these differences are often systematically larger between two regions divided by a national border than between regions within the same country. Our analysis takes account of this.

Finally, labour mobility between two regions (with or without a border) involves different combinations of choice of residence and workplace. An employee with residence and place of work in one region can become a cross-border commuter between two regions if he/she keeps their residence and moves their working place to another region or if he/she relocates their home to another region and maintains their workplace. In these two cases, the incentives (pull and push factors) are different. Moreover a complete move of home and workplace to the new region may happen, which will not affect the figures for commuters crossing national borders. Change of place of residence (migration) and commuting between home and workplace are, in other words, closely linked as decisions that affect mobility. Choices of residence place and workplace are closely linked to each other in a way that may both be substitutive and complementary in nature.

The following section describes the role of impediments to mobility and incentives (pull and push factors), especially those that arise in connection with mobility across national borders. It also describes the interaction between commuting and migration. Following a systematic review of mobility factors, a further section specifically describes the Fehmarnbelt Region and selected comparable regions. We look at the situation at the Danish/German land border and in the Øresund Region, both of which in recent years have been characterised by asymmetric commuting figures which have risen considerably – at least in one direction. Here, the incentive factors have played a crucial role. They have apparently been so significant that the barriers at the borders between Denmark and Germany or Denmark and Sweden have almost vanished, at least in one direction. We supplement these findings with a brief description of the conditions at the border between Holland and Northern Germany, in particular because this border region has the longest tradition for, and most extensive experience with, European co-operation.

Further on in this chapter follows a description of impediments to mobility and mobility incentives in the Fehmarnbelt Region, which takes its starting point in the situation over the past few years and the current situation with two fixed links in the western part of the Baltic area and the ferry link across the Fehmarnbelt. Here we focus on the region between the two agglomeration areas at each end, i.e. the link region between the two cities Hamburg and Copenhagen (including Lübeck, Ostholstein, Lolland-Falster and Southern Zealand).

The expected future reduction of border barriers and its impact on labour mobility in the Fehmarnbelt Region will already begin prior to the start of construction work for the fixed link, i.e. in the next few years. The processes will change their quality and intensity as a consequence of the special impulses during the construction phase. When the link is completed around 2020, the reductions in time costs, the introduced system of charges and the new infrastructure will once again impact on the Fehmarnbelt Region's labour market. This will occur as a direct consequence of, in part, the shorter distance, and in part, of a targeted effort to reduce the factual and psychological barriers that impede mobility across the border between Denmark and Germany. Finally, one can expect new impetuses for mobility due to the location of business and residential sites along the axis between Hamburg and Copenhagen.

The opportunities that will arise for the metropolises at both ends of the Fehmarnbelt axis in the form of stronger economic cooperation and mutual exchange of impetuses is a theme of its own. This process will occur in conjunction with the intensification of the typical labour mobility between the two large metropolises and will, in particular, focus on the highly qualified cross-border commuters that commute by train from an agglomeration area to a neighbouring metropolis, usually once a week. This type of labour mobility will be considered in connection with the commuting scenarios in the subsequent chapter.

BARRIERS TO MOBILITY ACROSS NATIONAL BORDERS

The geographical distance, administrative and legislative barriers as well as language, cultural and psychological barriers are realities for a labour market across national borders. This was discussed a few years ago in connection with an analysis of barriers to the Fehmarnbelt Region and documented by a large number of interviews with the region's players (Barten et al., 2006). In the meantime, four years have passed that have brought (with the participation of players and institutions from the region) important decisions about the fixed link across the Fehmarnbelt. At the same time, the commuting figures have risen considerably across the land border from Germany to Denmark and from Sweden across Øresund:

Commuters from Germany to Southern Jutland:
2003:   1,800
2005:   2,600 (Buch et al., 2008)
2008:   3,400 (see next chapter)

Øresund commuters from Sweden to Denmark:
2003:   5,700
2005:   8,800
2007:   15,700
2008:   19,100

Source: Ørestat

We argue that the increase is both due to a reduction in the impediments – either through intensive consulting activity or through bilateral agreements between the involved states – or due to a reduction of psychological barriers. In the case of the Øresund Region, the barriers have also been reduced as a result of the Øresund Bridge becoming a true constant in the minds of people. Growing incentives in the Danish/German border region because of greater differences in the labour market situation on both sides of the border and in the Øresund Region owing to regional differences in housing and living costs have also played a part. The impediments described in the barrier analysis, however, still significantly affect mobility across national borders.

It is easiest to describe the impact of the commuting distance between home and workplace. The actual length of a trip from home to workplace in one's own car, measured in monetary units for time consumption as well as the variable and fixed transport costs are, in the simple case – i.e. without waiting times because of ferries and with no other road or bridge charges – to a significant extent proportional to the geographical road distance. However, it is not the objectively established, but the perceived distance that is decisive in terms of the impact on decisions on mobility. According to empirical analyses of commuting behaviour, the perceived distance is related positively, but not linearly with the actual distance. An important reason is that the average number of journeys to the workplace per week falls when the commuting distance increases – i.e. that the percentage of weekend commuters increases with the distance. Transport costs per week, therefore, rise only slowly with the actual distance per journey. In addition subjective perceptions also play a role, e.g. interruptions of the journey or waiting time and not least a journey by ferry to a neighbouring region that is visible in the distant horizon across a distance that subjectively is felt to be significant.

With this non-linear relationship between the actually measured and the perceived distance (see Fig. 1), the relation between the decision to commute and the actual distance is also non-linear. The relation between the number of commuters and the actual distance has rather a convex shape (see Fig. 2).

FIGURE 1.
THE ACTUAL AND PERCEIVED DISTANCE FROM HOME TO WORK

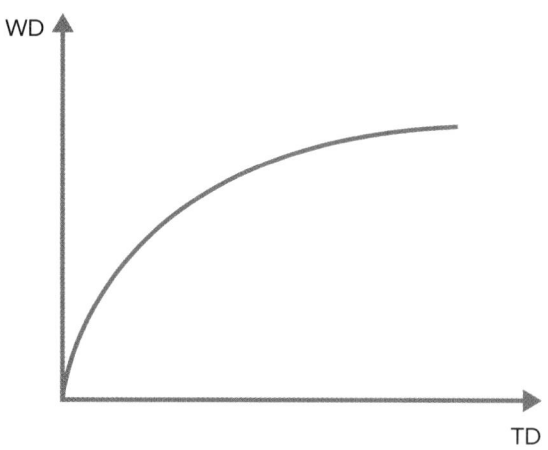

TD = the actual distance measured in monetary units
WD = the distance perceived by the commuter

FIGURE 2.
COMMUTER MOBILITY AND THE ACTUAL DISTANCE FROM HOME TO WORK

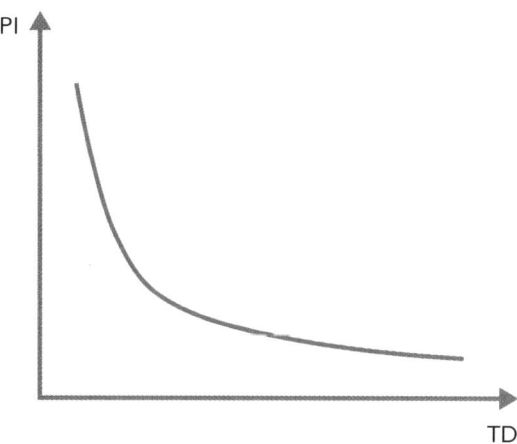

PI = commuting intensity (with the given incentives and barriers that are not dependent on distance and the given size of the home and work region): the share in total number of employed persons in the home region of commuters that leave their home region
TD = the actual distance of a car journey

Now we consider the barriers that are not dependent on distance but arise in connection with a change from home to workplace region. As the barriers related to moving to another country are particularly significant, we distinguish between domestic commuters who change region but not country and cross-border commuters. In an extreme case, the border barriers are so significant that mobility across the border is impossible (e.g. "the Iron Curtain"). With a given geographical distance and given commuter incentives (pull and push factors), there will be a positive and concave relation between commuting intensity and the integration of the two regions measured as an inverse function of the border impediments with the extreme cases of "Iron Curtain" and of complete integration ("single country"). The hypothesis is then that the reduction in border impediments will result in an increase in commuting figures.

The description and assessment of border impediments in the Fehmarnbelt Region, as contained in Barten et al., (2006), constitute the information framework that also applies

FIGURE 3.
COMMUTER MOBILITY AND INTEGRATION FOR TWO REGIONS

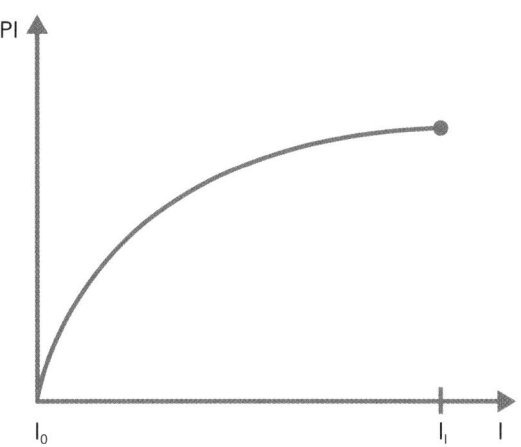

PI = commuter intensity (at a given commuting distance and given incentives)
I = integration between home and workplace region, extreme cases I_0 "Iron Curtain" and I_1 "single country"

today. In addition, there is a lot of information that the consultancy institutions for cross-border commuters make available through special events and personal conversations or through the Internet and in information brochures. We will limit ourselves here, therefore, to a systematic overview without describing the details, for instance those behind the administrative barriers[iii].

In principle, mobility barriers can occur at the beginning of a job in another region or during a home move across the border or they can impact permanently throughout the entire period of living/working in the neighbouring region. Barriers that appear permanent must, within this context, be generally classified as a more serious problem in respect of mobility-impeding effects.

Legal obstacles arise (a) as a consequence of different legal provisions and regulations which, in the final analysis, can only be reduced through legislative measures, (b) as a consequence of problems with administration and implementation by the responsible authorities which can be analysed and remedied locally and (c) as a consequence of information problems: the effect of the barriers on people's decisions depends on their subjective judgment and decisively on the knowledge about the issues in question. Thus a lack of information should be perceived as part of the mobility obstacles. Information on obstacles and how to overcome them can only reach (potential) cross-border commuters if such information is made available for and is requested by them – the bottleneck problem, therefore, is not always related to information supply. The information problem also depends on how transparent and especially how stable the regulations and institutions are over time. Measures aimed at reducing obstacles usually take their starting point in two strategies: (1) solution-oriented strategies, and (2) consultancy and information on the obstacles.

The following overview shows the most important obstacles to labour mobility between two countries. Within this context we establish different categories that relate to work or daily life in the other country. The importance of different categories of obstactles is then diffferent for a daily commuter that returns to his region of residence every day than it is for a weekend commuter that spends the whole week in the other region. It is even more different for a cross-border commuter that has chosen to live in a neighbouring country while keeping the workplace in the county of origin. In addition, the impact of the obstacles depends on personal characteristics (educational status, age and family situation) and whether the person is looking for a permanent job in the neighbouring region or just temporary employment. We analyse the following categories:

– Administrative obstacles
– Labour market obstacles
– Qualification obstacles
– Obstacles in relation to daily life and psychological barriers

Reductions to administrative obstacles, depending on their source, must be carried out by the EU, by the involved state or länder, by relevant institutions at national or regional levels or by the border region itself, i.e. by the municipalities and local institutions that are in direct contact with those who take the step of relocating across the border. In this respect, we are talking about mutual agreements concerning changes to legislation, rules and regulations that impede workforce mobility across the border, i.e. measures aimed at harmonising regulations and provisions for the case of change between the legal systems that are reliable and that are interpreted in the same way in all regions and at all times. A more important aspect within this context is the effort to create clarity and transparency and, in particular, to create stability of the regulations and ensure continually involved institutions and qualified persons, first and foremost because the learning process can then unfold with employees and consultancy staff.

The solution models for the qualification-related barriers partly take their starting point in the involved parties in relation to education at schools, universities, in companies and in the parties involved, such as the chambers of commerce, employer and industry organisations or trade unions. The success also depends crucially on whether the people being educated or trained are willing to make use of the provision for qualifications across national borders. The harmonisation model for joint professional education with qualifications that are recognised on both sides of the border is an effective concept. In addition, the mutual recognition of existing qualifications should not be ignored – it also includes additional qualifications (certificates) and certificates concerning further education. In other words, you can only eliminate the qualification-related barriers through a dual strategy of harmonisation (of new educational programmes) and recognition (of old qualifications).

The language barrier is an obstacle at the place of work and in daily life in a border region. This is a particularly important issue for people who move their whole life centre i.e. home and workplace or for people who, as weekend commuters stay in the neighbouring region during the week. The language barrier is also a problem for employees in the service sector, such as the health sector. Employees within the construction industry with lower qualifications or highly qualified people within management and science can, in principle, often manage with their own language or with English in a work situation. Advice and services to customers as well as everyday life are, however, in the long run only possible with a knowledge of the relevant country's language. Bottlenecks in connection with the possibilities to learn the neighbouring country's language are, however, often due more to demand than supply. There exist language courses, but their supply would increase if demand was greater. Teaching of the neighbouring country's language in school has, despite all the effort in border regions, not yet reached the necessary extent. The language barrier is not a problem of oral communication but also a problem of written information (forms, regulations and internet text) which still does not meet the standards for bilingual versions in all places.

The information and advice to people, who with their choice of residence or workplace are likely to become cross-border commuters or who have already gained their first commuter experiences can, however, in regions with a longer tradition for a labour market across national borders, e.g. at the Danish-German land border, in the border area between Germany and Holland or in the Øresund Region, draw on an experienced consultancy. Other regions can learn from this experience. All institutions make extensive written and internet-based information available, provide information events and courses as well as

personal consultations and are part of the network for the regional labour market and business institutions. Of special assistance in addition to individual advice are the easy-to-understand "what to do" lists for cross-border commuters where the necessary steps, their order, the involved institutions and the documents to be submitted and received when changing jobs from the home country to the neighbouring region are provided. The European portal regarding mobility EURES provides Danish-German cross-border commuters with such a compass. Finally, the reports of cross-border commuters on their own experiences where positive events in relation to working in the neighbouring country are often weighted higher than the problems to be solved at the start, should not be underestimated.

OVERVIEW: BARRIERS TO A CROSS-BORDER LABOUR MARKET

Category	Impediments and barriers (examples)	Comments
Administrative impediments Impediments due to various laws and regulations, different institutions and different interpretations of regulations	Tax system, particularly income tax Social insurance Pension and medical care insurance, widows' and/or orphans' pension and early retirement benefit State health insurance Family benefits (child and parent benefits)	The involved states' laws and regulations with regard to tax and social insurance: bilateral national agreements and separate regulations in the border region
Labour market barriers Barriers owing to different regulations and different institutions as well as language and cultural barriers	Unemployment insurance Regulations regarding employment contracts Regulations regarding job security Regulations regarding holiday and sick leave Regulations regarding industrial accidents and accidents on the way to and from work Company pensions, company or trade union benefits Payroll accounts and payment Language at the daily workplace (with colleagues and customers) Trade unions and works councils Working conditions (breaks and overtime) Job search and intermediation Requirements and expectations (further education, mobility and flexibility) Work culture (hierarchy, teamwork, duties, communication and autonomy) Application and negotiation culture	Employment law and unemployment schemes: legislation of the EU and of the states involved Bilateral national agreements and separate regulations in the border region
Qualification-related barriers Barriers in connection with mutual recognition of degrees and qualifications and in connection with different educational programmes	School leaving certificates (recognition) Professional qualifications University degrees Other qualifications and certificates Internships and further education	Educational systems in the involved states and countries: bilateral national agreements and separate regulations in the border region
Barriers in everyday life Barriers particularly for weekend commuters, or when the place of residence switches to another country	Private insurance (accident, life, health, personal liability and old-age pension) Personal documents, compulsory registration and daily bureaucracy Law of contract (house purchase and rental) Bank accounts and different currencies Regulations regarding use of vehicle Difference in the school system Daily language problems Cultural barriers (social attitudes and norms) Psychological obstacles (e.g. historically conditioned)	

In the already established border regions, the information and consultancy infrastructure largely comprises the following institutions:

– Information centres at the border (regional office offering commuter advice)

– EURES-advisors in the region (partly in local employment agencies of Bundesagentur fur Arbeit, at job centres, trade union offices or social centres)[iv]

– Local job centres, e.g. private or municipal employment bureaus; in Germany - the local offices of the Federal Employment Agency (for the recipients of ALG I) and the job centres of ARGE (co-operation of the local employment agencies and the local authorities) (for recipients of ALG II)

– Chamber of commerce and trade unions' information centres e.g., in respect of recognition of professional qualifications

– The Central Office for International Mediation (Zentrale Auslandsvermittlung (ZAV)) which is a job exchange scheme under the Federal Employment Agency in Germany; in Denmark: "Workindenmark" initiative for the foreign workers, supported by the Danish government

INCENTIVES FOR MOBILITY ACROSS NATIONAL BORDERS: PULL AND PUSH FACTORS

"If everything were alike, there would be no incentive for crossing borders" (Barten et al., 2006, p. 146). Mobility across regions and, especially, national borders arises because of the differences between neighbouring regions that constitute an incentive to leave one's own region (regardless of where to – the "push factors") or to be drawn towards a specific region (regardless of where from – the "pull factors"). For a commuter within the same country, it is, for instance, the differences between urban and rural areas that constitute an incentive to live near a city and work in the city. For cross-border commuters it is particularly the differences between the two countries in which their home and work region lies. These are mostly greater than between regions within the same country.

If one sets the individual factors that constitute an impediment or an incentive to mobility across national borders against each other, it becomes clear that, in addition to the factors that exclusively constitute an impediment (e.g. lack of language skills) and

MOBILITY INCENTIVES AS A CONSEQUENCE OF DIFFERENCES BETWEEN THE REGION OF ORIGIN AND THE TARGET REGION

Taxes, duties and state and municipality services	Working life	Daily life
Collection of taxes and duties	Earned income	House and property prices
State family benefits	Special benefits	Rentals, rental legislation and construction legislation
Other transfer payments	Job security	Other housing expenditure
Social insurance and pensions	Industry-related labour market situation	General living costs
Health services and health insurance	Formal working conditions	Life quality and leisure value (nature and culture)
Infrastructure provision	Career opportunities	School system
Law and order	Work culture	Life in society

factors that trigger an incentive to mobility (e.g. a higher salary in the neighbouring country) there are also factors that can include both. This, in particular, applies to many system differences between neighbouring countries especially relating to taxation and duties, social security or family benefits. The effort needed to become acquainted with these differences and handle the formalities related to working in a neighbouring country or moving home may initially constitute an impediment to mobility. The exploitation of taxation benefits or better social services in the neighbouring region can, however, also be an incentive to living or working there. There is, therefore, an in-built tension between mobility barriers and incentives that we will consider in more detail below. The strategy of handling impediments to labour mobility across national borders with extensive harmonisation of laws and regulations or other living and working conditions can, therefore, be completely counter-productive. Rather it should be an objective on the one hand to reduce particularly serious disparities, but on the other to allow differences between border regions as part of life's diversity and to communicate such differences and advise people accordingly.

The differentiation between mobility incentives based on push or pull factors is, for the most part, unclear. Often those persons who have moved their home and/or workplace from one region to another (i.e. from the region of origin to the target region) do not know whether they have left their region of origin because of unfavourable conditions or whether they have moved to the target region because of its favourable conditions – most often it was a direct comparison between the two regions that has led to the decision. In this respect, it is better to talk about incentives in general.

THE INTERACTION BETWEEN IMPEDIMENTS AND INCENTIVES

"When the undertaking is rewarding, barriers are easy to overcome" (Barten et al., 2006, p. 148). This sentence expresses the tension between impediments and incentives with regard to mobility across national borders. As a third component, people's knowledge about impediments and incentives comes into play. Only if the interaction between these three components is understood can you untangle apparent contradictions, e.g. why do people in a border region complain about a lack of information while the advisory bodies often note a lack of demand for available information.

Figures 4, 5, and 6 illustrate that the key lies with incentives. If they are small and if people are familiar with them, there is no particular motivation for mobility across national borders. Also, if people with no information are convinced that there are no incentives for moving across the border, they are unlikely to search for advice and information. In both cases, interest in the neighbouring region is small regardless of how high or low the border barriers are. Even small barriers then constitute a strong impediment to mobility across the border and when the barriers are high measures aimed at reducing them are of little importance. If the incentives in the neighbouring region (compared to one's own region) are considerable, people make use of the information and advice on the impediments connected to the change of region if this is necessary. The extent of mobility across national borders, therefore, depends on the barriers and the information provided on them.

Information plays a central and supporting role in cross-border mobility: firstly it makes people aware of incentives in the neighbouring region and thus stimulates their activity and, secondly, information reduces the limiting effect of a number of border impediments.

IMPEDIMENTS AND INCENTIVES OVER TIME

How will labour mobility, especially commuter flows across the border and, in particular, across the Danish-German border in the Fehmarnbelt Region develop over time? Here, too, we have to look at the three above-mentioned deciding factors relating to mobility

FIGURE 4.
INTERACTION BETWEEN BARRIERS, INCENTIVES AND INFORMATION

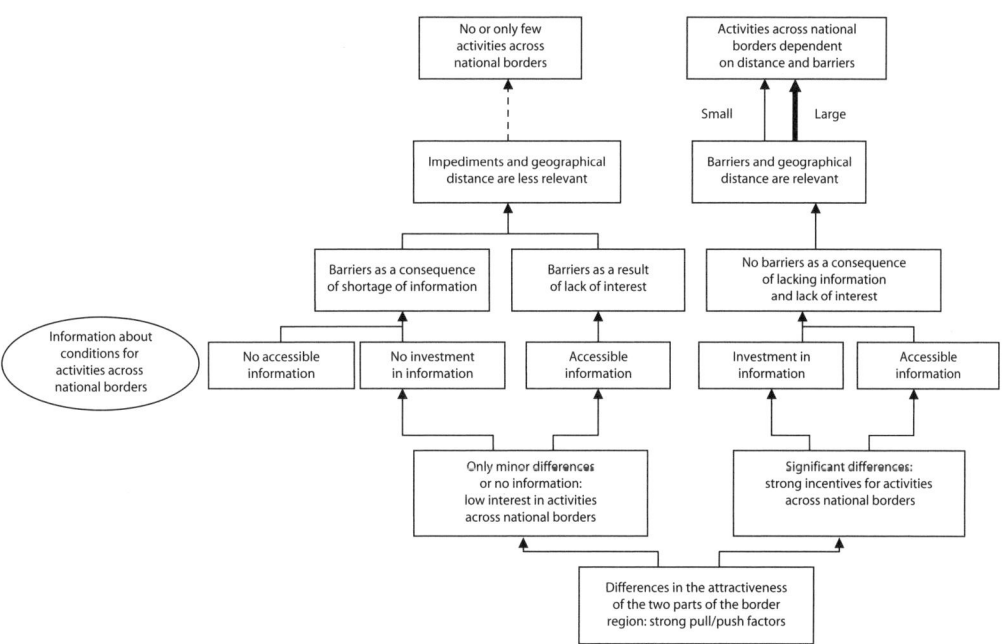

Inspired by Barten et al. (2006)

together, border barriers, incentives and information about the above two factors, and follow their changes over time. After the basic discussion about the development of impediments and incentives over time, there follows in the next section a specific examination of selected border areas, including the Fehmarnbelt Region.

In terms of mobility barriers, we regard a steady decline process as likely – whether through EU agreements and regulations, between the involved countries or between municipalities and institutions on both sides of the border. Within this context, it should be ensured that this is conducted in a smooth manner so that the information and advisory institutions will not be overly burdened. In addition, improvements to the provision of

FIGURE 5.
INTERACTION BETWEEN BARRIERS AND INCENTIVES AND THE IMPACT ON MOBILITY ACROSS BORDERS

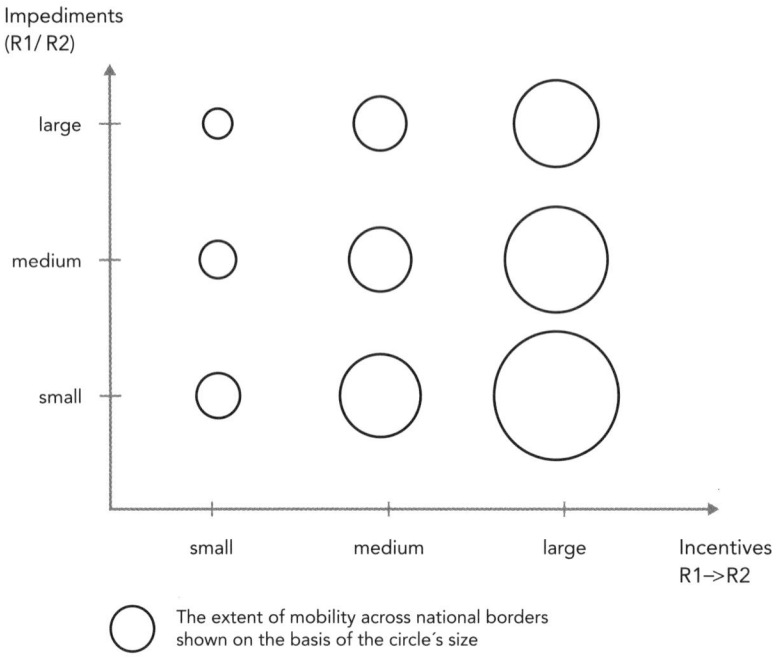

Border regions R1 and R2 and labour mobility from R1 to R2

advice and information through everyday work and the transfer of knowledge and through the exchange of experience between advisors which, in turn, will benefit from staff and institutional continuity. Moreover, we will follow the hypothesis that a rising number of commuters across national borders in itself can contribute to reducing impediments and improving information because commuters share knowledge and experience with each other and are happy to share their knowledge with prospective commuters.

The development in mobility incentives is, however, less clear. On the one hand, through better information about the benefits in the neighbouring region, they will become more significant. On the other hand, it could be that the incentives will be reduced due to the harmonisation of institutional and legislative regulations and through tendential levelling of prices or other key figures between ever closer linked regions. A possible example of the

FIGURE 6.
INCENTIVES AND BARRIERS TO MOBILITY ACROSS NATIONAL BORDERS THE IMPACT OF INCREASED INFORMATION

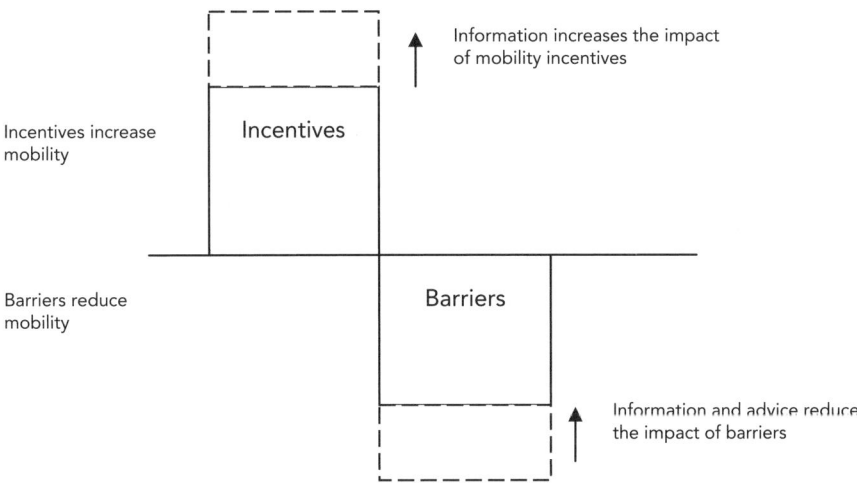

latter argument is the reduction of the differences in living costs, earned income, property prices or unemployment percentages on each side of the border – issues that are relevant, e.g. for the currently high number of commuters from Sweden to Denmark across Øresund or from Germany to Denmark across the land border.

Let us return to the barriers to mobility across the border: what can we expect in terms of the above-mentioned barriers? For the administrative and legislative barriers we expect, over the next few years, to see a marked reduction in impediments owing to the increasingly improved implementation of agreements between the involved countries and between the local organisations on both sides of the border, especially in the form of easily applicable and, above all, stable regulations that can be integrated into the involved institutions' advisory day-to-day work in the most uncomplicated way possible. User friendliness and stability are, in this connection, more important than a cascade of new regulations. Mutual learning processes for advisors in different border regions and between employees themselves will strengthen this trend.

In relation to labour market barriers we expect that many differences on both sides of the border will remain. They are, of course, not only an impediment, but also an incentive to mobilty across national borders. In this respect, the steadily improving information and advice for those involved, i.e. the employees and the companies, have first priority. Extensive experience from border regions with their already intensive labour market integration should be used in this connection. This means that, within this context, a considerable reduction of impediments can be expected over the years ahead. A more sustained problem will relate to language in daily working life, especially when the share of mobile workers in simple craftsmen occupations decreases and that of the occupations in the individual service sector increases.

In respect of qualification impediments, i.e. the mutual recognition of professional qualifications, it will be more difficult to reduce the barriers. Despite the many initiated measures, many labour market players complain – employees as well as employers – that there are considerable shortcomings in this area. Here we have to set up long-term strategies both in connection with the establishment of joint education programmes and in recognising existing qualifications. These must take their starting point on both sides of the labour market, i.e. employers and employees themselves. We expect that significant progress can be made here, at least within those professions that are involved in the construction of the fixed link across Fehmarnbelt.

Impediments relating to daily life in the neighbouring country are primarily relevant to weekend commuters and employees that move their home permanently to the other side of the border region. The impediments are less relevant to daily commuters who return to their life centre in the evening. Some impediments can be reduced quite easily and rapidly through advice, information, the communication of experience between the people involved and perhaps also through openness and adjustment to the changed environment. This concerns different ways of arranging daily life and the handling of different social norms. Other day-to-day problems in an environment that is initially foreign, in particular problems concerning a different language or different psychological barriers require more time and support, e.g. in the form of language courses and integration offers ("people-to-people").

In general, however, we are optimistic: many arguments speak for a societal integration process which once started, will strengthen itself through many impulses even if these are initially centred on the labour market. Impediments will be reduced even if this happens at different speeds within the individual areas and not without external impulses as a result of political and social institutions' active intervention.

INTERACTION BETWEEN COMMUTING AND MIGRATION ACROSS BORDERS

As already shown in the introduction, labour mobility between two regions comprises different combinations of the choice of home and workplace: relocation of home (migration) and commuting between home and workplace are closely linked decisions in terms of mobility.

(1) The classic case, which is determined by the labour market, is that an employee with a home and workplace in one region becomes a commuter between two regions in that he/she maintains their home and moves their place of work to another region and thus becomes a cross-border commuter.

(2) A working person who moves his/her home to another region while maintaining his/her workplace, however, is also a cross-border commuter. Here the reasons are better accommodation and life quality in the neighbouring region.

(3) Finally, there may be a complete relocation of home and place of work to the new region which will only be visible in the statistics for immigration and emigration and not in the commuting figures. In the following section, we show that the mentioned variants have a different significance according to region and time through examples from the border areas in the Fehmarnbelt Region.

Case (1): By moving the place of work to the neighbouring region, people become cross-border commuters between their home region and the region on the other side of the border. This scenario is relevant for the above-mentioned advantages of integrated, large labour markets, especially if the commuter flows go in both directions over a long time. For weekend commuters, social contacts may develop in the work region while daily commuters maintain their life centre in their home region.

Case (2): By relocating their home to the neighbouring region people start to commute from the "new" to the old home region and the old place of work will be maintained. This scenario has only secondary significance in terms of the establishment of a common labour market. It does, however, lead to a situation where the social network across the border can be developed if the integration into the new home region is successful. In this case, this will contribute to cohesion in the border region.

Case (3): A complete relocation of place of work and home to the neighbouring country most often means that one settles far from the old home and work region. The border region's labour market and cohesion effects come into force in the event of a relocation from one to the other side of the region, at least if the social ties to the "old" region are not loosened completely.

The correlation between commuting and immigration/emigration, therefore, appears on the one hand in case (2) and on the other in the time-related sequence that can often be observed in the form that a certain amount of time passes before a partial decision about the neighbouring region (scenarios 1 or 2) is followed by a complete relocation to the new region – or a complete return to the original home region.

THE INTEGRATION OF LABOUR MARKETS ACROSS NATIONAL BORDERS OVER TIME

The time pattern for increasing integration of labour markets across national borders follows, on the one hand, basic features that apply to all border regions, but, on the other hand, the development is also characterised by the individual regions' special conditions. In general, one can say that there exists "mobile" segments among the professions and qualifications of the employees and among the characteristics of workplaces. The impediments of cross-border employment, even involving a language barrier, are in these segments relatively small. On the one hand, this concerns the low qualifications or the teams of workers speaking the same language. The examples here could be the unskilled work in the agriculture (harvest helpers), assembly teams within the construction industry, or simple logistic operations (freight forwarding). On the other hand, this includes highly qualified work (management, research) in the departments, where international teams are created and where English is spoken.

At the other end, there are the language specific occupations within consultancy, other services, social professions, health services and teaching. Here linguistic barriers and cultural impediments have a special meaning in that they can only be reduced in the longer term. Correspondingly, it must be assumed that the labour market integration across the border, especially across linguistic borders, begins with the mobile professions and only later includes immobile segments.

For the Fehmarnbelt Region there is, in this respect, the special condition that the decade we have only just begun will be characterised by the fixed link's construction phase, by co-operation between different companies and different teams with a variety of professions and qualifications, but especially by companies and teams that can be characterised as "mobile" – e.g. groups of workers from the construction industry and related industries or international teams consisting of engineers and technicians who can be assumed to choose English as their common language platform. The process involving increased labour market integration is, therefore, not a steady process in this region as in many other border regions. It will rather be characterised by events around the dominant infrastructure project. By the end of the construction phase, the labour market in the region around Fehmarnbelt will certainly no longer be what it was.

WORKFORCE MOBILITY ACROSS NATIONAL BORDERS: REGIONAL EXAMPLES

For clarification of the above-mentioned impediments and incentives relating to mobility across national borders, we will initially look at the situation in border regions which, in part, are already characterised by significant commuter flows and, therefore, can function as a model for the future Fehmarnbelt Region. Therefore, we have described the situation at the Danish/German land border in a fairly detailed way because, in our opinion, it provides a sound basis for the Fehmarnbelt Region in many respects, not only with regard to adopting concepts and ideas, but also in respect of avoiding errors. The second border area described here is the Øresund Region. Both regions have, in recent years, been characterised by asymmetrical commuter figures which have clearly been increasing, at least in one direction. In this respect, unilateral commuter incentives apparently played a particular role and these have been so significant that the impediments at the German-Danish and Danish-Swedisch border respectively have been less significant, at least in one direction. We supplement these results with a brief description of the border area between Holland and Northern Germany since this region has the longest tradition for cross-border co-operation within the EU.

THE SITUATION AT THE DANISH/GERMAN LAND BORDER

The situation at the Danish/German land border, i.e. especially for the Flensburg Region on the German side and the former Sønderjylland Amt on the Danish side has been fairly well documented with regard to mobility across national borders, especially by research institutions within the region itself[vi]. In addition, the regional office of the Infocenter Grænse-Grenze in Padborg offers a broad range of material via the internet (www.pendlerinfo.org) and information brochures. Further information can be obtained from the websites for Foreningen Grænsependler (www.grenzpendler.dk) and EURES–consultants (www.eures-kompas.eu) and not least from local employment offices (www.arbeitsagentur.de) and job centres (www.jobnet.dk). In particular, the survey on cross-border commuters should be mentioned (Buch et al., 2008). Moreover, through personal interviews with Torben Dall Schmidt (Institut for Grænseregionsforskning, Syddansk Universitet Sønderborg) and Peter Hansen (Infocentre Grænse-Grenze) we have obtained much empirical data concerning mobility across national borders and about the current labour market situation at the Danish/German land border.

In recent years, a comprehensive and, in our opinion, professional advisory infrastructure for a mobile workforce at the Danish/German land border has been established which has expanded its capacity in line with the rising commuter figures but which, however, also makes its experiences available to other border areas, not least in the Fehmarnbelt Region. In particular, Infocenter Grænse-Grenze, a department of the regional office Sønderjylland-

Schleswig[vii] which was established in 2004 in Padborg, i.e. directly on the border, has taken over the day-to-day work with regard to information and advice to people who are confronted with institutional regulations in connection with moving workplace (or home) to the other side of the border. This is the first point of contact where problems are identified and guides people to appropriate partners in the advisory network in connection with more specific issues. The advisory service also covers the self-employed and employers.

Also the EURES-advisors that work in several places in the region (Flensburg, Breklum, Sønderborg, Aabenraa, Haderslev and Tønder) are helpful in terms of questions concerning the relocation of place of work or home across the border. They are, however, especially helpful with regard to searching for new employment on the other side of the border, e.g. by preparing regular lists of demanded occupations. In addition, employment advice is handed by traditional employment services, (regional offices under the state employment organisation in Germany and municipal job centres in Denmark) and ARGE job centres (for recipients of unemployment benefit "ALG II" in Germany.) On the basis of the above-mentioned main points, the relationship between these advisory institutions is, in our view, characterised more by co-operation than competition. Within the field of employment services, the project "Gramark" ("labour market across national borders") was implemented for the Flensburg and Westküste, i.e. on the German side, during the period 2001-2006.

Those responsible for the project were Wirtschaftsakademie Schleswig-Holstein, Ministerium für Justiz, Arbeit und Europa in Schleswig-Holstein and the business union Unterelbe-Westküste. "Gramark" had offices at the employment office in Flensburg and in the social centre in Leck. A private employment office currently operates under this name in Harrislee near Flensburg.

Finally, we should mention Foreningen Grænsependlere which is part of Foreningen af Europæiske Grænsependlere and which has the longest tradition in respect of providing assistance to cross-border commuters at the Danish/German land border. In the 1980s, the association was the first and at the time, the only point of contact. The association is a pioneer for all present advisory offices and representative of people who are active across the border, although the advisory function is today primarily handled by Infocentre Grænse-Grenze. The interests of German employees are handled by Verein Grenzgänger in Husum, while the interests of Danish employees are served by Foreningen af Europæiske Grænsependlere in Aabenraa.

Information about life and work in the Danish-German border region Syddanmark-Schleswig can also be found at the websites www.pendlerinfo.regionsyddanmark.dk and at www.grenzlandportal.eu. The website www.pendlerplus.com offers an intermediation service for journey sharing.

Overall, the impression is that assistance to people who are interested in moving their place of work or home across the border is diverse and extensive and there is a considerable signal value in the fact that the most important institution, Infocentre Grænse, is located where the two countries meet. There are, however, two points of criticism. Firstly, because mobility across this border started to evolve long ago, several parallel institutions were established in a way that was not completely transparent for people in search of advice and which were located in different places. A simple and centralized access to their information in the Internet is also missing. Secondly, even an apparently complete advisory infrastructure does not guarantee that necessary information is also received by people. The logical sequence – i.e. to collect information first and then decide – is not followed by many employees in their search for work on the other side of the border. This is certainly the experience of the information centre advisers. Even so, the structures at the Danish/German land border with their advantages and shortcomings are included here as an example of the future design of advisory services in the Fehmarnbelt Region.

The interviews with Torben Dall Schmidt and Peter Hansen focused on two issues: the development of mobility in the region across national borders until today and an assessment of the currently most important impediments and incentives and their future development – with regard to the latter, especially in the case of Peter Hansen.

The survey on cross-border commuters (Buch et al., 2008) describes the development of commuting across national borders between 1998 and 2005 based on a specific analysis, in part for commuters from Germany to Southern Jutland (the municipalities Aabenraa, Haderslev, Sønderborg and Tønder), and in part from Denmark to the Flensburg Region (Flensburg with the districts Schleswig-Flensburg and Nordfriesland). For commuters working in Germany, the figure for employees covered by national insurance has been used. The figure does not include the self-employed, civil servants and marginally employed persons. For an even better comparison, we only included those active in the labour force in Denmark with a minimum income of EUR 6,000 per year.

The number of commuters from Germany to Sonderjylland went up from 1,000 in 1998 to 2,600 in 2005, an increase of 150 per cent. At the same time, the number of commuters from Denmark to Flensburg region went up from 390 to only 540, an increase of 40 per cent.

If we look at more recent figures for commuters to Denmark we must make use of an estimate from Infocenter Grænse-Grenze, according to Peter Hansen's information which is based on a survey of Danish municipalities (cross-border commuter with health insurance certificate form E106). If, within this context, the same scale is used as in the analysis from Buch et al., (2008)[viii], one will get, in terms of the south-north flow (commuters from Germany to Southern Jutland) the following values that can be compared with the above figures: 2,940 in 2007 and 3,440 in 2009[ix], and in the opposite direction in accordance with the German employment statistics: 570 in 2007 and 490 in 2009.

Assuming that a relatively large part of the figures mentioned concern commuters between the two border regions, the results show a significant asymmetry for the labour market across national borders which has increased further in recent years. This asymmetry arose in the mid 1990s. Before that, the number of commuters from South Denmark to Germany was higher than in the opposite direction and in the period 1998-2001 they still grew at the same rate. Subsequently, however, the growth rate of the south-north flow was significantly higher while, in the opposite direction, commuter figures have stagnated since 2001.

The reasons behind the asymmetry (Buch et al., 2008) are clearly the incentives on the Danish side in the form of significantly lower unemployment figures and an increased shortage of labour since around 1996 and a stronger rise in net wages and salaries since 1999. In addition, the lower prices of property on the Danish side in the 1980s and 1990s persuaded many Germans to move their home to the Danish side and commute from Denmark to Germany. This incentive, however, has had a lesser impact since the late 1990s which has resulted in the percentage of Germans among the cross-border commuters from Denmark to the Flensburg region during the period 1999-2005 declining from 62 per cent to 38 per cent while the percentage of Danes has increased correspondingly. In the opposite direction the percentage of Germans among cross-border commuters from Germany to Southern Jutland during this period rose from 56 per cent to 70 per cent (the percentage of Danes fell correspondingly). In both directions, the labour market motive has therefore taken on greater significance while the motive for searching for better living accommodation (by maintaining the place of work) which was important in the early days, means less.

Bearing in mind the two countries' different labour market situations, the asymmetry in commuter flows should, at least initially, be seen as positive: the labour market in the two neighbouring regions benefits from the fact that labour mobility can even out the differences in both labour market balances which would otherwise display an even greater difference with regard to unemployment, workforce shortages or incomes between neighbouring regions. A long-term, permanent asymmetry should however, be regarded critically: the matching advantage from a large labour market will only impact fully when commuter mobility is not one sided but goes in both directions. Finally, the socio-political impulses from mobility across national borders in the form of a deepening of social contacts will become stronger if mobility is not just one way.

In respect of the strategy for reducing mobility barriers to be further developed in the Fehmarnbelt Region, Peter Hansen's statements concerning the impediments at the Danish-German land border were particularly valuable because they are based on a large number of conversations with advisors and information enquiries and therefore rest on broadly based experiences. These are some selected points:

Infocenter Grænse-Grenze is only consulted in approximately 25-35 per cent of all those instances where people are looking for work on the other side of the border. Many commuters do not make use of the information on offer and do not require advice until problems actually arise. Information deficit thus results from a mistaken attitude on the part of the commuters.

In connection with the many administrative regulations, the rapid shift between legal provisions, contradictions and omissions in the regulations, the different definition of concepts and the interpretation of regulations from municipality to municipality, long processing times on the part of the relevant courts and forms that rarely appear in two languages, are the most important problems, not just for those affected but also for the advisors. The lack of continuity also matches the fact that from May 2010, the EU once again changed the rules for "migratory employees in Europe" (EU Regulation 1408/71 and Directive 88/364, e.g. with regard to social security) which is a new "building site" for staff at the information centre. This is why it has been decided to employ a lawyer to assist advisors just as was done in the Øresund Region.

The strongly rising number of commuters from Germany to Denmark in recent years has resulted in an increasing need for advice to an extent that the relevant institution's capacity can rarely match. One example is that the cross-border commuters' tax centre in Tønder has a shortage of staff, especially compared with the corresponding institution in Øresund (SkatØresund).

For employees with several employment contracts in both countries (multi-jobbers), a number of problems relating to taxation and social security remain unclear and unresolved or the regulations put secondary cross-border jobs at a disadvantage. There should be fixed rules in accordance with the model in the Swedish-Danish border region.

Impediments due to language problems in daily working life are less serious within the construction and haulage sectors, but crucial within the service sectors, e.g. health and care for the elderly or within the teaching sector, which will become increasingly important in the future. Programmes that facilitate access to the neighbouring language are, therefore, more than ever, at the top of the list of strategies for reducing barriers.

With regard to the recognition of qualifications and skills in the neighbouring country, extensive individual examinations are still the rule. In addition, there are problems relating to extra certification (e.g. within the area of safety at work) which are in force on one side of the border, but not on the other. A joint Danish-German government initiative under preparation by the university in Flensburg can be expected soon (Professor A. Willi Petersen, Berufsbildungsinstitut Arbeit und Technik).

With regards to the advisory infrastructure in the region around the Danish-German land border and the opportunities for transferring such infrastructure to the Fehmarnbelt Region, there are, according to Peter Hansen, two points worth noting: (1) There should be focus on an intensive and well defined collaboration between the employment offices and the advisory services concerning border impediments to avoid double functions or even competitiveness. There must be a simple and transparent approach to the advisor network's Internet structure. (2) Concentration of the advisory offices at the border, i.e. directly at the Fehmarnbelt, is problematic since the population and work space density is very low here. Besides contact points at the ferry terminals and on the ferries or later at the fixed link, there should at least be information offices in the region's larger localities. Local basis of the advisory infrastructure is not as easy to build as in other border regions.

THE SITUATION IN THE ØRESUND REGION

The Øresund Region differs from many other, more peripheral border regions with a lower density in that the region comprises densely populated major city areas directly opposite each other on both sides of Øresund. Owing to its geographical structure, it can, therefore, neither be compared with the Danish-German region of Southern Denmark-Flensburg nor with the region around the Fehmarnbelt, but rather, for example, with the border regions Maas-Rhine, Rhine-Waal or Upper Rhine (Karlsruhe-Strasburg-Basel) which are very densely populated, albeit with the difference that the Øresund Bridge has been an effective transport link between the two parts of the region for only 10 years. Its function as a model for the Fehmarnbelt Region can thus only be inferred conditional upon this, also because the distance between the two cities of Hamburg and Copenhagen, which the fixed link will bring closer together, cannot be compared to the short distance between Copenhagen and Malmö.

With regard to the labour market situation across national borders in the Øresund Region, especially with regard to commuter flows, barriers and incentives for labour mobility as well as the consultancy and information structure, we have used the following sources: OECD Territorial Reviews Copenhagen (2009), Schmidt (2006), Matthiessen (2004) and the Øresundsbro Konsortiet (2009), which describes the region and particularly labour market conditions and trends across the border after the opening of the Øresund Bridge. Moreover, a wide range of selected internet sources provide additional information about the region's labour market as well as information and advice to cross-border commuters (see below).

The situation in the Øresund Region in 2003 is summarised by Schmidt (2006) as follows: mobility across the border (that is, across Øresund) has indeed increased in recent years, but is concentrated locally, asymmetrically and will remain limited and certainly far from national commuting figures. Border barriers remain an obstacle to cross-border dynamics and it requires more time and patience before the commuter volume approaches the scale of domestic commuting.

In recent years, the number of cross-border commuters has increased considerably. However, the asymmetries remain, and the overall numbers stay clearly under the levels of commuting from Zealand into the Capital Region. The commuter numbers developed as follows: From Sweden to Denmark (source: Ørestat): 3,800 (2001); 8,800 (2005); 15,700 (2007). From Denmark to Sweden: 500 (2001); 700 (2005); 1,400 (2007). With regard to the nationalities who commute, one finds that 45 per cent of commuters from the Swedish to the Danish side are Swedes, while 55 per cent are Danes (OECD, 2009). Commuting across Øresund lags far behind the figures for commuting from Zealand to the Capital Region. 66,000 people commuted from Zealand to their workplaces in the Danish capital in 2007 (OECD, 2009). The fact remains, however, that compared to the first year after completion of the bridge, the number of commuters from Southern Sweden to the Danish side more than quadrupled. The asymmetry of the two opposing flows in this connection was even stronger. The reasons for this development are mainly based on four points:

(1) During the 10 years of its existence, the Øresund Bridge has increasingly made an inroad into people's minds and, therefore, impacted on local decisions in the region, not least helped by increasingly user-friendly toll fees.

(2) The large number of Danes who have moved homes to the Swedish side and commute to a workplace on the Danish side is due to incentives to live on the Swedish side, in particular substantially lower property prices. Thus, a 140 m² one-family house in Copenhagen in 2007 was around 35 per cent more expensive than in Malmö, and by comparing equivalent average house prices in the four surrounding municipalities of Copenhagen and Malmö, the difference is as much as 75 per cent (average price in Scania is EUR 200,000 and in the Copenhagen area EUR 350,000). In this respect, the further development in price differences is also interesting for the anticipated commuter flows, especially when the spatial-economic principles would favour a reduction of the differences[x].

(3) The incentive to work on the Danish side relates not only the Danes who have moved homes to Scania, but also the Swedes who still live there and commute across Øresund. Increased labour shortage on the Danish side in recent years (at least until 2008) – a parallel to the Danish-German border – provided opportunities for work for southern Swedes and led to higher incomes on the Danish side. The demographic differences on both sides suggest that this labour market stimulus will be increased while economic knowledge into the fact that labour market data for two regions will be tendentially equalised by increasing exchange counts against this (Øresund Bridge, 2009 and OECD, 2009).

(4) As at the Danish-German land border, advisory and information structures for cross-border workers have intensified as part of increased mobility across Øresund with consultants building up experience, steadily expanding Internet offers as a number of border barriers were reduced through national bilateral agreements and a regional partnership.

Migration balance, i.e. change of residence from Zealand to Scania or in the opposite direction, also fits the picture of mobility across national borders in recent years: between 2002-2008, 22,500 people decided on a new home in Southern Sweden (this movement culminated in 2006/2007) while 10,300 moved from the Swedish to the Danish side (Øresund Bridge, 2009).

The information and advisory structure of the labour market across national borders in the Øresund Region rests on three pillars: (a) the EURES CrossBorder Øresund (b) the municipalities' regional job centres, and (c) Øresunddirekt. In addition, Workindenmark (with support from the Danish Government) serves all foreigners who are interested in working in Denmark through a central website (www.workindenmark.dk) and local offices (for example, in Høje Taastrup near Copenhagen for East Denmark).

As at the Danish-German land border, EURES concentrates more on advice related to the labour market while the Øresund Committee, with its consultancy services, aims more at tackling barriers related to moving from one side of Øresund to the other. Nevertheless, both organisations' written and Internet information covers both fields.

EURES CrossBorder Øresund is responsible for the Capital Region of Denmark and Scania and helps those people who wish to work or study on the other side of Øresund as well as employers looking for employees. To this end, a network of consultants and EURES offices has been established: two in Scania in Sweden and two in the Danish Capital Region. Here one can access databases showing vacancies in both regions. Additional activities include:

- Organising information seminars and "job markets" for job seekers and employers

- Preparation of information material on issues affecting cross-border commuters (national insurance, taxation, labour law, recognition of educational programmes and qualifications, living conditions, etc.)

- Preparation of a handbook for cross-border commuters dealing with practical questions from cross-border commuters in the Øresund Region

- Linking the website with databases that contain vocational training opportunities across national borders.

Information material and further information can be downloaded from the website (www.oresundsinfo.org). Partners in the EURES CrossBorder Øresund are the Danish national labour administration and the labour administrations in the regions of Greater Copenhagen, Frederiksborg and Roskilde, the national and regional Swedish labour administration (Scania) and trade union organisations, employer organisations and other organisations (academic and official organisations). Rickard Engleson from the job centre in Malmö is the coordinator.

Regional job centres are the traditional contact points for job-seekers and employers on each side of Øresund. Regional and national databases are used for the information service (www.jobnet.se and www.jobnet.dk) where job seekers can also retrieve information directly online.

The Øresunddirekt organisation is the third and perhaps most important information channel, especially its website www.oresunddirekt.dk. With its extensive information about the region and links to other websites, Øresunddirekt is a suitable entry point for anyone interested in working across national borders or moving to the other side of Øresund. An information centre has also been established in Malmö. In addition to the link to EURES and to the job centres and databases for job seekers, which can be managed from Øresunddirekt, this website and the information centre in Malmö are involved with all the problems that arise in connection with moving workplace or home across Øresund. The centre also works with other institutions in connection with specific issues, for example in the case of tax and national insurance issues particularly with the cross-border commuter centre, SkatØresund, that has its own website (via www.skat.dk) and also provides personal advice.

The above-mentioned institutions' experience in advising cross-border commuters or people who are interested in moving to the other side of Øresund shows that the language barrier presents only a minor problem – especially in comparison with the Danish-German border areas. This is the same with the cultural barriers (Øresund Bridge 2009). However, there are barriers caused by national differences in tax or national insurance regulations, labour legislation (e.g. protection against dismissal) or family services, which continue to require an advisory and information structure. And for people from the Capital Region, who have moved homes to Scania or are planning to do so, the distance to their workplace across Øresund (including the necessary bridge tolls) is often greater than from the direct area around Copenhagen. This disadvantage is only acceptable if it is offset by other benefits, e.g. in housing and living costs – this becomes evident by the still relatively low commuting figures from the Danish to the Swedish side of the Øresund Region.

The Øresund Region can only partially serve as a model for the region around the Fehmarnbelt, even if a future transport facility can be compared with the Øresund Bridge. Firstly, the geographical structures in the two regions differ significantly from each other at the point of crossing and secondly, there are no incentives for mobility across national borders because of the difference in the cost of land and housing, which constitutes a strong commuter incentive at Øresund. Also the magnetic effect from a large, elastic labour market in a city that lies directly at the border is lacking in the Fehmarnbelt's immediate surroundings.

On the other hand, the information and advisory structure around Øresund – like the structure at the Danish-German land border – provides a number of impulses for the construction of similar structures at the Fehmarnbelt, by providing a stronger impetus to mobility across national borders. In particular, Øresunddirekt's information and advisory

offering, with its internet service as an entry platform, can serve as a model for the region around the Fehmarnbelt, in that – for example – under the name "Femerndirekt" – it deals with the issues and problems that people, faced with making a decision on mobility, have to address and either solve themselves or pass on to affiliated institutions such as EURES, job centres or tax consultancy for cross-border commuters.

COMPARISON WITH OTHER EUROPEAN BORDER AREAS – SUCH AS GERMANY-THE NETHERLANDS

In Germany, the highest number of cross-border commuters is in the south-west part (neighbouring France and Switzerland) and at the border with the southern part of Holland and Belgium (especially Euregio Maas-Rhine). A major reason for the high figures is the high population density in these regions. The asymmetry in commuter mobility across national borders is primarily owing to differences in the labour market situation, incomes and prices of land and property. In respect of Germany, they result is a large surplus of commuters from France and Belgium[xi] as well as a large surplus of commuters to Switzerland.

With regard to the border areas in the Fehmarnbelt Region, the regions at the German-Dutch border are actually more interesting as reference points because the geographical structure and population density, at least in the northern part, the Ems-Dollart Region (EDR), have greater similarity with the central parts of the Fehmarn Region, and because cooperation across national borders in the adjacent area to the south, "EUREGIO" (Rhein-Ems-Ijssel, with the cities of Enschede, Gronau, Osnabrück and Münster), dates back to 1950 and thus offers extensive experience. Unlike the border areas in the Fehmarnbelt Region, commuter conditions between Germany and the Netherlands, at least in recent times, are relatively balanced in that until 2000-2001, there was still a significant surplus of commuters from the Netherlands to Germany. In total, around 15,000 people commuted from Lower Saxony and North Rhine-Westphalia to the Netherlands in 2005, in 2000 the figure was below 5,000 and in 2008, there were approximately 16,000 commuters. In the opposite direction, the estimated number of employees covered by national insurance, based on all those in active employment, presumably reached a similar value of 15,000-16,000 commuters to Lower Saxony and North Rhine-Westphalia. For commuters from Germany to the Netherlands, the incentives have been lower unemployment, various opportunities for part-time work, mini-jobs or part-time jobs and the fact that many Dutch people prefer to live on the German side, which can also be registered in connection with migration across the border (positive net migration in Germany, Technau 2006). Conversely, the lower Dutch incomes, at least compared to North Rhine-Westphalia, are an incentive for the Dutch to commute to the neighbouring country.

If one compares the sum of these two commuting figures with the number of jobs in the German-Dutch border region (measured by those active in the workplace this was 7.7 million in 2005), it results in a "commuter intensity" of 0.4 per cent. By way of comparison, the number of jobs in 2008 was around 280,000 in the border area at the Danish-German border (Schleswig and Southern Jutland). The total number of commuters in both directions in this area, according to our estimate, reached 3,500, leaving a commuter intensity of 1.2 per cent[xii]. Owing to the strongly rising commuting figures from the German to the Danish part of this region in recent years (in 2008 almost 3,200 commuters from south to north) commuter intensity is, therefore, higher than in the German-Dutch border region, albeit with strong asymmetry.

Technau (2006) formulates his conclusion on the basis of the statistics for the German-Dutch border area correspondingly: as the figures continue to move (apart from the border area around Aachen) at a low level, one cannot talk about a real labour market across national borders. This applies even to the relatively large EUREGIO (3.4 million inhabitants) with its long tradition as a border region, the strenuous efforts over several years to overcome border barriers and a relatively low language barrier. The number of commuters in the German part was just 2,000 in 2005. In the relatively sparsely populated EDR in the north (2.0 million inhabitants), just about 300 people commuted to the German part in 2005.

The border impediments and the strategies for overcoming them in the two border regions, EDR and EUREGIO, are shown In the presentation of the barrier analysis for the Fehmarnbelt Region (Barten et al., 2006). Therefore we are restricting ourselves to some key items for which we have analysed newer internet information further.

Typical for EDR and EUREGIO is that the offices are located in close proximity to the border – in EDR's case to Bunde (Germany) and Nieuweschans (Holland) and in EUREGIO's case in Gronau (Germany) at the former border crossing to Enschede (Holland). The other organisational characteristic is the close cooperation with EURES labour market consultancy. Since 2007, the two border regions have had a joint EURES partnership, Rhein-Waddenzee, with over 10 consultants of which four are at the EURES office in Gronau and one at the EDR office in Nieuweschans. Advisory and information service in the form of consultations, events, information brochures and the internet (digital counselling) is provided in close cooperation between the three institutions and comprises labour market consultancy (with the participation of local job centres in Germany, private recruitment agencies in Holland) and also all other issues relating to relocation to the neighbouring region[xiii].

Measures aimed at overcoming the border barriers – in addition to the advisory and information services – focus on the qualification and language barriers as well as mental distance. In this regard, an initiative for cross-border training with the title "Handwerk Fit für Europa" should be seen as a model as well as a land border project entitled "euregiofit" headed up by Westdeutscher Handwerkskammertag (WHKT see www.handwerk-nrw.de) and initially for Euregio "Rhine-Meuse-Nord." Here, potential students and recent graduates on both sides of the border have the opportunity to gain their first professional experiences in the neighbouring country, and at the same time small and medium-sized businesses achieve the benefits of being able to recruit new labour across the border.

The special factors in relation to the organisational structure in other border areas, in for example, the close and local co-operation at the EUREGIO and EDR offices with EURES consultancy and exemplary measures such as "euregiofit" show that it can be beneficial for the Fehmarnbelt Region to test whether the structures and strategies in other border regions are suitable as models for its own future structure.

THE CURRENT SITUATION IN THE FEHMARNBELT REGION

Unlike the situation at the Danish-German land border, there is no central facility such as Infocenter Grænse-Grenze in Padborg in the Fehmarnbelt Region. However, several organisations on both sides of the border collect relevant information to which potential cross-border commuters have access.

On the German side this is:

1) The Fehmarnbelt Bureau in Eutin (East Holstein)
   www.Femernbelt-portal.de
   Set up in 2008 as part of the Interreg IVa project, the office is the main address in the Lübeck-Ostholstein region and its neighbourhood for those who look for information or have specific questions about working in Denmark. The office provides free advice on the specific conditions regarding social security, health insurance, taxes, allowances and other similar issues. Besides individual advice, it organises regular information seminars.

2) Local offices of the Federal Employment Agency (Bundesagentur für Arbeit (BA)) or the ARGE offices (job centres) in Germany
   www.arbeitsagentur.de/nn_9114/Navigation/Dienststellen/RD-N/Luebeck/Luebeck-Nav.html
   These are the official employment offices for Germans seeking jobs in Denmark. The Central Placement Office (Zentrale Auslands- und Fachvermittlung (ZAV)) is responsible for finding jobs for applicants from abroad in German companies and, correspondingly, places German applicants with companies abroad. In addition,

the local job centres, which represent cooperation between local authorities and the Federal Employment Agency support long-term unemployed in their search for employment. In the Lübeck-Ostholstein region, these offices are available in Lübeck, Oldenburg in Holstein, Eutin, Neustadt and Timmendorfer Strand.

3) Partners in the European Employment Services' (EURES) network in Hamburg

Evangelische Auslandsberatung eV: ev-auslandsberatung.de/EURES.php

Raphaels-Werk: www.raphaels-werk.de/site/de/EURES.html

EURES partners also provide information and advice to prospective cross-border commuters and to businesses inviting applicants for employment abroad. Due to its location, the network is most likely to be of help to residents of the Hamburg area.

The number of relevant addresses in the region is, therefore, limited, which may, however, be seen as an advantage. As previously noted, the existence of several parallel institutions dealing with related issues at the land border may create confusion for potential users. A clear structure that is not overburdened with several similar links may form a solid basis for the future development of advisory services.

On the Danish side the relevant contacts are:

1) The Fehmarnbelt Bureau in Holeby (Lolland)

www.femern.info

This is expected to be the main address for Danes who are seeking information or have specific questions about working in Germany when labour mobility from north to south increases.

2) Local offices of the Danish Employment Service (job centres)

www.jobnet.dk

In the Lolland-Falster Region these offices are located in Nakskov, Nykøbing Falster and Vordingborg.

3) The partners of the European Employment Services' (EURES) network in the region

Work in Denmark-East: www.eures.dk.

We had the opportunity to discuss issues concerning labour mobility across national borders in the Fehmarnbelt Region with representatives of the Fehmarnbelt Bureau in Eutin (Sibylle Kiemstedt) and the employment office in Lübeck (Carsten Marzian). Here is an outline of our findings from the two interviews.

There is close co-operation and an efficient division of responsibility between the Fehmarnbelt Bureau and the BA offices. The Fehmarnbelt Bureau's role is primarily to provide advisory services relating to differences in the institutional framework (insurance, labour law, taxation, family allowances, etc.). Frequently, one consultation is sufficient to clarify all questions. Sharing experiences with Infocenter Grænse-Grenze in Padborg is an important factor which contributes to improving the quality of service to commuters. Actual job search activities are undertaken by the BA and the ARGE offices in Germany and the job centres in Denmark.

The information that was most difficult to obtain for our study was the current number of German and Danish cross-border commuters from the regions in the study area. In the interviews we did not get the exact figures, but we obtained some information which indirectly characterises commuter intensity in the immediate surroundings of the Fehmarnbelt. For example, the number of participants in the information seminars for cross-border commuters taking place in various locations in Ostholstein was always well below 100 individuals (including representatives of Danish employers). Furthermore, the number of telephone and personal consultations at the Fehmarnbelt Bureau in Eutin averages 2-3 per day (of which some are repeated and involve the same persons).

However, we should take into account that not all cross-border commuters contact the local advisers. A further interesting conclusion from our interviews is that commuters across the Fehmarnbelt who contact the advisory services for the first time are, in general, already better informed and better prepared for the various difficulties associated with working in Denmark than commuters across the land border. This is yet another reason for interpreting the very low number of people seeking help from the Fehmarnbelt Bureau with some caution.

Taking this into account and comparing the image of the Fehmarnbelt area with the corresponding description from the Infocenter Grænse-Grenze in Padborg, we can deduce that commuter flows across the Fehmarnbelt from South to North are probably 6-7 times less than the equivalent flows across the land border. Furthermore, assuming that 10-20 per cent of the commuters participate in the special information meetings in their communities, we can estimate that the number of commuters living in the immediate vicinity of East Holstein-Lübeck is the order of 200-300 people. This figure was not rejected as unlikely by the interviewee from the employment agency in Lübeck.

The occupational composition of commuters from Germany to Denmark has, in recent years, been dominated by craftsmen and construction workers due to the construction boom in Denmark which peaked in 2008. The number of such types of jobs has presently declined whereas the proportion of other occupations, primarily in healthcare, has risen.

However, the expected start of the construction of the fixed link will again increase the demand for the construction workers in the first place.

The likely reason why, as mentioned, commuters in the Fehmarnbelt area are better informed about the various aspects of working abroad, is the current extent of the border impediments. Overcoming such formidable impediments requires information. A long (and expensive) commuting trip to Denmark is an important factor determining the frequency of commuting. In fact, the vast majority of cross-border commuters who use this connection and who have contacted the Fehmarnbelt office are weekend commuters. They spend most of the week in Denmark, have accommodation there and thus have greater opportunities to participate in social events and acquaint themselves with life in Denmark.

An important prerequisite for participation in social life is knowledge of the local language. Compared to other border barriers such as legislation, the language barrier can only be reduced gradually. In many occupations within individual services (health, education and consultancy) knowledge of the local language is crucial. Currently, with a shift towards a larger share of German cross-border commuters employed in the individual service sector, the importance of the language barrier has increased and is expected to increase further in the future. One possible step towards reducing the language barrier in the Fehmarnbelt area (which is supported by the BA in Lübeck) is a broad introduction of Danish as a foreign language at schools in Ostholstein.

Apart from the interviews at the relevant institutions in the region, the additional information on the current situation in the Fehmarnbelt area derives from previous studies. There is presently a relatively modest number of studies on the labour market in the Fehmarnbelt area and on the perspectives of the fixed link compared to the number of studies focusing on to the Øresund Region or the Danish-German land border region. It is, however, worthwhile to present the conclusions of the two most recent publications.

Copenhagen Economics and Prognos (2006) (CE&P) have studied the dynamic and strategic effects of the fixed link specifically for the two regions on both sides of the Fehmarnbelt: Kreis Ostholstein and the former Storstrøms County. Especially interesting is the summary of the two regions' current strengths and weaknesses. The two regions are similar in terms of geographical and industrial structure and in terms of the economic and demographic trends that are characteristic of peripheral areas. Both have significant tourism potential for people on the opposite side of the Fehmarnbelt (especially the coastal area of Ostholstein). In other respects, the existing links are rather weak. Labour markets, for example, still appear to be largely segregated and have very low commuting levels. The reasons for this are the same as mentioned in our general discussion above: large distance, border barriers, lack of strong incentives for labour mobility.

With regard to the latter factor, it should be noted that income levels in the two regions are very similar although unemployment is significantly lower on the Danish side. There are no major differences in property prices in the regions[xiv]. This is clearly not the case with, for example, the Øresund Region. According to Copenhagen Economics and Prognos (2006) (CE&P) study, the low proportion of employees with higher education in the two regions around Fehmarnbelt in addition to other border impediments limits the integration of regional labour markets even after the opening of the fixed link. In spite of this, we still expect positive effects for the inter-regional labour market after completion of the fixed link.

A tempting scenario for both regions is the objective of hosting a major transport hub. If such a transport centre can be realised, the region will attract investment and new businesses and create new jobs and thus improve the region's employment situation. As for labour mobility, CE&P distinguish between direct and indirect effects of a fixed link. The direct effects relate to reduced travel time while the indirect effects are caused by higher growth in the metropolitan areas of Copenhagen/Malmö and Hamburg. This study, however, takes its starting point in the assumption that the increased cross-border commuting from north to south solely relates to Danes who choose to live on the other side of the Fehmarnbelt while retaining their original work place in their own region and, conversely, from south to north.

Barten et al. (2006) examined the barriers and potential for cooperation across national borders in the Fehmarnbelt Region. For us the most relevant part of this study addresses the scenarios for cross-border commuting between Denmark and Germany assuming full integration of the German and Danish labour markets, especially in respect of the impact of the completion of the fixed link. The scenarios show that a barrier-free labour market across national boundaries will lead to a much greater potential for commuting between the regions on both sides of the Fehmarnbelt. The majority of commuters still prefer short routes and distance has a significant impact on the estimated number of commuters. In this respect, the Fehmarnbelt crossing is at a disadvantage compared to the land border and this disadvantage can only slightly be mitigated through the time and cost savings offered by a fixed link where the level of user payment is an important factor. The relocation of existing, or the establishment of new, commercial and residential areas along the Hamburg-Copenhagen-axis in the direction of the Fehmarnbelt would also be crucial for intensifying mobility across the border. This would strengthen the agglomeration benefits and have a positive impact in the economies of the regions near the border.

SUMMARY

The benefits of a cross-border region with significant labour mobility between the two sides stem from the fact that commuters themselves contribute to reducing border barriers and promote social cohesion across the whole of the region. Moreover, such a new cross-border region will profit from the economic benefits of a large and diverse labour market.

Barriers to mobility in cross-border regions are created by geographical distance and other impediments to travel between two countries: administrative barriers, different labour market conditions, qualification barriers and other barriers in the daily lives of the populations of these regions. Furthermore, information about the conditions on the other side is often fragmented. Strategies and initiatives aimed at reducing border barriers are based upon two principles: (a) problem solving, such as harmonisation of regulations through bilateral agreements, and (b) information and consultancy. Strategic success also depends on the learning process of the labour force and of the consultants involved.

Cross-border labour mobility comes from differences between the two border regions. These provide an incentive for people to move to the neighbouring region. If the conditions on both sides were more or less the same, there would be no incentive to cross the border. However, if the incentives are sufficiently strong, the barriers can easily be overcome. So there is a link between barriers and incentives. The third component is the market's level of information concerning these two factors. On the one hand, the right level of information will raise awareness of the benefits of labour mobility and on the other it reduces the constraints on cross-border mobility.

For most of the mobility barriers, an ongoing process of reduction is likely, either through agreements and regulations or through sharing experiences, learning processes, information and advisory services. However, the reduction proceeds at a different pace for different barriers. In the long-run, the most important challenges will be language barriers, acceptance of qualifications and some psychological barriers.

We have selected some established cross-border regions with a long tradition for cooperation and often large numbers of commuters and have analysed current cross-border mobility, barriers and incentives as well as the information and advice provided to the labour force in relation to their relevance to the future situation in the Fehmarnbelt Region. Within the selected regions, the consultancy structure of organisations, advisory bodies and internet services frequently consists of an information centre, which helps to overcome the many barriers, supplemented by the institutions responsible for dealing with specific problems. In addition, there is labour market consultancy tailored to cross-border issues and manned by consultants.

At the Danish-German land border, commuter traffic from south to north has increased considerably in the past years whereas commuting in the opposite direction has stagnated at a low level. This asymmetric trend developed during the 1990s when labour market conditions on the Danish side improved considerably and unemployment rates began to fall below those of Germany. Particularly in recent years, the incentives inherent in the Danish labour market have been the main driver for cross-border mobility. In keeping with increasing cross-border commuting, a broad consultancy structure for the mobile labour force has been established around the information centre in Padborg. With its qualities and experience, but with some deficiencies, too, the consultancy structure can be a prototype or a case story upon which similar structures around the Fehmarnbelt could be established. Some additional elements would, however, have to be organised or located differently.

For the region around the Fehmarnbelt, the Øresund Region is not especially relevant as a prototype. First, the urban structure differs between the two regions, especially around the border areas. Secondly, the incentives for Øresund cross-border mobility have been driven by price differences for properties and homes, which are a strong factor in commuting from the Swedish to the Danish side of the Øresund. These incentives do not exist around the Fehmarnbelt, i.e. at the time of the analysis in 2010. Moreover, the attractiveness of a large and diverse labour market close to the border (which is part of the Øresund Region's character), does not exist around the Fehmarnbelt. At the same time, the information and consultancy structure around Øresund provides a large number of examples for building similar structures around Fehmarnbelt. In particular, the information service "Øresunddirekt" (website and information centre) could serve as a model for a similar information platform for the Fehmarnbelt Region.

Despite the strong incentives for labour mobility to North Zealand, the minor language barriers and a good consultancy structure, the number of commuters crossing Øresund from Sweden lags significantly behind those heading towards Denmark's capital from the Danish hinterland. This also applies to the prototype for all European border regions, the German-Dutch EUREGIO, although the consultancy services and the strategies for removing barriers have existed for many years. Even EUREGIO, therefore, is a far cry from being a fully integrated labour market with strong bi-directional mobility.

In the region surrounding Fehmarnbelt, the labour markets are presently almost completely separate. There are no sufficiently strong preconditions for achieving the level of cross-border commuting comparable to the levels at the German Danish land border or in the Øresund Region. On the one hand, a clear incentive for German commuters is provided by the favourable labour market conditions in Denmark. On the other hand, even with a fixed link, commuting distances between the large population and job centres will remain so great that mobility is likely to be largely limited to weekend commuters. If we apply today's perspectives, we expect no strong incentives for the increase of commuter activity because of regional differences in living costs, property prices, salaries and wages. Regional differences, which in other cross-border regions have led to considerable commuting, have not yet come into play.

We expect strong development of information and consulting infrastructure and further progress in removing the border barriers to take place simultaneously with the construction of the fixed link. An increase of the number in commuters can be expected as a result of interaction of these impulses. We quantify this impact using the scenarios of commuter mobility.

REFERENCES

Bundesministerium für Arbeit und Soziales (ed.), *'Dänisch-Deutsche Arbeitsgruppe zur Förderung der grenzüberschreitenden Mobilität'*, report, Copenhagen and Berlin, 2006

U. Barten, J. Bröcker, H. Herrmann & M. Klatt, *'Barrieren und Potenziale der grenzüberschreitenden Zusammenarbeit in der Fehmarnbelt Region'*, analysis, den Institut für Regionalforschung der Universität Kiel, J. Bröcker (ed.), Kiel, 2006, 41

T. Buch, A. Niebuhr, T. D. Schmidt & M. Stuwe, *'Grenzpendeln in der deutsch-dänischen Grenzregion – Entwicklung und Struktur 1998-2005'*, IAB regional report, Institut für Arbeitsmarkt- und Berufsforschung (Ed.), 008, 4

Copenhagen Economics ApS und Prognos AG (ed.), *'Regional Effects of a Fixed Fehmarn Belt Link'*, Copenhagen, 2006

G. Duranton. & D. Puga, *'Micro-foundations of urban agglomeration economies'*, in J.V. Henderson & J.-F. Thisse (ed.), *'Handbook of Regional and Urban Economics: Cities and Geography'*, Elsevier, Amsterdam, 2004, 2063-2117

European Commission, Directorate-General for Employment, Social Affairs and Equal Opportunities (Ed.), *'Employment in Europe 2006'*, Luxembourg, 2006

J. Heining & S. Möller, *'Wer sie sind, woher sie kommen, wohin sie gehen'*, IAB report, Institut für Arbeitsmarkt- und Berufsforschung (Ed.), 2009, 27

C. W. Matthiessen, *'The Øresund Area, Pre- and Post-Bridge Cross-Border Functional Integration, the Bi-National Regional Question'*, GeoJournal, 2004, 61, 31-39

OECD (ed.), *'The Competitiveness of Copenhagen'*, OECD Territorial Reviews, Copenhagen, 2009

T. D. Schmidt, *'Cross-Border Regional Enlargement in Øresund'*, GeoJournal, 2006, 64, 249-258

J. Technau, *‚Grenzpendlerzahlen – Niederlande – Deutschland 2005, Erhebung und Auswertung der Grenzpendlerzahlen'*, ordered by Euregio Gronau und dem Ministerium für Arbeit, Gesundheit und Soziales in NRW, Duisburg, 2006

L. Thormählen (ed.), *'Entwicklung europäischer Grenzräume bei abnehmender Bedeutung nationaler Grenzen – deutsch-dänische und deutsch-niederländische Grenzräume im europäischen Integrationsprozess'*, ARL work document, Hannover, 2004, 308

Øresundsbro Konsortiet, *'The Øresund Bridge and its region,'*, report, Copenhagen, 2009

NOTES

i   The concept "cross-border commuter" is currently used synonymously with the Danish term "grænsegænger". Previously, the term "cross-border commuter" was restricted to people who undertook a daily trip to their place of work which meant that he/she had a different tax status from those that commuted only during weekends. Today, this difference no longer exists. According to current EU regulations, a "cross-border commuter" is an employee who travels from his/her place of work to their home country at least once a week. Such persons, therefore, maintain their life interest in the home country where, in the main, they are covered by social security regulations. (see for example: www.Flensborg.de/wirtschaft-arbeit and the EURES cross-border commuter calculator: www.eures-kompas.eu).

ii In 2005, 0.6 per cent of all employees within the EU (EU-25) were cross-border commuters. Of these, 0.4 per cent were cross-border commuters within the EU-25 while 0.2 per cent worked outside the EU, e.g. in Switzerland or Norway. Source: Buch et al. (2008) and the EU report "Employment in Europe 2006" (2006). Countries with particularly large percentages of cross-border commuters were Belgium (2.6 per cent), Austria (1.3 per cent), France (0.9 per cent) and Sweden (0.8 per cent). Germany (0.4 per cent) and Holland (0.4 per cent) were somewhat below average while the EU report did not include figures for Denmark. In 2000, the percentage for the EU only accounted for 0.2 per cent (source: Buch et al., 2008, Heining & Moller, 2009).

iii Only one detailed description of border barriers (problem descriptions and solutions) exists – in a brochure from Infocenter Grænse-Grenze in Padborg which is regularly updated. The final report from the Danish-German working group concerning the promotion of mobility across national borders is no longer quite up-to-date. Nevertheless, it is informative and contains proposals for action. Presented by former Danish Prime Minister Anders Fogh Rasmussen and former German Chancellor Gerhard Schröder's personal representatives, it was published by Bundesministerium für Arbeit und Soziales (2006).

iv EURES (European Employment Services) is the European portal for labour force mobility. EURES was founded in 1995 for the purpose of overcoming barriers to mobility in border regions and increasing commuter numbers. By late 2009, the number of EURES partnerships stood at 22 with over 700 EURES advisers across national borders. Within the individual EU border regions, the EURES advisers offer job seekers personal advice and, therefore, supplement the extensive internet information provided at the European EURES portal. The advisers provide information about the labour market (vacancies), living and working conditions as well as education and higher education opportunities on "the other side" in border regions. EURES Cross Border Denmark-Germany is responsible for the Danish-German border regions with Poul Hansen Frank in Sønderborg as coordinator. The EURES-partners are the official employment service in Germany (Bundesagentur für Arbeit) and the Danish job centres, trade unions on both sides and business and employer organisations. The Danish-Swedish border region around Øresund (the metropolitan region in Copenhagen and Scania) is a further EURES border region with a similar structure and similar responsibilities. Ses EURES' website: ec.europa.eu/eures.

v "You find things that are better than death everywhere." (Grimm, J., Grimm, W., Die Bremer Stadtmusikanten, German fairy tale.).

vi Organised by Institut for Grænseregionsforskning at the University of Southern Denmark in Sønderborg (Torben Dall Schmidt), in part-collaboration with the working group Nord (Arbeitsgruppe Nord) at the Institute for Labour Market and Business Research (Institut für Arbeitsmarkt- und Berufsforschung) under the official employment agency in Germany (Bundesagentur für Arbeit) (Annekatrin Niebuhr and Tanja Buch) and ongoing research for Schleswig-Holstein at the Institute for Regional Research, (Institut für Regionalforschung) at the University of Kiel (Hayo Herrmann and Ann-Christine Schulz). The Danish-German border areas and, in particular, labour mobility across the border is also analysed in the barrier analysis for the Fehmarnbelt Region (Barten et al., 2006) and in a publication from the Academy for Area Research and Federal Planning (Akademie für Raumforschung und Landesplanung) (Thormählen 2004). The authors include Ludwig Thormählen, Michael Schack, Konrad Lammers and Hayo Herrmann.

vii The regional office is Region Southern Jutland-Schleswig's joint secretariat for the Regional Council and from 2007, for the Regional Assembly, the Board of Directors, the committees and the professional groups.

viii The individual steps as seen by Peter Hansen on the basis of figures from the Danish municipalities will be explained in the following chapter (commuting scenarios). According to Peter Hansen, an income threshold (which was seen as necessary by Buch et al. (2008)) with a view to comparing the figures from the German employment statistics result in the information centre's estimate (which is used in the chapter about "commuting scenarios") being reduced by another 10 per cent in order to calculate commuters with lower incomes.

ix In 2008, the figures for north-bound commuters were temporarily significantly higher than in 2007 due to the improved economic trends and the significant shortage of labour in Denmark whereas, in 2009, they declined once more because of the economic crisis and the ensuing fall in the shortage of labour in Denmark. In 2009, however, they remained above the level of 2007.

x Source for property prices: Øresundsbron (2009), Øresund Trends 2008 (www.tendensoresund.org) samt Värderingsdata AB og Realkreditrådet. The selected surrounding regions to Malmö are: Landskrona, Eslöv, Svedala and Trelleborg, while the surrounding regions to Copenhagen are: Elsinore, Hillerød, Roskilde and Køge.

xi Commuting to Germany from the neighbouring countries has been analysed by Heining & Möller (2009) on the basis of the number of employees in Germany covered by national insurance and living abroad during the period 2000-2005. If you calculate the figures for the level for all those active in the labour force, in all probability, around 50,000 commmuted from France to Germany in 2005. From Belgium it was approx. 7,000 and in the opposite direction fewer than 1,000 commuters.

xii Statistical sources regarding commuters to the German-Dutch border area: Technau (2006) and internet information from www.grenzpendler.nrw.de. The commuting figures between Denmark and Germany stem from the status-quo-estimate for 2008 as described in the following chapter. For Germany, the figures for people of working age derive from the official statistics (calculation of workforce) and in the case of Holland and Danmark from Eurostat. The relevant Danish-German border region consists of the Flensborg region (the City of Flensburg plus the districts Schleswig-Holstein and Nordfriesland) and the former Southern Jutland County.

xiii Border commuting advice within EUREGIO is also provided through www.grenzpendler.nrw.de by Nordrhein-Westfalen's Ministry of Employment (Arbeitsministerium). The "border commuter portraits" discuss commuter experiences across national borders.

xiv Average house prices from Danish municipalities derive from "Øresund Trends 2008" (www.tendensoresund.org) for 2007. According to this source, a home in one of the four municipalities bordering the Fehmarnbelt with a living area of 140 m^2 costs approx. EUR 175,000 on average. By comparison: on the German side of the Fehmarnbelt, the price of a similar size property in 2007 was the same except for the areas on the coastline, the city of Lübeck and the densely populated Kreis Stormarn, where house prices are higher.
Source: Brief internet descriptions of house prices per sq. m. in selected German municipalities at "immobilienbewertung.Immoblllenscout24.de".

CHAPTER 6
CROSS-BORDER MOBILITY: COMMUTING SCENARIOS FOR 2020

JOHANNES BRÖCKER, HAYO HERRMANN & ARTEM KORZHENEVYCH

The purpose of the present chapter is to evaluate the commuting potential across the Fehmarnbelt following the opening of the fixed link and assuming that appropriate steps have been taken to integrate the labour markets of the German and Danish regions separated by the Fehmarnbelt. In the following, we shall present the results of a simulation for the year 2020 carried out by the team of researchers at the Institute for Regional Research at the University of Kiel.

We begin by presenting the data sources and describing the procedures used to estimate missing data. The approach underlying the scenario construction is then briefly described. In addition to the status quo scenario for 2020, four scenarios of cross-border mobility are presented: 1) implementation of the fixed link; 2) implementation of the fixed link plus moderate integration of the labour market; 3) implementation of the fixed link plus high integration of the labour market; 4) implementation of the fixed link plus high integration of the labour market plus additional integration effects on the Hamburg-Copenhagen axis.

This analysis is then augmented by a study of long-distance rail commuting with an application to the Hamburg-Copenhagen case.

BUILDING A DATABASE OF GERMAN AND DANISH COMMUTERS

The first step in the analysis is the collection of data on cross-border commuting between Germany and Denmark in recent years. Unfortunately, official statistics in the two countries do not provide much information on this issue. Bundesagentur für Arbeit reports for each German municipality the number of employed persons with place of residence in Denmark. Danmarks Statistik, however, reports only the total number of people employed outside Denmark that includes ship crews at sea rather than cross-border commuters. None of the official statistics offices provides detailed data on commuters between Germany and Denmark on regional level. Moreover, the available information only includes commuting destinations, but neither their origin nor the actual routes taken.

TABLE 1.
ESTIMATED NUMBER OF PEOPLE RESIDENT IN GERMANY AND WORKING IN DENMARK (2008)

City of Copenhagen	140
Frederiksberg municipality	300
Copenhagen County	510
Frederiksborg County	300
Roskilde County	510
West Zealand County	140
Storstrøms County	460
Funen County	510
Southern Jutland County	3,430
Ribe County	1,350
Vejle County	2,170
Ringkøbing County	310
Aarhus County	260
Viborg County	310
Northern Jutland County	890
Total	11,590

Source: Calculations based on data from Infocenter Grænse-Grenze in Padborg

A further problem is that German employment statistics (from where the commuting data derives) only comprise individuals entitled to social security payments and, therefore, do not cover civil servants (Beamte), the self-employed, or marginally employed persons. As a result, some commuters (national as well as cross-border) are excluded. In contrast, Danish national commuting data is based on a broader definition of commuter. Later, we will have to adjust for such differences in order to arrive at a consistent combined database.

The survey data provided by the Infocenter Grænse-Grenze in Padborg was of great help in terms of building a database of cross-border commuting. For each Danish municipality, they document the number of people in employment living outside Denmark, (excluding Sweden and Norway[i]). These are primarily German citizens although commuters from Poland and other EU countries cannot be entirely excluded. Based on their experience, the authors of the survey deduct 20 per cent from the original figures to allow for possible book-keeping errors, and another 20 per cent to account for commuters to Denmark from

TABLE 2.
ESTIMATED NUMBER OF PEOPLE RESIDENT IN DENMARK AND WORKING IN GERMANY (2008)

Flensburg, Kreisfreie Stadt	320
Kiel, Kreisfreie Stadt	10
Lübeck, Kreisfreie Stadt	10
Nordfriesland	100
Ostholstein	10
Schleswig-Flensburg	230
Hamburg	30
Rest of Germany	850
Total	1,560

Source: Calculations based on data from the Bundesagentur für Arbeit

countries other than Germany. As a result, the estimated number of people living in Germany and working in Denmark in 2008 is around 11,600. Table 1 shows the corresponding regional totals calculated from data at municipality level.

Please note that we are using the old (pre-2007) administrative districts ("amt"=county) for Denmark. One reason is that the differences in size between the German and Danish regions are then less pronounced than under the new system. A second reason is that the distance data for Denmark used for our calculations is based on the old system of municipalities and counties.

In order to draw conclusions on the distribution of cross-border commuters to Denmark according to their places of residence in Germany, we have to make a number of assumptions. We assume, for instance, that the number of commuters to Denmark from each municipality is proportional to the number of commuters from these municipalities to the German regions in the vicinity of the Danish-German border. We also assume that commuters to Jutland are distributed similarly to commuters to the Flensburg region (northern

Schleswig-Holstein) and that commuters to Zealand are apportioned in the same way as commuters to the Lübeck-Ostholstein Region.

As far as commuters in the north-south direction are concerned, German employment statistics for 2008 show that 1,250 people liable for social security contributions are living in Denmark and working in Germany. In order to account for the omitted groups of employed individuals, we applied a homogenous markup of 25 per cent on this value, resulting in 1,560 commuters in the north-south direction (see Table 2). To identify commuters' residential addresses, the same method was used as for the flows in the opposite direction. The pattern of commuting to the border-close regions inside Denmark was assumed to reflect the pattern of cross-border commuting.

Additional information used to identify the distribution of residential addresses of cross-border commuters stems from interviews conducted in Lübeck, Eutin, and Padborg. A full list of assumptions used to construct the commuter database can be found in the Technical Appendix to this report (Bröcker, Herrmann & Korzhenevych, 2010).

The steps described so far resulted in the calculation of the row and column sums of the actual commuter matrix for the year 2008. The external data sources provided us with the numbers of working places occupied by cross-border commuters for all regions in the study area (column sums). Furthermore, our own calculations provided the number of residents of every region who work on the other side of the border (row sums). As the next step, we wish to determine the commuting flows between all places of residence and places of work.

Our approach is based on the gravity model and thus on the notion that regions with many jobs attract many commuters from other regions; that regions with many residents generate many commuters to other regions; and that commuter flows decrease with distance. The application of this methodology requires two stages: calibration and simulation (scenario evaluation). The details of this process are described in the Technical Appendix.

A point of particular importance in this approach is the construction of an interregional distance matrix for calculating the cheapest routes between all pairs of regions. In fact, we are able to create such a matrix at municipality level. We have obtained detailed road network data for Schleswig-Holstein, as well as for the whole of Denmark, which enabled us to determine distance costs for car travel between each of the over 1,100 municipalities on the German side as well as between 271 (pre-2007) municipalities on the Danish side. To determine the costs of cross-border commuting, however, we had to identify the border-crossing points and calculate the costs involved separately. Transit between the German and Danish road network in our model occurs at four points:

1. Passage Bov-Handewitt (motorway)

2. Passage Tønder-Süderlügum (local road)

3. The Rødby-Puttgarden ferry crossing across the Fehmarnbelt (60 minute ferry trip, including average waiting time)

4. The Rostock-Gedser ferry crossing (135 minute ferry trip, including average waiting time)

The cost calculation is based on the parameters reported in the Danish Ratios Catalogue (Transport-og Energiministeriet, 2006). The cost of car usage is DKK 1.89 per km (EUR 0.265 per km). Moreover, we calculate time costs on the part of commuters by using a value-of-time parameter of DKK 64 per hour (EUR 8.30/per hour).

The price of the ferry ticket is also included in the total cost for both ferry routes. In the case of Rødby-Puttgarden, the one-way ticket for boarding with a car costs EUR 64. There are no discounts for frequent users. However, if we apply this price of the crossing in the commuting cost matrix and perform the calculations using the gravity function, the predicted number of cross-border commuters across the Fehmarnbelt appears to be much lower than the actual number suggested by the interviewed experts. We interpret this as an indication that commuters will find a way to reduce their travel costs by either sharing rides or by boarding the ferry without a car and using public transport on the other side of the border. We are able to reproduce a reasonable figure for commuters across the Fehmarnbelt by assuming an average cost of half the actual fare (i.e. EUR 32). Similarly, half the fare for the Rostock ferry i.e. EUR 45, was applied.

Table 3 contains the estimated cross-border commuting matrix. It displays the absolute number of commuters between 10 zones. The values on the diagonal of this matrix also include everyone working in the region of residence. The zones in this and the following tables are defined in the box below.

Due to a deficit of reliable numbers and due to the significant weight of our own assumptions about the distribution of commuters, this matrix should not be interpreted as the most probable point estimate. It is a good representation of the orders of magnitude and of the relative sizes of the commuter flows. It will mainly serve as a reference point for comparison between the scenarios.

GERMAN ZONES

SH North:	Flensburg, Schleswig-Flensburg, Nordfriesland
LÜ-OH:	Lübeck, Ostholstein
HH hinterland:	Lauenburg, Stormarn, Segeberg
Rest of SH:	Kiel, Neumünster, Plön, Rendsburg-Eckernförde, Pinneberg, Steinburg, Dithmarschen
HH City:	Hamburg
Rest of DE:	Germany apart from Schleswig-Holstein and Hamburg

DANISH ZONES

CPH+hinterland:	City of Copenhagen, Municipality of Frederiksberg, Copenhagen County
Rest SL:	Roskilde County, Vestsjællands County, Frederiksborg County
SA:	Storstrøms County
Rest of DK:	Funen County, Southern Jutland County, Ribe County, Vejle County, Ringkøbing County, Aarhus County, Viborg County, North Jutland County

This matrix presents some important information. First, it suggests that the labour markets of Germany and Denmark, in particular in the Fehmarnbelt area, are largely separated. People mostly commute to the neighbouring regions in their home country. These numbers far exceed the numbers of cross-border commuters. Secondly, even against this background, it is impossible to ignore the huge differences between the cross-border flows in the north-south and in the south-north direction. As set out in the previous chapter, the current market situation (described by the pull and push factors) is the main factor underlying the asymmetry of cross-border commuting. Thirdly, there are substantial differences in the degree of mobility across the land and the sea border between Germany and Denmark, with roughly six times more commuters at the land border in both directions.

Because our methodology allows to identify the cheapest route (a sequence of links in the road network) between any two locations, we can calculate the number of cross-border commuters who actually use the Fehmarnbelt crossing. We estimate the current

TABLE 3.
COMMUTERS IN THE FEHMARNBELT AREA: 2008 ESTIMATES, ABSOLUTE NUMBERS

From\To	SH North	LÜ-OH	HH hinterl.	Rest SH	HH City	Rest DE	CPH+ hinterl.	Rest SL	SA	Rest DK
SH North	142,670	620	700	12,540	2,480	5,710	250	220	80	7.740
LÜ-OH	360	123,260	7,920	5,730	8,200	7,640	80	110	80	90
HH hinterl.	600	12,990	140,510	15,570	103,920	17,230	60	70	40	150
Rest SH	8,490	5,330	15,660	384,480	70,570	20,310	150	160	100	870
HH City	760	2,710	37,540	20,240	588,100	42,040	30	30	20	80
Rest DE	7,910	18,360	27,940	21,620	161,340	31,030,340	380	360	150	280
CPH+ hinterl.	0	10	0	0	10		170	574,870	61,200	2,980	7,790
Rest SL	0	0	0	0	0		130	158,740	324,770	6,080	4,750
SA	0	0	0	0	0		40	16,560	16,340	111,060	1,270
Rest DK	640	10	0	10	30		510	16,310	5,440	900	1,541,220

Source: Data from Bundesagentur für Arbeit, Danmarks Statistik and own calculations

number to be around 1,650 in the south-north direction, and around 350 in the north-south direction.

An interesting finding is that the share of commuters across the Fehmarnbelt to the two closest Danish regions along the Hamburg-Copenhagen axis (Storstrøms County and Roskilde County) is more than twice that of the regions' share of jobs in the Zealand region. By contrast, the proportion of commuters to other counties in Zealand (in particular, Copenhagen) is lower than the proportion of jobs available there. This suggests that the physical distance is important to commuters crossing the Fehmarnbelt in a south-north direction and that this commuter flow may be significantly influenced by the construction of the fixed link.

We will now examine how the construction of the Fehmarnbelt fixed link and further political initiatives may impact on these findings.

THE SCENARIOS

To simulate commuting flows across the Fehmarnbelt after the opening of the fixed link, we must first update the reference situation from 2008 to the situation following the project's completion. As several earlier studies, including Barten et al. (2006), have chosen 2020 as a future reference point for analysing the Fehmarnbelt project, we will do the same. To construct the future reference situation, it is necessary to recalibrate the estimated commuter matrix for 2020. To do this, we assume that the number of jobs in the German and Danish regions will develop at constant growth rates until 2020.

    The aggregate growth factor for the number of people in employment in Germany is taken from a labour market forecast by Schnur and Zika (2007). Based on the trends for the period 1991 to 2007, they predict that by 2020, the number of people employed in West-Germany will be only 2.8 per cent higher than in 2007. In the case of Denmark, the 2020 prediction is based on forecasts from Danmarks Statistik for the economically active popu-

TABLE 4.
EMPLOYED PERSONS ACCORDING TO PLACE OF WORK AND PLACE OF RESIDENCE

	2008		2020	
Region	According to place of residence	According to place of work	According to place of residence	According to place of work
SH Nord	173,600	161,500	171,000	158,600
LÜ-OH	153,400	163,300	152,800	160,400
HH hinterl.	290,700	230,200	308,600	245,100
HH City	691,600	934,600	746,700	1,016,200
Rest SH	506,100	460,200	507,700	454,100
Rest DE	31,268,700	31,124,100	32,074,900	31,917,600
CPH+ hinterl.	666,600	786,800	678,000	802,000
Rest SL	327,600	260,600	320,300	250,100
SA	147,200	128,700	147,000	128,700
Rest DK	1,710,500	1,685,700	1,685,000	1,659,100

Source: Data from Bundesagentur für Arbeit, IAB (2007), Danmarks Statistik and own calculations

lation by age group and municipality of residence. For Denmark as a whole, the economically active population is expected to shrink by 1.8 per cent by 2020 compared to 2008. Assuming stable participation and unemployment rates in Denmark, we aggregated the data for the age groups in order to calculate the regional totals and assess the corresponding employment growth factors.

The resulting growth factors for each region are then applied to all commuter flows in the respective column of the commuter matrix. This corresponds to assuming that the relative weights of all regions of residence, in terms of the number of commuters to a given destination, remain unchanged between 2008 and 2020. We make this assumption because a deeper study of different urbanization and industry allocation scenarios is beyond the scope of this report. The projected numbers of employed persons and jobs in the study area for 2020 are given in Table 4.

Reflecting the general projection of the population dynamics, the figures show that the number of people in work will decline in many rural areas while large cities will continue to grow. As far as the number of commuters across the Fehmarnbelt is concerned, this type of status quo calculation does not predict any significant deviation from current levels.

The regional totals of employed persons according to place of work and place of residence for 2020 are kept fixed in the scenario calculations below. This fixes the row and column totals in the commuting matrix to be estimated for each scenario. The question to be examined is, therefore: how the spatial correspondence between the places of residence and the places of work (and thus commuter flows) will change as a result of the completion of the Fehmarnbelt fixed link and the reduction of border barriers, given the pre-defined number of employed residents and jobs in every region. Note that the invariance of the totals implies that the increase of some commuter flows would be offset by a reduction in other commuter flows. If the number of commuters from one origin to a given destination increases as a result of the changes modelled in the scenarios, this necessarily means that commuter flows from other origins to the same destination will decrease in order to match the pre-determined number of jobs in that destination.

While long-term processes, such as the development of new residential areas, shifts in company location or the emergence of new business areas along the Fehmarnbelt axis will also generate new commuter flows, this is not assessed in this analysis. The simulated scenarios, which take the distribution of jobs and population as given, can thus be interpreted as the first phase of the adjustment of the cross-border labour market that will take place soon after the project's completion. Other effects brought about by the shift or emergence of new business and residential sites would then constitute a second phase and materialise in the medium to long-term.

Official German and Danish statistics on internal commuter flows provide no information on the frequency of commuting (daily, weekly, seasonal). It is, therefore, not possible to distinguish between these categories of commuters on the basis of this data. This is also the reason why, although the reported number of commuters decreases with distance, they do not reach zero after achieving a certain "critical distance", which would be the case with daily commuters. We regard this data problem to be of little significance with respect to the impact of the Fehmarnbelt fixed link on cross-border labour mobility. The majority of the cross-border commuters using this route are weekly commuters, and this will remain so after the opening of the fixed link.

IMPACT OF THE COMPLETION OF THE FIXED LINK

Pure Infrastructure / No Integration Scenario. To model the impact of a fixed link on cross-border labour mobility, we introduce a change to the inter-regional distance matrix on the

TABLE 5.
COMMUTERS CROSSING THE FEHMARNBELT IN A SOUTH-NORTH DIRECTION
PURE INFRASTRUCTURE / NO INTEGRATION SCENARIO

	Status Quo 2020			No Integration / CF			No Integration / LF		
From\To	CPH+ hinterl.	Rest SL	SA	CPH+ hinterl.	Rest SL	SA	CPH+ hinterl.	Rest SL	SA
SH North	90	40	60	130	70	80	210	130	110
LÜ-OH	80	110	70	90	130	90	130	170	140
HH hinterl.	60	70	40	60	80	50	80	110	70
Rest SH	140	150	90	170	180	110	220	240	160
HH City	30	30	20	40	40	20	50	50	30
Rest DE	220	210	90	220	210	80	210	200	80
Sum	620	610	370	710	710	430	900	900	590

CF: current fare, LF: low fare

link between Rødby and Puttgarden. The fixed link will reduce travel time by car to 15 minutes (including a stop at the terminal) from the current 60 minutes (including waiting time at the ferry). The time costs will fall correspondingly. At this early stage, it is, however, difficult to estimate the toll levels for frequent users, such as weekly commuters. We will, therefore, present a Current Fare (CF) version of this scenario, which maintains the current price level (EUR 32 one way, under the cost-sharing assumption) and a Low Fare (LF) version assuming a multi-ticket priced at EUR 20 per crossing. Thus in the first case, one would only see the effect of the travel time saving, while in the second case, the impact of a lower price would be evident. The chosen price for frequent use is comparable to the level at the Øresund Bridge (currently EUR 19).

Tables 5 and 6 show the projected cross-border commuter flows in the south-north and the north-south direction for status quo 2020 (without the fixed link) and Current Fare and Low Fare versions of the No Integration scenario (with the fixed link).

Table 5 indicates that the number of people using the Fehmarnbelt link to commute to Denmark will rise slightly (+15 per cent) due to the cost reductions stemming from the fixed link with the total increasing from 1,600 to 1,850 commuters. The proportion of commuters from Germany to Denmark using the Fehmarnbelt will rise from 14 per cent to 16 per cent once the project has been implemented. A price reduction of almost 40 per cent

TABLE 6.
COMMUTERS CROSSING THE FEHMARNBELT IN A NORTH-SOUTH DIRECTION PURE INFRASTRUCTURE / NO INTEGRATION SCENARIO

	From\To	SH North	LÜ-OH	HH hinterl.	Rest SH	HH City	Rest DE
Status Quo 2020	CPH+ hinterl.	0	10	0	0	10	170
	Rest SL	0	0	0	0	0	140
	SA	0	0	0	0	0	40
No Integration / Current Fare	CPH+ hinterl.	0	10	0	0	10	170
	Rest SL	0	0	0	0	0	140
	SA	0	0	0	0	0	40
No Integration / Low Fare	CPH+ hinterl.	0	10	0	0	10	180
	Rest SL	0	10	0	0	0	150
	SA	0	0	0	0	0	50

(from EUR 32 to EUR 20) would, however, have a more pronounced effect. The total number of commuters would rise to 2,400, i.e. 50 per cent increase compared to the status quo level. Of this number, 38 per cent would commute to Greater Copenhagen and 25 per cent to Storstrøms County. These shares are roughly the same as in the status quo.

The number of commuters in the opposite direction is currently much lower and is not expected to rise significantly after the opening of the fixed link. The status quo level of some 370 commuters from Denmark to Germany using the Fehmarnbelt link will not be affected under this scenario where the price of crossing the link remains unchanged. A decrease in the toll fee merely results in a 10 per cent increase. This strongly supports the argument that limitations on workforce mobility in a north-south direction are caused less by physical distance than by the absence of other incentives for cross-border mobility. These incentives are apparently weak on the German side at the present time.

On numerous occasions, the German and Danish authorities have reiterated that one of the sought-after results from the construction of a fixed link is the emergence of a cross-border labour market in the Fehmarnbelt area. As a consquence, we shall primarily be interested in seeing the effects of the investments on workforce mobility between the regions in the Hamburg-Copenhagen axis, which includes the Lübeck-East-Holstein region as well as Hamburg with its north east hinterland on the German side, and nearly the whole Zealand on the Danish side.

Besides illustrating the already mentioned generally low mobility of people in a north-south direction, the numbers in Table 6 point to another asymmetry in the current and projected pattern of labour mobility in this area. Only a small share, namely 5 per cent of Danish commuters across the Fehmarnbelt travel within the boundaries of the Fehmarnbelt Region (in the opposite flow, the proportion is 30 per cent), with the rest finding employment in other German regions. This pattern will be retained with the construction of the fixed link. Apparently, both the time-saving and cost-saving effects generated by the link are not sufficient to alter the picture noticeably.

To understand the reasons for this, one has to imagine a situation where distance costs alone are not the determining factor in decisions to seek employment abroad, where border barriers are more or less symmetrical and where there are no incentive differences in the destination regions. A plausible outcome would then be an even distribution of cross-border commuters to the regions in the country of employment, with more people choosing to go to the major agglomerations. And, in fact, the observed proportion of commuters from Zealand that travel to Schleswig-Holstein and Hamburg via the Fehmarnbelt is in line with the proportion of these two federal states in the total number of employed persons in Germany (6 per cent). Thus, we can argue that these regions do not provide any particular incentive for Danes seeking jobs in Germany, and the physical proximity does not act as an incentive either.

By contrast, over 50 per cent of Danish commuters across the land border to Germany are employed in the three counties close to the border (Flensburg, Schleswig-Flensburg and Nordfriesland). A further 3 per cent are employed in Hamburg, which again corresponds to the relative weight of the Hanseatic City within the total German workforce. 43 per cent are employed outside Schleswig-Holstein and Hamburg. In general, we can argue that the special conditions that attract a disproportionately large number of Danish commuters to the Schleswig-Holstein/Hamburg region currently exist only in the immediate vicinity of the land border. This is unlikely to change dramatically after the opening of the fixed link.

THE EFFECTS OF LABOUR MARKET INTEGRATION

The figures in the previous section confirm the findings from other studies, i.e. that some important barriers to cross-border commuting, especially in the Fehmarnbelt Region, do not relate to distance, but are rather a question of language difference, legislation, information as well as a lack of incentives. In order to establish a fully functional cross-border labour market, these barriers must be reduced. As regional and central governments on both sides of the border are indeed working on this problem, we can expect some major input here over the next decade. This is why we are going to present a set of scenarios for further steps towards the integration of the labour market between the regions in the area under consideration.

As mentioned before, the size of the commuter flows in our model depends on the following factors: the size of the labour market in the region of origin and in the destination region, the distance between the regions expressed in cost terms (monetary as well as time-related costs) and other factors influencing labour mobility of which the precise composition is unknown. The influence of the latter category is measured by comparing the expected number of commuters (by taking only size and distance effects into account) to the actual number of commuters between regions on the basis of the data for the reference year 2008. As a result, it is possible to calculate a set of region-pair specific multipliers that we shall refer to as integration factors. All other things being equal, a higher integration factor implies larger commuter flows between the regions. These factors are generally higher for domestic flows than for cross-border flows. In the case of commuter flows between Germany and Denmark, these factors comprise both the influence of incentives for cross-border mobility and the influence of various border barriers. Differences in the integration factors can then be explained by differences in incentives, in barriers or both. We do not have information that allows us to distinguish between the reasons for these differences.

Despite this, we shall use the integration factors for the purpose of an analysis of the workforce's mobility. The aim is to test how the cross-border commuter flows will respond to ever greater integration between the German and Danish labour markets. By greater integration we mean both reduced border barriers and additional incentives such as new industrial and commercial areas that specialise in cross-border partnerships. This is why the multipliers described above provide a good indication of the level of integration between the regions. We shall conduct a series of experiments where the difference between the average level of integration factors for cross-border commuter flows and the average level of integration factors for domestic commuter flows will be gradually reduced.

It is difficult to quantify the policy measures that, in our view, will reduce border barriers or increase the incentives for cross-border mobility and to express them in terms of a percentage increase of the integration factor. As a result, the numerical assumptions upon which the integration scenarios are based cannot be interpreted literally. Ideally, we would have preferred to evaluate the relative significance of the different factors which

evaluate the level of the workforce's cross-border mobility. However, as the basic data on cross-border commuting between Germany and Denmark is sparse and lacks precision, the chances of implementing an investigation of this type are low.

Moderate Integration Scenario. In this scenario, we assume that 15 per cent of the difference between the cross-border integration level and the internal integration level in Germany, as measured by the average level of the respective inter-regional integration factors, will be eliminated and that the Fehmarnbelt fixed link is completed. As in the case of No Integration Scenario, we will use two price options for the crossing: EUR 32 (CF version) and EUR 20 (LF version). The results are given in Tables 7 and 8 below.

TABLE 7.
COMMUTERS CROSSING THE FEHMARNBELT IN A SOUTH-NORTH DIRECTION MODERATE INTEGRATION SCENARIO

	Status Quo 2020			Moderate Integration / CF			Moderate Integration / LF		
From\To	CPH+ hinterl.	Rest SL	SA	CPH+ hinterl.	Rest SL	SA	CPH+ hinterl.	Rest SL	SA
SH North	90	40	60	140	70	80	220	130	120
LÜ-OH	80	110	70	100	130	100	130	180	150
HH hinterl.	60	70	40	70	80	50	90	110	70
Rest SH	140	150	90	170	190	120	230	250	170
HH City	30	30	20	40	40	20	50	50	30
Rest DE	220	210	90	230	220	90	220	210	90
Sum	620	610	370	750	730	460	940	930	630

CF: current fare, LF: low fare

When comparing tables 7 and 8 above with tables 5 and 6 (the No Integration scenario), the general impression is that the number of commuters in a south-north direction is fairly similar in the two sets of tables whereas the number of commuters in a north-south direction is notably larger in the Moderate Integration scenario. In fact, the commuter flows from Germany to Denmark in this scenario increase by an average of only 5 per cent while the counter flow increases by more than 30 per cent. The explanation lies in the different starting points for the integration factors. The region pair specific multipliers for the flows in a south-north direction are higher in the status quo situation which shows that the incentives determining the decision to work abroad are currently much stronger for German commuters. Thus a 15 per cent step towards a common reference point for the integration level is smaller for the German origins.

Furthermore, the strong increase in the number of commuters from Denmark to Germany in the integration scenario (in contrast to the small effect of the infrastructure scenario only) is due to the fact that the vast majority of the current commuters are basically

TABLE 8.
COMMUTERS CROSSING THE FEHMARNBELT IN A NORTH-SOUTH DIRECTION MODERATE INTEGRATION SCENARIO

	From\To	SH North	LÜ-OH	HH hinterl.	Rest SH	HH City	Rest DE
Status Quo 2020	CPH+ hinterl.	0	10	0	0	10	170
	Rest SL	0	0	0	0	0	140
	SA	0	0	0	0	0	40
Moderate Integration / Current Fare	CPH+ hinterl.	0	10	0	0	10	230
	Rest SL	0	10	0	0	0	180
	SA	0	0	0	0	0	60
Moderate Integration / Low Fare	CPH+ hinterl.	0	10	0	0	10	240
	Rest SL	0	10	0	0	10	190
	SA	0	10	0	0	0	60

insensitive to a reduction in travel time across the Fehmarnbelt because they work some considerable distance from the link. The large relative growth, however, does not result in a large number of commuters as the initial levels are very low. Overall, this scenario predicts an increase in the number of commuters from Germany to Denmark across the Fehmarnbelt of up to 2,000 people at the current fee level and up to 2,500 people if toll fees are reduced. In the opposite direction, the figure would be 500 and 550 people respectively. The proportions of commuters using the land border crossing and the Fehmarnbelt will remain the same as in the No Integration scenario.

High Integration Scenario. In a stronger integration scenario, we assume that 30 per cent of the difference between the cross-border integration level and the internal integration level in Germany, as measured by the average level of the respective inter-regional integration factors, will be overcome and that the Fehmarnbelt fixed link is completed. Again, we employ two price options for the crossing: EUR 32 (CF version) and EUR 20 (LF version). The results are given in Tables 9 and 10.

TABLE 9.
COMMUTERS CROSSING THE FEHMARNBELT IN A SOUTH-NORTH DIRECTION
THE EFFECT OF THE HIGH INTEGRATION SCENARIO

	Status Quo 2020			High Integration / CF			High Integration / LF		
From\To	CPH+ hinterl.	Rest SL	SA	CPH+ hinterl.	Rest SL	SA	CPH+ hinterl.	Rest SL	SA
SH North	90	40	60	150	70	90	240	140	120
LÜ-OH	80	110	70	100	140	100	140	190	160
HH hinterl.	60	70	40	70	90	50	90	120	80
Rest SH	140	150	90	190	200	130	250	270	180
HH City	30	30	20	40	40	20	60	50	30
Rest DE	220	210	90	250	240	100	240	230	90
Sum	620	610	370	800	780	490	1,020	1,000	660

CF: current fare, LF: low fare

TABLE 10.
COMMUTERS CROSSING THE FEHMARNBELT LINK IN A NORTH-SOUTH DIRECTION
THE EFFECT OF THE HIGH INTEGRATION SCENARIO

	From\To	SH North	LÜ-OH	HH hinterl.	Rest SH	HH City	Rest DE
Status Quo 2020	CPH+ hinterl.	0	10	0	0	10	170
	Rest SL	0	0	0	0	0	140
	SA	0	0	0	0	0	40
High Integration / Current Fare	CPH+ hinterl.	0	10	0	0	10	310
	Rest SL	0	10	0	0	10	250
	SA	0	0	0	0	0	80
High Integration / Low Fare	CPH+ hinterl.	0	10	0	0	10	330
	Rest SL	0	10	0	0	10	270
	SA	0	10	0	0	10	90

The same line of reasoning as in the previous case seems to apply here. Again, commuter flows in a north-south direction are affected relatively more, but the absolute growth in commuter numbers is higher in the opposite direction. Commuter flows from Germany to Denmark in the High Integration scenario will increase by an average of 6-7 per cent while the flows from Denmark to Germany will rise by more than 30 per cent. This pattern seems robust and we will not present further scenarios of this type. However, it is worthwhile analysing a complete commuter matrix for one of the integration scenarios.

One can consider the reduced toll fee level (EUR 20 per trip) for commuters using the Fehmarnbelt link as the likely future price level. Table 11, therefore, shows the absolute commuter figures as calculated for the Low Fare version of the High Integration scenario. Overall, we expect a total of 12,900 commuters from Germany to Denmark with 2,700 of them (21 per cent) using the Fehmarnbelt link. In the opposite direction, we expect 3,000 commuters, 750 of whom (25 per cent) will cross the Fehmarnbelt. These figures represent a significant difference compared to the starting point (2008) primarily in respect of the commuter flows in a north-south direction. In fact, the flows in this direction are expected to more or less double. In the south-north direction, a growth of 60 per cent in the number of commuters across Fehmarnbelt is expected under this scenario.

Axis Integration Scenario. The establishment of stronger links between the two metropolitan areas of Hamburg and Copenhagen is seen as a desirable outcome of the Fehmarnbelt project and of the political steps taken to promote wider cooperation in the area. In the following, we shall present a scenario with stronger integration along the Hamburg-Copenhagen axis. This will be followed in the next section by a study of long-distance rail commuting with fast trains between the two metropolises.

We assume that in addition to 30 per cent growth in the general integration level between Germany and Denmark, a further 30 per cent of the distance to the integration level inside Germany will be eliminated for the labour market along the Hamburg-Copenhagen axis. On the German side, this includes the Lübeck-East-Holstein region and the Hamburg metropolitan region, including three neighbouring counties (the HH hinterland region in our zonal system) and on the Danish side, all counties in Zealand. As before, we allow for two price options for the Fehmarnbelt crossing: EUR 32 (CF version) and EUR 20 (LF version). The results are given in Tables 12 and 13.

TABLE 11.
COMMUTERS IN THE FEHMARNBELT REGION: 2020 ESTIMATES
HIGH INTEGRATION / LF SCENARIO

From\To	SH North	LÜ-OH	HH hinterl.	Rest SH	HH City	Rest DE	CPH+ hinterl.	Rest SL	SA	Rest DK
SH North		139,560	600	730	12,320	2,670	5,800	340	270	130	8,050
LÜ-OH	350	121,130	8,470	5,660	8,880	7,790	140	200	160	100
HH hinterl.	580	12,690	149,490	15,350	112,900	17,620	90	120	80	160
Rest SH	8,290	5,240	16,480	378,700	76,630	20,720	250	270	180	910
HH City	750	2,650	40,170	20,500	639,400	43,040	60	60	30	80
Rest DE	7,800	18,030	29,820	21,510	175,690	31,820,780	390	380	150	300
CPH+ hinterl.	10	10	0	0	10	330	586,210	60,580	2,840	7,800
Rest SL	10	10	0	0	10	260	160,310	316,440	5,800	4,770
SA	0	10	0	0	0	90	16,770	16,190	106,140	1,290
Rest DK	1,180	30	0	20	50	980	16,510	5,290	850	1,519,410

This scenario entails growth in commuting within the Fehmarnbelt Region in a south-north direction of 40 per cent and in the opposite direction of 30 per cent. The growth is partly compensated by a reduction in the number of commuters from other locations, primarily the rest of Germany and Denmark (as the totals in the commuter matrix cannot be adjusted). Overall, however, it is clear that the specific assumption of closer integration in the regions in the immediate vicinity of the Hamburg-Copenhagen axis has a strong effect on workforce mobility. This can be interpreted as proof of the desirability of inter-regional co-operation agreements that reduce administrative and other types of barriers to cross-border commuters. Such agreements may be significantly easier to achieve than agreements at federal or national levels. If they genuinely facilitate cross-border mobility, they may be even more efficient.

TABLE 12.
COMMUTERS CROSSING THE FEHMARNBELT IN A SOUTH-NORTH DIRECTION
AXIS INTEGRATION SCENARIO

	Status Quo 2020			Axis Integration / CF			Axis Integration / LF		
From\To	CPH+ hinterl.	Rest SL	SA	CPH+ hinterl.	Rest SL	SA	CPH+ hinterl.	Rest SL	SA
SH North	90	40	60	150	70	90	230	140	120
LÜ-OH	80	110	70	120	170	120	200	270	220
HH hinterl.	60	70	40	80	110	60	130	160	100
Rest SH	140	150	90	180	200	120	240	260	170
HH City	30	30	20	50	50	30	80	80	40
Rest DE	220	210	90	250	240	90	230	220	90
Sum	620	610	370	830	840	510	1,110	1,130	740

CF: current fare, LF: low fare

TABLE 13.
COMMUTERS CROSSING THE FEHMARNBELT IN A NORTH-SOUTH DIRECTION
AXIS INTEGRATION SCENARIO

	From\To	SH North	LÜ-OH	HH hinterl.	Rest SH	HH City	Rest DE
Status Quo 2020	CPH+ hinterl.	0	10	0	0	10	170
	Rest SL	0	0	0	0	0	140
	SA	0	0	0	0	0	40
Axis Integration / Current Fare	CPH+ hinterl.	0	10	0	0	10	320
	Rest SL	0	10	0	0	10	250
	SA	0	10	0	0	0	80
Axis Integration / Low Fare	CPH+ hinterl.	0	20	0	0	10	350
	Rest SL	0	20	0	0	10	270
	SA	0	10	0	0	10	90

COMPARISON OF SCENARIOS

Table 14 provides a summary of commuter flows across the Fehmarnbelt as predicted by different scenarios described above.

Figures 1-3 compare the projections of the Status Suo scenario (SQ), the Pure Infrastructure scenario (NI) and the two integration scenarios, High Integration (Hi) and Axis Integration (AI), for workforce mobility in the Fehmarnbelt area. All policy scenarios are included in the Low Fare version. We present the predicted number of commuters in a south-north direction across the Fehmarnbelt separately for three aggregation areas: East-Holstein-Lübeck, Hamburg, including its north-eastern hinterland and all of Schleswig-Holstein/Hamburg. The two destination areas on the Danish side are Storstrøm County and the rest of Zealand (excluding the areas under Storstrøm County). Commuter flows in the opposite direction are not included in the illustrations because the flows are too insignificant and the changes only marginal in absolute values.

COPENHAGEN-HAMBURG: WEEKLY RAIL COMMUTERS

One part of the mobile labour force, namely those who – generally once a week – commute between the major agglomerations and usually do so by train or plane, occupy a special position. Such individuals work in specialised jobs in the metropolises, mainly within management, finance and business services, culture and media, research and development, and higher education. They have specific personal characteristics (age, education, skills, etc.) which differ from those of the average commuter. Consequently, they display different mobility patterns, e.g. a more pronounced willingness to commute over long distances.

In the case of Germany, where the metropolitan regions are spread evenly across the country (from Hamburg to Munich, from Cologne to Dresden), there are a considerable number of commuters between the metropolises. This large number of commuters over relatively long distances does not appear in other circumstances, e.g. in the case of commuting from rural areas to small or medium-sized cities, even in relative terms (commuting intensity). For commuters from the Munich area (city plus suburbs) to other major West German cities (Hamburg, Cologne, Frankfurt, Stuttgart), the figure lies between 2,000 and 4,000. For commuters from the Hamburg area (to Cologne, Frankfurt or Munich), the number is between 2,500 and 4,400.

TABLE 14.
SUMMARY OF SCENARIO RESULTS

Commuter flows	Fare	Scenario				
		Status Quo	No Integration	Moderate Integration	High Integration	Axis Integration
From Germany to Denmark across the Fehmarnbelt	Current	1,600	1,850	1,940	2,070	2,180
	Low	n.a.	2,390	2,500	2,680	2,980
From Denmark to Germany across the Fehmarnbelt	Current	370	370	500	680	700
	Low	n.a.	410	540	750	790

The high commuting figures between the German metropolises are evidence of the integration of the urban labour markets that has developed over many years and of the willingness of certain types of employees to seek work in distant metropolises rather than in their home region. The large labour markets offer many advantages (such as risk sharing, matching benefits, better exit options, knowledge transfer). This is why, in addition to the scenarios mentioned above, we have carried out further calculations specific to this type of workforce mobility.

The case involving weekly long-distance commuting (by train) is particularly interesting for the calculation of future workforce mobility between Hamburg and Copenhagen although current figures do not indicate this. According to the status quo figures for commuting in 2008, the starting point is fewer than 100 commuters from Hamburg to Copenhagen and even fewer commuters from Copenhagen to Hamburg. Below we briefly present the construction of the calculations and afterwards we present the results. Please refer to the Technical Appendix for further details on the methodology.

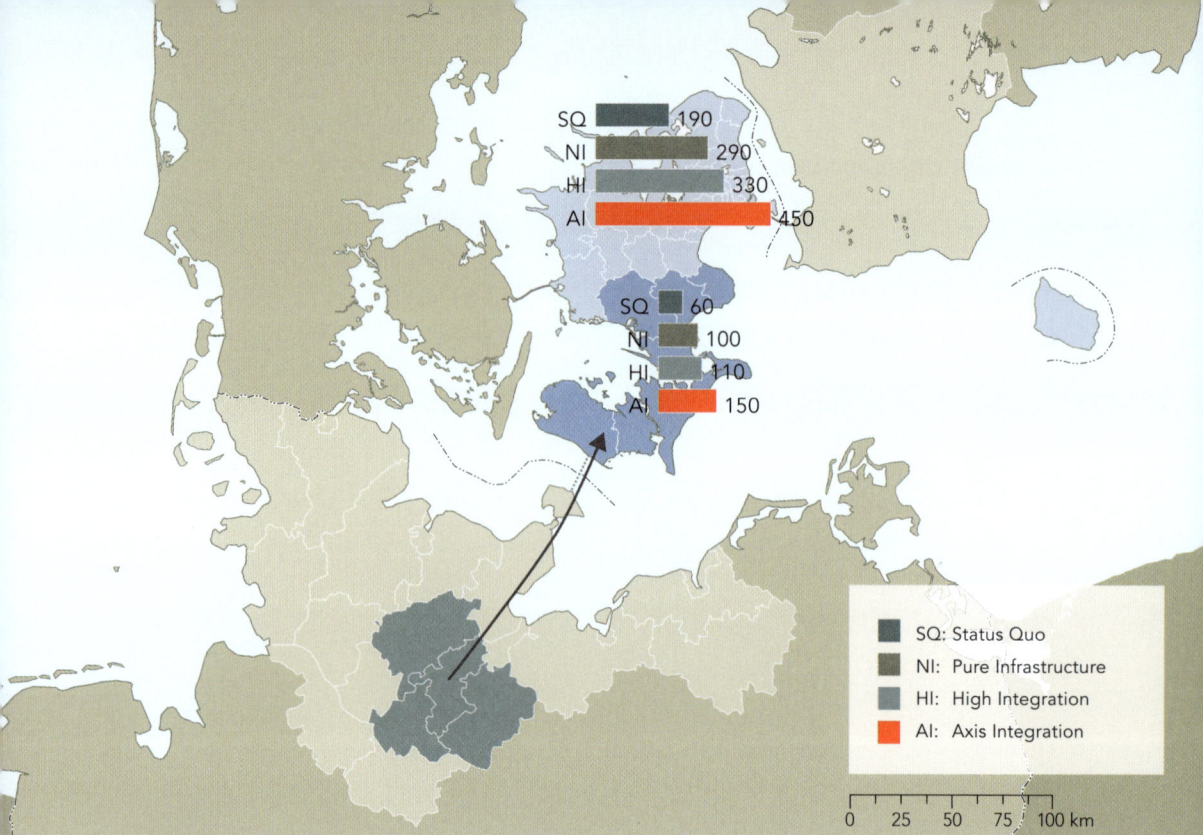

FIGURE 1.
COMMUTERS FROM REGION HAMBURG (WITH ITS NORTH-EASTERN HINTERLAND) TO DENMARK ACROSS THE FEHMARNBELT
COMPARISON OF SCENARIO RESULTS (WITH LOW FARE)

Note: Flows in the opposite direction within the Fehmarnbelt area are very small and are not shown on this map.

We use the simple gravity model, which was introduced in the previous chapter:

$$I_{ij} = \gamma \cdot \frac{M_i^{a_i} \cdot M_j^{a_j}}{f(d_{ij})}$$

I_{ij} are the commuters from the residential metropolis i to the job metropolis j, M is the mass or the size of the metropolises, as measured by the number of employees at the place of residence and at the place of work; d_{ij} is the distance between the metropolises.

On this basis, we estimate an ordinary least-squares gravity regression. It takes into account the masses of the source and destination region and the distance between them, but it does not consider other barriers or asymmetric mobility incentives.

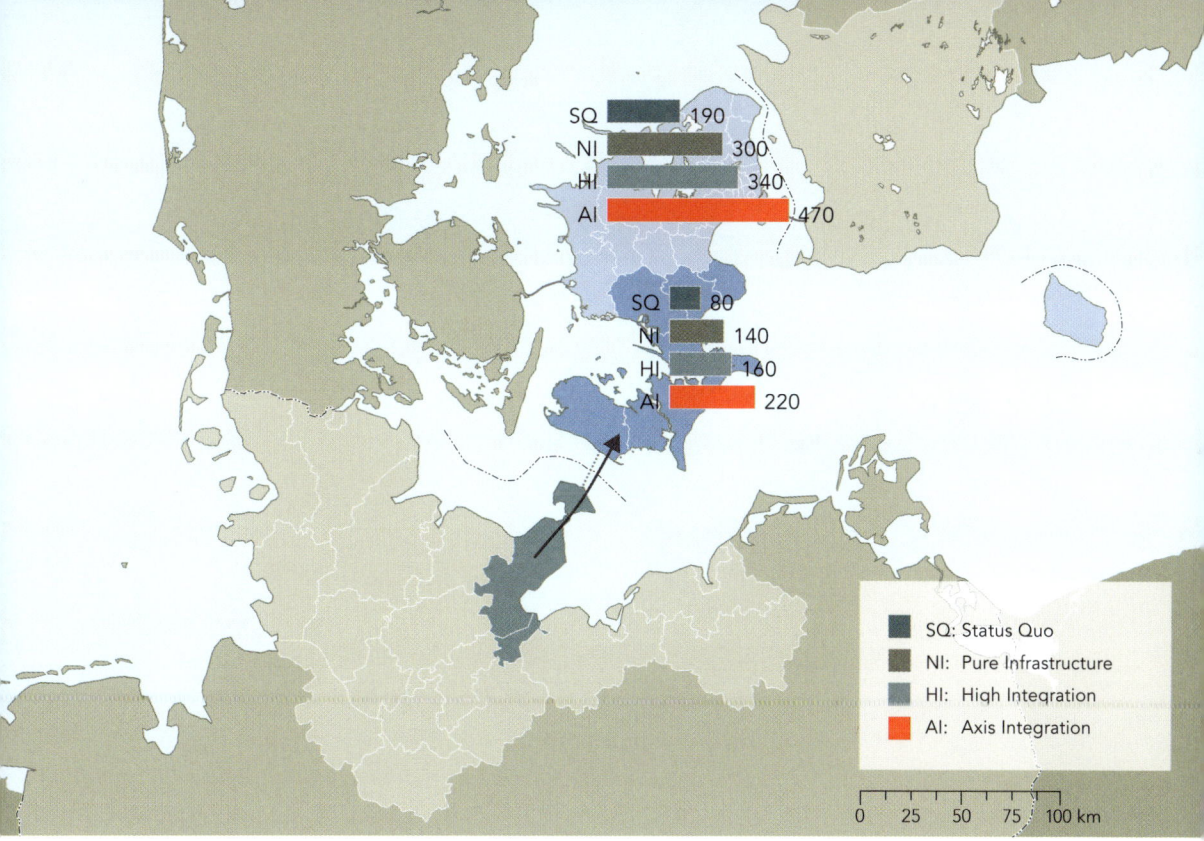

FIGURE 2.
COMMUTERS FROM REGION LÜBECK-OSTHOLSTEIN TO DENMARK VIA THE FEHMARNBELT COMPARISON OF SCENARIO RESULTS (WITH LOW FARE)

Note: Flows in the opposite direction within the Fehmarnbelt area are very small and are not shown on this map.

The coefficients of the gravity regression are estimated on the basis of the numbers of commuters between the West German metropolises in 2008. These estimates are then used to evaluate the number of commuters between Hamburg and Copenhagen – assuming that the commuters here act similarly to those between the German cities.

Concerning the source and destination masses, we also include the employees living in the suburban areas of the city in the source mass (the residential region), while the mass of the commuters' destination (job region) largely relates to jobs within the city. The distance between the regions is calculated as the cost of a one-way train trip (monetary travel expenses, plus time costs, plus public transport costs) measured in EUR.

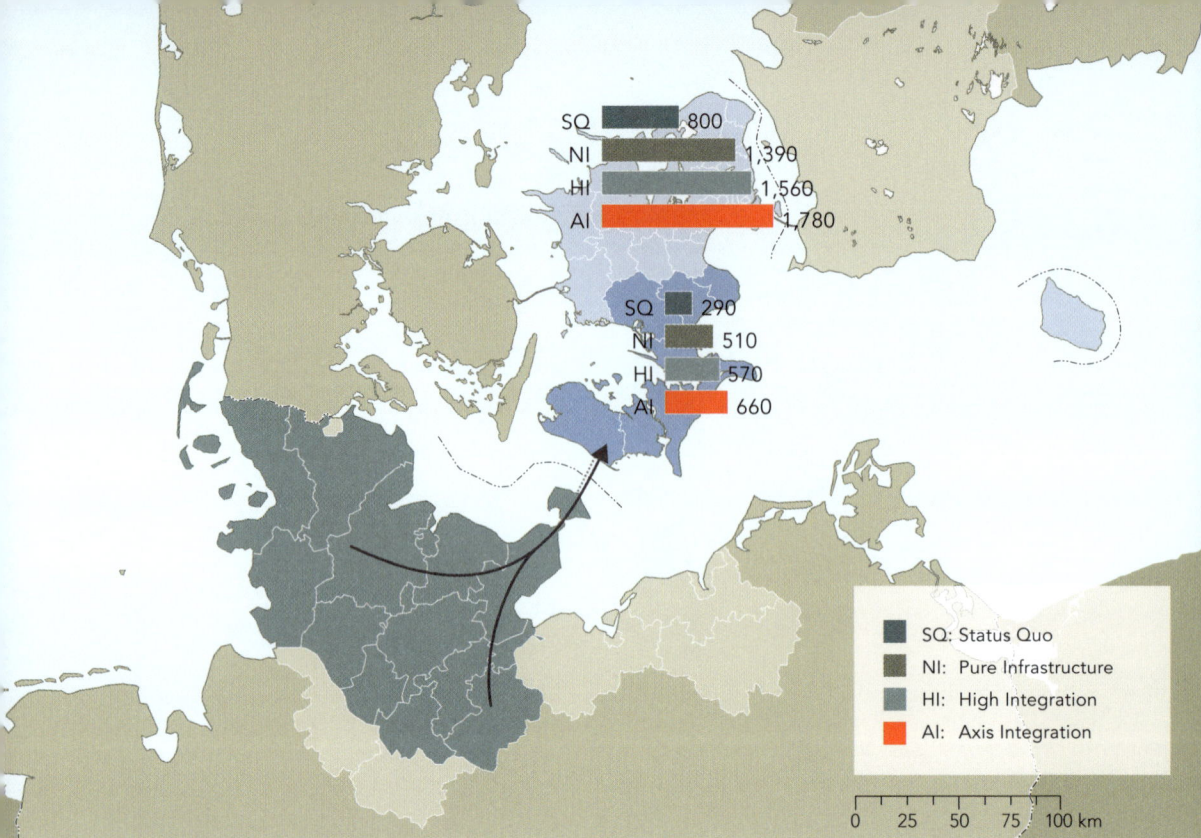

FIGURE 3.
COMMUTERS FROM SCHLESWIG-HOLSTEIN AND HAMBURG TO DENMARK ACROSS THE FEHMARNBELT
COMPARISON OF SCENARIO RESULTS (WITH LOW FARE)

Note: Flows in the opposite direction within the Fehmarnbelt area are very small and are not shown on this map.

The regression analysis shows a stable relation between the masses of the respective metropolises, the distance between them and the number of commuters. The estimated values of the coefficients are statistically significant and have the expected signs.

The distance between Copenhagen and Hamburg is calculated for five different constellations, characterised by three factors. 1) the type of the Fehmarnbelt link (TF = train plus ferry, TFL = train across the fixed link) 2) the duration of a one-way train trip (in minutes), and 3) the price (with a discount card 'Bahncard50') of a one-way trip by train, (EUR 40 or EUR 60).

TABLE 15.
PROJECTION OF LONG-DISTANCE COMMUTING BETWEEN COPENHAGEN AND HAMBURG

Flow Setup	Hamburg → Copenhagen		Copenhagen → Hamburg	
	no barriers	reduced barriers	no barriers	reduced barriers
TF 280 60 (current case)	2,040	(740)	3,140	(960)
TFL 180 60	2,500	910	3,840	1,180
TFL 180 40	3,530	1,280	5,440	1,660
TFL 150 60	2,670	970	4,110	1,260
TFL 150 40	3,840	1,400	5,910	1,810

The name of each setup is constructed as follows: Trip by train via ferry (TF) or fixed link (TFL), duration of a single train journey in minutes, one-way train fare in EUR
No barriers: full integration scenario (commuter figures as if both metropolises were in the same country)
Reduced barriers: barriers according to "high integration scenario" (low fare case))

For all five setups, we estimated the commuter figures from Hamburg to Copenhagen, and in the opposite direction, always for two cases:

(I) Case "no barriers": Here the behaviour of commuters is identical to that within Germany, e.g. we consider Hamburg and Copenhagen as two metropolises with no border barriers between them and as if, for many years, they have been metropolises within one country. The commuter figures are a fictional upper limit of what might be expected after the complete removal of all border barriers (including language barriers) and after a long period of adjustment.

(II) Case "reduced barriers": Here we assume that the level of border barriers, as calculated above in the High Integration scenario (Low Fare case), are already considerably reduced compared to the current situation, i.e. the border barriers between Denmark and Germany are 30 per cent lower than today.

The estimates of commuter numbers reported in Table 15 are higher for the north-south direction than for the south-north direction. This asymmetry exists only because of the difference in the size of the two metropolises and not because of asymmetric incentive factors that are not included here.

The estimated commuter figures in the case of reduced border barriers (High Integration scenario) and ferry operation are given in parentheses and are not very likely because the reduction of current barriers to the level of the high integration scenario is linked to the effect of the construction and the opening of the fixed Fehmarnbelt link. For the scenario with ferry operation, the figures from our status quo calculations are more realistic. In both directions, the level is significantly below 100 people.

The comparison of the five setups in Table 15 indicates that commuter figures depend more on price than on the duration of the train journey. Whether the journey takes 180 or 150 minutes is less important. This applies particularly to weekend commuters who are likely to dominate the city-to-city mobility patterns, but not for daily business travellers between the metropolises.

In the case of strong barrier reduction following the opening of the fixed Fehmarnbelt link for which we have adopted the high integration scenario with symmetric incentives, we can expect about 1,000 commuters to Copenhagen and nearly 1,300 to Hamburg for the 150 minute and EUR 60 combination, i.e. around 2,300 per week in total, and 1,400 and 1,800 respectively (3,200 per week in total) for the 150 minute and EUR 40 combination. The allocation between the two directions can be changed by allowing for asymmetric incentives on the two sides of the border, but this was not the point of the above analysis.

The numbers for "no barriers" case are fictitious, they are in any case not likely for the near and medium future, but refer to the cooperation structures built over a long time between the German cities. Between Copenhagen and Hamburg, such a situation would be only possible in the long-run in the case of complete overcoming of all border barriers including the language differences.

SUMMARY

The German and Danish labour markets, particularly in the Fehmarnbelt Region, are largely separated – as is common to many other border regions in Europe. Cross-border commuting between the two countries is characterised by significant differences in the flows between north-south and south-north directions. This is owing to the current market situation where the Danish side offers better opportunities for cross-border employment. The absence of systematic, statistical information about cross-border commuters in the Fehmarnbelt Region severely limits the scope of our analysis. Nevertheless, we estimate that some 11,600 individuals work in Denmark and live in Germany while 1,600 individuals work in Germany and live in Denmark (2008).

Compared to the German-Danish land border, the Fehmarnbelt connection currently has roughly six times fewer commuters in both directions. We show that the longer commuting distance is an important factor limiting commuting in a south-north direction. This flow, therefore, would be significantly affected by the construction of the fixed link. For commuters in the opposite direction, however, travel patterns seem to depend much less on physical distance, but more on opportunities for cross-border employment (e.g. as offered by the German metropolitan regions).

Fare levels at the fixed link will be an important factor in the development of future commuting patterns. Assuming a special fare of, e.g. 20 EUR per passage for commuters on the new link, the immediate effect on commuter figures from Germany to Denmark would be in the order of a 50 per cent increase.

We mentioned above that physical proximity does not currently play a decisive role for Danish commuters to Germany as the majority work some distance from the border. This commuter category will, therefore, not be seriously affected by the fixed link in itself. However, we believe that steps towards the integration of the labour markets (e.g. reducing administrative barriers) would have a strong effect on such commuters. In particular, we wish to emphasise the importance of inter-regional co-operation agreements that are much easier to achieve than agreements at governmental level and that may be significantly more efficient.

The role of the Fehmarnbelt fixed link in a new cross-border labour market will be substantial. Nevertheless, forecasts based on the experience from the labour markets at the Danish-German land border and in the Øresund Region are unrealistic in the short-term. Long distances will remain an important factor in limiting cross-border labour mobility in the area. Hopes for greater economic co-operation in general and cross-border commuting in particular are based on the creation of a new transport hub near Fehmarnbelt, which would attract investment and generate employment in the region. The possible effects hereof can be inferred from our integration scenarios of which the most favourable predicts a doubling of current commuter numbers.

We present a new assessment of commuting potential across the Fehmarnbelt once the fixed link is commissioned and the necessary policy steps taken reduce the psychological distance between the German and Danish regions separated by the Fehmarnbelt. The team presents a status quo scenario, which is an update from the 2008 assessment for 2020 as well as four cross-border commuting scenarios:

– implementation of the fixed link

– implementation of the fixed link + moderate integration of the labour market

– implementation of the fixed link + high integration of the labour market

– implementation of the fixed link + high integration of the labour market + additional integration effects on the Hamburg-Copenhagen axis

FIGURE 4.
COMMUTING ACROSS THE FEHMARN BELT IN 2020 ALTERNATIVE SCENARIOS

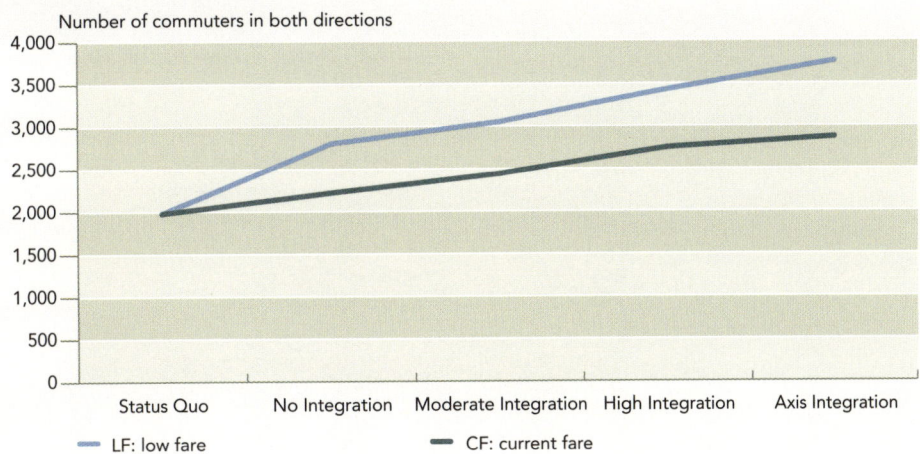

Figure 4 summarises the estimated commuter flow in both directions across the Fehmarnbelt as envisaged in the various scenarios. We argue that these would mainly be weekly commuters. Please note that prices are per person.

One part of the mobile labour force, namely those who – generally once a week – commute between the major urban areas and usually use trains or fly, are in a special position. This group specialises within particular jobs in the metropolises, mainly in high-skilled activities in the service sectors usually within management, finance and business services, culture and media, research and development, and higher education. Since they have specific personal characteristics (age, education, skills, etc.) which differ from those of the average commuter, they show different mobility patterns, for instance in the form of a greater willingness to commute over long distances. In Germany, fairly large numbers of commuters travel between the major cities so we have made further calculations specifically for this group. The actual flows are very small. Less than 100 individuals commute from Hamburg to Copenhagen and even fewer from Copenhagen to Hamburg. In Figure 5, we have calculated the potential flow between two metropolises with increased train speed and cost structures and we have used the assumptions of High Integration scenario.

FIGURE 5.
CALCULATION OF WEEKLY TRAIN COMMUTING BETWEEN COPENHAGEN AND HAMBURG IN 2020

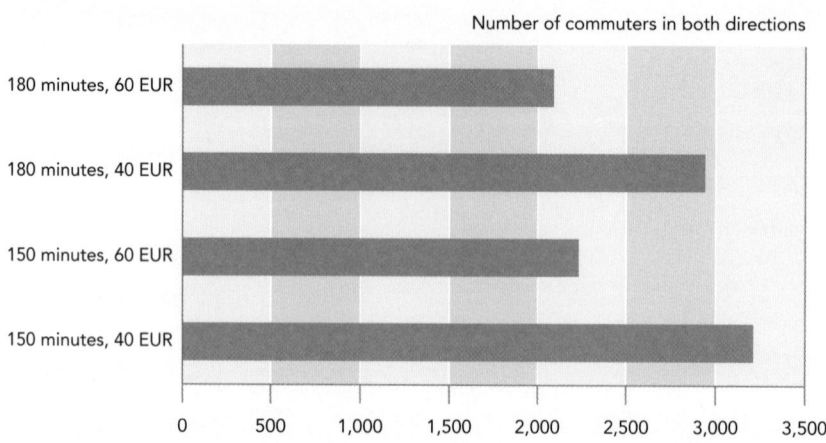

Note: Price with discount card (Bahncard50)

In the event of a strong barrier reduction following the opening of the Fehmarnbelt link, and in the event of symmetric incentives, we can expect commuter figures of about 1,000 to Copenhagen and nearly 1,300 to Hamburg for the 150 minute journey and 60 EUR fare, i.e. 2.300 per week. For the 40 EUR fare, the result will be 1,400 and 1,800 respectively (3,200 per week in total).

The links between the labour markets in the metropolitan regions, Hamburg and Copenhagen, are currently very weak with current travelling times being 280 minutes with ferry fares of 60 EUR. In addition to the dramatically shorter train travelling times generated by the Fehmarnbelt link, significant efforts to diminish border barriers are needed to achieve the numbers projected by our study of long-distance rail commuting.

REFERENCES

U. Barten, J. Bröcker, H. Herrmann & M. Klatt, *'Barrieren und Potentiale der grenzüberschreitenden Zusammenarbeit in der Fehmarnbelt Region'*, Institut für Regionalforschung der Universität Kiel, Kiel, 2006, paper, no. 41

J. Bröcker, H. Herrmann & A. Korzhenevych, *'Technical Appendix to The Fehmarnbelt Fixed Link: Regional Development Perspectives'*, www.femern.com, Copenhagen, 2010

P. Schnur & G. Zika (ed.), *'Die Grenzen der Expansion'*, Institut für Arbeitsmarkt- und Berufsforschung, Nürnberg, 2007, IAB abstract, no. 26

Transport- og Energiministeriet (ed.), *'Nøgletalskatalog – til brug for samfundsøkonomiske analyser på transportområdet'*, Copenhagen, 2006

NOTES

[i] Every cross-border commuter working in Denmark receives a health insurance card from the respective municipality (a so-called Form E 106). The survey has included all instances where this card has been issued. As this rule does not apply to the residents of Sweden and Norway, they were not included.

CHAPTER 7
CLUSTERS IN THE ECONOMY: POTENTIAL NEW INTERACTION

HAYO HERRMANN & CHRISTIAN WICHMANN MATTHIESSEN

The consequence of Michael Porter's (1990, 1998, 2003) cluster theory policy which, in turn, builds on agglomeration theory, especially the theory about localisation economies, is a series of political agendas. The background of the cluster concept is empirical. First, a large proportion of the world's economic output is produced by a small number of industrial core regions. Second, firms with similar focus are often located in the same place. Third, these two agglomeration processes tend to be cumulative and fourth, certain agglomerations are extremely innovative.

Empirical analysis of clusters has led to a new policy which, to a certain extent, is based upon but has outgrown traditional policy areas such as regional policies, science and innovation policies, industrial policy and policies aimed at attracting investment. The cluster policy sets a micro-focused agenda in contrast to old macro-focused paradigms which were built on industry concepts and subsidies. Location and distance play important roles in understanding the development and function of clusters and the analytical work is often focused on local or regional environments. The same applies to the identification of what

is important, ranging from technology and innovation to regional foundations to networks and business relations. Powerful technology clusters linked to effective cluster policies are increasingly becoming a central determinant for regional competitiveness together with macro-economic conditions, market accessibility and institutional, legal and political conditions.

A cluster consists of a group of leading and complementary companies (small and large), research and educational institutions, financial institutions, consultancy institutions (e.g. technology transfer institutions), government bodies and cluster management , all with a common production and/or technology focus, located within daily co-operation range (the definition of clusters is based on Sölvell, Lindqvist & Ketels (2003). The composition of players and the networks' structure are shown in Figure 1 and a more detailed illustration of the types of players is presented in Figure 2.

FIGURE 1.
ACTORS FORMING A CLUSTER

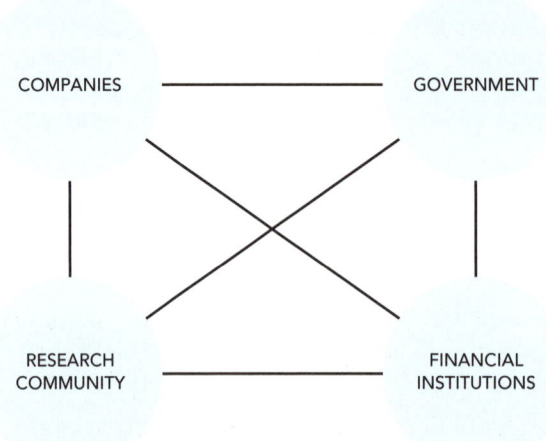

Based on Sölvell, Lindqvist & Ketels (2003)

The underlying driver behind a cluster formation is the interaction between co-existence and competition. Cluster formation is enhanced when strong, leading companies show the way. Clusters are often identified as the international competitive parts of the local economy, but can also be competitive on a smaller scale. Cluster analysis comprises a systematic view of production, services and public activities and of learning, innovation and knowledge sharing. Focus is on common interests in the form of production factors and infrastructure as well as confidence-building and optimization of networks between companies and supporting institutions.

In this chapter, we identify and present the clusters in the Fehmarnbelt Region and point out potential cross-border co-operation. Taking our starting point in the work by others, we will look at the literature and the statistics on the subject. The cluster analytical

FIGURE 2.
LOCAL AND REGIONAL ACTORS FORMING A CLUSTER

background material on Germany is more comprehensive and detailed than on Denmark and Sweden, which is reflected in the chapter's varying degree of detail about the sub-regions. Based on this, we will present our own views. The rationale is that co-operation must overcome a number of barriers, including geographical (land-sea) and national as well as barriers owing to a lack of information.

In a political set-up, the emphasis is on improving the conditions for clusters (often supported by cluster management bodies) rather than focusing on selected industries or a single company. Subsidies are avoided and seed-money is the preferred development tool. A cluster initiative and the institutional framework for such a cluster management organisation should focus on a balanced input from the commercial world and (local/regional/national) authorities.

Dynamic clusters (of a certain size) are critical to regional success. According to Sölvell, Lindqvist & Ketels (2003), these are typically characterised by:

- dynamic competition, not least from new firms, which could be spin-offs from existing companies

- local rivalry, which stimulates upgrading and change and creates the foundation for a more advanced supplier base

- local and trans-regional co-operation, organised between institutions and/or informally

- strong incentives to reduce uncertainty (technical as well as economic),

- access to increasingly specialised and advanced production factors in the form of human capital, financial capital, infrastructure and access to universities and research institutions

- links to related industries, sharing pools of talent and new technological advancements

- local demand

- geographical proximity

Strong clusters are creative and innovative, which means that they raise the level of competitiveness for the companies within the cluster. Clusters must be dynamic for regional success. Moreover, they have to have a certain size relative to the regional economy in order to impact on regional growth. This means that although small dynamic clusters can be successful, they have little potential for impacting on the region. Face-to-face contact is crucial for the exchange of intangible knowledge and creation of new knowledge. Face to face interaction is also important, especially between key persons (managers, researchers, and teachers), but also generally between the different units (firms, institutions).

Companies are shaped by the national and regional economic environment, which consists of four pillars: national legacy and culture, geographical position, local institutions

FIGURE 3.
PORTER´S DIAMOND – LOCAL AND REGIONAL ECONOMIC DEVELOPMENT

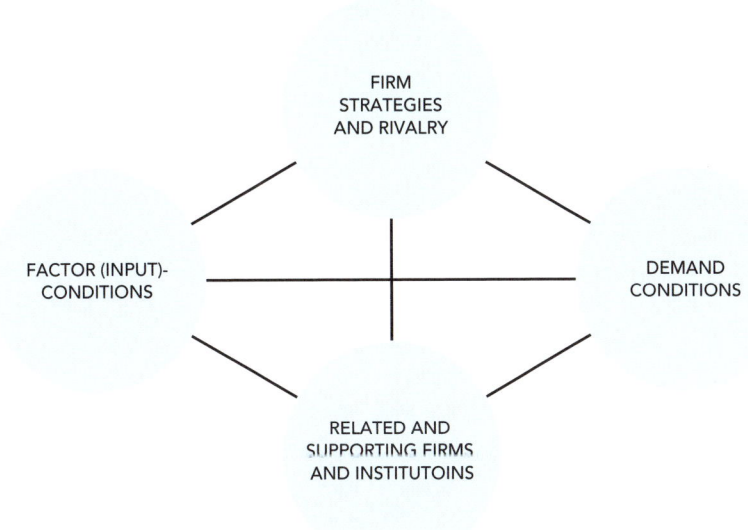

Source: Porter (1990, 2002)

and legal framework (Sölvell, Lindqvist & Ketels, 2003). The local and regional economic framework plays a key role in driving innovation and upgrading competitive advantage. Michael Porter calls the local or regional economic environment "the diamond." This is where clusters develop, see Figure 3.

Initiatives to create organisations to support the formation and development of clusters ("cluster management organisations") are common in the developed world (Sölvell, Lindqvist & Ketels, 2003). Cluster initiatives evolve over time and vary from information gathering and dissemination, cluster analysis, networking, lobbying, export promotion, regional branding to innovation. They can be offshoots of well-established organisations, including industry organisations, chambers of commerce or local/regional government departments. Isaksen & Hauge (2002) find that the most common cluster initiatives and administrative bodies comprise public relations, teaching, research and development, joint marketing and branding. They also point out that cluster initiatives and cluster management organisations are highly sensitive to local conditions and traditions adapted to the local resource base.

DENMARK

Danish regional development policy has been based on cluster analysis since Michael Porter's research was commonly recognised. This policy remains current in 2010. Each region and their growth forums[i] identify a series of clusters based on in-depth analytical work which, however, is often affected by political prioritisations. The aim is to strengthen regional competitiveness in a global context. Cluster identification focuses on the private sector although global competitiveness is not only a private sector issue. The hospital sector and the universities, for instance, participate as suppliers in the global market for surgery or with regard to international students.

The Zealand archipelago comprises four larger islands connected by bridges and a series of smaller inhabited islands with ferry connections to the main islands. The region also includes the island of Bornholm, which is part of Region Hovedstaden (the Capital Region of Denmark) but has its own growth forum. Three growth forums (Vækstforum Hovedstaden, Vækstforum Sjælland, and Vækstforum Bornholm) cover the Danish part of the Fehmarnbelt Region. Like the three other Danish growth forums, they interact with the Ministry for Trade and Industry and the relevant directorate (Erhvervs- og Byggestyrelsen).

The Ministry and the Directorate act on national level and provide analyses on national growth clusters although clusters should have a regional or even local constraint in order to build up close and personal networks. In this chapter, we will focus on clusters with a clear regional focus.

Identification of competitive clusters must also take into account that the regional division of this part of Denmark is not in accordance with economic, regional logic nor converge with regional labour markets' forms and logic. The Capital Region comprises only parts of the Greater Copenhagen labour market. The five municipalities in Region Zealand are clearly parts of the functional Greater Copenhagen region, Solrød, Greve, Roskilde, Lejre and Køge, which belong under the Region Zealand in that more than 33 per cent of employees commute to the Capital Region. Other studies claim that the entire island of Zealand is one labour market (By- og Landskabsstyrelsen, 2007).

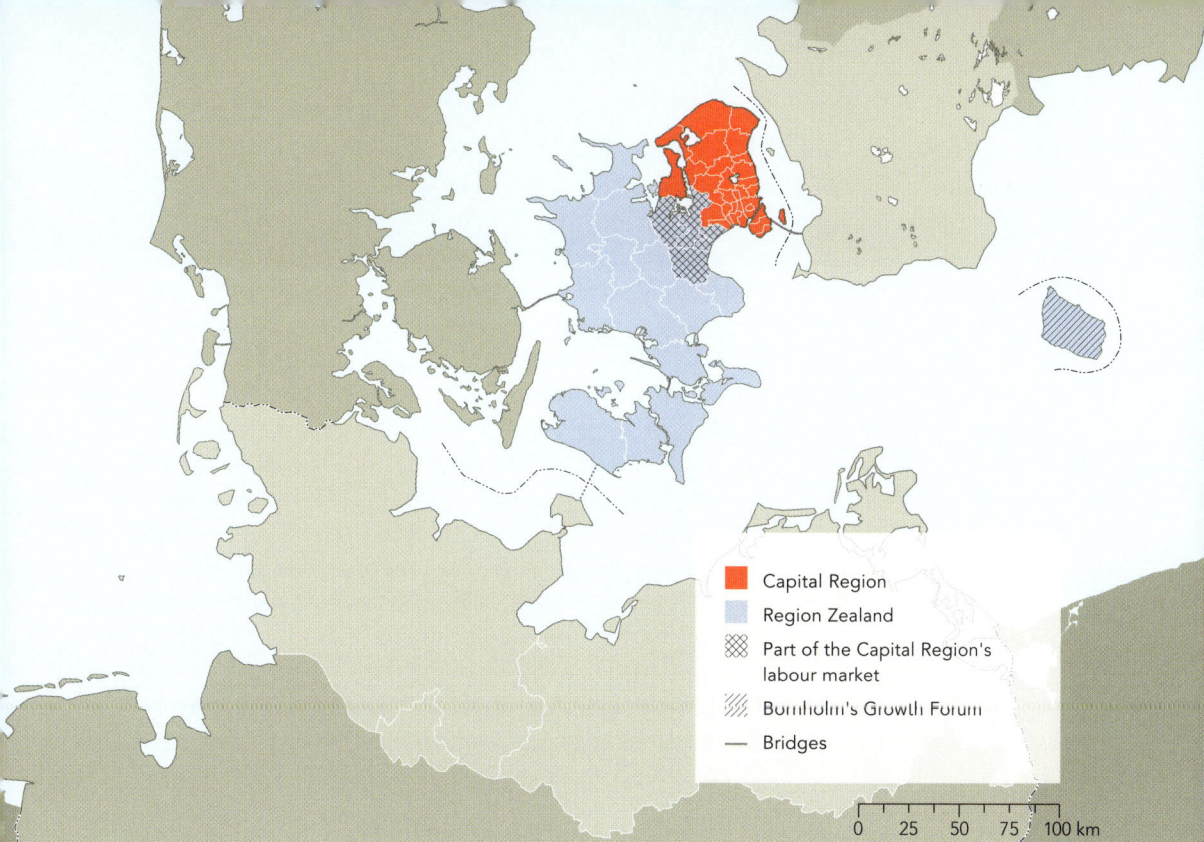

FIGURE 4.
TWO REGIONS, THREE GROWTH FORUM AREAS

Note: Some Region Zealand municipalities are part of the Greater Copenhagen labour market.

CAPITAL REGION

The Capital Region is Denmark's only metropolis. Copenhagen is a giant on the national scene and is the only Danish city competing in the rivalry between international metropolitan areas. The functional urban unit (Greater Copenhagen) has 1.8 million inhabitants and more than 1 million jobs. With 1.6 million inhabitants, the Capital Region covers most of the functional urban unit although part of Region Zealand is a logical part of the metropolitan region, see above. More than half of all Danes with higher education live in the

Capital Region and more than 40 per cent of GDP is generated within the region where 33 per cent of all Danish jobs are located. 85 per cent of all foreign investments in Denmark are found within the region.

The Capital Region has a strong university sector, including the University of Copenhagen, Denmark's Technical University, Copenhagen Business School and a number of smaller higher educational institutions. In addition, there are a number of research institutions and research organisations.

Compared to other metropolitan areas within the OECD area as selected by the organisation for its recent territorial review of Copenhagen (2009), employment in the largest economic sectors demonstrated a specialisation pattern, which in general terms is not substantially different from other metropolitan areas in the OECD. The average metropolitan region displays a high rate of specialisation compared to the national average and has a high representation of financial services, business services, transport and communication. It appears, however, that Copenhagen's specialisation in financial and business services and transport is less extreme than the average for the OECD metropolitan database[ii].

The Capital Region[iii] has a working population of 945,000. Of these, 1 per cent is employed in resources, 9 per cent in manufacturing, 6 per cent in construction, 18 per cent in trade and hotels, 7 per cent in transport and communication, 22 per cent in financial and business services and 36 per cent in other services. Global employment is estimated at 30 per cent. OECD's territorial review of Copenhagen (2009) lists different cluster examinations of Copenhagen using a variety of methods. The number of clusters varies between 6 and 18, which is reflected in the calculation of the number of employees within the clusters. It is, however, not entirely clear what the term "cluster" actually covers. The term appears to range from the identification of specialisation patterns and commercial positions of strengths to agglomerations to genuine clusters as defined in accordance with Michael Porter and his associates' definitions.

An overview of clusters (or rather of areas of competence)[iv] by the Danish Agency for Science, Technology and Innovation under the Ministry of Science, Technology and Innovation (Forsknings- og Innovationsstyrelsen, 2008) identifies 10 areas within the Capital Region's growth forum. Without specifically referring to the cluster concept, the overview uses the term "clusters." The largest areas are information and communication technology, transport and logistics, construction, bio-health, business services, film and television, design, energy, games and food. Another analysis by the Ministry of Economic and Business Affairs also concerns clusters, and also focuses on fields of competence rather than on well defined clusters. This report highlights biopharma with its 18,000 employees and a very high level of specialisation. Information technology and communication with 35,000 employees, medical equipment with 4,000, entertainment with 8,000, transport with 21,000 are listed together with business services (32,000) and financial services (40,000) (Ministry of Science, Technology and Innovation, 2008).

The most recent analysis of Greater Copenhagen clusters identifies the life science/health cluster as the flagship (Oxford Research 2009). Set up in 1997, this cluster was initiated by the Øresund Region's public organisations on a cross-border basis in order to mobilise and increase commercial positions of strength within pharmaceutical activities, medical equipment and biotechnology. It is characterised by a healthy business environment with extensive collaboration between life science companies, academic researchers and clinicians and constitutes a fully integrated biotech cluster with more than 100 biotech companies with own research and development, major research and development based pharmaceutical companies, medico-technical companies, relevant service providers and clinical research organisations and 10-12 experienced life science research institutions – all varying in size and specialisation.

In addition to this health-oriented cluster, there is one cluster under Business Tourism, i.e. a cluster based on hotels, restaurants and conference venues. The attractions of Copenhagen (Tivoli, museums, zoo, concert halls etc) also contribute together with transport/logistics activities. Direct employment within the field totals 2,000. Film/television accounts for around 2,000 key jobs within production companies, the media, theatres and universities and are centred around the Danish Film Institute. Although not a distinct cluster, the area has the potential to develop into one.

The Greater Copenhagen clusters include many of Denmark's leading companies. Life science/health, for instance, comprises Novo Nordisk, Lundbeck, Coloplast and Leo Pharma.

Within the food cluster are Carlsberg, Danisco and Christian Hansen. With its ports, airports and infrastructure the transport and logistics cluster also includes the world's leading container company, Mærsk, and a plethora of traffic and transport companies such as DSV, DSB and SAS. The IT cluster's leading player is TDC and the environment cluster comprises Novozymes, ISS and DONG. The business-financial cluster includes a number of large banks, among which is Danske Bank. Nordea and Nykredit are also among the heavyweight financial groups while TrygVesta is the country's largest insurer. The group also includes a number of large consulting and service companies such as Deloitte and KPMG. Finally, the business tourism cluster includes travel operators such as SAS, infrastructure owners like Copenhagen Airports, hotels and experience companies such as Tivoli.

FIGURE 5.
GREATER COPENHAGEN CLUSTERS

Fields with cluster characteristics:
– Life science/health
– Food
– Transport and logistics
– Information and communication technology
– Environment
– Business services - finance
– Business tourism

Fields with few cluster characteristics:
– Film/television
– Design
– Games
– Energy
– Clean tech/green technology
– Family tourism

REGION ZEALAND

In a Danish context, the region is characterised by low productivity and migration of globally oriented business to other regions, by the challenge of attracting highly skilled labour to regional employment, by problems in maintaining highly qualified employees in the region and by the fact that innovation is centred on a few – but very – innovative companies with close links to Greater Copenhagen's academic world. In contrast to the generally low status (low productivity, low wages) of the area, Region Zealand is characterised by a high level of prosperity (per capita income). This is, in part explained by the large number of highly qualified commuters with jobs in the Capital Region. Municipalities with a high percentage of commuting to the Capital Region have high per capita income. And, as mentioned, parts of Zealand belong to the Copenhagen labour market. From this point of view, it is a great asset to have the large Greater Copenhagen labour market with a strong public services sector with high growth rates (Copenhagen Economics, 2005)[v] as a neighbour. In addition to the problematic industry structure, Region Zealand suffers from the fact that it has an ageing population while younger people move away from the area and the number of people in employment is lower than the average for Denmark. In addition, per capita income growth is also below the Danish average. On the other hand, the workforce is experienced and well educated and the number of newly established companies is above the Danish average although most of them are small, non-innovative firms with a low rate of survival (Vækstforum Sjælland, 2009). Region Zealand comprises Roskilde University and the Risø research institution.

The number of employees within Region Zealand (2008) is 350,000 (Statistikbanken, 2010). Of these, 4 per cent are employed within resources, 12 per cent in manufacturing, 9 per cent in construction, 19 per cent in trade and hotels, 5 per cent in transport and communication, 12 per cent in financial and business services, and 38 per cent in other services. For 2004, Copenhagen Economics identified a number of competence areas and found close to 55,000 (Copenhagen Economics 2005)[vi]. They identified ten areas that each had more than 2,000 employees. This was compared with the national growth average for the same areas, and regional differences were identified.

Region Zealand comprises relatively few global competitive growth areas and the majority of new jobs are created within the public sector and low-income parts of the private sector. The positive deviation from this picture is accounted for by the pharmaceutical industry, which is growing in respect of employment as well as in terms of income. This sector is an offshoot of the strong pharmaceutical sector in Greater Copenhagen. The IT sector is also growing in the number of employees. Most other industries within Region Zealand which are competing globally are losing jobs.

A comparison with Danish growth figures revealed that Region Zealand achieved relatively rising growth figures within pharmaceuticals, machinery and food. However, it is only within pharmaceuticals where Region Zealand's growth is significantly above the national figures. Although IT services are growing fast, according to Copenhagen Economic, the Zealand area is losing market share in relation to the Danish IT sector.

Growth policy in Region Zealand follows two main tracks. One focuses on changing the industrial structure, the other on improving the competitiveness of existing firms. The existing clusters are fundamental for regional growth, while there is political focus on new and growing clusters.

The Danish Agency for Science, Technology and Innovation (Forsknings- og Innovationsstyrelsen 2008) identifies nine focus areas within Region Zealand. This ambitious list comprises energy and environment, medico/health, agriculture, plant and seed cultivation, tourism and experience economy, transport and logistics, construction, food and aquaculture. Another analysis by the Ministry of Economic and Business Affairs provides

FIGURE 6.
FIELDS AND PROFILE AREAS ZEALAND AND BORNHOLM CLUSTERS

ZEALAND
(MINUS GREATER COPENHAGEN)
Fields with some cluster characteristics
- Pharma/medico products
- Construction
- Information and communication technology

BORNHOLM
Profile areas
- Agricultural products (organic)
- Family tourism (summer)

Profile areas
- Logistics
- Food
- Clean tech / green technology
- Tourism

further information on the Zealand clusters. This report lists the areas of medical equipment with 1,500 employees in the core area and with a relatively high degree of specialisation. The report also lists biopharma with 3,500 employees, energy with 3,000, plastics with 2,500, agricultural products with 1,500, food with 10,000, entertainment with 1,500 and construction with 13,000 employed within their core areas.

Based on the analysis mentioned above, we find that three areas display some cluster characteristics. Two of these, pharma/medico, and information and communication technology are part of the Greater Copenhagen clusters which, in turn, are part of the Øresund Region clusters. Construction can be defined as a Region Zealand cluster with certain cluster characteristics. We also identify "profile areas" whose components have a uniform production focus and are located near each other. They can be seen as potential clusters, but they are currently rather strategic marketing objects.

GROWTH FORUM BORNHOLM

Bornholm is a very small labour market (43,000 inhabitants, 18,000 employees) and is considered peripheral in a Danish and European context. The population has been decreasing for decades, unemployment is high, income per capita low, qualification levels are low and there are few persons in the job-active age groups. The island is well connected to Sweden and Denmark by ferries and to Copenhagen by frequent air connections. The small labour market is oriented towards agriculture and food products, tourism (summer) and the public sector (being a closed economy there is an over-representation of certain public activities). Bornholm has its own growth forum although the island is part of the Capital Region. Growth Forum Bornholm's strategy is based on a "Bright Green Island" concept and focuses on organic food and sustainable tourism (Growth Forum Bornholm, 2008).

SCANIA

Employment in Scania comprises half a million individuals (measured as work year 2008). The majority of employment is non-cluster affiliated, but contributes to the level of production. Specific companies can be very competitive – even world leading – without being part of a cluster or concentration of related firms. Nilsson, Svensson-Henning & Wilkenson (2002) have analysed the part of the Scania labour market, which has been termed clusters, cluster-affiliated or co-located in cluster discussions. Altogether this part of the economy comprises almost 200,000 jobs within 16 industrial groups. With a more narrow definition (without public and private health care personnel) they identified 100,000 jobs of this type. To identify their cluster status, they analysed the 16 industrial groups in respect of:

- co-location and critical mass in Scania
- strategic interaction
- a high level of research and development
- growth potential

In the comprehensive analysis of the 16 industrial segments, six areas of Scania's economy can be characterised as clusters (in whole or in part). Only two of these areas showed distinct cluster characteristics (food, life science) while four fields demonstrated some cluster characteristics (wood, hospitality, ITC, packaging). Eight areas could not be characterised as clusters (transport & logistics, music, machinery, games, film, marine industry, graphic industry, plastics) and two areas had to be considered profile areas and could not be characterised as clusters (design, environment).

FIGURE 7.
SCANIA CLUSTERS

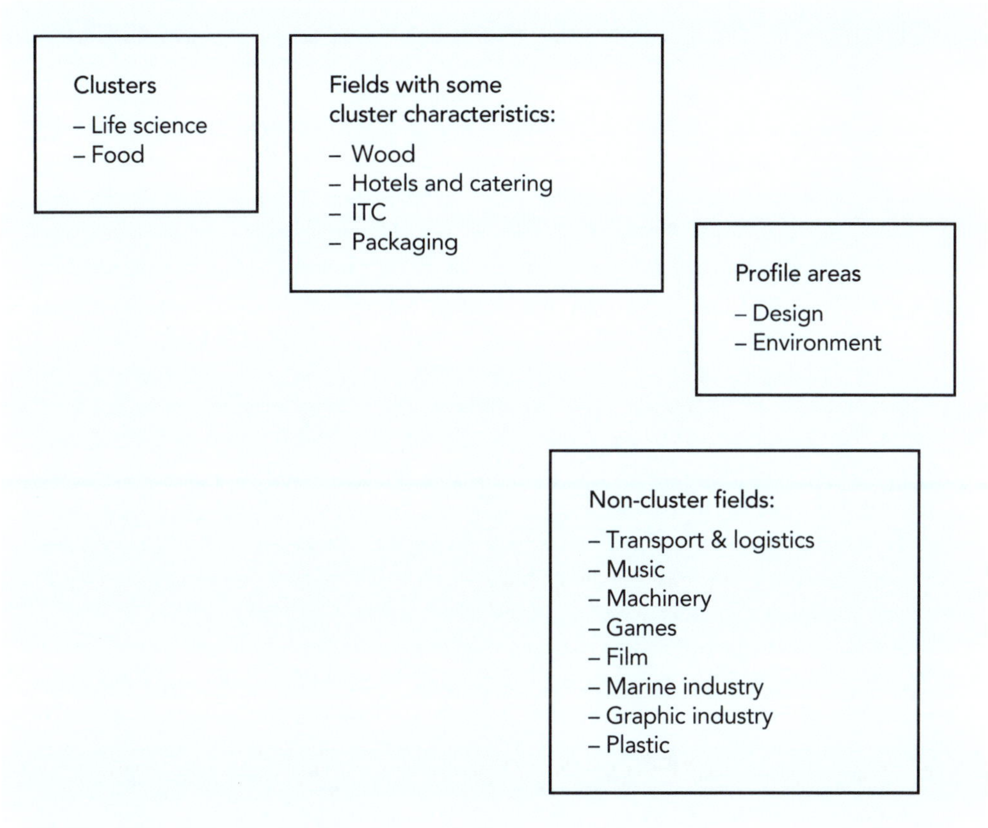

Clusters
– Life science
– Food

Fields with some cluster characteristics:
– Wood
– Hotels and catering
– ITC
– Packaging

Profile areas
– Design
– Environment

Non-cluster fields:
– Transport & logistics
– Music
– Machinery
– Games
– Film
– Marine industry
– Graphic industry
– Plastic

Based on Nilsson, Svensson-Henning & Wilkens (2002)

The group "areas with certain cluster characteristics" comprise wood, tourism, ITC and packaging. The wood industry has around 6,000 employees, hospitality 11,000, information and communication technology 13,000 and packaging 7,000. The category "profile areas" (design, environment) has the ability to strengthen the image of the region and its production without displaying the characteristics of a cluster. Design comprises 1,000 jobs and the environment is a large group which, according to Nilsson, Svensson-Henning

& Wilkenson (2002), cannot be calculated accurately. Both types have the potential to develop into clusters either through local strategies or by cross-border co-operation. The group "real clusters" possesses all the characteristics of a cluster. The two genuine Scania clusters (food, life science) are presented below.

The broad food sector has a strong position in Scania, where agriculture accounts for 43 per cent of the land, and where 25-30 per cent of the workforce are directly or indirectly linked to the food sector. The food cluster employs 38,800 (Nilsson, Svensson-Henning & Wilkenson, 2002) and is centred on raw material and food production with a base in research, development and higher education in conjunction with supporting industries, official bodies and intermediary organisations. Some of the cluster companies are also directly involved with retail activities (bakeries, restaurants) and operate in a demanding local market which is rapidly turning towards organic products. Moreover, large national retail chains play a central role in terms of cluster behaviour (Ahold/ICA, Coop, Axfood).

Scania's agricultural sector has high standards and a high yield compared to the Swedish average. Grain, beet, oil plants and livestock are primary products, which form part of the production of sugar, oil, starch, meat (processed, canned or frozen), milk products, bread and spirits (Arla, Procordia, Nestlé, Skånemejerier, Van den Berg Foods, Danisco). The support functions include chemicals, fertilizers, livestock feed, vets, agricultural machinery and repair industries, and packaging machinery (Tetra Pak) together with logistics and parts of the environmental sector. The products are aimed at local, regional and Baltic markets but also global (Absolut Vodka, Tetra Pak).

A number of higher education institutions are present in Scania, including the Swedish Agricultural University, Lunds University, Högskolan Kristianstad and some smaller institutions. Some of the larger companies operate their own research and development units. Research parks like Ideon also play a part. The public sector is represented by the Swedish grain and seed control unit and organisations like the Ideon Agro Food and the Scania Academy of Food are closely involved in cluster activities. The key elements of the cluster are dispersed across the Scania Region with some relatively strong concentrations in small and medium-sized cities while supporting industries, research and development and some public sector institutions are mainly located in the Malmö-Lund area and medium-sized cities such Helsingborg and Kristianstad.

Scania Region's flagship is the life science cluster. The region has a strong international profile in terms of health-related products and services and the key companies operate in a tough global competitive environment and do so successfully. This life science cluster is characterised by a highly educated, specialised labour force rewarded with good salaries. The real driver behind the cluster is the health care sector, which is a large and mainly public sector administered or funded by regional government in a highly controlled market.

The health industries focus on pharmaceutical and biotechnical products based on own research and research at universities and in research parks. The life science cluster in Scania comprises 100,000 jobs, including in the public and private health care sector. Health care carries out its own research, especially at the university hospitals in Lund and Malmö. Moreover, the sector provides skills and innovation to the cluster's key companies and shares part of the labour market with them.

Not including the health sector, the number of employees in Scania totals 30,000 (Nilsson, Svensson-Henning & Wilkenson, 2002). Hospitals and other suppliers of health services reflect the population distribution hierarchically. The primary health sector is distributed across municipal and suburban centres and the hospital sector is concentrated in the major urban centres. Manufacturing and related companies are centred on the largest cities and towns and often near universities. This means that cluster activities are concentrated on Western Scania, especially the Malmö-Lund area. The central part of the cluster consists of pharmaceutical companies (Pharmacia, Astra), medico-technical firms

(Gambro, Becton Dickinson) and biotechnical companies (Active Biotech). These work in close contact with university research at Lund's University, Malmö Högskola, the associated research parks (Ideon, Medeon) and Wallenberg Laboratories in Lund. The life science cluster is innovative and comprises hundreds of new innovative companies of which some are in need of incubators. Many are short-lived while some grow into large manufacturing or service companies. Risk capital and capital owners also take part in the cluster as do ordinary financial institutions. Business to business services comprise consultants, patents, market analysis, clinical tests and providers of IT/communication, logistics, media and public relations and specialised accountants.

THE ØRESUND REGION

Cluster organisations are not as well defined in Denmark and Sweden as in Germany. An exception to this rule is the Øresund Region although it has no formal governing body. The Øresund Science Region is the cross-border, cluster facilitating organisation that develops the strong sectors in Zealand and Scania on a "triple helix" basis[vii]. The organisation was established in 1997 by universities, major companies, regional authorities and local governments and has a staff of 40 who work with existing clusters and develop new ones. The Øresund Science Region is financed by the region's universities, regional and national governments, the EU and a membership of more than 1,000 companies. Øresund Science Region's main platforms are the Medicon Valley Alliance, Øresund Food, Øresund Logistics, Øresund IT and the Øresund Environment Academy.

The cluster flagship is the Medicon Valley Alliance (formerly Medicon Valley Academy), a partnership that is conceptually located in the interface between commerce and industry and the academic world. Medicon Valley Alliance is a Danish-Swedish non-profit, fee-based member organisation, which aims at creating synergies and value for the members, which include universities, hospitals, human life science companies and business service providers. Established in 1997, Medicon Valley Alliance's membership comprises more than 300 life science companies, 10 universities and higher education institutions and 32 hospitals. The organisation is committed to facilitating economic growth, increased competitiveness and employment in the Øresund Region by 1) establishing local and global platforms for networking; 2) organising communication and branding activities, teaching and seminars on business and business-related subjects as well as documentation and benchmarking.

Øresund Food is a knowledge based Danish-Swedish network organisation, uniting research, business and authorities within the food value chain. High priority is given to the application of food products in disease prevention and treatment as well as opportunities for more efficient food processing. The network has 78 members from research and education, authorities, industry and organisations within the food value-chain. It coordinates and participates in several multidisciplinary projects within food, pharma, ICT and environment. It 1) carries out skills mapping and match-making; 2) organises informal meetings, seminars, workshops and conferences; 3) gives attention to increased investments in food-related research and development, and 4) focuses on lobbying and marketing the region.

Uniting Danish and Swedish players within the logistics sector, Øresund Logistics works in close co-operation with universities, industries and authorities. Its main aim is to advance logistics and supply chain management in the Øresund Region as well as to promote the region as the main access and logistics centre for Scandinavia and the Baltic Rim. The network includes approximately 1,200 representatives from infrastructure owners, logistics providers, manufacturing companies, local, regional and central government, consultants and universities. Øresund Logistics supports logistics in the Øresund Region in four ways: 1) Networking activities, seminars, conferences, workshops; 2) By boosting knowledge about logistics; 3) By identifying and initiating research and development projects and 4) Branding the Øresund Region as the main gate to the Nordic area.

Øresund IT is the platform for the information and communications technology cluster and aims at promoting and supporting development in the region with its more than 100,000 IT employees, 12,000 companies, 8,000 students and 500 university researchers within the fields of information and communication technology. The organisation has 100 members from hardware and software companies, providers of business services, local and regional government and the universities. Its main aim is to 1) facilitate knowledge and contacts by marketing the Øresund IT cluster in publications, newsletters and on the Internet; 2) provide meeting-places, such as seminars, networks and conferences; 3) match-making; 4) gathering and disseminating information, and 5) identifying and initiating research and development projects.

The Øresund Environment Academy is tasked with contributing to making the Øresund Region a world leading environmental cluster within sustainable energy, construction and the environment. The organisation comprises 150 members from business, the R&D community and authorities and can create new contacts that facilitate the development of new research and innovation projects in the region. The Øresund Environment Academy 1) promotes dissemination, innovation and commercialisation of environmental knowledge and research; 2) arranges workshops, network meetings and seminars; 3) attracts funding, and 4) provides a forum for networking and knowledge exchange.

Other fields are considered as potential clusters. Nanotechnology is already a factor at the universities and attracts considerable attention from the authorities due to the decision to place the huge European research facility (European Spallation Source) at the

FIGURE 8.
THE ØRESUND REGION CLUSTERS

Clusters
– Medicon Valley Alliance
– Øresund Food
– Øresund Logistics
– Øresund IT
– Øresund Environment Academy

Profile areas
– Design
– Nanotechnology

Based on Øresund Science Region (2009)

University of Lund. The European Spallation Source will be the world's most powerful research facility for materials and life science with neutrons and will be built during the coming decade at a cost of EUR 2.5 billion.

SCHLESWIG-HOLSTEIN AND HAMBURG

In the analysis of the German clusters we have used a range of different sources[viii]. The starting point for the innovation policy regarding clusters in Germany was the "BioRegio" tender announced by the German Ministry for Education and Research (BMBF) in 1995. Under this subsidy programme, which was to run until 2005, the biotechnology sector in Germany was to be strengthened through the creation of regional pools of research institutions (including universities). This was the background for the formation of "BioRegions" in Germany, where the idea of clusters was pursued and promoted. This first initiative was taken in the late 1990s, followed by another BMBF subsidy programme named "InnoRegio" which was launched within the context of the innovation policy for the new länder (former East Germany). This programme, which was not limited to any single type of technology, fostered innovation networks mainly in regions outside the large metropolitan areas, where the economic structure was primarily based on small and medium-sized firms. The aim was to lay foundations for these regions' long-term competitiveness (Schrader, Laaser, Soltwedel, 2007; Herzberg, 2006).

In 2004, Schleswig-Holstein became one of the first German länder to include cluster strategy into the agenda of regional economic policy, using the term "cluster." In 2005, the traditional German regional policy programme (GA = Gemeinschaftsaufgabe zur Verbesserung der regionalen Wirtschaftsstruktur – "Incentives to improve regional economic structure") adopted the promotion of clusters as an additional element of assistance at regional level.

As mentioned above, the strategic definition of cluster policy and cluster management takes place first and foremost at federal level. Nevertheless, the elements and networks of individual clusters are, to a certain extent, linked to the regions, and in the case of the competence centres, these elements are linked to particular locations – which, of course, is a key feature of a cluster: its spatial concentration.

The German part of the Fehmarnbelt Region is dominated by the Hamburg metropolis, which is the high income service centre for the entire area, offering a broad spectrum of high-quality business services, research and development and higher education institutions as well as media services. A large number of industrial firms are located on the outskirts of Hamburg. Here, industrial density and the potential for clusters as well as for technological networks are significantly higher than in other parts of the Schleswig-Holstein/Hamburg area. Regarding employment trends over the past decade, we expect to see a positive trend for the whole Hamburg region.

The other regions in Schleswig-Holstein around the centres of Lübeck, Kiel and Flensburg show a much lower industrial density. Most notably, their industry structure is marked by the tertiary sector. However, only Kiel can be considered as a service centre with high quality functions and trans-regional relevance. In addition, services are mostly household-oriented (social, health and public services) and on average less high grade than in Hamburg. Key figures for the economic power and per capita income are below German average. Without new initiatives, future employment growth will be below the growth rates of the western part of Germany – as has been the case during the past ten years. Given a loose network of small and medium-sized industrial firms, specialisation on particular industries and technologies as well as the formation of technological clusters could be a way of compensating for difficult structural conditions – especially when regions cooperate with clusters in other areas.

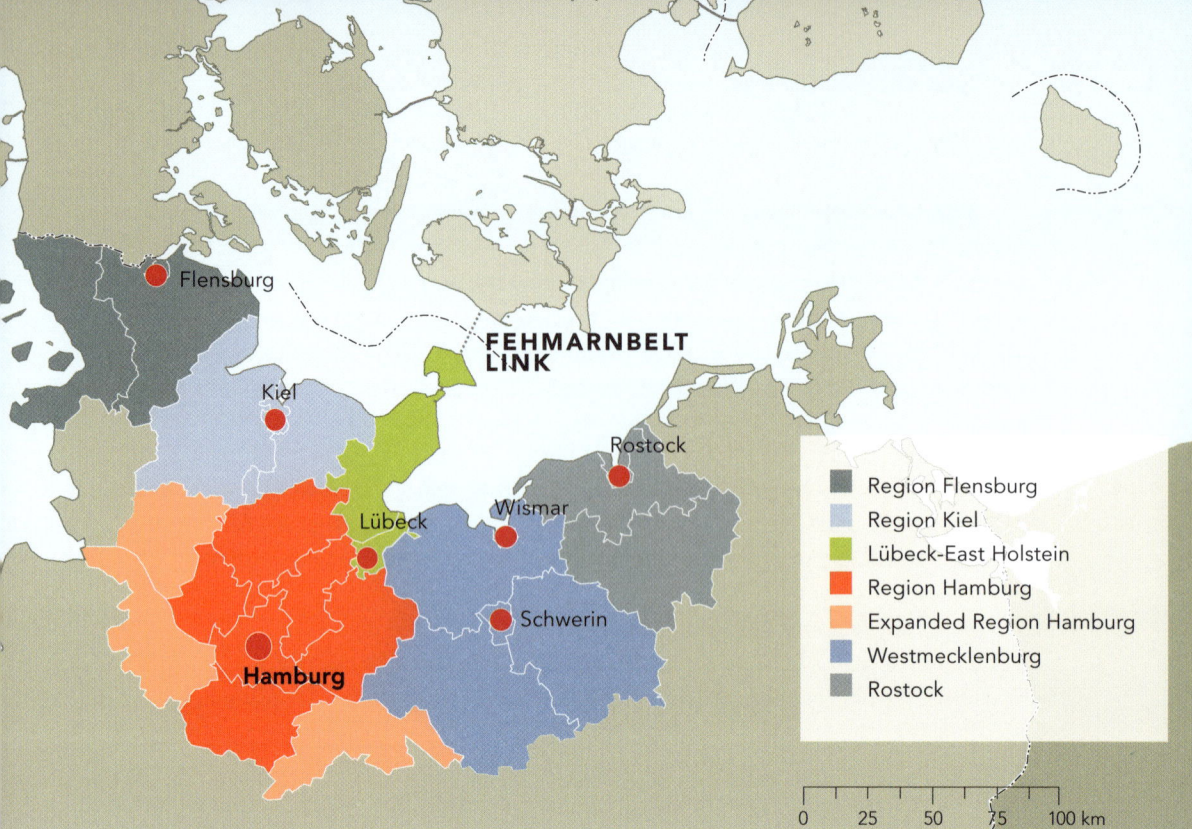

FIGURE 9.
THE NORTH-GERMAN PART OF THE FEHMARNBELT REGION

The cluster policy in Schleswig-Holstein and its integration into regional economic policy was introduced to the public as a new element of economic policy in the ministry's report for 2004. The report listed segments (industries or technologies) in the Schleswig-Holstein economy which could benefit in particular from federal subsidies. The choice of these segments was largely determined by existing structures and growth cells of the regional clusters. The following features were taken into account:

– substantial nucleus (industry, technology, goods)
– network of core enterprises, subsidiaries and complementary institutions
– local or regional focus
– critical mass of the cluster
– adequate labour market
– universities and vocational colleges matching with the cluster firms

- perspectives for future cluster development
- cluster awareness in the region
- impact from the cluster on regional growth

Since then, the cluster strategy in Schleswig-Holstein has been an important part of its policy for promoting innovation and growth. It has been continued even after the change of government in Schleswig-Holstein in 2005 although it lost its dominating position in the state's economic policy.

Together with the introduction of the cluster strategy in Schleswig-Holstein's policy in 2004, a concept for cluster creation was launched. It was developed by the Ministry of Economic Affairs and comprised three stages: (1) preparation, (2) formation, and (3) evaluation and adjustment. Subsequent to the preparatory phase, eight clusters were assigned to receive support from federal subsidies.

FIGURE 10.
CLUSTERS IN SCHLESWIG-HOLSTEIN

- Life science
- Maritime economy
- Food industry
- Information technology
- Micro and nanotechnology
- Wind energy and renewable energy
- Chemical industry
  (without pharma)
- Tourism

Source: List of State Government Schleswig-Holstein (2004)

This list was recently extended to include two further clusters based on the growing co-operation between Schleswig-Holstein and Hamburg: the logistics cluster and the aviation cluster, both of which are key industries in Hamburg. Although tourism is a key factor in Schleswig-Holstein's economy and receives a great deal of assistance, it cannot be compared with other, more technologically defined clusters. This could be the reason why tourism sometimes misses out in the lists of clusters found in publications and on the internet.

A further element in the innovation and network policy of the state is the creation and promotion of spatially or thematically narrowly defined competence centres. To a certain degree, the state also supports educational and research institutions in their applications for "excellence initiatives" (an initiative of BMBF). Here the objective is to gather the research potential within the country and achieve a world leading role within the selected areas. This has already succeeded in the fields of maritime and medical research (the excellence initiatives "Future Ocean" and "Inflammation of Interfaces").

In Schleswig-Holstein, the Minister of Economics is responsible for promoting and monitoring the clusters. For the individual clusters, the task lies with the respective cluster management institutions. At state level, the "Business Development and Technology Transfer Corporation" (WTSH) and the Chambers of Commerce (IHK) in Schleswig-Holstein also undertake cluster monitoring. At local level, this task is shared by the institutions for business support (or by regional development agencies) of the administrative districts (Kreise) and the big cities.

Regional institutions that represent a group of adjacent districts are now playing a very limited role, particularly since the end of the "KERN" partnership (technology region KERN around Kiel, Eckernförde, Rendsburg, and Neumünster) in 2008. Recently, the successor organisation, the "Wirtschaftsförderungsgesellschaft" (regional development agency) of Kiel, Kreis Rendsburg-Eckernförde and Kreis Plön replaced the KERN partnership.

FIGURE 11.
CLUSTERS IN HAMBURG

- Aviation
- Logistics
- IT and media
- Harbour services
- Life science

However, there is still a close partnership link between all parts of the Hamburg metropolitan region, including the districts of Southern Schleswig-Holstein. In the light of the decisions concerning the Fehmarnbelt link, future concepts also refer to an economic area "Fehmarnbelt" on the German side, stretching from Kreis Ostholstein via Lübeck to the area between Lübeck and Hamburg, also including Hamburg in a wider sense.

The assistance of the state consists primarily of financial aid towards the management of the cluster management units and support for infrastructure development with special focus on the clusters. The support for the cluster management was designed as start-up aid and aims at enabling self-financing of the cluster after some years. A support programme, which was initially limited to three years, can be extended for a further three years following evaluation.

In Hamburg, a cluster policy was launched by Hamburg's Senate for the 2004-2008 programme, which aimed at directing the city's economic policy towards "perspective fields", including aviation, ports and logistics, IT and media as well as life science. The policy was focused on infrastructure development, research and development, qualifications, support for marketing and network creation.

Cluster management in Hamburg is undertaken by the senate's management, i.e. state government level, by the Hamburg Business Development Corporation (HWF) and by initiatives for some of the most important clusters (life science, logistics, aviation). The performance of the clusters in Hamburg is also monitored by the Chamber of Commerce. Moreover, the "Süderelbe AG" on the southern bank of the River Elbe should also be mentioned. "Süderelbe AG" is responsible for location management and, especially, for cluster management of Hamburg's southern hinterland from Cuxhaven via Stade and Harburg to Lüneburg. Here, focus is on the logistics (port), maritime economy, food industry and aviation clusters.

Cluster policy and management of neighbouring spatial units are commonly characterised by the co-existence of competition and co-operation. Both Schleswig-Holstein and Hamburg have often announced their intention to further extend their co-operation regarding the cluster policy owing to large overlap between the existing clusters. The willingness to extend the collaboration was reiterated by the Hamburg and Schleswig-Holstein chambers of commerce in 2009. Such co-operation already exists within the life science cluster, for which a common cluster management has been created, the North-German Life Science Agency (Norgenta GmbH).

Furthermore, organisational efforts have been initiated in order to establish co-operation within the aviation and logistics clusters. In the aviation cluster, it would be logical to assign Hamburg leadership because of the role that aviation plays in the city and the dominant position of the leading company, Airbus. In addition, the creation of a maritime cluster is also on the agenda for Hamburg. In this case, a partnership with Schleswig-Holstein in the form of joint cluster management would also make sense. Thus, an organisational fine-tuning would be appropriate for the life science and aviation clusters. Both chambers of commerce, therefore, recommend the strengthening of cross-state co-operation in the form of joint cluster management.

Although the promotion of "clusters" is not, literally speaking, part of the state economic policy in Mecklenburg-Vorpommern (MVP), network support still plays an important role. In practice, there is little difference between this strategy and cluster policy. The support of networks in MVP is based on the view that in the most important industries and technological sectors in Mecklenburg-Vorpommern, networks emerge naturally from impetuses from the economy and science institutions. The Ministry of Economic Affairs subsequently supports these initiatives during a certain limited period for the purpose of creating stable, self-financing structures. Most of these networks ("competence networks") are both technologically and regionally more narrowly defined than the clusters in Schleswig-Holstein. Mostly, they are industry-specific and only in a few individual cases do they encompass several industries. In Schleswig-Holstein, many of these networks would be referred to as local "competence centres" rather than clusters.

The Mecklenburg-Vorpommern's Ministry of Economic Affairs lists a total of 20 economy-related networks or competence centres, focused on maritime economy as well as life science and health industries. The two networks "Maritime Allianz" and "BioCon Valley" correspond to the cluster managements in Schleswig-Holstein and Hamburg. Further economic industries on the list are IT, vehicle manufacturing (parts suppliers), ports and logistics as well as environmental technology. In the IT industry, the functions of the network management were handled by the "IT Initiative MV". Many network organisations and competence centres are located in and around Rostock with more minor activities centred on locations like Greifswald or Schwerin.

In addition to the above-mentioned industries, the agriculture and food industries play an important role in Mecklenburg-Vorpommern. The "Agrarmarketing MVP" facilitates co-operation within the network. In the tourism and hospitality sector, which constitutes a very important tertiary factor for Mecklenburg-Vorpommern, networks play a certain role in marketing, but a "tourism cluster" is not yet part of the economic policy of the state.

Intensive co-operation between clusters or networks in Mecklenburg-Vorpommern and Schleswig-Holstein or Hamburg is only sporadic, if at all. There is still a long way to go before mutual coordination of cluster or network support has been achieved, not to mention the organisational merger of cluster management as one sees between Schleswig-Holstein and Hamburg.

MAIN CLUSTERS IN SCHLESWIG-HOLSTEIN AND HAMBURG

The description of the clusters in the economic areas of Schleswig-Holstein and Hamburg is based on a plethora of information sources comprising reports about particular clusters and about the entire cluster structure in both states, other information from cluster management and the cluster supervising organisations (internet or written sources) and finally from personal discussions with cluster rmanagers. Based on this premise, tabular overviews for eight clusters were prepared. More detailed information sources are also contained in these tables. The overviews are presented in an appendix as a working document (www.femern.com). The presentation of the clusters in this section centre on:

- Cluster focus, type of cluster
- Industries and technologies involved
- Cluster management, key firms, research
- Cluster size, regional focus
- Growth potential. Present and future problems
- Links between Schleswig-Holstein, Hamburg and Mecklenburg-Vorpommern

The order of the clusters presented below is not accidental, but is a consequence of the selected criteria, i.e. absolute size (e.g. measured by the number of jobs), relevance to the overall economy in Schleswig-Holstein/Hamburg, network characteristics (is the cluster "complete"?), the intensity of the links between Schleswig-Holstein and Hamburg and the actual or potential links within the Fehmarnbelt Region, especially between Schleswig-Holstein/Hamburg and the region of Copenhagen/Malmö in the Øresund Region.

FIGURE 12.
CLUSTERS IN SCHLESWIG-HOLSTEIN AND HAMBURG

- Life science (including the health sector)
- Logistics
- Maritime economy
- Food industry
- Aviation and aircraft production
- Information technology and media
- Microtechnology
- Wind power and renewable energy

The life science cluster (including the health sector)[vii] is divided into (a) medical engineering and (b) pharmaceuticals and medical biotechnology. In terms of the production chain, life science is linked with (c) health industry (doctors, clinics, rehabilitation, wellness and spa clinics). All three areas have a prominent role in the states of Schleswig-Holstein and Hamburg – also compared to other German states. The technical field (medical engineering) is mainly located in large cities (Lübeck, Hamburg, Kiel), the biomedical sector is strongly represented in Lübeck and in Southern Schleswig-Holstein whereas health care coverage is more ubiquitous. But here as well, the cities of Hamburg, Lübeck and Kiel with their university hospitals play a leading role. The close integration between Schleswig-Holstein and Hamburg is obvious regarding the fact that Norgenta GmbH is responsible for the cluster managements in both states, having introduced the brand "Life Science Nord". The importance of the life science and health sector is also reflected in the many highly efficient companies led by Dräger Medical in Lübeck, the largest industrial employer in Schleswig-Holstein, and in the specific focus of the universities towards excellent medical skills and research, particularly in Lübeck and Kiel, but also in Hamburg. The universities are complemented by a number of top class research and educational institutions, particularly in Hamburg and Lübeck. This network of production, skills and research has achieved global leadership in several medical research fields.

Even in a purely quantitative sense, life science and the health sector play a formative role in the total economy in both states, particularly in Schleswig-Holstein. In the life science sector there are about 16,000 employees working in Schleswig-Holstein and about 10,000 in Hamburg. In the health sector, the number of employees in both states exceeds the 100,000 mark. Together, Schleswig-Holstein and Hamburg occupy third place behind Bayern and Baden-Wuerttemberg in respect of medical technology in Germany. They also have a distinguished position among all European regions.

The logistics cluster with more than 100,000 employees in Schleswig-Holstein/Hamburg, multiple links between the logistics industry in the two states, (especially between Lübeck and Hamburg,) and with existing links to the logistics cluster in the Øresund Region, will be increasingly important as the fixed Fehmarnbelt link proceeds. The North German logistics cluster takes second place among the networks listed here, although it was included only two years ago under the state governments' regional cluster concept[ix]. The entire logistics industry is a production and service chain with two main pillars (a) forwarding and trade logistics on land and (b) maritime logistics (shipping, port operations) which are also an essential part of the maritime cluster. In addition to the core services of transport, handling and storage, the additional services by logistics service providers ("value-added services") are gaining importance. Cluster managements are active in Schleswig-Holstein, for the Hamburg area (divided into northern and southern metropolitan region) and especially for the region of Lübeck-Ostholstein. Hamburg, with its international seaport and airport, forms the heart of the logistics cluster. Not only is the largest member of the logistics network, the HHLA (Hamburger Hafen und Logistik AG), with 3,500 employees located here, but Hamburg is also home to a wide range of educational and research facilities within the logistics sector. Nearly 70,000 people are employed in logistics in Hamburg. Throughout the entire metropolitan region the number is likely to exceed 100,000. In Schleswig-Holstein, we estimate the numbers to be approx. 30,000 to 40,000 employees, including about 12,000 employees in the south of the state (belonging to the Hamburg metropolis) and nearly 9,000 employees, each in the regions of Lübeck and Kiel. Lübeck-Travemünde with its Baltic Sea port forms a main area of maritime logistics in Schleswig-Holstein. Long-term prospects for logistics and, particularly, for value added services are still favourable due to the continuing globalisation and segmentation of production. However competition between the different logistics networks, particularly in North Western Europe, is intense. The logistics cluster in Schleswig-Holstein and Hamburg has specific specialisation advantages in the areas of health care logistics, logistics for the food industry, press and printing logistics and maritime logistics.

The maritime cluster is a composite cluster, which consists of several partial networks and has a broad range of content. General focus is on maritime subjects, especially maritime navigation, port services, shipbuilding and marine engineering, but also marine equipment suppliers and service providers, oceanography (blue biotechnology), marine food (and fishing), aqua and mariculture and marine tourism[x]. The Hamburg metropolitan region is the centre of the North German network, albeit the identification of people with the maritime industry is also very strong in Schleswig-Holstein and in particular in the Baltic cities of Lübeck, Kiel and Flensburg, not least because of the historical roots of the maritime economy.

Within the maritime cluster, distinctions must be made between industries and areas that are clearly maritime and industries whose production is only partially oriented towards the maritime segment. Moreover, the logistical element of the maritime cluster is an integral part of the logistics cluster, and one can find offshore technology also as part of the wind power cluster. In this respect, the exact scale of the cluster is difficult to quantify. In the uniquely maritime areas, we have registered about 20,000 employees in Schleswig-Holstein and about 30,000 employees in Hamburg, a further 20,000-30,000 employees are outside this core area, most likely within the maritime industry. Because of Schleswig-Holstein's regional policy's focus on cluster promotion over many years, a cluster management has been in existence since 2005 while in Hamburg it is still under construction. Many classic cluster elements such as educational and research facilities, network-supporting institutions or special maritime service providers, are strongly represented in Hamburg but are also present in the maritime locations in Schleswig-Holstein. The outlook for the cluster is considered positive due to the long-term growth of the maritime industry. On the other hand, other segments of the maritime industries face strong worldwide competition, particularly conventional shipbuilding. An answer to this challenge is (a) a stronger specialisation on elements (e.g. special shipbuilding, ship construction, nautical engineering, offshore engineering), where assembly and research and development are spatially linked to each other and (b) a strengthening of external relations, on the one hand, with the maritime network in Mecklenburg-Vorpommern and on the other, with other EU locations in Denmark, Norway, The Netherlands or the United Kingdom.

The food cluster typically represents a value-based chain from agricultural production via food processing and through to marketing, retail and restaurants. Indirectly, this cluster also includes specific manufacturing production, such as mechanical engineering, refrigeration, canning and packaging technologies as well as logistics[xi]. Schleswig-Holstein's share of the agriculture market is above the German average and the food sector is the third largest manufacturing industry in the state. In this respect, the food cluster in Schleswig-Holstein is more significant than in Hamburg. However, Hamburg accounts for a share of the marketing (wholesale), complementary services and specific educational and research institutions. Furthermore, the southern area of the metropolitan region of Hamburg is strongly influenced by a network of intensive agriculture and food processing, especially in fruit growing. Within the region of Schleswig-Holstein, the Lübeck-Ostholstein region has an intensive network of food industries with some internationally operating companies as well as educational and research institutions. Here the cluster management for Schleswig-Holstein and particularly for the Lübeck region was founded in 2006 ("FoodRegio", a department in the Lübeck's business development agency). Later, a second management body emerged in Flensburg

("Network of excellence for food"), which initially focused on the food industry in the northern part of Schleswig-Holstein, but recently has become more representative of the state as a whole. A third management unit, the "Süderelbe AG", is responsible for Hamburg's southern hinterland, co-operating closely with FoodRegio in Lübeck. Within the core of the food cluster, excluding agriculture, retail and hospitality, close to 40,000 people work in Schleswig-Holstein's food industry, including more than 11,000 in the region of Lübeck-Ostholstein. In Hamburg we have registered around 20,000 employees. Represented by its management FoodRegio, Lübeck's network is both a member of the "German Food Net" which is the management of all German food clusters and, therefore, maintains contact with the food industry in Mecklenburg-Vorpommern. FoodRegio is also a co-initiator of closer orientation towards the Baltic Sea region and an original member of the Baltfood network for the food industry.

The aviation and aircraft cluster is clearly focused on Hamburg and on three leading firms located in the hanseatic city. With over 20,000 employees, Airbus is the largest company in Hamburg. Together with the Lufthansa Technik and Hamburg Airport, Airbus has a key role in the cluster. After Seattle and Toulouse, Hamburg is the world's third largest area for the aircraft industry (Pfahler & Lublinski 2003). The aviation cluster relies on two main pillars: aircraft, with a diverse network of small and medium suppliers across the metropolitan region, and all aspects of airport operations (including logistics). In the aircraft industry, the cluster has its focus in interior design (cabin interior systems) and in all stages of the life cycle of an aircraft (maintenance, repair, modification), showing parallels with the maritime cluster in the interior construction (cabins for passenger ships) – a particular advantage of the combination of the two clusters at one location. Overall, almost 30,000 people work in these two cluster areas in Hamburg. Moreover, the workforce within the supplier industries in the Hamburg area, especially in the northern part of Lower Saxony but also in Schleswig-Holstein, here in excess of 2,000 jobs. In addition to the main firms that control the cluster together with the Hamburg Ministry of Economic Affairs and Labour, the clusters have many educational and research facilities in Hamburg, making the city a world-leading location for training in the aeronautical professions. Although further expansion of the aviation industry seems certain with its two components mentioned above, the prospects of the aviation industry cluster in the Hamburg region still depend on the location decisions of its main corporations.

The information technology (IT) and media cluster consists (a) of a technological part of information technology (IT), sometimes called "information and communication technology (ICT)", which is composed of equipment and software technology, and (b) of the

tertiary part of the media industry (television, film, print media, music, publishing, public relations). As a cross-section technology, IT is spread over many industries. In Schleswig-Holstein, the technology has no specific regional focus, aside from the fact that it is more present in urban than in rural areas. In Schleswig-Holstein, about 24,000 employees work in the IT industry with more than 30,000 in Hamburg. In Hamburg, the media industry is an important factor with around 35,000 jobs compared with Schleswig-Holstein's 15,000. In Hamburg, the share of media employees in the overall economy is more than twice as high as in Germany so Hamburg is the leading media location in the northern part of Germany. This is supported by several educational and research institutions, which are located in Hamburg in large numbers and great variety and relate particularly to the media sector. However, Kiel and Lübeck are also locations for education and research in the IT and media segments. The connection between the two sections results on the one hand from "media convergence", i.e. the increasing integration between technology (IT) and contents (media) and on the other, from the co-operation between the two network managements, the Digital Industry Association of Schleswig-Holstein (DiWiSH) and the initiative "hamburg@work". Both have links to the network in Mecklenburg-Vorpommern, represented by the IT Initiative (ITI-MV).

The micro-technology cluster consists of several elements: the most important are micro and nanotechnology, power electronics, silicon technology, micro-sensorics or semi-conductor physics. They form the input for a variety of production lines, including medical, environmental and transport engineering, IT, machinery, vehicle or electric motors and they are, therefore, also part of other clusters, IT, life science (nano-biotechnology) or food, for example. In the south-western part of Schleswig-Holstein, a micro-technology cluster is established in Itzehoe with approx. 700 employees. Because of its relatively small size it should rather be called a competence-centre although it clearly has the qualities and vision for achieving a cluster size. The cluster management comes under the Innovation Centre Itzehoe (IZET) and its main enterprise, Vishay Siliconix, is located close to a number of spin-offs. The third pillar is the Fraunhofer Institute for Silicon Technology (ISIT), a research institution of excellence located at an adjacent site. Thus, geographical proximity between research, production and management is second-to-none. Outside Itzehoe, close relations have been established with educational and research competencies at the University of Kiel and the TU Hamburg-Harburg through the network of the North German Initiative for Nanomaterials (NINa).

The wind power and renewable energy cluster is of outstanding importance in Schleswig-Holstein and centred on the west coast and Fehmarn. Currently, nearly 2,600 wind turbines produce an estimated 40 per cent of the state's electricity requirements. The wind power cluster not only includes generation of energy by wind but it also affects many other industries, starting with mechanical and electrical engineering to measuring and control instruments as well as many other technologies. Moreover, it includes a service chain with regard to the development and construction of wind turbines, their installation and maintenance as well as energy storage and power supply. In this process, Schleswig-Holstein is rather focused on production, installation and maintenance, while Hamburg is more focused on management, planning and consulting. Since wind power is used on land as well as increasingly offshore there are overlaps between the wind power and maritime cluster. Within Schleswig-Holstein, the west coast and especially the city of Husum have particular focus on the cluster, with the Network Agency "Windkomm" and key companies such as Vestas and RePower Systems located here. Their headquarters, however, lie outside the region (Vestas is based in Randers, Denmark). Husum is home to the world's most important trade fair "Wind Energy" and a large number of medium-sized firms based here are part of the wind cluster supply chain. Education and research facilities, however, are mainly located in the cities of Kiel and Flensburg. This also applies to other forms of renewable energy, such as the bio-energy sector. For the west coast of Schleswig-Holstein and Husum, the cluster has a significant regional impact, but for Schleswig-Holstein/Hamburg in general its influence is relatively modest compared to other clusters. Around 9,000 employees in Schleswig-Holstein and approximately 2,000 employees in Hamburg work in the wind energy and renewable energy sector.

STRONG CLUSTERS: CO-OPERATION OPPORTUNITIES

Scania, Zealand, Bornholm, Schleswig-Holstein, Hamburg and Mecklenburg-Vorpommern each have their own industrial profiles and focus on specific clusters and their development. While these regions differ, their clusters, nevertheless, have fairly similar focus. The objective of this chapter is to identify clusters of potential co-operation. The obvious strategy is based on the fact that life science and health are important industrial sectors in most parts of the Fehmarnbelt Region. This corresponds to the research focus of many universities and is reflected in the cluster policy of the relevant organisations. The industrial sectors of food and of information technology (plus the media) are also widely present in the Fehmarnbelt Region. These play major roles in the regional economies and are subject to further cluster development efforts. A fourth area with partnership potential is logistics with focus on the maritime segment while wind energy/green technology is a fifth area, with tourism (inclusive of business tourism) competing the list of six main clusters. Other sectors are strong but only in parts of the region. Maritime industry plays an important role in all north German regions. Nanotechnology is important in Schleswig-Holstein and Scania and the financial sector (with business to business services) – in Copenhagen and Hamburg, where the cultural segment is important, as are airport related activities. Aviation is strong in Hamburg but we have been unable to identify supplementary elements in other parts of the Fehmarnbelt Region although such development would be desirable due to the central role of the industry.

Life science/health is present as a cluster in all regions. The external relations of the Schleswig-Holstein/Hamburg life science cluster are closely oriented towards neighbours in the Baltic Sea region, especially with the life science network in Mecklenburg-Vorpommern (BioConValley). Based on the participation in the ScanBalt network (meta-cluster life science in the Baltic Sea region), connections have been established to one of the strongest life science clusters in Europe, the Medicon Valley of the Øresund Region. With the expansion of this link, not least inspired by the upgrading of the transport corridor between Hamburg-Lübeck and Copenhagen-Malmö and promoted by the two networks' different and complementary priorities, a "twin" life science cluster in the Fehmarnbelt Region would achieve an absolute top position in Europe.

Food networks and clusters across the Fehmarnbelt Region are partners as well, particularly between North Germany and the Øresund food network together with the Scania industry of food products innovation. Objectives and recommendations for the future are the establishment of a common cluster management for the region of Schleswig-Holstein and the metropolitan region of Hamburg and an intensification of relations with the Øresund food network, for which a fixed Fehmarnbelt link could serve as a catalyst.

The information technology (IT) and media cluster should focus on co-operation between the Hamburg and the Copenhagen parts of the Fehmarnbelt Region, especially with regards to the media sector, as Hamburg and Copenhagen are the two most important media locations in the Western Baltic Sea area. Despite the fact that the language barrier is particularly relevant here, there is considerable potential for co-operation which can be increased by the establishment a fixed Fehmarnbelt link.

Links to the logistics networks in the Baltic Sea region are supported by the LogOnBaltic network. In connection with the future upgrading of the Fehmarnbelt corridor, co-operation between the logistics cluster of Northern Germany and the Øresund Region is a growth factor in the promotion of and coordination of the logistics industry, especially along the Fehmarnbelt corridor. The aim is to form a "Fehmarnbelt logistics cluster" connecting the two centres of gravity, Hamburg/Lübeck and Copenhagen/Malmö.

The generation and use of renewable energy (wind) is a growing segment in the world economy. Although international competition has intensified significantly in recent years, there are competitive bases in Denmark, the Netherlands and Germany (Lower Saxony, Mecklenburg-Vorpommern) and these relationships are ever increasing. There are currently partnerships between Northern Germany and Southern/Western Denmark's large companies and between the University of Flensburg and the University of Southern Denmark (together with regional development agencies) within the "FURGY" project ("Future Renewable Energy"). This could be a pattern for co-operation between the German and the Danish part of the Fehmarnbelt Region, and should include companies and research institutions in Region Zealand.

Tourism is important to the regional economies but is a sector in which the regions are considered competitors. Hamburg and Copenhagen compete when it comes to metropolitan tourism (including business tourism – i.e. meetings, conferences, events. The two metropolises also compete for cultural tourism and for families looking for a metropolitan

FIGURE 13.
POTENTIAL CLUSTER COOPERATION

Present in all regions:
- Life science/health
- Food
- Information technology (plus the media)
- Logistics (with focus on maritime)
- Wind energy/green technology
- Tourism (inclusive of business tourism)

Present in some regions:
- Financial sector (with business services)
- Cultural sector (media)
- Airport related activities, civil aviation
- Nanotechnology
- Maritime industries

product. The many fine beaches and coastal areas of the Fehmarnbelt Region are also attractive destinations, especially for families but also for water-based sports. Although competition is a key element, co-operation opportunities should be examined and common cluster development placed on the agenda.

Nanotechnology cluster relations between Northern Germany and Scandinavia or Denmark are mainly linked to the University of Southern Denmark in Sønderborg. Given the strong competition between the micro-technology clusters in Germany, e.g. in Saxony, building cooperative links with other networks makes sense. There is currently considerable pressure on establishing partnerships within material technology/nanotechnology in relation to a number of existing and planned research facilities in megaformat. Regarding the future changes to the Fehmarnbelt Region, there will be opportunities for potential co-operation with the Øresund Region (for more details, see Chapter 8).

Finally, we believe that partnership opportunities for Copenhagen and Hamburg should be tested in respect of financial and related services and for the cultural sector in general. Work within the cultural sector could also be related to the media world. The same is the case with airport-related activities.

REFERENCES

Bornholms Vækstforum,'*Erhvervsudviklingsstrategi 2007 – 2010. Det unikke Bornholm. Vækst via kreativitet og kvalitet!*', 2008

By- og Landskabsstyrelsen, '*Danske bebyggelsers regionale erhvervsfunktioner*', 2007

Copenhagen Economics, '*Udgangspunkt for vækst i Region Zealand. De første skridt til et faktabaseret grundlag*', 2005

Danmarks Statistik, Statistikbanken, 2010

Erhvervsfremmestyrelsen, '*Kompetenceklynger i dansk erhvervsliv*', 2001

FORA, '*Baggrundspapir om regionens stærke klynger*', 2008

Forsknings- og Innovationsstyrelsen, '*Den danske erhvervsstruktur – udviklingstendenser og dynamic*', 2008

Georg & Ottenströer, Regionomica, '*Regionales Entwicklungskonzept in Folge einer festen Fehmarnbelt-Querung*', intermediate report, Hamburg, Berlin, 2009

Handelskammer Hamburg, Industrie- und Handelskammer Schleswig-Holstein, '*Eckpunkte-Papier zu einer gemeinsamen Clusterpolitik in Hamburg und Schleswig-Holstein*', Hamburg, Kiel, 2009

H. Herrmann & K. Krey, '*Innovations- und Technologiepotentiale in Schleswig-Holstein und Hamburg*', J. Bröcker (Ed.), '*Beiträge aus dem Institut für Regionalforschung der Universität Kiel*', 2007 No. 42

J. Herzberg, '*Clusterbasierte Wirtschaftsförderungsstrategien in strukturschwächeren Regionen (unter beispielhafter Betrachtung clusterpolitischer Strategien in Schleswig-Holstein)*', Diploma Thesis, Institut für Geographie, Universität Hamburg, 2006

Institut für Arbeit und Technik (IAT), '*Gesundheit ist Zukunft, Die Gesundheitswirtschaft in Schleswig-Holstein – Entwicklungsfelder und Handlungsempfehlungen*', report ordered by Ministerium für Soziales, Gesundheit, Familie, Jugend und Senioren des Landes Schleswig-Holstein, Gelsenkirchen, 2009

A. Isaksen & A. E. Hauge, '*Regional Clusters in Europe*', Brussels, European Commission, 2002, Observatory of European SME's no. 3

ISL- Baltic Consult, '*Cross Border Exchange – Logistische Potenziale des Landes Schleswig-Holstein in der VIKING-Region*', report ordered by Ministerium für Wissenschaft, Wirtschaft und Verkehr des Landes Schleswig-Holstein, Lübeck, 2005

Kompetenznetze Deutschland – Networking for Innovation, Benchmarking des Kompetenznetzwerkes Ernährungswirtschaft Schleswig-Holstein, Berlin, 2009

MC Marketing Consulting, dsn – 'Projekte und Studien für Wirtschaft und Gesellschaft, Maritime Technologien Schleswig-Holstein', report ordered by Ministerium für Wissenschaft, Wirtschaft und Verkehr des Landes Schleswig-Holstein, Kiel, 2006

M. Nilsson, M. Svensson-Henning & O. Wilkenson, 'Skånska kluster och profilområden – en kritisk granskning', Region Skåne, 2002

Nord/LB, Ernst Basler + Partner, MR Gesellschaft für Regionalberatung, 'Maritime Industrie in der Metropolregion Hamburg', report ordered by Behörde für Wirtschaft und Arbeit der Freien und Hansestadt Hamburg, Hanover, 2009

OECD Territorial Reviews, Copenhagen, Denmark, 2009

Oxford research, 'København på det finansielle verdenskort', København, 2009

W. Pfähler & A.E. Lublinski, 'Luftfahrt-Cluster Hamburg Norddeutschland. Bestandsaufnahme, Perspektiven und Vision für die Zulieferindustrie', Peter Lang, Frankfurt/Main, 2003

M.E. Porter, 'The Competitive Advantage of Nations', London, Macmillan, 1990

M.E. Porter, 'On Competition', Boston, Harvard Business School Press, 1998

M.E. Porter, (2003), The Economic Performance of Regions. Regional Studies, vol. 37, 6 & 7

J. Revilla-Diez & O. Brandt, 'Clusterstudie Ernährungswirtschaft in Schleswig-Holstein, Expert Report by Geographisches Institut, Universität Kiel', report ordered by Ministerium für Wissenschaft, Wirtschaft und Verkehr des Landes Schleswig-Holstein, Kiel, 2005

K. Schrader & C-F. Laaser, R. Soltwedel et al., 'Potenziale und Chancen zum Aufbau einer gemeinsamen Wirtschaftsregion Schleswig-Holstein und Hamburg', report ordered by Staatskanzlei des Landes Schleswig-Holstein, Kiel, 2007

Ö. Sölvell, G. Lindqvist & C. Ketels, 'The Cluster Initiative Greenbook', Stockholm, Ivory Tower AB, 2003

VDI/VDE Innovation + Technik, dsn – Projekte und Studien für Wirtschaft und Gesellschaft, 'Evaluation für Clustermanagements', report ordered by Ministerium für Wissenschaft, Wirtschaft und Verkehr des Landes Schleswig-Holstein, Berlin, Kiel, 2008

Økonomi- og erhvervsministeriet, 'Baggrundsrapport til regionalpolitisk vækstredegørelse', 2008

Øresund Org, Øresund Org is the common brand for activities run by Øresund University and Øresund Science Region, www.oresund.org

NOTES

[i] Growth Forum is the regional organisation on economic growth. Denmark is devided into 6 such bodies, each composed of politicians and industrial and organisational leaders.

[ii] From the OECD Metropolitan database the following cities (functional urban regions) were selected for comparison with Copenhagen: Vienna, Brussels, Prague, Athens, Oslo, Lisbon, Paris, Budapest, Seoul, Madrid and London.

[iii] Including Bornholm

[iv] The term "competence field" is not precisely defined, but covers a group of industries related by their production focus.

[v] Copenhagen Economics (2005): The Copenhagen Economics definition of clusters is very wide.

[vi] The term "competence field" is not precisely defined, but covers a group of industries related by their production focus.

[vii] Cooperation between companies, universities and government

[viii] Main references for the description of the clusters are: Schrader, Laaser, Soltwedel (2007), Herrmann, Krey (2007), Herzberg (2006) and Handelskammer Hamburg (2009), plus special internet information, mainly from Federal State Governments and Cluster Managements, as well as expert reports and our interviews with the cluster managers. Expert report for the Life Science Cluster: Institut für Arbeit und Technik (2009).

[ix] Expert Report for Logistics Cluster in Schleswig-Holstein: ISL – Baltic Consult (2005).

[x] Expert Reports for the Maritime Clusters in Schleswig-Holstein and Hamburg: MC Marketing Consulting, dsn (2006), Nord/LB, Ernst Basler+Partner, MR (2009).

[xi] Expert Reports for Food Cluster in Schleswig-Holstein: Kompetenznetze Deutschland (2009), Revilla-Diez (2005)

8

CHAPTER 8
THE WORLD OF SCIENCE: CENTRES, NETWORKS, DEVELOPMENT OPPORTUNITIES

SØREN FIND, CHRISTIAN WICHMANN MATTHIESSEN
& ANNETTE WINKEL SCHWARZ

Today's society is often described as a knowledge-based society because knowledge and information are key input and output and because innovation and creativity carry a premium. The knowledge economy is characterised by the increasing speeds at which information and knowledge spread along many and changing channels. The knowledge economy is a network economy characterised by a mixture of centre hierarchies and diffuse interaction. Cohesion and proximity play a role, as does critical mass. Decision-makers believe that the productivity and competitiveness of cities and regions are increasingly linked to the development and distribution of knowledge and that no region can thrive economically without some form of link-up to innovative sources.

In the new economic geography, the productivity carrying infrastructure will increasingly comprise communication channels, with cities and regions regarded as centres in the network. The driver of prosperity will no longer be access to resources and capital, but to intellectual and creative ideas distributed across various types of networks. More than ever before, growth and prosperity will be dependent on the ability to create ideas and knowledge. It could be said that this is all about being linked to intellectual capital as closely as

possible. The build-up of human capital is a significant factor behind the success or failure of cities and it is the accessibility to knowledge and skills that plays the biggest role for companies in growth. Research is a main driver behind the world's development and change. The world of science is a complex system that, however, resembles other productive systems in that input is transformed into output. Accessibility to the output of the world of science is crucial to the success or failure of cities, regions and countries.

More and more, universities, research institutions, companies and political leaders are interacting in the effort to create a sound knowledge base for their city, region or nation. This is because a local knowledge base is of rising importance to local economic growth, and a high and growing investment level in research and development has a value for other sectors. The commercial spin-off of research results shows that there is significant interaction between local/regional universities and local/regional growth. The promotion of local knowledge takes place regardless of the fact that many believe that distance plays an increasingly insignificant role and that access to knowledge and information is becoming universal. There has, indeed, been a remarkable fall in communication and transport costs in recent decades, which has resulted in the emergence of long-distance networks.

In a city-related context, the science-producing entities are often metropolises (e.g. Berlin, Stockholm, the Øresund City[i], Hamburg) although cities with lesser status also play a role within the scientific world. These can be cities organised around universities and campuses (such as Cambridge, Heidelberg, Uppsala) or possibly major cities without metropolis status where research linked to local commercial activities is an important part of the city's profile (e.g. Gothenburg, Dresden, Eindhoven). Moreover, there are many current examples of how governments at various levels promote urban development by establishing research growth centres (e.g. Aalborg, Umeå and Lübeck).

Centres that comprise research and science are, per definition, creative and innovative. Even small and medium-sized cities have the ability to create ideas and transplant them to local commercial life and even small knowledge centres comprise an often overlooked function as import centres for innovation. This is because scientists need to be updated on the latest research and methodology – otherwise they will not be taken seriously. Active scientists spread their knowledge to the local community not only through the graduates they educate, but also through formal and informal networks.

Proximity is important. If you ask scientists about their individual co-operation patterns they will often answer that these are global. However, if summed up, it is revealed that distance is the best explanation of interaction between regions. Synergies between ideas and direct face-to-face communication remain important factors behind productivity and superior to other types of contact – you will only build trust in another person if you maintain eye contact. Trust is, in fact, particularly important for joint innovation processes. Owing to its complexity, strategic planning requires proximity and the same applies to the micro-adjustment of plans and agreements. Knowledge is often codified and, therefore, commonly available, but non-tangible knowledge requires proximity in order to be exchanged. Finally, cultural proximity plays a role. Common norms and values facilitate partnerships.

Scientific results are produced by both academic researchers and researchers in private companies, organisations and public institutions. Scientific results are presented in the form of publications or patents. In this chapter, we focus on the world of science and take our analytical starting point in urban regions. We begin by analysing global research centres and the development in science's overall urban system from 1996-1998 to 2006-2008. We measure the size of cities in scientific output and we examine growth conditions and partnership relations in order to establish the roles of cities in the Fehmarnbelt Region. The result is summarised in diagrams showing the roles of cities. We detail the analysis for Denmark, Sweden and Germany and focus on the major knowledge centres in the Fehmarnbelt Region, the Øresund City, Hamburg, Kiel, Rostock and Lübeck with a few excursions to Stockholm-Uppsala and Berlin. Specialisation profiles for the major knowledge cities in Scania, Zealand, Schleswig-Holstein, Hamburg and parts of Mecklenburg-Vorpommern provide opportunities for determining potential partnership relations that may develop the region.

DATA

Measuring the scope of scientific productions or output is difficult. For the purpose of this report, we have used bibliometric methodology. Science Citation Index is a registration of all scientific papers and articles within natural science, medicine and technology in the world's 6,500 most cited scientific journals and other key international research publications. The individual bibliometric entities (papers) are given with detailed bibliographical information, including the author's institutional address, categorisation according to scientific discipline and registration of citations. Bibliometric methods are criticised because they comprise a number of inherent error sources. For instance, there is a difference between publication tradition from country to country, from institution to institution and from scientific discipline to scientific discipline. The English language occupies a key role, which favours English-speaking scientists. Despite these shortcomings, bibliometric methodology is, in general, believed to be the best way to register output of scientific results. The number of patents could also have been used, but this is even more complex. The use of the bibliometric analysis method is described in more detail in Matthiessen & Schwarz (1999) and Matthiessen, Schwarz & Find (2000, 2002 (a) and (b), 2006, 2010)[ii].

Based on these data, each paper is registered according to the city the author gives as the base of his/her institution. We have attempted to provide a spatial demarcation of cities, i.e. as functional units which, in practice, means that we have included the cities' daily hinterland. This, in turn, means that the cities are defined as urban regions so that, for instance, Copenhagen comprises the current metropolitan area with its approximately 1.8 million inhabitants. Moreover, we have combined neighbouring cities into one unit if the distance between their centres is less than 45 minutes of land transport. We have defined the world's approximately 100 largest conurbations measured in scientific output. If there are several authors from different cities, the publication incorporates all given cities[iii].

FIGURE 1.
THE WORLD'S 30 LARGEST COUNTRIES MEASURED BY POPULATION (2010[iv]) AND IN SCIENTIFIC OUTPUT WITHIN THE NATURAL SCIENCES, MEDICINE AND ENGINEERING (2006-2008[v])

Population: the area of countries is proportional to the population figures

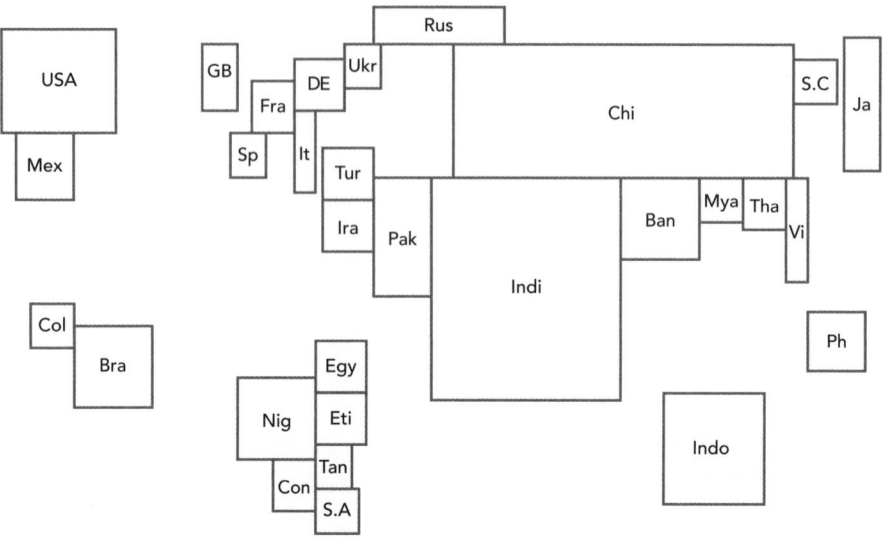

Scientific output: the area of countries is proportional to the number of papers

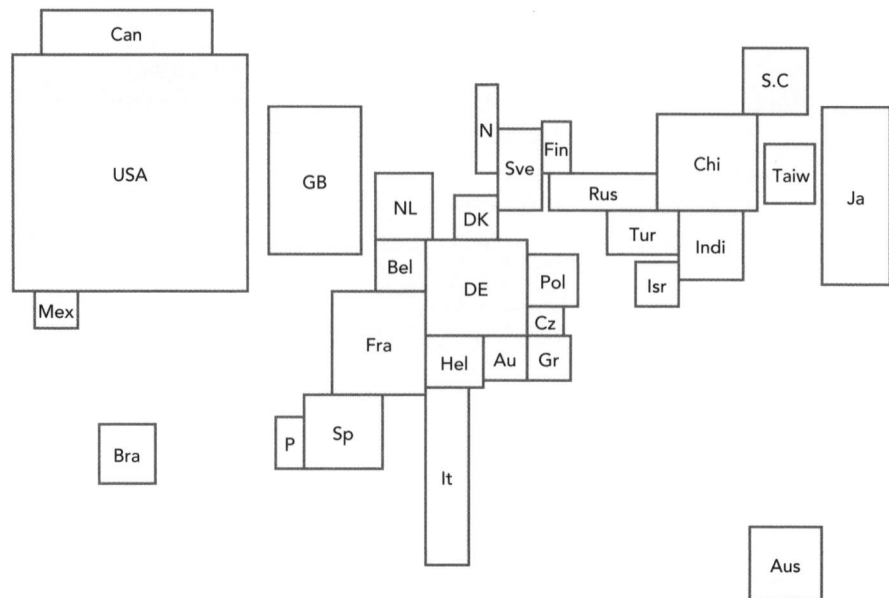

In this way, we have combined bibliometric methodology with a spatial demarcation of the city regions and have thus achieved an indicator of the individual city's scientific production.

HEAVY RESEARCH CENTRES: A GLOBAL PERSPECTIVE

In general, a country's size is measured by area or population. With regard to the latter, Europe is a small continent and even European countries that appear large are small seen within a global context. In terms of population figures, the largest European country (Russia) is the world's ninth largest. With 81.9 million inhabitants, Germany is 14th and Sweden with 9.1 million is 85th. Denmark's population of 5.4 million ranks 106th in the world. However, if a country's size is measured by scientific output for the period 2006-2008, the picture looks different. Europe is now a major continent, the UK is the second largest in the world and with 301,779 papers Germany ranks third. Sweden is 18th with 64,742 papers while Denmark, which produced 37,623 papers over the period, is 24th. Figure 1. shows the world's 30 largest countries measured by population or scientific output.

Measured by research results within medicine, technology and natural science, the world's 30 largest cities account for approximately 36 per cent of global scientific production. This reflects a formidable concentration that has been growing at considerable pace. Between 1996-1998, the number of papers totalled 2,790,000 of which 33 per cent derived from the 30 largest research centres. From 2002-2004, the corresponding figures were 3,140,000 and 35 per cent and for the period 2006-2008, the figures were 3,960,000 with 36 per cent relating to academia's top 30 cities. The growth figure for the world's top 30 research centres is 54 per cent from 1996-1998 to 2006-2008 against corresponding growth figures for the entire world's scientific output of 41 per cent. The concentration pattern and the increasing level of centralisation of research results indicates that large centres have certain advantages. These include interaction between many different research fields, major institutions and companies on a large scale. There is also a market for innovation and for selling strongly specialised products. Researchers are creative people and, therefore, also creative consumers whether they work in the academic world or in research-oriented companies. Creative consumer opportunities are concentrated on the large cities which, in addition, are also often well placed within the world's networks, such as air traffic networks.

Scientific centres are concentrated in specific parts of the world, namely North America, Europe (especially Northern Europe) and South East Asia (see Figure 2). Between 1996-1998, the list of the world's scientific heavyweights included 15 European, 13 North American and two Asian centres. The corresponding figure for 2006-2008 comprises 12

FIGURE 2.
THE SCIENTIFIC WORLD'S GLOBAL CENTRES
TOP 30

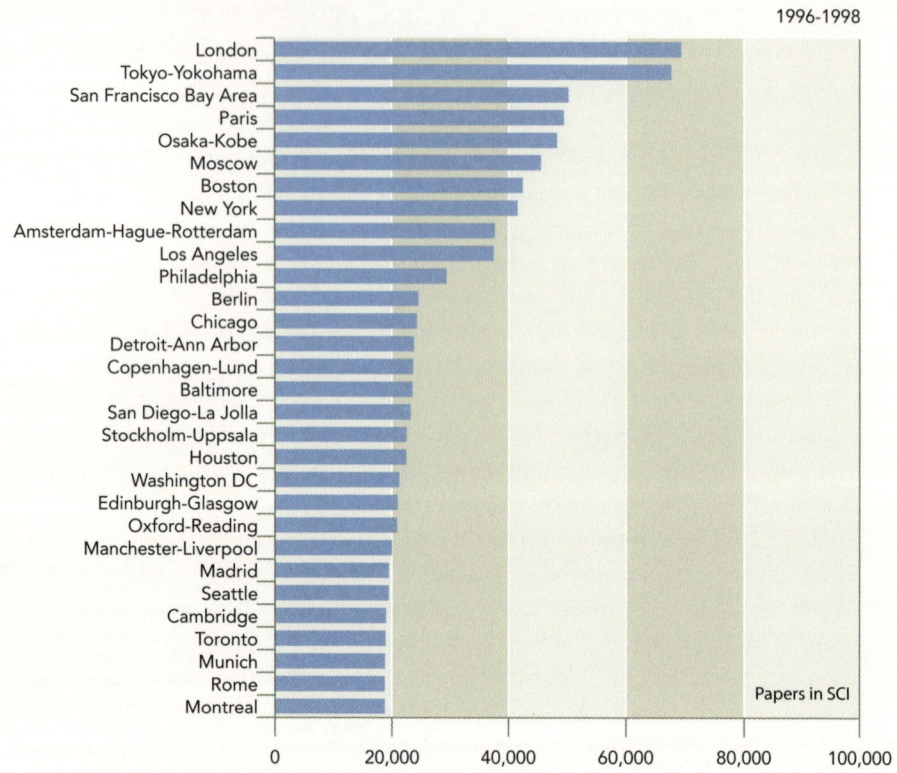

European, 12 North American, five Asian and one South American centre. Tokyo-Yokohama and London rank top for all three periods. These are of equal size and in a class of their own, but between 1996-1998 and 2006-2008 switched places in favour of the Japanese centre. These two cities are the real world cities in terms of research. On the level below them, there are nine centres in each of the diagrams. Between the periods 1996-1998 and 2006-2008, this group included San Francisco, Paris, Osaka-Kobe, Boston, New York, the Amsterdam Region and Los Angeles. In the period 1996-1998, Moscow and Philadelphia were members of the group although between 2006-2008 they were superseded and replaced by Beijing and Seoul. Between them, the two top levels in 1996-1998 comprised

FIGURE 2. (CONTINUED)
THE SCIENTIFIC WORLD'S GLOBAL CENTRES
TOP 30

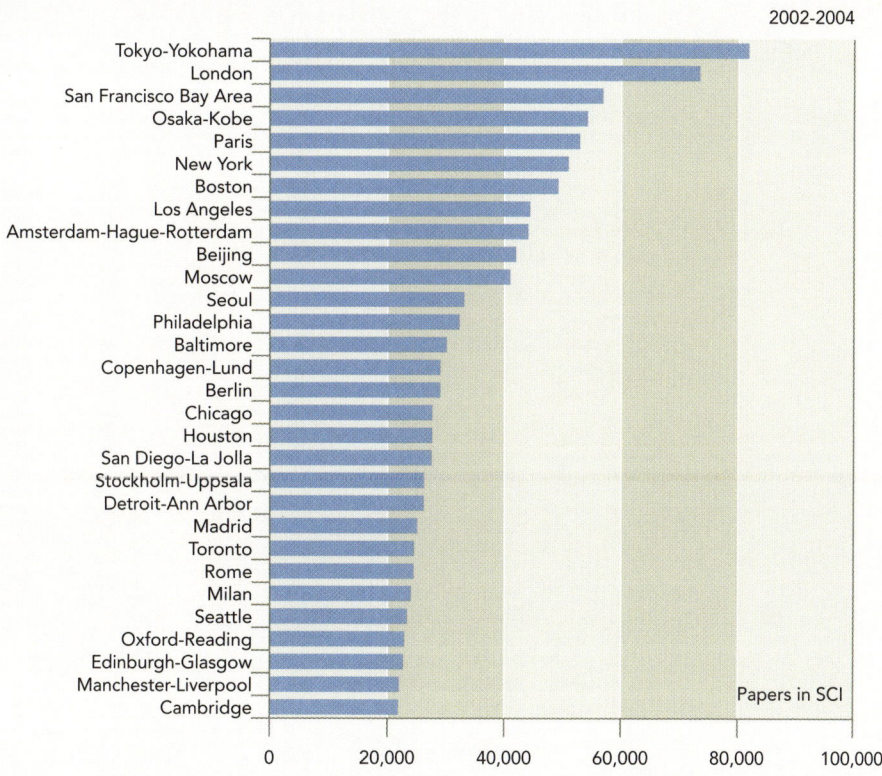

five North American, four European and two Asian centres. 10 years later, the top levels comprise three North American, three European and four Asian centres. Worldwide there is a third level comprising Berlin, Copenhagen-Lund and Stockholm-Uppsala. The diagrams show that although a considerable inertia is noticeable in the three top 30 lists, there are also dramatic movements both upwards and downwards. The traditional scientific "centres of gravity" in Europe and North America are under pressure from new Asian and South American centres. Moreover, North European cities have come under pressure from Southern European cities.

FIGURE 2. (CONTINUED)
THE SCIENTIFIC WORLD'S GLOBAL CENTRES
TOP 30

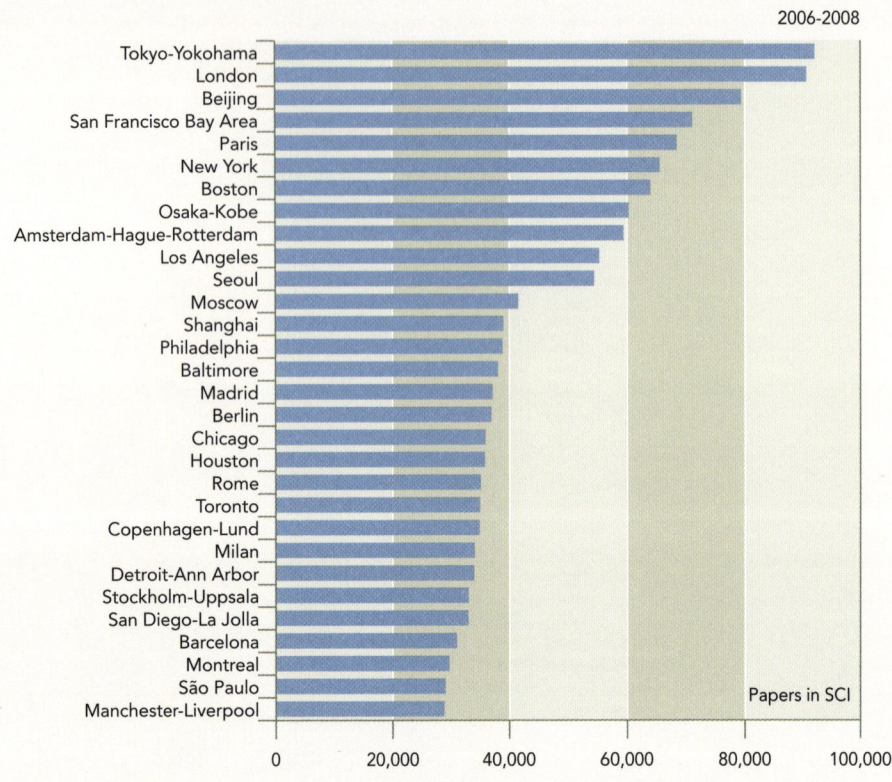

The top 30 lists pinpoint the winners and losers, with the big winners being Beijing, Seoul, Shanghai and São Paolo. None of these was in the 1996-1998 top 30 list, but advanced more than 25 places to their prominent positions in 2006-2008. Before long, Beijing can be expected to join the two current members of the very top level. Madrid, Rome, Milan and Barcelona are also among the winners group, although they have advanced less dramatically than the four previously-mentioned cities. As there are winners there are also losers. At the top 30 level, the loser group comprises 12 centres, all from Northern Europe and the United States. Among the losers are Moscow, Copenhagen-Lund, Detroit-Ann

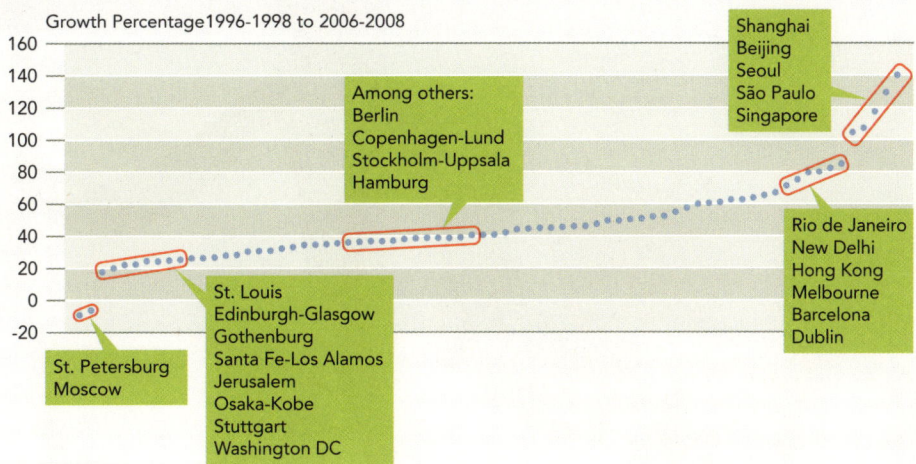

**FIGURE 3.
SCIENTIFIC GLOBAL CENTRES
TOP 75**

Arbor, Stockholm-Uppsala, San Diego-La Jolla and Manchester-Liverpool. Washington DC, Berlin, Chicago, Edinburgh-Glasgow, Oxford-Reading and Cambridge also belong to this category.

If the number of large cities is extended from the above top 30 to the top 75 and the real growth figures are calculated, the development pattern is further illustrated, see Figure 3. The major winners are the four Asian cities and São Paolo followed by one South American, two Asian, one Australian and two European centres. The losers are the two Russian cities, which are in minus, and three North American, three European, one Japanese and one Israeli centre. In terms of growth, the major cities in the extended Fehmarnbelt Region are in the lower centre of the field.

SCIENTIFIC CO-OPERATION: GLOBAL NETWORK

The weight of scientific production is an attribute variable which describes the role of the city on the scientific map. Collaboration between scientists from different cities, as expressed by co-authorships of publications presented in the world's leading scientific journals is a network variable, which describes networks and centres and thus indicates which

centres play leading roles and which centres play secondary roles. A scientific partnership that leads to a publication in an international scientific competitive journal is an expression of a strong partnership. Not only have there been discussions about doing something and planning it, but the plans have been executed and the results presented to scientists worldwide. In Figure 4 for each of the world's 40 largest research centres, relative co-operation with 39 others, as expressed by co-authorships (percentage) in relation to the size of the city, is shown. The figure shows how strongly the collaboration is influenced by the English language. English centres followed by North American cites (with Washington DC as the exception) account for the largest degree of cooperation. Next follow the European centres while the lowest level of cooperation is represented by the rapidly growing new Asian centres together with Sydney (which is the exception to the rule regarding the English language's impact on co-operation frequency) and São Paolo.

We have analysed the collaboration patterns between the world's 40 largest scientific centres by linking observed collaboration to what is expected. The expected collaboration between two research centres is calculated as the proportion of the overall observed

FIGURE 4.
SCIENCES' GLOBAL CENTRES
STRONG COLLABORATIVE RELATIONSHIPS (2006-2008)

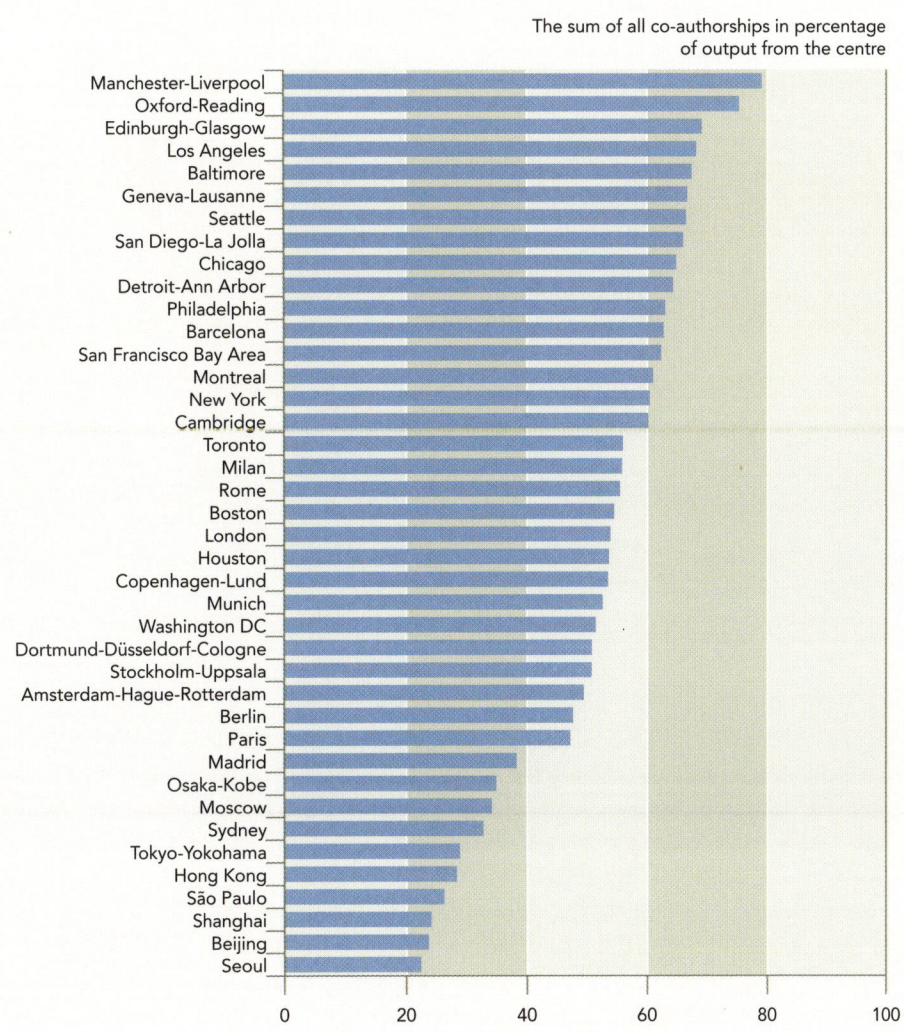

Top 40 cities measured as the total number of co-authors from the 39 other largest global scientific centres. The figure denotes this value as a percentage of the city's overall scientific output measured by papers.

**FIGURE 5.
SCIENCES' GLOBAL CENTRES
TOP 40 CITIES**

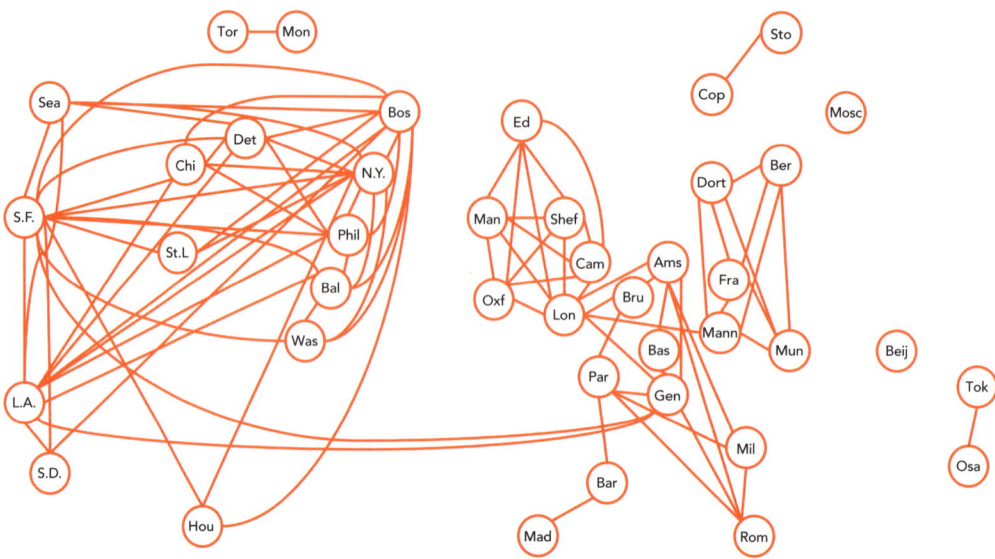

Co-authorships 1996-1998
Strong links
Top 40 centres measured according to output

co-authorships for all the cities in the analysis characterised by the number of papers that the smallest of the two centres' scientists have published. Next, we have calculated the relationship between the observed and expected co-authorships for each city pair. We have isolated the largest over-representations, i.e. 4 per cent of all city pairs and constructed map-like diagrams which illustrate strong collaborative patterns[vi].

Centres with many strong collaborative relationships play a leading role while centres with few are subordinate because it has to be assumed that there is a quality assessment concealed behind the choice of collaborative partners. One co-operates with people for whom one has respect and the summation, therefore, demonstrates the centre hierarchy. Three diagrams each illustrate the structure and together the development in collaborative

**FIGURE 5. (CONTINUED)
SCIENCES' GLOBAL CENTRES
TOP 40 CITIES**

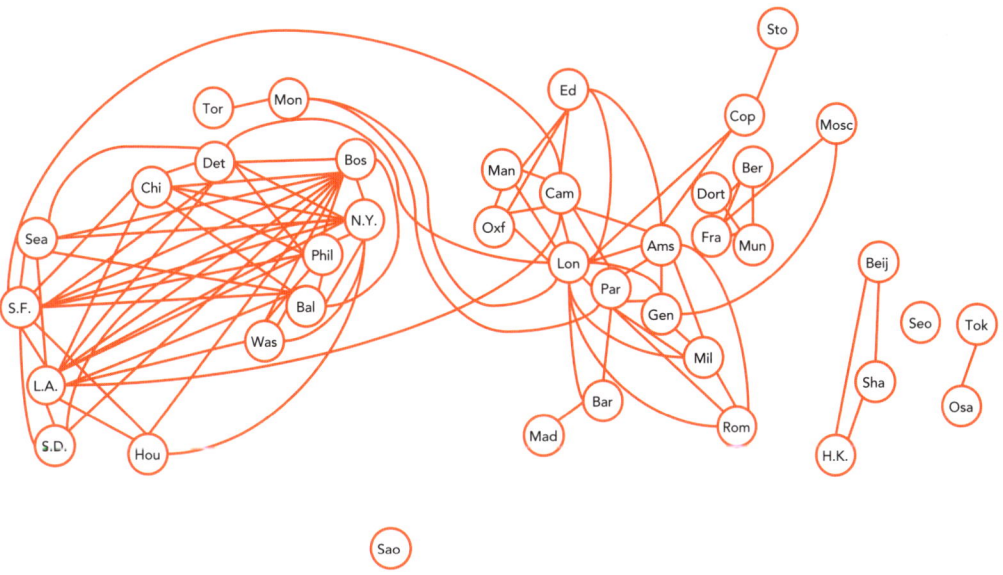

Co-authorships 2002-2004
Strong links
Top 40 centres measured according to output

patterns, see Figure 5. Each diagram shows the collaborative relationships that comprise at least twice as many papers as expected. The map–like diagrams show that national collaborative patterns prevail over international ones. If there is more than one city in a country, partnerships particularly take place inside national borders. Major countries, USA, UK, Germany and China are significant in all three diagrams. Countries with two cities in the top 40 generally account for strong national interaction. The picture of strong collaborative relationships changes to a limited extent over time. The number of intercontinental relationships is extremely limited, but shows an interesting trend over time. Between 1996-98, there were only heavy collaborative relationships between Geneva-Lausanne (home of CERN, the international nuclear physics facility) and the two Californian centres, San Francisco

**FIGURE 5. (CONTINUED)
SCIENCES' GLOBAL CENTRES
TOP 40 CITIES**

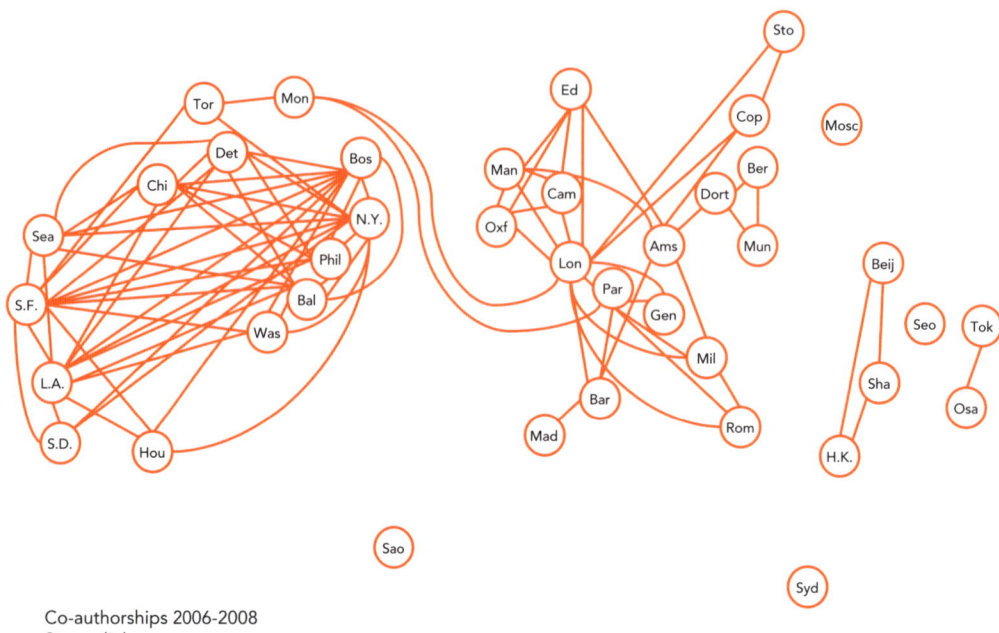

Co-authorships 2006-2008
Strong links
Top 40 centres measured according to output

and Los Angeles. For the period 2002-2004, Geneva-Lausanne's role has been taken over by Cambridge. London interacts with Detroit-Ann Arbor and with Montreal, which also collaborates with Paris. Between 2006-2008, there are only heavy intercontinental partnerships between, on the one side, Montreal and on the other London and Paris respectively. Montreal's bilingualism is also noticeable. All three diagrams with their strong co-authorship links highlight five leading cities, i.e. the San Francisco Bay region, Boston, Los Angeles, New York and London. The latter accounts for the only identified development trend at this level, i.e. a strengthening.

It is clear that national interaction accounts for more and heavier interaction than international interaction does. National borders play a role in the way in which scientists collaborate. They understand each other's language, research grants come out of national budgets and national foundations support their own citizens. Many organisations, institutions, companies and associations are nationally based and culturally-historically rooted so it is easier to work together with fellow nationals from the same country. Military considerations may even exclude international collaboration. International collaboration, however, accounts for an important and growing part of overall scientific collaboration. International interaction is higher on many agendas and there are many structures that promote such interaction. International companies and organisations aim at ignoring national borders, at least when they are able to protect their results. And although by far most universities are nationally rooted, there are many incentives to international partnerships within the world of academia. The EU promotes cooperation between research groups from the union's different countries and even demands such collaboration. The same is the case with the United Nations and the organisation's many specialised agencies, including UNESCO. The latter provides a mandate for the global scientific unions which aim to promote international cooperation and which often initiate or drive research. Similar endeavours take place within the Nordic countries and within ASEAN. This also applies to many NGO partnerships with regard to international research tasks. Research is increasingly global.

In Figure 6, we have isolated international co-authorships and presented them in three diagrams where collaborative relationships are given for city pairs, where observed international co-authorships are more than one and a half times larger than expected. The three map-like diagrams resemble each other significantly and, therefore, show a considerable degree of inertia as is the case when all co-authorships are part of the analysis. Europe is considerably more prominent in the international scene than the rest of the world and constitutes a strong, multi-nucleus research system where London, the Amsterdam region and Paris are the leading centres. The three cities form a particularly dominating centre in relation to other European heavyweights. On the level below, there is only one European centre, Geneva-Lausanne, that plays an important role. It is noticeable that American centres with strong traditions for significant scientific output are as absent on the international scene as they are. Only San Francisco, is, in fact, a major player although the position of Los Angeles and New York is rising. Canadian cities also show growth in terms of international cooperation. Moreover, the figure shows that the number of strong intercontinental links is fairly constant and limited to approximately 15. In addition, it is noticeable that European cities on the level below the four leading centres of 10 have better international

**FIGURE 6.
SCIENTIFIC GLOBAL CENTRES
TOP 40 CITIES**

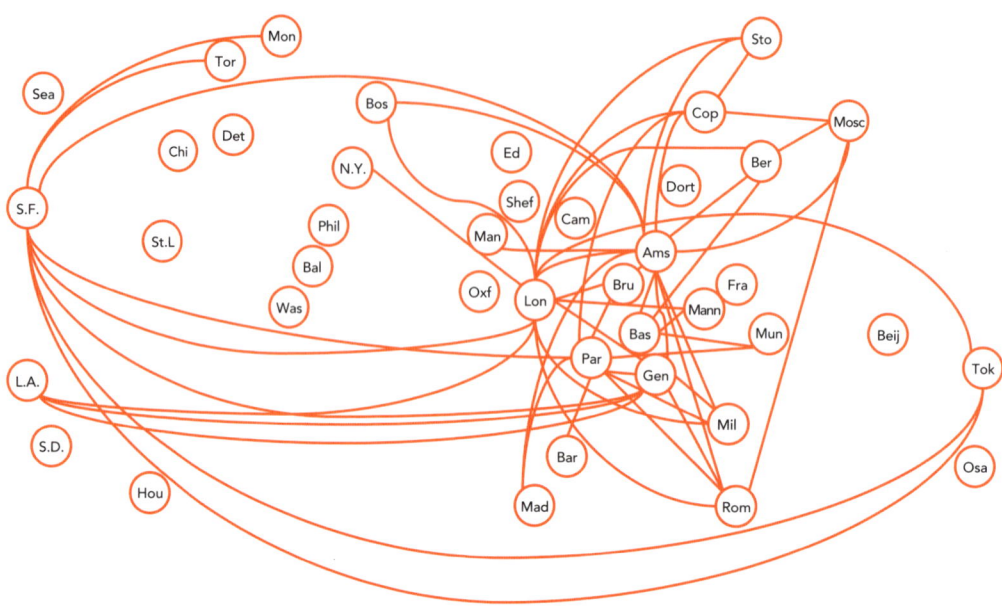

Co-authorships 1996-1998
Strong links
Top 40 centres measured according to output

links than their American colleagues and that the newly arrived strong cities outside North America and Europe are poorly linked to the international scene. Finally, it is noticeable that in contrast to other European cities, Moscow appears to be disconnected from the international level.

The analysis of international, scientific strength, links and network position is summarised in Figure 7, which has been inspired by Taylor's models of world city systematics (2004, 2007), see Chapter 4.

Taylor works on the basis of an analysis of the cities' international business-to-business service companies and defines a hierarchy of cities where control and dominance deter-

**FIGURE 6. (CONTINUED)
SCIENTIFIC GLOBAL CENTRES
TOP 40 CITIES**

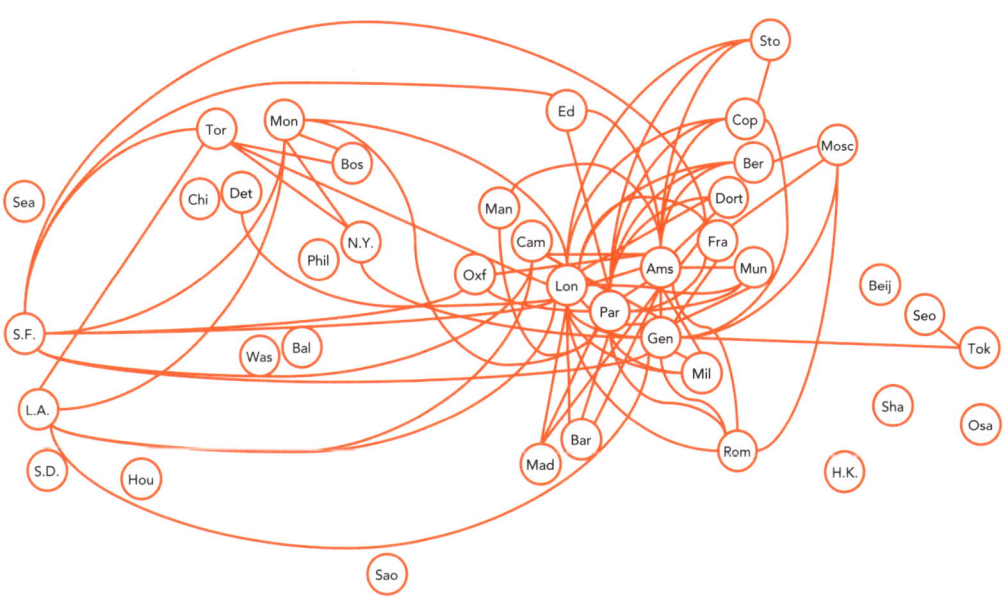

International co-authorships 2002-2004
Strong links
Top 40 centres measured according to output

mine levels. He also works with bands (families, cliques) where partnership profiles decide the grouping. Although we do the same, within the scientific world it is not entirely appropriate to talk in terms of control and dominance. One can, however, show the leading cities and those that are subordinate in respect of overall collaboration. As a result, the cities can be grouped in levels. By identifying the individual city's partners within the scientific environment, different bands can be created. The diagram presents a simple model.

**FIGURE 6. (CONTINUED)
SCIENTIFIC GLOBAL CENTRES
TOP 40 CITIES**

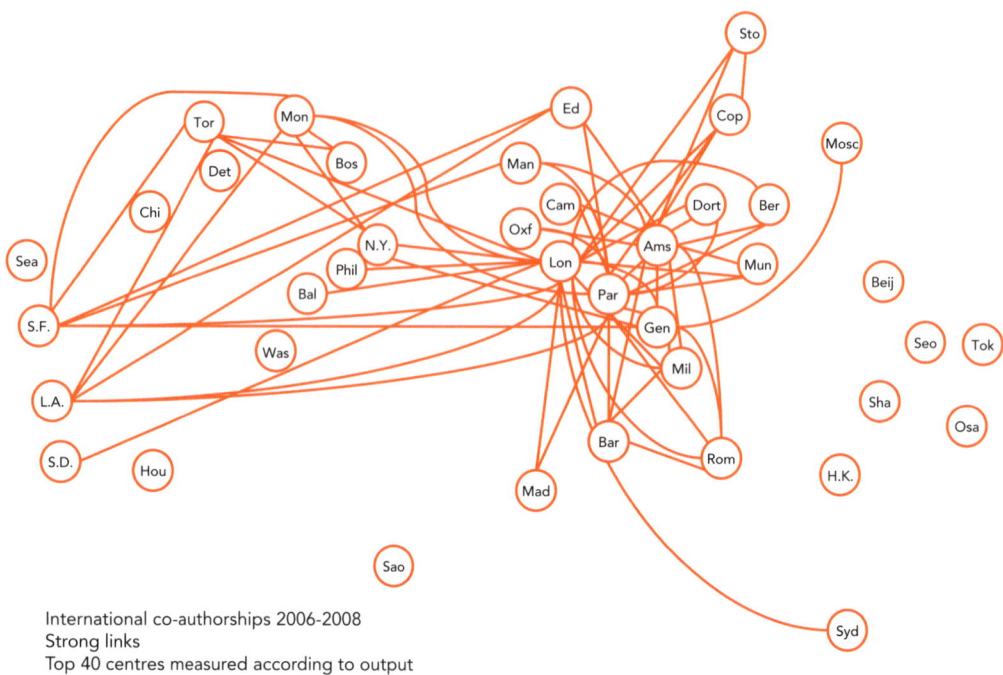

International co-authorships 2006-2008
Strong links
Top 40 centres measured according to output

The upper level comprises global research centres including five cities linked to other cities across the world and which form the lodestars of research. London, the Amsterdam region, Paris and the San Francisco Bay area are each leaders within their own bands. Geneva-Lausanne also has a top level position and a worldwide network rather than a real collaborative band. This city region's position is determined by the international nuclear research facility CERN. The figure also shows four bands and research second level centres within each of these bands. London has the dominant role within the British band with Edinburgh-Glasgow on the second level. The Amsterdam region plays a leading role within the North European band where Copenhagen-Lund and Stockholm-Uppsala are at the second level.

FIGURE 7.
THE GLOBAL SYSTEM OF RESEARCH CENTRES HIERARCHIES AND BANDS

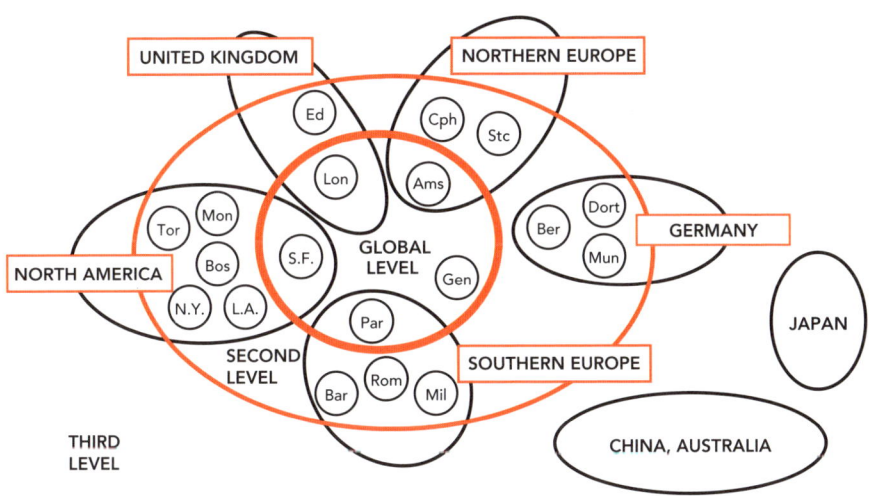

Science's world cities
Levels and bands: a model based on output, international collaboration and nodality
Source: As inspired by Taylor (2004, 2007)

Paris is the top metropolis for the Southern European band in which Barcelona, Rome and Milan occupy the second level. Finally, there is a German band outside the first level centres, but with strong interaction with the triad of leading European major cities. Part of the picture comprises a North American band in which San Francisco ranks among the world's first level cities while Boston, New York, Los Angeles, Montreal and Toronto can be found on the second level. Finally, there is a more isolated Chinese-Pacific level and an equally isolated Japanese band in which no cities have positions in the two upper levels. It should be noted that Beijing is well on its way upwards measured by volume, but not by network relationships.

FIGURE 8.
SCIENTIFIC CENTRES IN DENMARK, SWEDEN AND GERMANY RANKED ACCORDING TO SCIENTIFIC OUTPUT
TOP 30

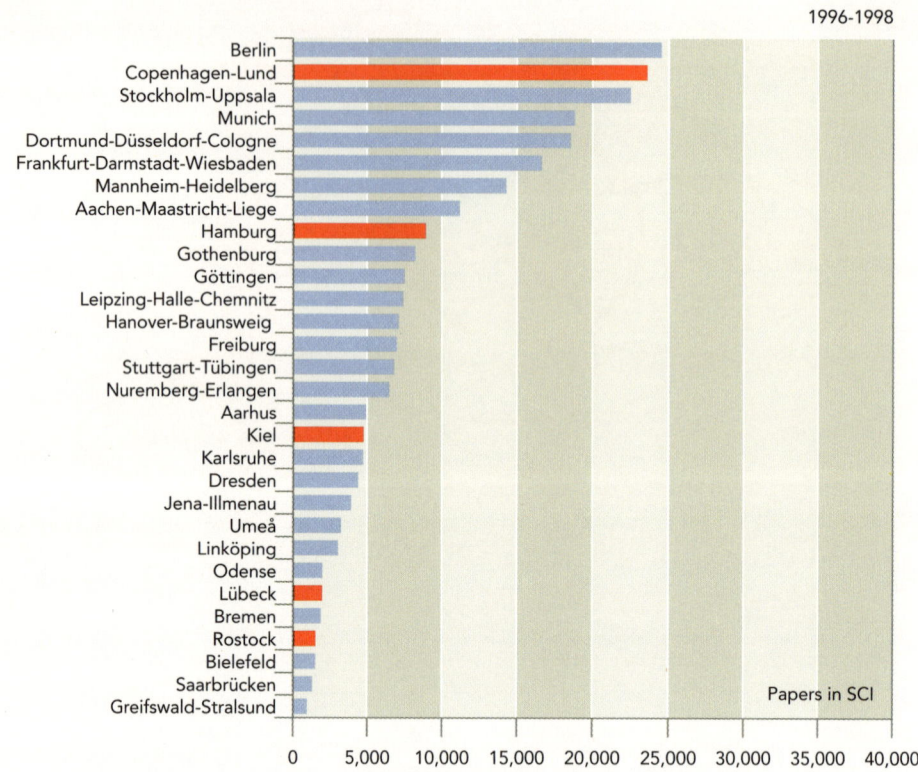

DENMARK, SWEDEN AND GERMANY: RESEARCH CENTRES

As has been made clear above, neither Denmark, Sweden nor Germany has global centres at the upper level on the world scene. Despite strong concentration in the capitals, Denmark and Sweden are too small to operate on such levels while Germany's decentralised structure and Berlin's historical *deroute* mean that the German centres cannot make an impact at the top level. By contrast, Germany accounts for three significant global second level centres while Denmark and Sweden each have one. The level below this comprises seven German and one Swedish centre while the rest of the cities on the three nation top 30 list

FIGURE 8. (CONTINUED)
SCIENTIFIC CENTRES IN DENMARK, SWEDEN AND GERMANY RANKED ACCORDING TO SCIENTIFIC OUTPUT
TOP 30

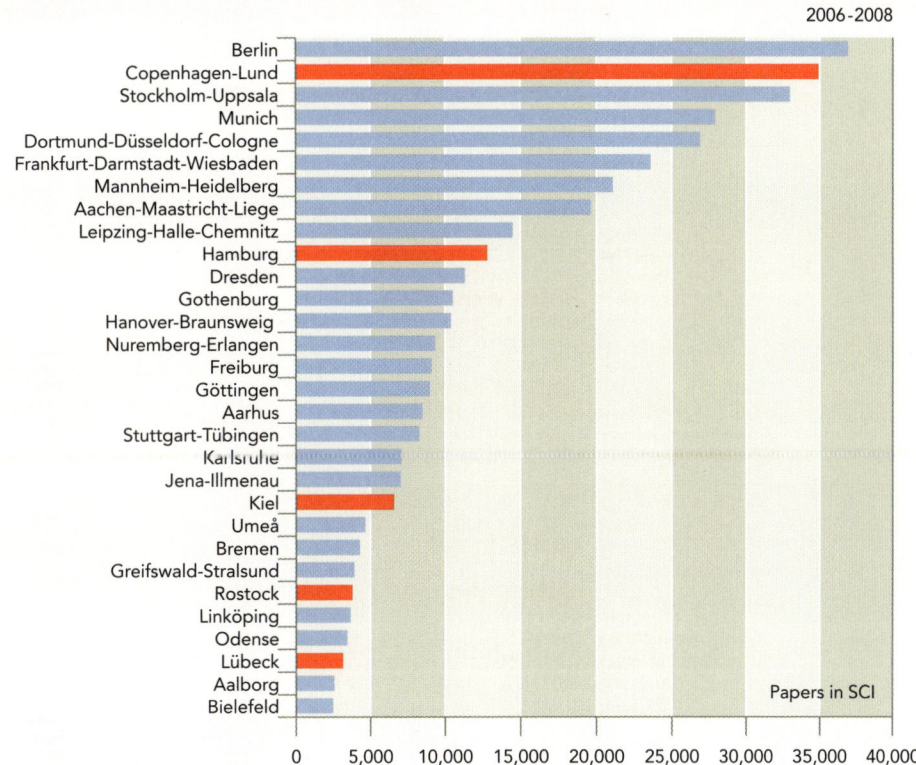

may be regarded as regional research cities. Two of the cities on the list are cross-border regions, i.e. Copenhagen-Lund and Aachen-Maastricht-Liege.

The 30 largest scientific centres in Denmark, Sweden and Germany appear in Figure 8. As expected, by far the majority are German. The Øresund City ranks among the very largest while Hamburg and Kiel are in the three countries' middle group. Rostock and Lübeck belong among the smaller centres. There is a clear inertia in the ranking and the eight largest centres appear in the same sequence in 1996-1998 and in 2006-2008. A few East German cities have advanced a couple of places.

FIGURE 9.
SCIENTIFIC CENTRES IN DENMARK, SWEDEN AND GERMANY
TOP 30

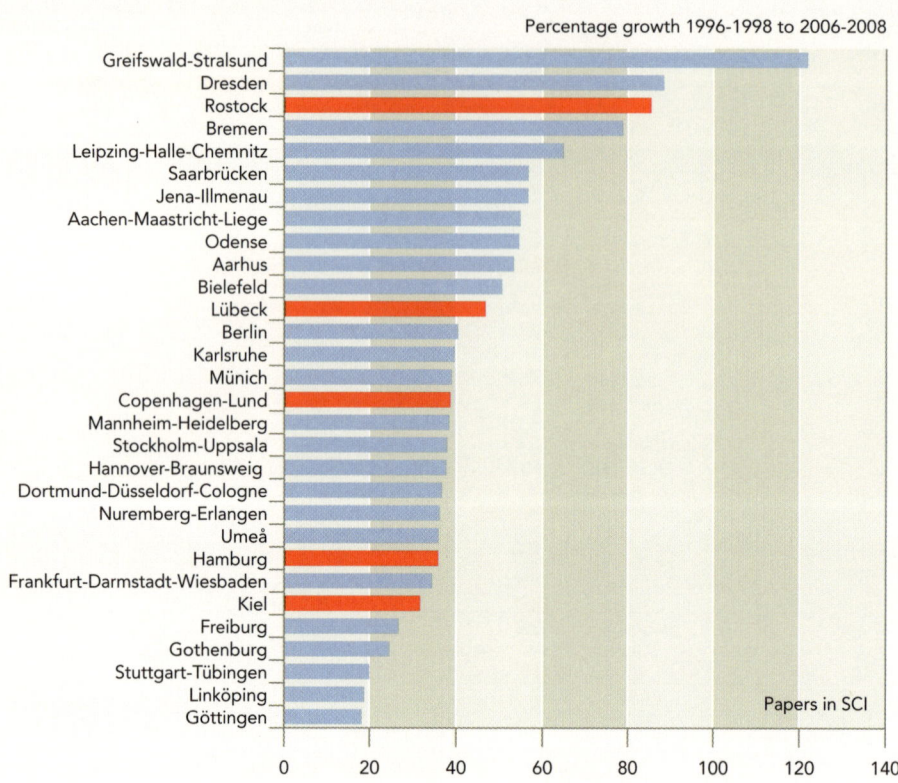

With regard to growth there are significant differences (see Figure 9). Over a time span of 10 years, such growth varies between plus 18 per cent to plus 122 per cent. The three largest scientific centres in Denmark, Sweden and Germany have grown at almost the same rate and, in terms of growth, are found in the middle group where we also find Lübeck and Hamburg. The Øresund City has seen growth of 39 per cent, (see the diagram). Stockholm-Uppsala has grown by 38 per cent and Berlin by 40 per cent. The relative strength between the three centres thus remains unchanged. The big losers are Göttingen, Linköping, Stuttgart-Tübingen, Gothenburg and Kiel while the winners are Greifswald-Stralsund, Aalborg, Dresden and Rostock.

Four global knowledge centres play essential roles and, therefore, affect the structure and development of the Fehmarnbelt Region. First and foremost, this is the case with Øresund City (Copenhagen-Lund) and Hamburg, but also two other cities outside the Fehmarnbelt Region, i.e. Stockholm-Uppsala and Berlin. These two cities are strong current and potential partners for Copenhagen-Lund and Hamburg. If you look at co-authorships with the global top 40 cities, you might expect a greater weight for the German than for the Scandinavian cities because national collaborative relationships generally carry greater weight than international collaborative relationships and because there are more German cities in the top 40 list. Hamburg's research community also accounts for the relatively strongest relationships and when co-authorships are measured as the overall number of co-authors in the other 39 cities calculated as a percentage of the city's own scientific output measured in papers 2006-2008, Hamburg's figure is 66 per cent. The corresponding figure for Øresund City is 54 per cent which means that part of the co-operation with Stockholm is within the national border (also applies the other way). Stockholm-Uppsala's collaboration

FIGURE 10.
COLLABORATION PROFILE FOR FOUR LARGE CITIES (2006-2008)
THE THICKNESS OF THE LINES IS PROPORTIONAL TO THE STRENGTH OF COLLABORATION

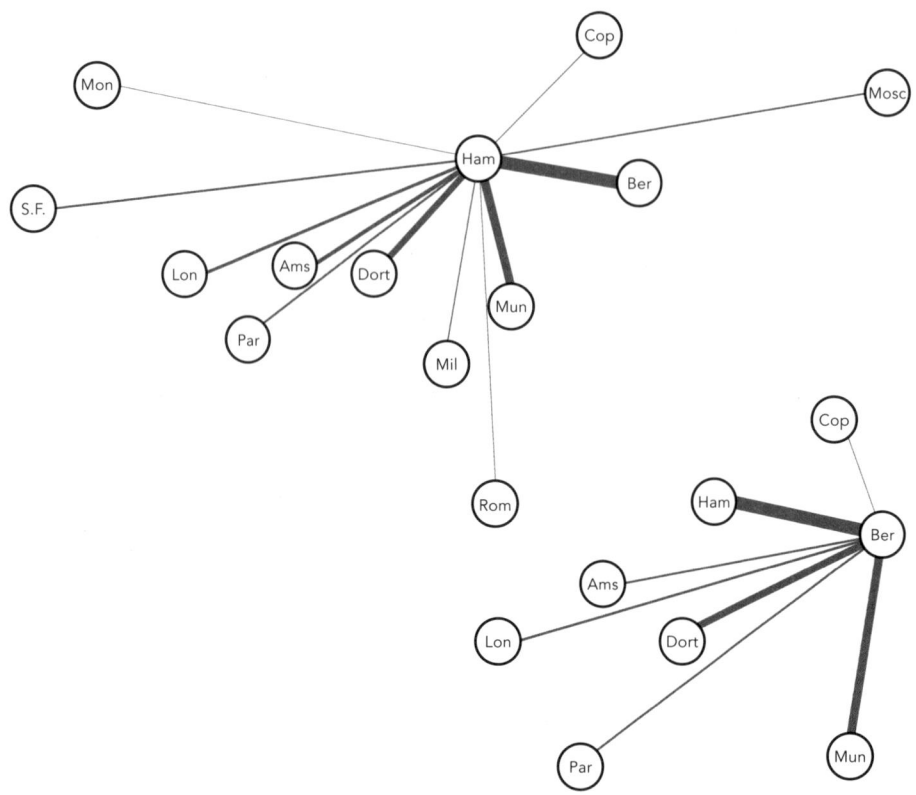

percentage with the other top 40 cities is 51 per cent while, strangely, Berlin lies at the bottom with 48 per cent (which may not be all that surprising considering the city's long isolation). At the major city level, Copenhagen-Lund's strongest co-operation partner is Stockholm-Uppsala while Hamburg's most important links are with Berlin – which in both cases also applies the other way.

Figure 10 shows the four major cities' strongest links measured by co-authorships with the world's 40 largest research cities. All four cities have excellent relations with the European top centres, London, Paris and the Amsterdam Region. Moreover, Hamburg and

FIGURE 10. (CONTINUED)
COLLABORATION PROFILE FOR FOUR LARGE CITIES (2006-2008)
THE THICKNESS OF THE LINES IS PROPORTIONAL TO THE STRENGTH OF COLLABORATION

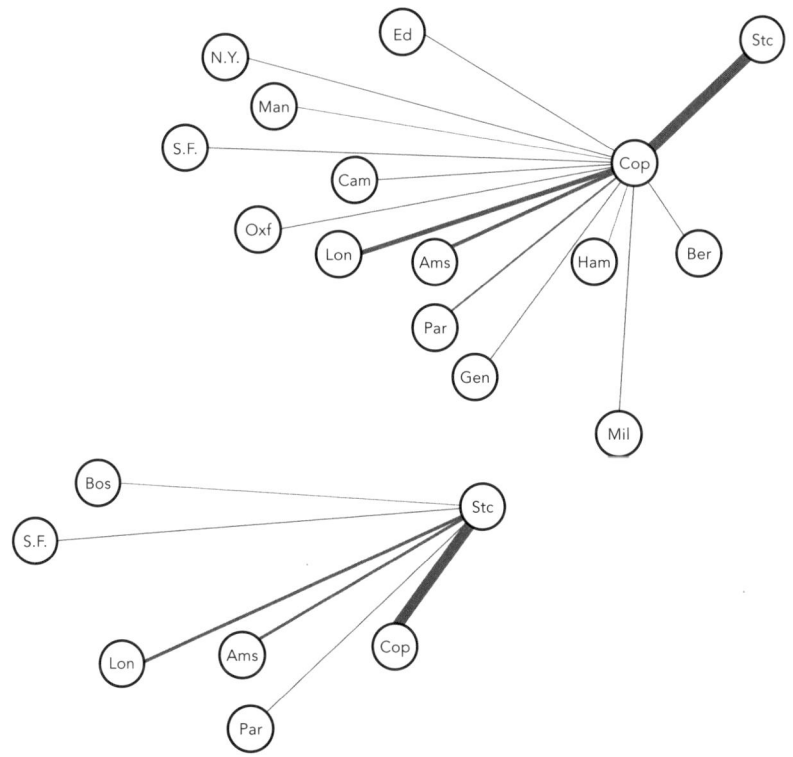

Berlin have excellent relations with the other two German top centres, Munich and Dortmund-Dusseldorf-Cologne and both of them account for moderately strong links to Copenhagen-Lund whereas they are not linked to Stockholm-Uppsala. In addition, Hamburg has relatively strong interaction with the San Francisco region, Moscow and Milan and moderate interaction with Montreal and Rome. Stockholm-Uppsala has moderately strong links to San Francisco and Montreal while Copenhagen-Lund, in addition to the links mentioned here, has moderately strong links to the San Francisco region, New York, Edinburgh-Glasgow, Cambridge, Oxford-Reading, Geneva-Lausanne and Milan. The Øresund City accounts for the most comprehensive network, followed by Hamburg, while Stockholm-Uppsala and Berlin have fewer strong links.

FIGURE 11.
COLLABORATION PROFILE WITH THREE NORTHERN GERMAN RESEARCH CITIES (2006-2008)
THE THICKNESS OF THE LINES IS PROPORTIONAL TO THE STRENGTH OF COLLABORATION

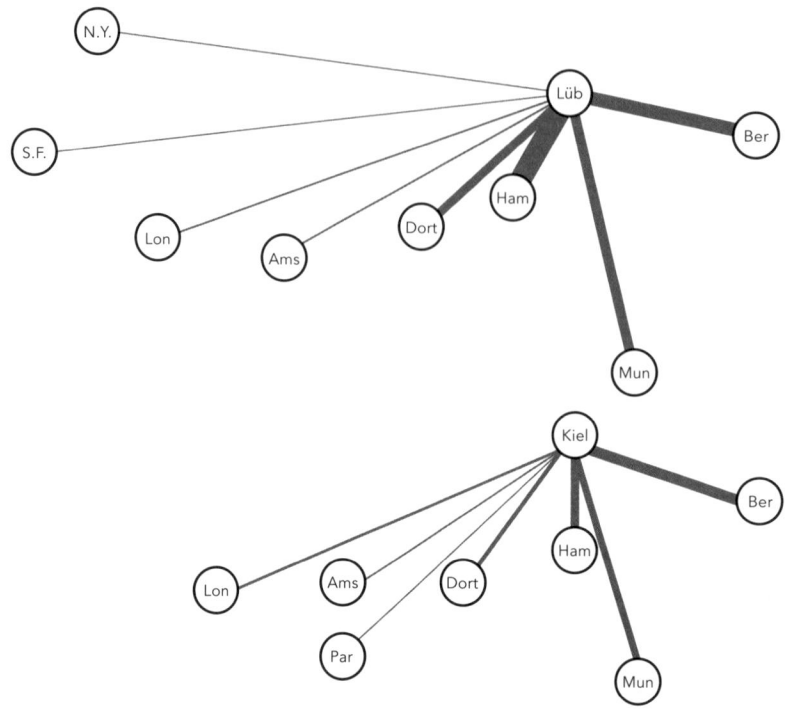

The three smaller research cities, Kiel, Lübeck and Rostock also have links to the 40 largest global cities, see Figure 11. All are solidly linked to the three global German centres and to Hamburg (as included in the analysis). Kiel and Rostock have their strongest links to Berlin while Lübeck, to a significant extent, collaborates with Hamburg. Kiel presents Hamburg as its second strongest partner followed by Munich and Dortmund-Dusseldorf-Cologne. Kiel also has fairly strong links to London and two more moderate links to the Amsterdam region and Paris. Lübeck's high level collaboration with Hamburg is supplemented by important and more or less equally strong links to the three global German centres and the city has moderately strong links to two of Europe's three top centres (The Amsterdam

FIGURE 11. (CONTINUED)
COLLABORATION PROFILE WITH THREE NORTHERN GERMAN RESEARCH CITIES (2006-2008)
THE THICKNESS OF THE LINES IS PROPORTIONAL TO THE STRENGTH OF COLLABORATION

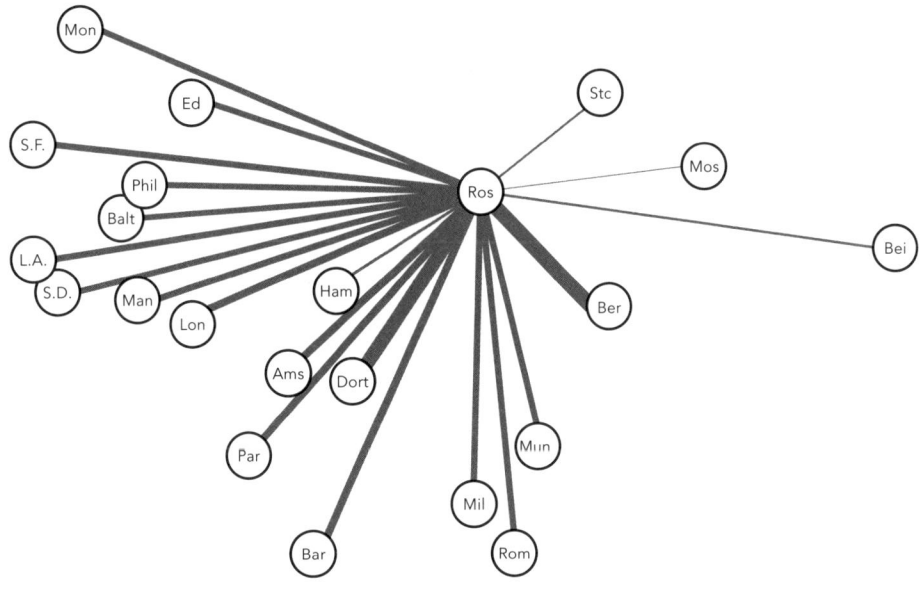

region and London) and to the American cities San Francisco and New York. Rostock's collaboration profile is rather special. Firstly, Rostock's collaborative relationships are particularly comprehensive. Secondly, the city's research has a strongly international profile i.e. a significant collaborative level with half of the world's scientific centres. It is notable that Rostock's partners include European, North American and Asian centres. Thirdly, Rostock's research community is almost detached from Hamburg compared to those of Kiel and Lübeck. This is probably a consequence of Rostock's history under the DDR and the then established ties to East German centres as well as its professional scientific profile.

FIGURE 12.
THE RESEARCH CENTRE SYSTEM: DENMARK, SWEDEN, GERMANY HIERARCHIES AND BANDS

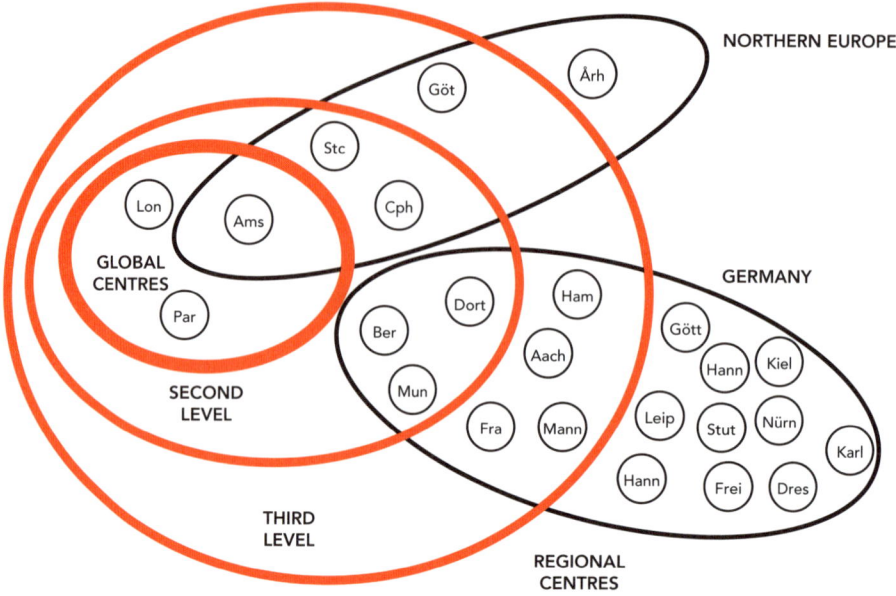

Source: As inspired by Taylor (2004, 2007)

In Figure 12, we have continued the Taylor-inspired modelling of the research cities in Denmark, Sweden and Germany. The categorisation is less well-founded than the model of the overall urban system because the database is incomplete. The European triad of leading research centres is presented at global level and to this triad, two bands have been linked together, a Northern European and a German one. Five cities from the three countries are placed on the second level with five on the third while eleven cities are designated as regional centres on a fourth level. The other centres are, in a global context, quite small and include Rostock and Lübeck. The model also sets out how Copenhagen-Lund, Berlin and Hamburg are placed at a fairly high level in mutual research collaboration.

The two main axes identified above, the Scandinavian and the North German, can and should be supplemented by a third main axis whereby the moderately strong axis between Hamburg and the Øresund City is boosted. This means that these two centres can further strengthen relations to their already well developed networks, providing both supplementary and complementary opportunities. Potentially, it can be assessed that a strengthening of the link between Hamburg and the Øresund City can result in these two centres rising to the research dominant level that is currently accounted for by Europe's main centres, London, Paris and the Amsterdam region. Enhanced interaction of this type, between the global third level centre, the Øresund City, and the regional research city Hamburg requires a strong effort and mutual respect. Hamburg's strong international position can contribute to this.

THE FEHMARNBELT REGION'S RESEARCH CENTRES: SCIENTIFIC SPECIALISATION

Scania, the Zealand archipelago, Schleswig-Holstein, Hamburg and parts of Mecklenburg-Vorpommern comprise five urban regions in which the region's research activities are concentrated. Together the Øresund City, Hamburg, Kiel, Rostock and Lübeck account for 1.53 per cent of the world's scientific output – a substantial figure considering the region only comprises 0.10 per cent of the world's population. With an output 34,909 papers in 2006-2008, the Øresund City ranks far above the other centres. Hamburg produces 12,361 papers, Kiel 6,324 papers, Rostock 3,578 and Lübeck 3,009. The five centres have different specification profiles, but also a number of similarities. Between them, Copenhagen-Lund has a strong position within health-related science and in the geoscience area. Hamburg focuses on the health sciences, Kiel on geosciences, health sciences and marine research, in which Rostock is also active. Lübeck is almost 100 per cent focused on health sciences.[vii]

In order to qualify the evaluation of the five research centres' scientific specialisation profiles and, therefore, their positions of strength, we have carried out an analysis of their composition of disciplines within pharmaceutical research, the natural sciences and technical sciences. Each paper has been categorised under one or several disciplines out of the total 172 disciplines comprised by the categorisation[viii]. The size of the disciplines varies widely measured by the number of papers registered for each of them. Worldwide the smallest discipline has 1,661 papers and the largest 353,024. There are 58 disciplines within health-oriented research, 48 within engineering sciences, technology and materials, 12 focus on agriculture, fishery and forestry, 22 aim at the hard natural sciences, physics, chemistry and mathematics, 13 are geosciences and 19 are biosciences. Moreover, for each city we have calculated each discipline's deviation from the discipline's global output. This has resulted in a measurement of the strength of the individual discipline in each city measured in relation to the discipline's average output.

For each city, we have then ranked the disciplines according to strength. Copenhagen-Lund's strongest scientific discipline is endocrinology and metabolism while Hamburg's is physics: particles and fields. For both Kiel and Rostock, oceanography comes first while Lübeck's prime area is dermatology. The cities' top disciplines are ranked in Figure 13

FIGURE 13.
CHART SHOWING RANKING ACCORDING TO THE FIVE CITIES' TOP DISCIPLINES (2006-2008)

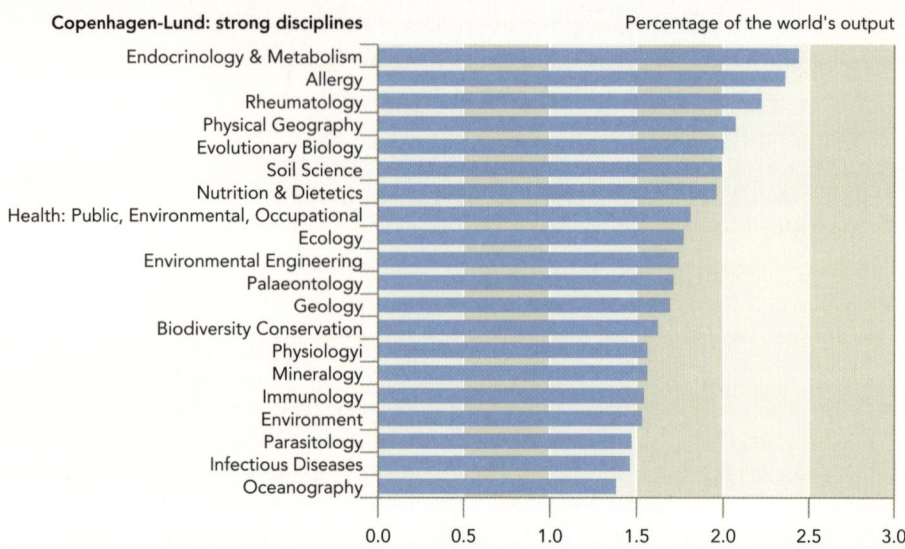

where, for each city, the 20 strongest disciplines have been included albeit only disciplines with more than 100 per cent stronger production than the global average for the discipline.

Copenhagen-Lund's position of strength primarily lies within health research. The strongest discipline is endocrinology and metabolism followed by allergy research and rheumatology. Lower down the top 20 list there are several health scientific disciplines such as nutrition and dietetics and health: public and environmental and industrial, physiology, immunology, parasitology and research into infectious diseases. The geosciences also have a strong position in the Øresund City, with physical geography occupying fourth place while earth science is number 6, palaeontology and geology 11 and 12, with mineralogy further down the list. A third prominent area for research is the natural environment which includes the discipline evolutionary biology (5), organic research (9), environment technology research (10), biodiversity (11) and environmental science (17). The Øresund City is strongly oriented towards health research, geoscience and the natural environment.

FIGURE 13. (CONTINUED)
CHART SHOWING RANKING ACCORDING TO THE FIVE CITIES' TOP DISCIPLINES (2006-2008)

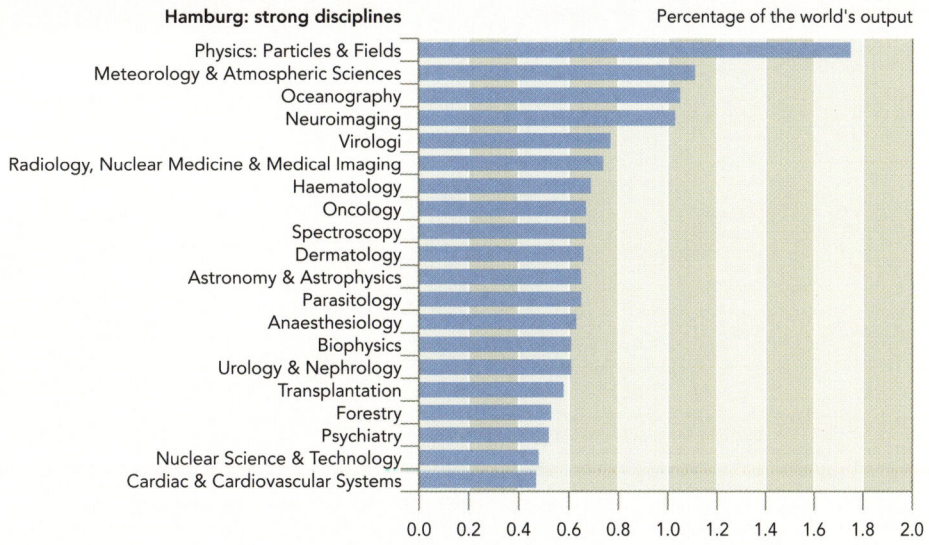

Like the Øresund City, Hamburg's scientific community focuses on health-oriented research. Of the 20 strongest disciplines, 14 are registered as medical research. In fourth position, there is research into neuroimaging followed by the next six places – virology, radiology and nuclear medicine and chemical medicine, hematology, oncology, spectroscopy and dermatology. In 12th place is parasitology followed by anesthesiology, biophysics, urology and nephrology and transplant research. Psychiatry ranks 18th and the discipline of cardiac and cardiovascular systems research is 20th. Even though Hamburg's strong research activities are primarily directed towards health issues, the absolute top positions are taken up by natural science. Number one is physics: particles and fields, number 2 is meteorology and atmospheric science while number 3 is oceanography. Ranked 11th is astronomy and astrophysics while nuclear research takes up 19th position. Only forestry is an exception to the fact that Hamburg primarily focuses on health and secondly, traditional natural sciences.

FIGURE 13. (CONTINUED)
CHART SHOWING RANKING ACCORDING TO THE FIVE CITIES' TOP DISCIPLINES (2006-2008)

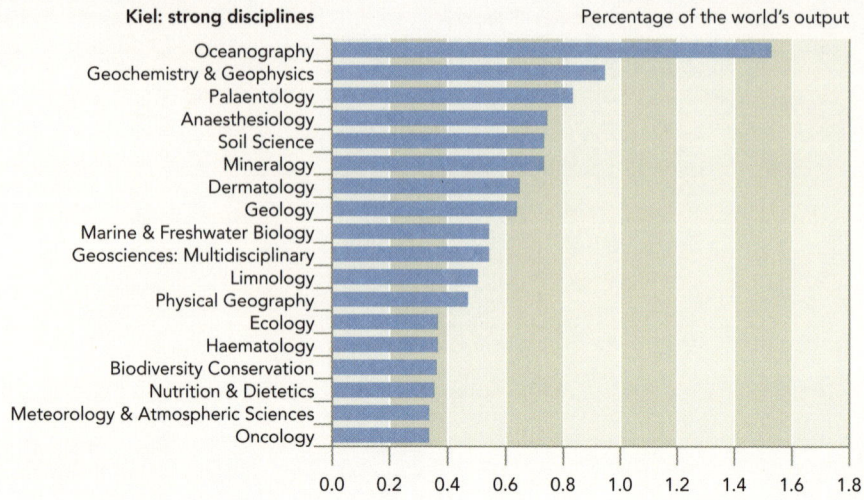

Kiel's strength is centred on the geosciences, health and ocean and freshwater research. Eight of the city's strong disciplines are geosciences, number 2 and 3 are geochemistry and geophysics and palaeontology. Number 5 is soil science with mineralogy as number 6 and geology as number 8. 10th place is occupied by multidisciplinary geosciences while number 12 is physical geography and number 17th meteorology and atmospheric science. Health orientated research also has a strong position, but only within a small number of disciplines. Anesthesiology comes in 4th with dermatology 7th, hematology 14th, research into nutrition and dietetics 16th and oncology 18th. Moreover, Kiel's scientific based research has a strong focus on oceanic and freshwater environments with oceanography at the top. Marine and freshwater biology hold 9th position and limnology 11th. Two natural science disciplines, ecology (13) and biodiversity research (15) break with the picture of geoscience, health-orientated and water environment research as focus areas for the specialisation profile.

FIGURE 13. (CONTINUED)
CHART SHOWING RANKING ACCORDING TO THE FIVE CITIES' TOP DISCIPLINES (2006-2008)

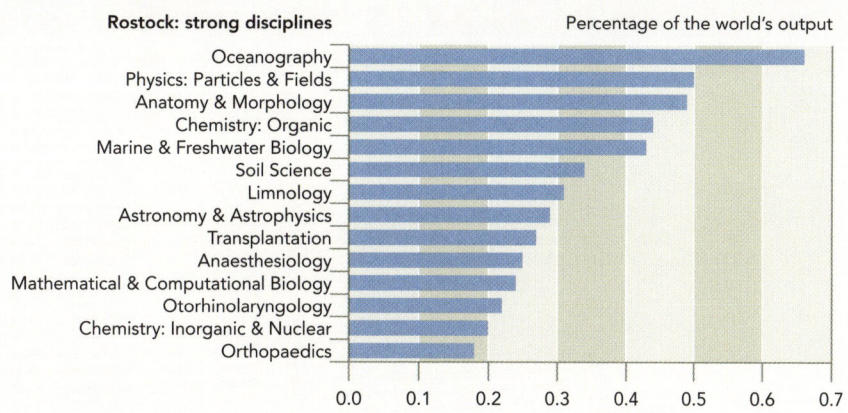

Rostock's specialisation profile reflects strong focus on ocean and freshwater environments, with oceanography at the top, marine and freshwater biology in 5th position and limnology as 7th. Another focus is on natural science where the disciplines physics: particles and fields (2), anatomy and morphology (13), organic chemistry (4), astronomy and astrophysics (8), biology: mathematics (11) and inorganic chemistry (13) also play a part. Health-oriented research also has a position of strength, including transplantation (9) and anesthesiology as 10th, otorhinolaryngology as 12th and orthopedics as 14th.

Lübeck is completely specialised within medical research. All the city's top disciplines are directed towards health-oriented science.

FIGURE 13. (CONTINUED)
CHART SHOWING RANKING ACCORDING TO THE FIVE CITIES' TOP DISCIPLINES (2006-2008)

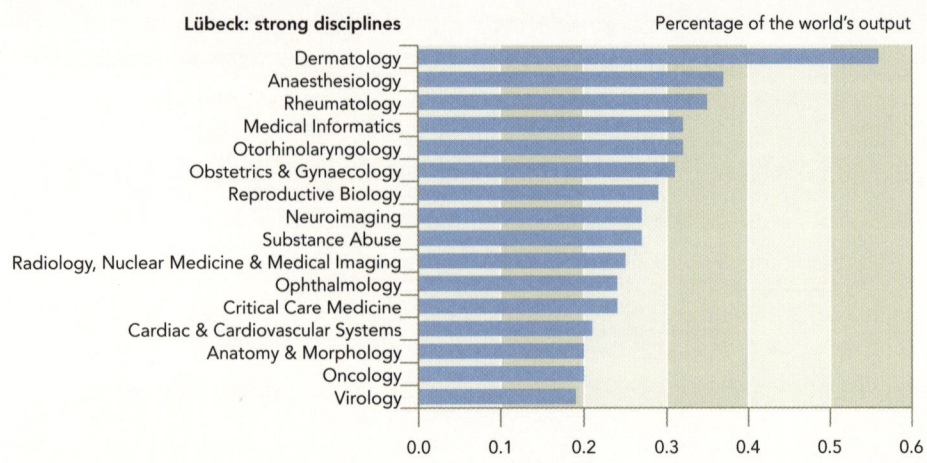

THE FEHMARNBELT REGION'S STRONG DISCIPLINES: POTENTIALLY SUPPLEMENTARY AND COMPLEMENTARY GROWTH PROMOTERS

We have reduced the number of scientific disciplines from 172 to 163 by eliminating very small disciplines (<5,000 papers on a global scale 2006-2008). In addition, for each city we have identified the strength of all disciplines and eliminated disciplines with weak positions in all the cities. This means that, by and large, all technical, engineering scientific, business-oriented and chemical disciplines, together with materials research and thermodynamics, are removed. We have also eliminated disciplines that are particularly weak in either the Øresund City or gathered in the Fehmarnbelt Region's German cities. This concerns, for instance, physiology (which has a strong position in the Øresund City, but a very weak posi-

FIGURE 14.
SCIENTIFIC DISCIPLINES WITH STRONG POSITIONS BOTH NORTH AND SOUTH OF THE FEHMARNBELT

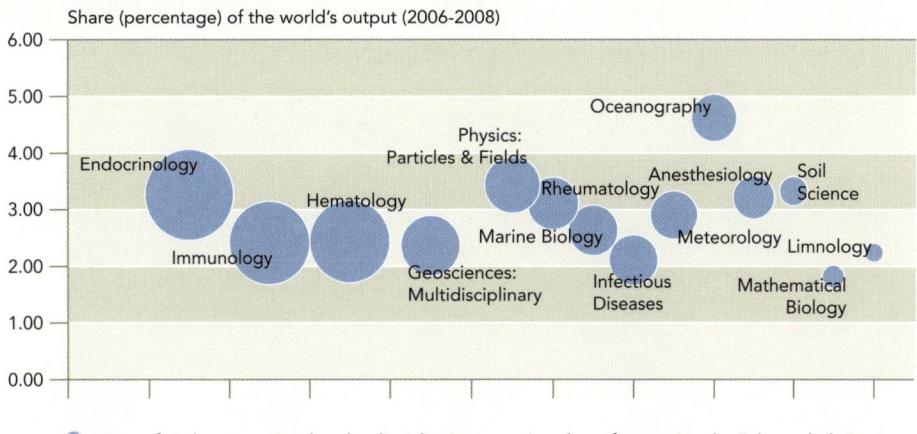

tion in the German cities) and inorganic chemistry (which has a strong position in the German centres, but is very weak in the Øresund City). 36 disciplines have strengths that rank from middle to very strong on both sides of the Fehmarnbelt.

14 of these disciplines supplement each other and are strong on both sides of the Fehmarnbelt. These top disciplines appear in Figure 14 where the disciplines are ranked on the X-axis according to the size of the disciplines in the whole of the Fehmarnbelt Region while the rank order on the Y-axis gives their strength measured against the discipline's global strength. The higher the stronger. The 14 disciplines represent the disciplines where north and south can supplement each other. The scientific centres on both sides of the Baltic are very strong internationally and further collaboration could enhance their strengths.

FIGURE 15.
SCIENTIFIC DISCIPLINES THAT ARE STRONG EITHER NORTH OR SOUTH OF THE FEHMARNBELT. NONE OF THESE DISCIPLINES ARE WEAK

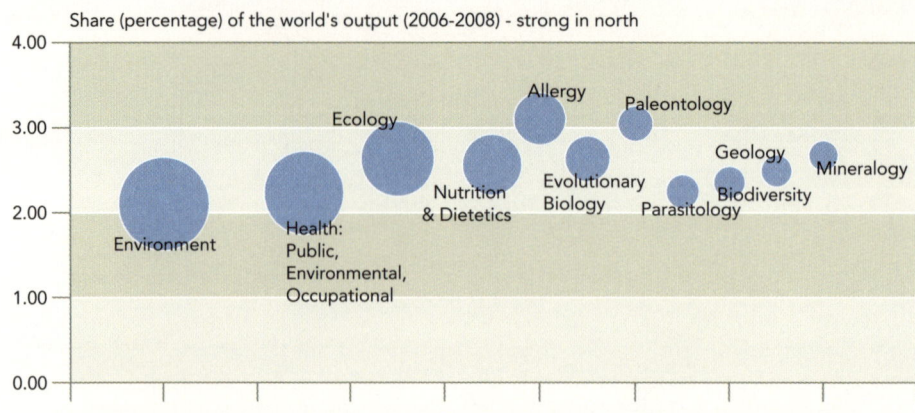

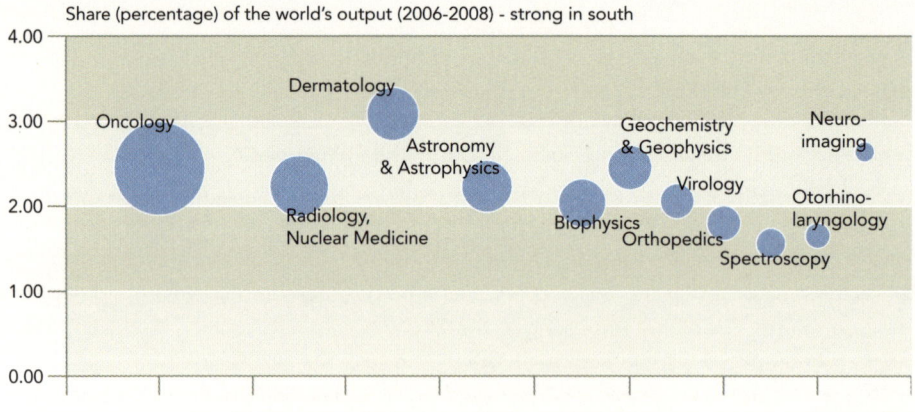

22 disciplines are strong on the one side and have medium strength – but not weakness – on the other side of the Fehmarnbelt. These disciplines have complementary potential. The disciplines are presented in Figure 15.

It is obvious to bring scientific players within the same discipline together to examine potential new partnership opportunities. The disciplines appear in the diagram below and proposals are presented with regard to from which city environments' lead partners can be appointed, i.e. from among the relatively strongest. It should be noted that a large environment almost per definition will be stronger than a small one. This is why the Øresund City appears more often than the German centres while the two smallest environments, Rostock and Lübeck, only appear rarely. That the small environments, nevertheless, have as strong positions as they do within certain disciplines demonstrate that they have been successful at pursuing their niche policies.

DISCIPLINES WITH POTENTIAL FOR COLLABORATION. RANKED ACCORDING TO STRENGTH WITHIN THE FEHMARNBELT REGION: STRONG ENVIRONMENTS BOTH IN THE NORTH AND SOUTH: POTENTIAL SUPPLEMENTARITY

Discipline	Strongest environments
Oceanography	Kiel, Rostock
Soil science	Kiel
Marine biology	Kiel, Rostock
Anesthesiology	Lübeck
Physics: particles and fields	Hamburg
Endocrinology and metabolism	Øresund City
Immunology	Øresund City
Infectious diseases	Øresund City
Meteorology and atmospheric science	Hamburg
Limnology	Øresund City
Rheumatology	Øresund City
Hematology	Hamburg
Geosciences: multidisciplinary	Øresund City
Biology: mathematics	Øresund City

DISCIPLINES WITH POTENTIAL FOR COLLABORATION. RANKED ACCORDING TO STRENGTH IN THE FEHMARNBELT REGION: STRONG ENVIRONMENTS SOUTH AND MEDIUM-STRONG IN THE NORTH: POTENTIAL COMPLEMENTARITY

Discipline	Strongest environments
Neuroimaging	Hamburg
Virology	Hamburg
Radiology, nuclear medicine, medicinal chemistry	Hamburg
Oncology	Hamburg
Dermatology	Lübeck
Astronomy and astrophysics	Rostock
Geochemistry and geophysics	Kiel
Otorhinolaryngology	Lübeck
Biophysics	Hamburg
Orthopedics	Hamburg
Spectroscopy	Hamburg

DISCIPLINES WITH POTENTIAL FOR COLLABORATION. RANKED ACCORDING TO STRENGTH IN THE FEHMARNBELT REGION: STRONG ENVIRONMENTS NORTH AND MEDIUM-STRONG IN THE SOUTH: POTENTIAL COMPLEMENTARITY

Discipline	Strongest environments
Allergy research	Øresund City
Evolutionary biology	Øresund City
Nutrition and dietetics	Øresund City
Health: public, environmental, industrial	Øresund City
Ecology	Øresund City
Paleontology	Øresund City
Geology	Øresund City
Biodiversity	Øresund City
Mineralogy	Øresund City
Environmental research	Øresund City
Parasitology	Øresund City

For a number of the above disciplines, there are already existing partnerships to build on. Of the five cities' overall output of 60,181 papers in 2006-2008, 391 have authors from both the northern and southern parts of the Fehmarnbelt Region. This is a small number, but individual disciplines show partnerships at a level that offer development perspectives. The disciplines that currently collaborate include, in particular, a number of health-oriented disciplines. Oncology is in a class of its own – in part because this discipline generally has a tradition for very comprehensive collaborative relationships and even publishes papers with multiple authors and in part because the oncology discipline enjoys a genuine position of strength in the Fehmarnbelt Region. Among the other disciplines currently involving collaboration are, as expected, a number of the areas' strong disciplines. Within the field of health research this applies to health: public and environment and industrial, genetics and heredity, hematology, endocrinology and metabolism, immunology, rheumatology and nutrition and dietetics. Within the natural sciences, this concerns biochemistry and molecular biology, geosciences, multidisciplinary, environment, physics: multidisciplinary, meteorology and atmospheric science and physics: particles and fields. We recommend a more in-depth analysis of existing collaborative relationships.

NANOSCIENCE AND NANOTECHNOLOGY

There are currently a range of initiatives aimed at strengthening research within and around nanoscience and nanotechnology. No fewer than four new scientific avant garde facilities in the form of gigantic experimental facilities are under establishment, two in Hamburg – European XFEL (experimental facility that generates extremely fast x-ray flashes) and PETRA (synchrotron x-radiation facility) – and two in the Øresund City – European Spallation Source (European experimental facility based on the world's strongest neutron source) and MAX IV (Synchrotron radiation facility). Altogether, we are talking about double digit billion investments (in kroner) and the development of new contacts and collaborative relationships with the world of business and industry.

The perspectives for research into materials science and for life science research are considerable and there is a significant readiness within the business sectors that have the potential to participate in and benefit from the planned research. To boost development, a number of stakeholders propose an alliance of scientific hubs to comprise approximately 15 university cities from Oslo via Gothenburg, Lund and the Danish university cities to Kiel, Rostock and Hamburg called "The Science Corridor". The proposal presents some problems not just because of the proposed corridor's extreme length (750 km) but also because the discipline nanoscience and nanotechnology does not currently have a position of strength in terms of research, at least not in those research centres within the area from which we have data on the strength of the disciplines. The four Northern German centres (Hamburg, Kiel, Rostock, Lübeck) produced 146 papers in 2006-2008 within the discipline (far below the average global production in relation to their size) and the Øresund City 335 (the average) while Berlin, which is not part of the vision, accounted for 475 papers (just over 50 percentage points above the global average).

Using the same methodology as employed to indicate science's system of centres, we have shown the weight of nanoscientific and nanotechnological research in Figure 16 where the output is registered for 2006-2008. The picture of this discipline's heavy centres is entirely different from the normal picture of scientific heavyweights. The absolute top position measured in output belongs to Beijing which together with the four other Asian centres, Tokyo-Yokohama, Seoul, Osaka-Kobe and Shanghai, constitute the upper level. Below this level are six cities, San Francisco, Moscow, Singapore, Berlin, Paris and Los Angeles. The Øresund City is number 24. We have also demonstrated collaborative relationships within the discipline in Figure 17. Three cities play leading roles. Berlin is the world's most important centre followed by Moscow and San Francisco. Cambridge and Geneva-Lausanne also occupy important positions. Four sub-systems are in evidence, one

FIGURE 16.
**NANOSCIENCE AND NANOTECHNOLOGY RESEARCH'S GLOBAL CENTRES
TOP 30**

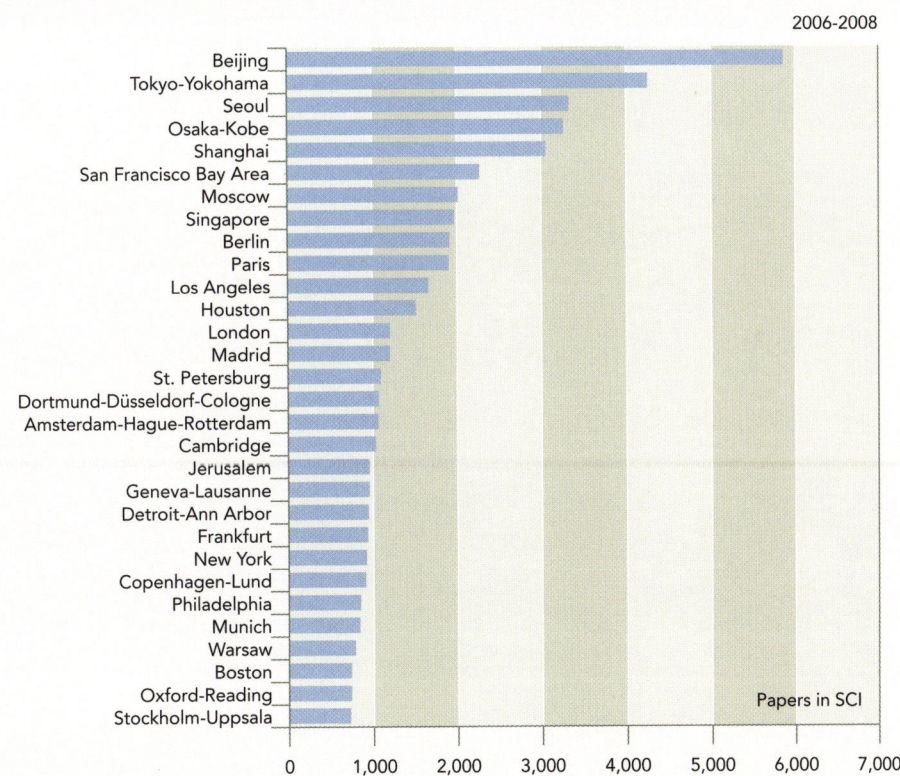

strong European, one American, one Asian-Australian and one British. Within the European sub-system, Berlin plays the main role followed by Moscow and Geneva-Lausanne. On the level below, we find other Swiss and German cities together with Copenhagen-Lund which, therefore, play a role as a centre for nanoscience and nanotechnology at the level below the top cities.

FIGURE 17.
NANOSCIENCE AND NANOTECHNOLOGY
TOP 40 CITIES

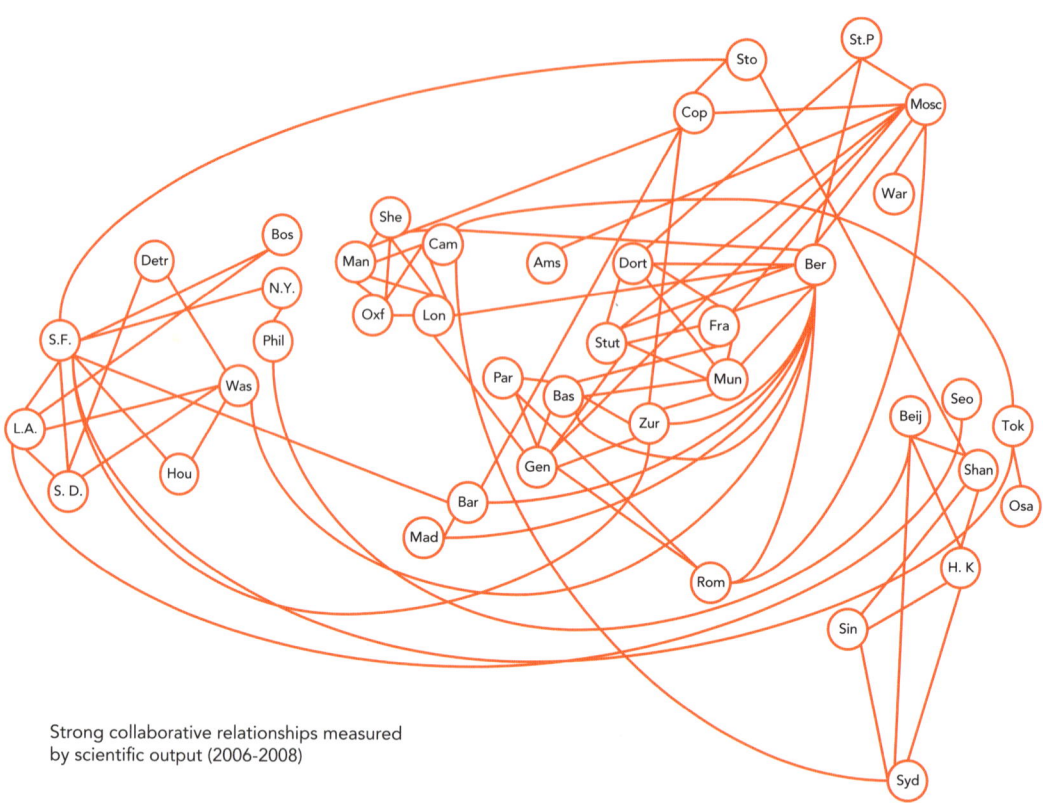

Strong collaborative relationships measured by scientific output (2006-2008)

It can be stated that the effort within the fields of nanoscience and nanotechnology is based on current productive strength at a level below the top level and it is doubtful whether it is expedient to exclude the only Danish-Swedish-German environment with demonstrated strength, Berlin, from "The Science Corridor" alliance. Since Berlin also plays a leading role within the discipline's network and, in this respect, is the world's leading city, the recommendation is to include the city in the science corridor.

SUMMARY

The Fehmarnbelt Region comprises five scientific centres. The Øresund City belongs to the group of Europe's scientific metropolises; Hamburg and Kiel are research cities on a slightly lower level while Rostock and Lübeck belong to the group of regional research centres.

Denmark, Sweden and Germany are international heavyweights in the world of science. The same applies to a number of metropolises of which three German urban regions (Berlin, Munich, Dortmund-Düsseldorf-Cologne), one Swedish (Stockholm-Uppsala) and one Danish-Swedish (The Øresund City) feature on the international top 40 list. None of these centres, however, has a place among the world cities' global top level, but are considered second level centres. It is also notable that in terms of growth these cities are not doing particularly well. Asian and South European cities are overtaking our centres and racing up to the upper global levels. However in terms of the networks, characterised by partnerships with scientists from other top 40 cities, they have a strong position and in this respect Danish, Swedish and German metropolises are not losing ground.

Research partnerships between scientific environments in different cities will accelerate and international collaboration is showing particularly high rates of increase. Analysis of the global level shows that cities with international profiles in the form of bilingualism (Montreal, the Øresund City, Aachen-Liege-Maastricht) have an advantage in so far as international collaboration is concerned. They have primary contact with more than one network.

Three European cities have leading positions in the global networks: London, Paris and the Amsterdam region are the continent's world cities. The largest centres in the expanded Fehmarnbelt Region (Berlin, the Øresund City, Stockholm-Uppsala, Hamburg) are well linked to the leading triad and each account for consistent international partnership profiles. The links between the four major centres are such that Berlin and Hamburg are each other's largest partners on a global level and the same is the case with the Øresund City and Stockholm-Uppsala. In addition, there are moderately strong collaboration axes between the Øresund City and Hamburg and between the Øresund City and Berlin, but not between Stockholm-Uppsala and the two German cities.

The two main axes, the Scandinavian and North German, can and should be supplemented by a third main axis which would strengthen the moderately strong axis between Hamburg and the Øresund City. This means that the two centres can further strengthen the links to their already well-established networks, which in turn, will offer supplementary as well as complementary opportunities. Potentially, a strengthening of the link between Hamburg and the Øresund City will mean that these two centres together will raise themselves to a research domineering level which will be actually drawn by Europe's main centres. This, however, will require some effort, but it is an inspiring challenge to develop a strong link between Hamburg and the Øresund City as currently exists between Hamburg and Berlin and between the Øresund City and Stockholm-Uppsala. We recommend that the three regional North German centres, Kiel, Rostock and Lübeck, become part of such efforts.

The five research centres have different profiles, but also share some common features. The Øresund City's position of strength is primarily based on health research, geosciences and the natural environment. In Hamburg, focus is on health together with traditional natural science. Kiel's strength is centred on the geosciences and marine science. Rostock also focuses on marine science, while Lübeck has a specialisation profile, which exclusively focuses on health.

We have analysed the opportunities for collaboration by isolating those disciplines with potential for developing new links and which can either supplement or complement each other. We have also pointed to obvious opportunities for strengthening the interaction between the centres in order to achieve gains. On the backdrop of positions of strength, north as well as south of the Fehmarnbelt, a number of marine disciplines (oceanography, marine biology, limnology) health-science fields (anesthesiology, endocrinology & metabolism, immunology, research into infectious diseases, rheumatology, hematology) geo-science areas (soil science, meteorology and atmospheric science, geosciences: multidisciplinary) and two traditional natural science disciplines (physics: particles and fields; biology: mathematical) would be able to supplement each other at a high level.

Similarly, it should be recommended that disciplines that are strong on one side of the Baltic Sea and medium strong on the other, aim for complementary interaction. This is the case with a range of health-science disciplines where neuroimaging, virology, radiology, nuclear medicine, chemical medicine, oncology, dermatology, otorhinolaryngology, biophysics, orthopaedics and spectroscopy are strong in the south and medium strong in the north while allergy research, nutrition & dietetics, health: public and environment and industrial and parasitology are strong in the north and medium strong in the south. This also applies to some geosciences where the south is strong within geochemistry and geophysics, while the north is strong within paleontology, geology and mineralogy. Finally, there are development opportunities for complementary disciplines within some of the traditional natural science disciplines where astronomy and astrophysics are strong in the south while north is strong within the disciplines evolutionary biology, ecology, biodiversity and environmental research.

With regard to collaborative relationships, it should be noted that these are currently at a low level between the northern and southern parts of the Fehmarnbelt Region. Of the five cities' combined output of 60,181 papers in 2006-2008, 391 have authors from both the northern and southern part of the Fehmarnbelt Region, largely between the Øresund City and Hamburg. However, it should also be pointed out that there are opportunities for mobilising partnerships based on uniform positions of strength and that, in addition, there are strong grounds for focusing on a range of scientific disciplines where one part of the region has a strong position while the other only has medium strength. There are reasons for optimism, but a serious effort is needed. Such efforts comprise focus on the development of more partnership-oriented frameworks and on information about each other's respective advantages. We also recommend further analysis of existing partnership relations.

REFERENCES

C. W. Matthiessen & A. W. Schwarz, 'Scientific Centres in Europe, An Analysis of Research Strength and Patterns of Specialisation Based on Bibliometric Indicators', Urban Studies, 1999, 36 (3), 453-477

C. W. Matthiessen, A. W. Schwarz & S. Find, 'Research gateways of the world, an analysis based on bibliometric indicators', in Å. E. Andersson & D. Andersson (ed.), 'Gateways to the Global Economy', Cheltenham, Edward Elgar, 2000

C. W. Matthiessen, A. W. Schwarz & S. Find, 'The Top-level Global Research System, 1997-99: Centres, Networks and Nodality. An Analysis Based on Bibliometric Indicators', Urban Studies, 2002 (a), 39 (5-6), 903-927

C. W. Matthiessen, A. W. Schwarz & S. Find, 'The ups and downs of global research centres', Science Magazine, 2002 (b), 297, 5586, 1476-1477

C. W. Matthiessen, A. W. Schwarz & S. Find, 'World cities of knowledge - research strength, networks and nodality', Journal of Knowledge Management, 2006, 10(5), 14-25

C. W. Matthiessen, A. W. Schwarz & S. Find, 'World Cities of Scientific Knowledge: Systems, Networks and Potential Dynamics. An Analysis Based on Bibliometric Indicators', Urban Studies Journal, 2010, 47(9), 1879-1897

P. J. Taylor, 'World City Network, a Global Urban Analysis', Routledge, 2004

P. J. Taylor, 'World City Network, a Global Urban Analysis', Routledge, 2007

Thomson Reuters Web of Science, Science Citation Index (SCI), 2009

Wikipedia, 2010

NOTES

ⁱ Øresund City: Greater Copenhagen, Greater-Malmö-Lund and Greater Helsingborg. The frequently used expression Copenhagen-Lund is used in the diagrams about the Øresund City.

ⁱⁱ Sources for the figures: Thomson Reuters Web of Science (2009): Science Citation Index, SCI. Data processing : DTU Analysis and Research Promotion Center, D'ARC.

ⁱⁱⁱ In this chapter, we consider the Øresund City as one urban region because the academic world has structured itself as one entity under the name The Øresund University and because, to an increasing extent, the city region forms one entity for research and development. For example, the key clusters in Michael Porter's interpretation have been created across the national border. Greater Copenhagen alone accounts for 25,623 papers 2006-2008, while the corresponding figure for Malmö-Lund is 12,548. The total figure for the Øresund City is less because joint author papers are only included once. Of these, there are 1,355 across Øresund. Therefore, the Øresund City's output was 36,816 papers 2006-2008.

^{iv} Wikipedia 2010.

^v Outside Europe and North America, we have only recorded data on scientific output for a number of selected countries. Hence the reduction to the Top 30.

^{vi} Diagrams with partnership patterns have been drawn to resemble maps. No dimensional accuracy nor north-south and east-west order has been carried out although this was aimed at. The diagrams were simply drawn arbitrarily. City names have been given as identifiable abbreviations as far as possible. Each diagram comprises the 40 largest cities measured by scientific output during the given period.

^{vii} Insert assessments are based on the subsequent analysis.

^{viii} Thomson Reuters Web of Science (2009).

CHAPTER 9
THE POTENTIAL EFFECTS OF THE FIXED FEHMARN LINK ON HOUSE PRICES IN THE HAMBURG-COPENHAGEN CORRIDOR: APPLYING EAST ASIAN LESSONS TO NORTHERN EUROPE

DAVID EMANUEL ANDERSSON, ÅKE E. ANDERSSON,
ZOLTAN KETTINGER & OLIVER F. SHYR

The Fehmarnbelt link is scheduled for completion in 2020. It represents one of the most substantial infrastructural investments in Northern Europe. In many ways, this link can be viewed as the third and final phase – after the Øresund Bridge and the Storebælt Bridge – of the integration of Scandinavia into the continental European road and rail network. The inauguration of the Fehmarnbelt link will have major effects on inter-regional time distances, regardless of whether it is a bridge or a tunnel. For the first time, the time distances between the main Scandinavian centres and nodes in Northern Germany will correspond to equivalent nodal distances south of the Baltic Sea.

Investments in new transport links tend to have a number of effects that adhere to a predictable qualitative structure (Banister, 2007). The immediate impact of a new transport link is an improvement in the overall accessibility of the affected region as well as relative accessibility changes among various nodes within that region. Accessibility improvements tend to give rise to agglomeration economies at various levels of spatial aggregation, which in turn alters the feasibility of establishing new firms and specialised clusters according to industry-specific accessibility considerations. New demand from investors and employees within these expanding industries restructures regional land and property markets, with a predictable increase in land values that reflects overall accessibility improvements. It is also possible that there will be secondary effects, such as new property development schemes

that raise the demand for transport services, which in some cases may lead to increasing congestion problems in the transport system and a demand for further infrastructural investments. Interestingly, new congestion may therefore sometimes signal the unanticipated dynamic success of a new transport link, since the most valuable links are those that trigger substantial agglomeration economies with numerous previously unknown entrepreneurial opportunities (Andersson, 2005).

There are also a number of contextual conditions (Banister, 2007) that act as constraints on the economic opportunities that are facilitated by improved accessibility. Most of these constraints are institutional. Linguistic and other cultural barriers may, for example, slow down processes of inter-regional integration and urban enlargement. When two or more nation states are involved, there are also formal institutional differences that may influence spatial patterns. For example, Danish housing regulations make it more difficult for residents of other countries to own holiday homes in Denmark than in Germany or Sweden. On the other hand, labour market regulations tend to be less flexible in Germany than in Denmark, which makes Denmark a more attractive recipient of certain types of foreign direct investment. All such institutional differences have the effect of channelling location decisions away from the spatial pattern that could be expected within a uniform institutional framework.

The most established method for estimating the effects of differentiated accessibility on land values is hedonic price (bid price) estimation (Rosen, 1974). Property transactions are then modelled as representing the sale or rent of a number of attributes, where each attribute is associated with an implicit price that can be estimated on the basis of within-sample variability in attribute levels. The implicit prices associated with one attribute will tend to be influenced by other attribute levels, since real-world property tends to be associated with costly repackaging of attributes and non-constant returns to scale. The preferred hedonic price functions are, therefore, non-linear, ranging from logarithmic models – which yield estimates of mean attribute elasticities – to more complex data-specific functional forms such as iterative maximum likelihood functions.

It is common to divide the set of property attributes into three distinct categories: structural, neighbourhood, and accessibility attributes. Even if the research question is limited to the effect of relative accessibility on sales prices or rents, it is often necessary to include an exhaustive set of structural and neighbourhood attributes in the estimated hedonic price function. This is because there are often non-zero correlations between accessibility and other attributes. For example, less accessible housing tends to be associated with larger floor areas and lots. In addition, it is common for socio-economic neighbourhood attributes to be spatially distributed in ways that reflect the trade-offs between access and space among different categories of buyers or renters (Andersson, Shyr & Fu, 2010).

A relatively large number of hedonic studies have estimated the effect of urban transport accessibility on residential property prices (e.g. Dewes, 1976; Gatzlaff & Smith, 1993; Al-Mosaind, Dueker & Strathman, 1993; Cervero, 1994; Bollinger & Ihlanfeldt, 1997; Cervero & Landis, 1997; Henneberry, 1998). Studies of the relative price effects of major bridges, tunnels or long-distance rail are much less common. The most relevant recent studies are all from East Asia and concern combined expressway-tunnel investments in Hong Kong and Taiwan (Yiu & Wong, 2005; Shyr & Andersson, 2009) as well as accessibility to a new inter-regional high-speed rail (HSR) line in Taiwan (Andersson, Shyr & Lee, 2009; Andersson, Shyr & Fu, 2010; Andersson & Shyr, 2010). It is to these East Asian studies that we turn next.

THE EFFECTS OF KEY INFRASTRUCTURAL INVESTMENTS

Yiu & Wong (2005) show that the expected accessibility effects of a new tunnel in Hong Kong were capitalised in house prices several years before the completion of the project. In the Hong Kong case, this allowed the government to partially fund the construction of the tunnel by selling property that benefited from the improved access in the vicinity of the tunnel. Hong Kong is, however, a special case, since all land is owned by the government,

TABLE 1.
TIME COSTS, MONEY COSTS AND DAILY PASSENGER VOLUMES BEFORE AND AFTER THE OPENING OF THE XUESHAN TUNNEL (2006)

Mode	January-May		June-December		Change	
	Car	Bus	Car	Bus	Car	Bus
Time cost (minutes)	90	170	45	50	-50%	-71%
Money cost (USD)	7.00	6.81	4.00	4.06	-43%	-40%
Daily passenger volume	30,648	355	45,763	5,494	+49%	+1,448%

Source: Shyr & Andersson (2009)

which sells long-term leaseholds to the highest bidder. This may be one reason why Hong Kong's urban transit (MTR) also has been unusually profitable. The MTR is operated by a corporation which controls most of the land around the stations of the MTR network. It has, therefore, been able to profit from a combination of low passenger fares and high rental payments in accessible locations. In addition, high population densities have made high-frequency train services possible.

Shyr & Andersson (2009) provide an analysis of a new tunnel and motorway investment which is a closer analogy to the fixed Fehmarn link: the Xueshan project, which includes the world's fifth-longest road tunnel. After more than a decade of construction work, the Xueshan Tunnel and National Freeway No. 5 were opened in 2006. The completion of the tunnel resulted in a reduction in the time distance from northern Yilan County to eastern districts of Taipei City from 90 to 45 minutes. Before the completion of the tunnel, connections between the two regions (Taipei and Yilan) consisted of two narrow two-lane roads with average speed limits of about 50 km per hour. The Taipei metropolitan region had a population of about 6.7 million in 2005, while Yilan County had a population of 460,000. Table 1 shows travel times, money costs, and passenger volumes before and after the opening of the tunnel in 2006.

It has become increasingly obvious to both buyers and sellers of real estate that Yilan has become a feasible spatial option for Taipei-bound commuters. Yilan's land value index rose by about 10 per cent between 2002 and 2007, as compared with increases of less than 5 per cent nationally as well as in the Taipei metropolitan area. Land values account for between 30 and 50 per cent of the total property value in Taiwan.

Shyr & Andersson (2009) used disaggregated data from four different time periods to estimate the timing and magnitude of the accessibility effect that is associated with the Xueshan tunnel and motorway. In each case, they used logarithmic hedonic price functions with almost identical variable specifications.

Because the investment cost was initially underestimated, the inauguration date of the tunnel was postponed several times during the construction period. In order to assess the house price effects of the tunnel project over the 15-year construction period, Shyr & Andersson employed three hypotheses that were based on Yiu & Wong (2005):

1. The distance-to-Taipei effect will increase at an increasing rate as the completion date approaches.

2. After the completion of the tunnel, the distance-to-Taipei effect will exert a greater influence on house prices than distance-to-local-centre attributes, which would then imply that Yilan County is a new sub-region of an enlarged Taipei functional urban region.

3. The price effect of the distance-to-Taipei attribute should increase more in Yilan County than in other equally distant locations that have not received substantial investments in transport infrastructure.

Table 2 shows the results of the estimations as regards the distance-to-Taipei variable, which measures the shortest road distance from the property to the Taipei 101 skyscraper in the centre of Taipei. All price data refer to contractual sales prices. A negative but insignificant price-distance elasticity is first estimated for the period that begins slightly more than four years prior to the completion of the project, while the first significant price-distance elasticity is estimated for the subsequent time period. The greatest effect is estimated for the final period, which includes the opening of the tunnel in May 2006. It is noteworthy that the price-distance elasticity is as high as -.46, which implies that a halving of the distance to central Taipei – within Yilan County – was associated with a 46 per cent price increase in the 2006-2007 period. This is a very strong accessibility effect, which testifies to the pull of very large regions (the Taipei metropolitan area – excluding Yilan – has a population of almost seven million and a per capita gross regional product that exceeds the national per capita GDP by about 40 per cent).

On the other hand, the estimated price-distance elasticities associated with the distance to the two main population nodes within Yilan County declined between 1992 and 2007 from -.20 to -.13 and from -.12 to -.07, respectively. The implication is that housing

TABLE 2.
ESTIMATED DISTANCE-TO-TAIPEI ELASTICITIES FROM YILAN COUNTY

Time period	1992-1994	2002-2003	2004-2005	2006-2007
Status of project	Beginning of construction	4 years before completion	2 years before completion	Completion
Estimated distance-to-Taipei elasticity	+0.190	-0.139	-0.436	-0.458
t-value	0.338	-0.760	-3.540	-4.989
Sample size	298	245	674	967
Mean distance to Taipei 101 (km)	78.7	57.1	57.9	54.8
Minimum distance	64.8	41.3	39.6	39.9
Maximum distance	96.7	72.5	74.0	84.3
Standard deviation of distance	8.5	7.4	7.4	7.1
Number of control variables	17	16	20	20

Source: Shyr & Andersson (2009)

that is especially suitable for Taipei-bound commuting commands a substantial price premium over less accessible housing. A further implication is that Yilan County now constitutes a sub-region of Taipei's functional urban region, rather than the separate region that it no doubt was before the construction of the Xueshan Tunnel and Freeway No. 5.

Shyr & Andersson (2009) conclude that all three of their hypotheses are supported by the results, since a comparison with other peripheral areas around Taipei shows that the increase in the slope of the estimated price-distance gradient is greater in Yilan County (to the east) than in Keelung (to the north) or Taoyuan (to the south-west). Neither of the two latter regions experienced any equally dramatic reductions in periphery-to-core commuting times during the 1992-to-2007 period.

Shyr & Andersson (ibid.) conclude that Yilan County can be expected to receive increasing investments in residential property in the coming years, since house prices are still much lower than in Taipei and also because air and noise pollution levels have so far remained low. A stable spatial distribution of the region's population can only be expected when the combined effects of emergent congestion, pollution, and house price increases reach the accessibility-adjusted levels of the regional core and its western outskirts.

FIGURE 1.
TAIWAN'S HIGH-SPEED RAIL

THE EFFECTS OF HIGH-SPEED RAIL LINKS: ESTIMATES FROM TAIWAN

Taiwan's high-speed railway was inaugurated in early 2007, and consists of eight stations in seven metropolitan regions (see Figure 1). It traverses the 345 km between Taipei and Kaohsiung (Zuoying) in about 90 minutes. This makes Taiwan's high-speed railway an especially appropriate case study from the Fehmarnbelt link perspective, since the distance between Hamburg and Copenhagen is 288 km as the crow flies.

The high speed rail station in Taipei is co-located with the old railway station and the main transit interchange, but all other stations are located on newly developed suburban land. There has, therefore, been a reshuffling of the relative accessibility of urban neighbourhoods, with the exception of Taipei. The new time distances between several of the metropolitan regions are in many cases short enough to enable the integration of previously separated housing and labour markets. Several of these regions are now accessible

TABLE 3.
EXAMPLES OF TIME DISTANCES BY HIGH-SPEED RAIL AND CONVENTIONAL RAIL, MINUTES

Regional combinations	High-speed rail (HSR)	Conventional rail (TRA)	Change
Taipei – Kaohsiung (Zuoying)	96	280	-66%
Taipei – Hsinchu	34	65	-48%
Taipei – Taichung	52	135	-62%
Hsinchu – Taichung	26	65	-60%
Hsinchu – Chiayi	52	134	-61%
Taichung – Chiayi	26	70	-63%
Taichung – Tainan	43	115	-63%
Chiayi – Tainan	19	42	-55%
Chiayi – Kaohsiung (Zuoying)	34	75	-55%
Tainan – Kaohsiung (Zuoying)	17	33	-49%

Source: HSR and TRA schedules (2009)

from one another in less than 50 minutes (one way), which a host of empirical studies identify as a threshold associated with a sudden drop in commuting frequencies (Andersson & Andersson, 2008). The Taipei metropolitan area – as conventionally defined – is now within the reach of daily commuters from the Taoyuan and Hsinchu areas. Taiwan's third largest metropolitan area, Taichung, has for the same reason become a feasible choice for daily commuters from Hsinchu, Chiayi, and Tainan.

Table 3 provides an overview of time distances by rail before and after the completion of the high speed rail (road time distances are usually longer than time distances by conventional rail, due to Taiwan's congested road network). Table 4 gives population figures for these metropolitan areas as well as the time distance from the central business district to the high-speed rail station by means of public and private transport.

TABLE 4.
METROPOLITAN AREA POPULATIONS AND ACCESS TIME IN MINUTES FROM CBD TO HSR STATIONS

HSR station	Metropolitan area population (million)	Access time to CBD (car)	Access time to CBD (public transport)
Taipei	6.7	0	0
Banciao	6.7	-	-
Taoyuan	1.9	20	30
Hsinchu	0.8	20	30
Taichung	2.3	25	15
Chiayi	0.3	30	40
Tainan	1.2	30	40
Kaohsiung (Zuoying)	2.7	20	15

Source: National Statistics, Republic of China (Taiwan) (2008)

Official delimitations of metropolitan areas – which correspond to the population figures in Table 4 – usually employ historical observations of commuter flows between outlying areas and an urban core with greater daytime than residential population. Typically, a peripheral area is included in a metropolitan region as long as the proportion of core-bound commuters exceeds a specific but arbitrary threshold. There are, however, other ways of defining a metropolitan region; a more forward-looking way is to measure how far away a regional centre impacts land values by making it more expensive than in genuinely rural areas. Should such an impact be present it would imply that market participants expect centre accessibility to be a valued attribute among participants in various property markets – an indication of functional economic integration. For example, adding the population of Yilan County to the Taipei Metropolitan Area yields a regional population of 7.2 million, while the economic integration of Taipei, Yilan, Taoyuan, and Hsinchu would yield a functional urban region with a population of almost 10 million.

Taiwan's seven metropolitan areas reflect the process of economic development as it has manifested itself on the island. One driving force has been the core of the Taipei metropolitan area, which specialises in the production of knowledge services in fields such as finance, marketing, trade, entertainment, and basic research. The other important driving force is the development and manufacture of high technology products – both producer

TABLE 5.
ANNUAL PER CAPITA INCOME AND AVERAGE HOUSE PRICE,
TAIWAN'S METROPOLITAN AREAS (2007)

Urban area	House price per sqm in USD	House price index (Chiayi=100)	Disposable income in USD per person	Income index (Chiayi=100)
Taipei	1,826	204	15,130	161
Taoyuan	976	109	10,649	113
Hsinchu	1,144	128	14,169	151
Taichung	1,149	128	11,664	124
Chiayi	895	100	9,390	100
Tainan	956	107	10,261	109
Kaohsiung (Zuoying)	918	103	11,451	122

Source: Andersson, Shyr & Lee (2009), Urban and Regional Development Statistics 2008, Urban and Housing Development Department, Executive Yuan (per capita income)

and consumer goods – which is centred on Taiwan's three science parks in Hsinchu, Taichung, and Tainan. There are also some high-value-added economic activities in the major metropolitan areas of Kaohsiung and Taichung, particularly in logistics (Kaohsiung) and higher education (Taichung). But most Taiwanese still work in traditional family firms that make standardised goods or engage in personal services such as retailing. The traditional economy is particularly evident in the southern half of the island, which has been under cost-cutting pressure in recent years due to the increasing availability of low-cost labour in mainland China.

Table 5 shows average per capita income and average house price per square metre in each of the seven metropolitan regions. Taipei and Hsinchu residents have incomes that are on average between 20 and 60 per cent higher than in the other five regions. House prices reflect these differences to some extent, the difference being that it is income per square metre rather than income per person that becomes the clinching factor. There are basically three house price levels in Taiwan: high in Taipei; moderate in Hsinchu and Taichung; and low in much of the rest of the island. However, the table does not show the sharp differentiation within the Taipei region, where the central business district exhibits land values that are several times higher than the Taipei region as a whole.

The Hsinchu region is particularly interesting: a medium-sized region with higher incomes than Taiwan's second and third largest cities but with house prices at similar levels. Hsinchu's economic success is in large part due to the Hsinchu Science Park, which is Taiwan's largest and oldest science park. Its 150,000 workers – almost 20 per cent of the region's total population – make up about 1.3 per cent of Taiwan's labour force but accounted for more than 3 per cent of GDP and 8.5 per cent of exports in 2004 (Chen, 2005). The park is an important node in the information technology industry, with especially strong linkages to Silicon Valley and Guangdong in Southern China. Two of Taiwan's twelve research universities are also located in Hsinchu, both of which have taken an active part in the development of manufacturing capabilities such as the production of integrated circuits.

The location of the high-speed rail station is perhaps not as peripheral as is implied by Table 4, since the access time refers to the traditional city centre rather than the Hsinchu Science Park, with the latter arguably being the new economic centre of Hsinchu. The park is located in the eastern part of the region, with an access time of only about 10 minutes to the HSR station – a considerably shorter time distance than from the science parks in Taichung and, especially, Tainan (about 30 minutes).

The economic structure of Taiwan's metropolitan areas is a relevant concern when considering the impact of high-speed rail accessibility, since the attractiveness of high-speed rail commuting is not only a function of time distance, but also a function of ticket affordability and differences in real house rents and wages in various origin-destination pairings, from the point of view of the individual with her specific skills and opportunity costs. One may expect people to react to long-term, stable differences in local wage rates by commuting or by moving to the higher-wage location. Other relevant factors, such as educational opportunities, service quality and purely subjective factors may of course reinforce or weaken the propensity to move.

Andersson, Shyr & Fu (2009) estimated the relative implicit prices of high speed rail, central business district, and Science Park accessibility in five of Taiwan's seven metropolitan regions (Taoyuan, Hsinchu, Taichung, Chiayi, and Tainan). They used a logarithmic hedonic specification, which implies that all estimated accessibility attributes may be interpreted as average price-distance elasticities.

One way of looking at the spatial orientation of the five metropolitan areas is by comparing the impacts of the various estimated accessibility attributes on residential property prices. Table 6 shows that four traditional city centres, three high-speed rail stations, and two science parks have substantial and highly significant impacts on sales prices in their respective housing markets. Andersson, Shyr & Fu infer that none of the five regions exhibits an unambiguously monocentric character. They also note that all of the included nodes emerged from substantial infrastructural investments: first in traditional railway stations, then in science parks, and finally in high-speed rail stations.

TABLE 6.
RANKING OF NODES ACCORDING TO HEDONIC ESTIMATES OF AVERAGE PRICE-DISTANCE ELASTICITY; TAOYUAN, HSINCHU, TAICHUNG, CHIAYI AND TAINAN REGIONS (2007)

Node	Region	Estimated price-distance elasticity	t-value	Sample size	Control variables
Hsinchu HSR station	Hsinchu	-.18	-8.99	846	10
Chiayi city centre	Chiayi	-.14	-6.09	683	10
Taichung city centre	Taichung	-.11	-8.18	1,486	10
Tainan city centre	Tainan	-.11	-6.97	1,550	10
Taichung HSR station	Taichung	-.09	-5.80	1,486	10
Hsinchu science park	Hsinchu	-.09	-5.47	846	10
Tainan science park	Tainan	-.08	-3.55	1,550	10
Chiayi HSR station	Chiayi	-.08	-3.40	683	10
Hsinchu city centre	Hsinchu	-.06	-4.08	846	10
Tainan HSR station	Tainan	-.04	-1.95	1,550	10
Taichung science park	Taichung	-.03	-1.79	1,486	10
Taoyuan city centre	Taoyuan	-.01	-1.28	1,180	12
Taoyuan HSR station	Taoyuan	-.01	-0.48	1,180	12

Source: Andersson, Shyr & Fu (2009)

Table 6 shows that in the case of Hsinchu, high-speed rail station accessibility has a greater impact on house prices than either science park or CBD accessibility. The estimated high-speed rail accessibility effect thereby testifies to the economic importance of the Hsinchu-Taipei linkage for the Hsinchu Science Park. All three distance effects are however substantial and statistically significant. The estimated hedonic price function lends support to the notion that Hsinchu's city centre and science park nodes have been transformed into outlying sub-centres in an enlarged northern metropolitan region. We may interpret high-speed rail accessibility as a proxy for accessibility to Taipei's as well as Taichung's central business districts. Since the new high-speed rail link has resulted in feasible commuting opportunities between Hsinchu and two of Taiwan's three largest cities, it seems that high-speed rail investments may contribute to urban enlargement processes that in some cases yield partially overlapping metropolitan areas.

High-speed rail station accessibility is also associated with clear price-distance gradients in Taichung and Chiayi. The price effect reflects the dramatic reduction of time distances to other metropolitan areas. It is now possible to live in Taichung and work in the Hsinchu Science Park or in the centre of Taipei, which are the areas with Taiwan's best-paying employment opportunities. Chiayi represents a classic example of a low-wage, low-cost area from which it has now become feasible to commute to Taichung, which has a wage level that is about 25 per cent higher than Chiayi.

In the Taoyuan and Tainan regions, high-speed rail accessibility has so far only had minor effects on residential property prices. While in Tainan the traditional city centre area has retained its predominance, Taoyuan has maintained its unusual character of having two small centres for which few people express a willingness to pay. The small or negligible high-speed rail accessibility effects in Taoyuan and Tainan reflect a factor that is present in both regions: the low intra-regional accessibility of their high-speed rail stations and the resulting lack of any real accessibility improvements. Centre-to-centre commuting by conventional train from Taoyuan to Taipei and from Tainan to Kaohsiung imposes lower money and time costs than high-speed rail commuting. It is only in a few suburbs that the high speed rail has effected real improvements in commuting opportunities. Those suburbs are however considered unattractive by the most likely high-speed rail commuters: professionals in knowledge services (i.e. the high-speed rail stations are located in low-income neighbourhoods).

Both of the studies from Taiwan show that accessibility improvements tend to raise house prices and that such improvements may additionally result in enlarged or overlapping functional urban regions. But there are also limits to the lessons that may be drawn. Taiwanese and other Asian households tend to have greater income elasticities of demand for accessibility than for space (Andersson & Shyr, 2010), which makes accessibility between different urban cores more relevant to high-income households than the accessibility of low-density areas to urban centres. In addition, it is very unusual for Taiwanese households to own a holiday home such as a summer cottage, unlike in Scandinavia or Germany. Improved accessibility to scenic spots such as seacoasts, lakes, and forests is therefore more likely to trigger new property development and new consumer demand in a European than in an Asian context.

THE HAMBURG-COPENHAGEN CORRIDOR: THE HOUSING MARKET BEFORE THE LINK

The length of the Hamburg-Copenhagen corridor is about 288 km, which is approximately the same length as the Taipei-Kaohsiung corridor in Taiwan or the Gothenburg-Malmö corridor on the Swedish west coast. But unlike the corridors in Taiwan and Sweden, the Hamburg-Copenhagen corridor has a population that is heavily concentrated at its southern and northern ends. The main reason for this lopsided population distribution is the bottleneck at the Fehmarnbelt, where the only mode of transportation prior to the

opening of the Fehmarnbelt link is a ferry service. At present, the ferry crossing takes almost one hour.

According to standardised European Union definitions, the Hamburg functional urban region ("larger urban zone") had a population of 3.2 million, while the corresponding population for the Copenhagen region was 1.8 million. The area between the Hamburg and Copenhagen regions is however sparsely populated by European standards. The only major city is Lübeck, with a population of 215,000 in 2005. By contrast, the population of the German island of Fehmarn was only 13,000 in the same year, while the largely rural municipality of Lolland (opposite Fehmarn in Denmark) had a total population of 67,000, which includes several small towns, each with fewer than 15,000 permanent residents. The largest urban node in the Danish part of the corridor is Næstved, located 71 km south of Copenhagen, with a population of only 42,000. Nykøbing Falster has 17,000 inhabitants in its urban area.

The low population density of the area between Lübeck and Næstved is reflected in low property and land prices by western European standards. On Lolland, average sales prices for residential property ranged from about EUR 900 to about EUR 1,350 per square metre in 2009 (see Figure 2). On the other side of the Fehmarnbelt – the island of Fehmarn and North-Eastern Holstein – the corresponding figures ranged from about EUR 850 to about EUR 1,600 for the most part, with the exception of some coastal communities on the mainland, where the average sales price reached almost EUR 2,000 in 2009 (see Figure 2). By both Danish and German standards, house prices on Lolland, Fehmarn, and the German Baltic coast are unusually affordable.

By contrast, central areas of both Hamburg and Copenhagen are very costly. The highest sales prices were recorded in the centre of Hamburg, with an average sales price per square metre of EUR 5,830. The maximum average sales price on the Danish side was not much lower with an average sales price per square metre of EUR 5,645 in central Copenhagen. The two sides of the Fehmarnbelt are roughly symmetrical: unit sales prices of EUR 5,000 or more at the two terminal nodes of the new connection, each of which generates a downward-sloping price-distance gradient. These gradients end in Southern Zealand and halfway between Hamburg and Lübeck, respectively.

While house prices are even lower in southern Lolland than on Fehmarn, this does not imply that it is necessarily cheaper to live on Lolland, since households do not only consume housing. According to the Economist Intelligence Unit, the cost of living was 31 per cent higher in Copenhagen than in Hamburg in 2007, if housing costs are excluded. According to the Central Intelligence Agency, Denmark's average cost of living was 33 per cent higher than Germany's in 2009. As regards households with normal spending patterns, one can therefore unambiguously conclude that Fehmarn and North-Eastern Holstein are the lowest-cost locations within the Hamburg-Copenhagen corridor.

Although Germany and Denmark are both members of the European Union and do not have any bilateral barriers against flows of people, capital, goods or services, there are still many institutional differences that on balance make Denmark a more expensive location. For example, Danish land-use regulations make it extraordinarily difficult to initiate new commercial property development, and the Danish value-added tax is among the world's highest and most comprehensive. One of the effects of Denmark's unusually stringent land-use regulations is that the number of property developers and retailers is much smaller in Denmark than in Germany, and there is therefore less competition in these sectors. The predictable consequence is that German developers and retailers are under greater cost-cutting pressures than their Danish counterparts. From a consumer perspective, Germany is a more attractive location, assuming equal house prices and equal language capabilities. On the other hand, Denmark is often a more attractive location for workers, since Danish wage rates tend to be higher. It is thus more likely that people will choose to live in Germany and work in Denmark than the reverse combination.

The map (Figure 2) gives a clear indication of the existence of price-distance gradients that are centred on Hamburg and Copenhagen, even though we have not checked for

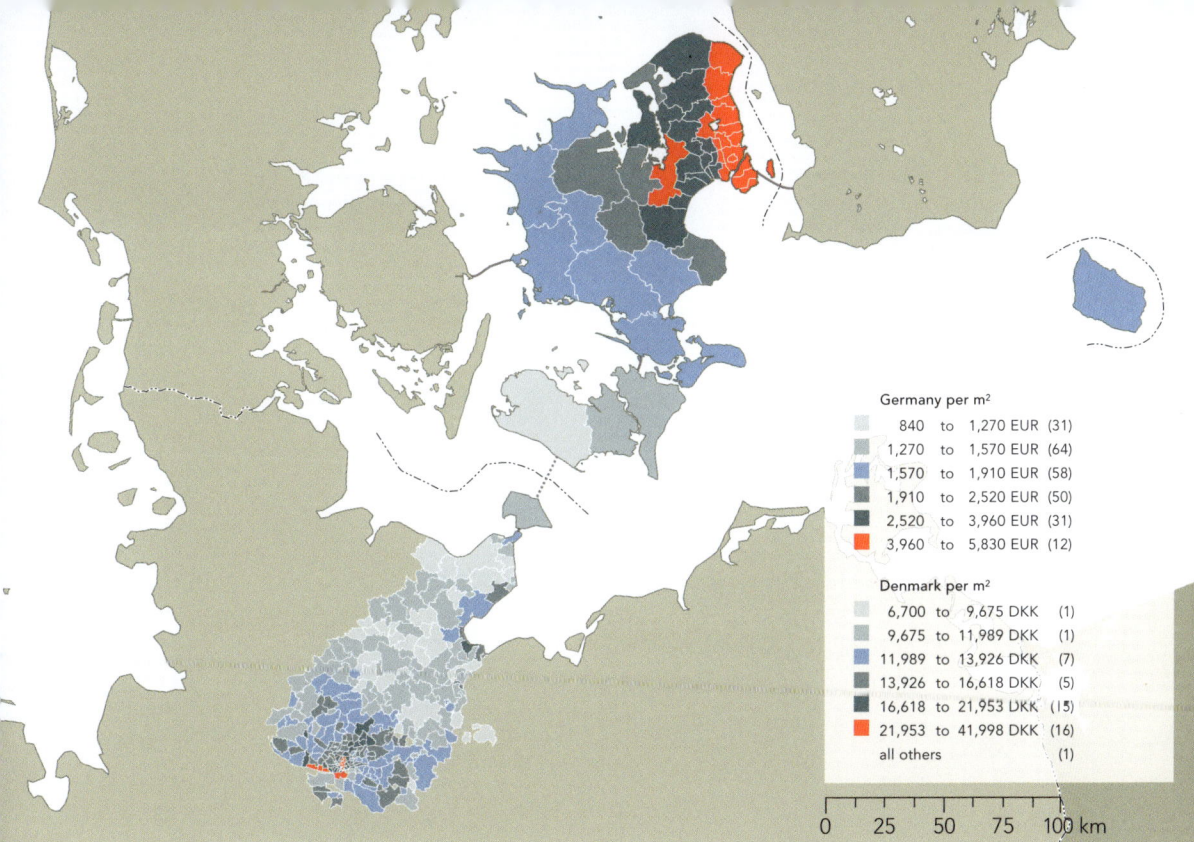

FIGURE 2.
SALES PRICES PER SQUARE METRE IN ZEALAND AND IN THE HAMBURG-FEHMARN CORRIDOR (2009)

various spatially dependent countervailing factors. For the purpose of analysing spatial economic factors in more detail, we estimated a hedonic price function for the Hamburg-Fehmarn part of the proposed road-and-rail corridor. While we did not estimate an analogous function for Zealand and Lolland, it is reasonable to assume that the accessibility effect will be of a similar order of magnitude, since the overall price structure is so similar on both sides of the Fehmarnbelt. The analysed region in Germany includes the Bundesland of Hamburg and most of eastern Schleswig-Holstein, including Lübeck but not Kiel.

The observations on asking prices and structural attributes (floor area and age of dwelling as well as quality dummy variables) were obtained from a number of commercial estate agents that operate in Northern Germany, and encompass 7,556 dwellings that were offered for sale and 2,600 dwellings that were offered for rent. All observations refer to housing units that were actively marketed but had not yet been sold in December, 2009.

TABLE 7.
HEDONIC PRICE FUNCTION FOR OWNER-OCCUPIED HOUSING IN THE HAMBURG-FEHMARN REGION (DEPENDENT VARIABLE: NATURAL LOGARITHM OF ASKING PRICE IN EUR) (2009)

Variable	Coefficient (b)	t-value
Constant	7.544	
Structural attributes		
Floor area (log)	1.017	132.430
Age of dwelling (log)	-.073	-24.621
Low quality (dummy)	-.243	-8.280
Normal quality (dummy)	-.067	-5.645
High quality (dummy)	.089	8.137
Special features (dummy)	.349	15.973
Neighbourhood attributes		
Good reputation (dummy)	.307	13.349
District income (log)	.064	12.864
District unemployment (log)	-.149	-16.156
Accessibility		
Distance to CBD (log)	-.134	-20.622

R^2=.775; N=7556

The socio-economic data are based on official statistics from the Federal German Statistical Office and the Statistical Office of Hamburg. Income data refer to city districts within Hamburg and municipalities in Schleswig-Holstein. Unemployment data again refer to city districts in Hamburg, but were only available at the state level (Bundesland) in Schleswig-Holstein. Hamburg districts with a good reputation were identified in discussions with a number of Hamburg residents. The accessibility variable corresponds to approximate distances between individual dwellings and the central station of Hamburg, using the shortest road distance as calculated by Google Earth.

Table 7 gives estimated attribute effects using asking prices for owner-occupied housing. All structural variables have substantial and significant effects with the expected signs. The reason that all condition dummies (i.e. low, normal, and high) yielded significant effects was that a subset of the database did not include sufficient information regarding the condition of the property. The results imply that these observations on average had a better condition than units classified as "normal." All socio-economic variables are also significant, with reputation (image) and local unemployment rates being more important than average incomes as price determinants within the city of Hamburg (the income level was the only distinguishing feature for areas in Schleswig-Holstein).

The estimated distance elasticity was -.134, which implies that a halving of the distance – measured as road distance in km – is associated with a 13.4 per cent price increase. This is a very credible estimate by international standards. For example, in the slightly smaller metropolitan area of Taichung the average distance elasticity is -.11 (see Table 6). Estimates from other metropolitan regions with population sizes of between one and five million also tend to produce elasticity estimates in the -.1 to -.2 interval, which implies that the real effect is likely to fall within this range.

A problem with the distance measurement used for the hedonic price functions reported in Tables 7 and 8 is that it is based on geographical distance rather than time distance, which is the variable that is most relevant to households and other users of property. In other words, the estimated price-distance gradient should be interpreted as the effect of the geographical distance, given the present state of the transport infrastructure. Since improvements to road and/or rail networks can be expected to result in shorter time distances, one should expect that such improvements result in a "flattening" of the geographical price-distance gradient as well as a larger area being affected by it, other things being equal (i.e. the price-distance gradient should remain constant in time-distance terms). As a corollary, a halving of all time distances to the regional node with the best general accessibility is associated with a doubling of the geographical radius from the centre to the periphery of the region, if a region is defined as an area with a maximum time distance to the centre. The exact configuration of the transport system – including average speeds on roads and railways and the location of motorway ramps and railway stations – tends to be the main influence on the process of urban enlargement. The transport system is the key factor in this process since expected commuting times determine the feasibility of daily commuting, which drives the integration or fragmentation of labour and housing markets.

Table 8 gives the results of the estimated hedonic price function for rental housing in the Hamburg-Fehmarn region. While the attribute effects all have the same direction as in the hedonic price function for the owner-occupied housing market, the relative importance of attribute categories is different. Generally speaking, structural and neighbourhood characteristics are less important for renters than for buyers, while accessibility is more important. This is not unexpected, since the population of renters has socio-economic

TABLE 8.
HEDONIC PRICE FUNCTION FOR RENTAL HOUSING IN THE HAMBURG-FEHMARN REGION (DEPENDENT VARIABLE: NATURAL LOGARITHM OF RENT IN EUR) (2009)

Variable	Coefficient (b)	t-value
Constant	2.776	
Structural attributes		
Floor area (log)	.992	96.059
Age of dwelling (log)	-.049	-14.218
High quality (dummy)	.162	6.870
Special features (dummy)	.101	9.678
Parking (dummy)	.046	5.194
Neighbourhood attributes		
Good reputation (dummy)	.158	7.691
District income (log)	.014	3.048
District unemployment (log)	-.125	-11.837
Accessibility		
Distance to CBD (log)	-.182	-29.388

R^2=.883; N=2600

features that distinguish them from buyers. For example, a mixed multinominal logit model for the German housing market showed that a 10 per cent increase in household income was associated with a 4.01 percentage point increase in the probability to buy rather than rent housing. It also showed that a household with the average German income is associated with a 48.6 per cent probability of choosing owner-occupied housing (Börsch-Supan, Heiss & Seko, 2001).

The demand for rental housing can therefore be expected to reflect the demand of low-income households to a greater extent than the market for owner-occupied housing. There also tends to be a positive statistical association between household income and car ownership rates, which in general should make us expect low-income households to be more concerned about access to public transport access points than high-income households. Moreover, accessibility in public transport networks tends to be more sensitive to variations in population density than is the case for private transport networks. Socio-economic differences therefore explain why the rental housing market is associated with a steeper rent-distance gradient than the owner-occupied housing market.

In the Hamburg case, a halving of the road distance to the city centre of Hamburg is associated with an 18.2 per cent increase in rents, which is substantially greater than the 13.4 per cent increase in asking prices for owner-occupied housing. This no doubt reflects the considerable benefits of an urban location to users of public transport systems. This conclusion is reinforced by the similarity of the two price-distance gradients if only observations within the City of Hamburg are included: the estimated price-distance gradients are then -.202 for the rental market and -.236 for the owner-occupied market. For the regional urban core, it is likely that road accessibility exhibits greater variability than rail accessibility, due to high-density congestion effects.

The policy implication is that rental housing in the form of small apartments is most appropriate in high-density urban areas and around transit stations, while owner-occupied housing in the form of large single-family homes is least appropriate in those locations. The reason for this is not only that high land values imply high-density development. There is also the additional reason that the typical renter benefits more from high density than the typical home buyer, given present rates of car ownership in different income segments.

THE HOUSING MARKET AFTER THE FIXED LINK: THREE SCENARIOS

The exact features of the rail link between Hamburg and Copenhagen have still not been decided at the time of writing. This makes it worthwhile to discuss likely effects of various options. We have decided to analyse the effects of the fixed Fehmarnbelt link in terms of three scenarios: a minimum-cost option (Scenario 0); an Øresund-inspired commuter railway (Scenario 1); and a high-speed rail option (Scenario 2). These three options can be expected to affect property markets and commuting flows in distinct ways. Tables 9 and 10 summarise possible time distance and house price effects.

Scenario 0 implies that the overriding priority is to minimise investment costs. The likely new effects of such a strategy lie beyond regional housing markets, and thus cannot be analysed on the basis of the empirical results that are presented in this chapter. Long-distance transport by lorry is likely to be rerouted from the Storebælt Bridge, and there is likely to be a moderate increase in the number of Germans buying second homes in Southern Sweden. Both these effects are difficult to forecast. On the other hand, overall long-distance traffic flows are likely to be similar no matter which strategy is ultimately adopted. If the only infrastructural improvement is a new road-and-rail bridge or tunnel, it would imply that no urban enlargement processes will take place on either the German or Danish side of the Fehmarnbelt. This would also imply that time distances would remain the same with the exception of the Fehmarnbelt itself, with roads being generally faster than rail transport. House prices would remain largely unaffected by the link, and the average road speed would remain approximately 90 km per hour on the German side and 95 km per hour on the Danish side.

If Scenario 1 is adopted, it implies that the fastest commutes will be by train rather than car for those locations that are in close proximity to railway stations. The average speed for trains – including stops at stations – is then expected to increase to about 100 km per hour. In this case, one can expect modest house price increases in peripheral areas, as well as a small but non-negligible share of commuters that are bound for Hamburg and Copenhagen in towns such as Lübeck and Næstved. It is likely that there will be opportunities for property developers to increase construction of new single family homes near commuter rail stations, especially on Southern Zealand and in the area around Lübeck.

The most dramatic effects are almost certain to appear if Scenario 2 – with a new high-speed rail link – is adopted. Using the same strategy as in Taiwan would imply eight stations and an average speed of 165 km per hour for those trains that stop at all stations. Express services between Copenhagen and Hamburg would then take about 90 minutes, at an average speed of 220 km per hour. In this case, it would be reasonable to expect a flattening of the price-distance gradients around Copenhagen and Hamburg, as well as a substantial enlargement of their respective functional urban regions. House prices could be expected to increase by about 8 per cent in most regions, including the peripheral islands of Fehmarn and Lolland. It may even be possible for some workers in central Copenhagen to relocate to Fehmarn, which is likely to be attractive as it is associated with much lower prices of both land and consumer goods (the one-way time distance would be about 70 minutes).

The scenarios presented in Tables 9 and 10 are based on an extrapolation of the hedonic price function for owner-occupied housing in the Hamburg-Fehmarn corridor. Its reliability depends on several assumptions. First, we assume that the price-distant gradient remains constant in time-distance terms. Second, we assume the same price level for property in Copenhagen as in Hamburg, as well as identical price-distance gradients. The use of observations from the German side of the Fehmarnbelt implies that the Hamburg-Fehmarn price effects are more reliable than the Copenhagen-Lolland effects, other things being equal.

Socio-economic variation has been disregarded in all scenarios: the implication is that all areas have the same average incomes and unemployment rates. In this context, it is worth noting that the highest incomes are associated with the two metropolitan areas, and that both the highest and the lowest unemployment rates tend to be found in inner-city neighbourhoods. Consequently, the Hamburg and Copenhagen indices are pure accessibility indices, unlike real-world land price indices that tend to be higher in the most central neighbourhood – the central business district – due to high household incomes and low unemployment rates. A pure accessibility index is advisable in the face of major infrastruc-

TABLE 9.
TIME DISTANCES ACCORDING TO THREE SCENARIOS

Station	Distance from Hamburg	Distance from Copenhagen	Time from Hamburg (Scenario 0)	Time from Hamburg (Scenario 1)	Time from Hamburg (Scenario 2)
Bad Oldesloe	47 km	282 km	31 mins.	28 mins.	17 mins.
Lübeck	65 km	264 km	43 mins.	39 mins.	24 mins.
Fehmarn	146 km	183 km	97 mins.	88 mins.	53 mins.

			Time from Copenhagen (Scenario 0)	Time from Copenhagen (Scenario 1)	Time from Copenhagen (Scenario 2)
Nykøbing Falster	201 km	128 km	81 mins.	77 mins.	47 mins.
Næstved	258 km	71 km	45 mins.	43 mins.	26 mins.
Køge	287 km	42 km	27 mins.	25 mins.	15 mins.

			Time Hamburg-Copenhagen (Scenario 0)	Time Hamburg-Copenhagen (Scenario 1)	Time Hamburg-Copenhagen (Scenario 2)
Copenhagen central	329 km	329 km	220 mins.	195 mins.	120 mins.

Source: Google Maps, authors' calculations

TABLE 10.
HOUSE PRICE INDICES ACCORDING TO THREE SCENARIOS

Station	Scenario 0	Scenario 1	Scenario 2
Hamburg central	100	100	100
Bad Oldesloe	60	61	64
Lübeck	57	58	62
Fehmarn	51	52	56
Nykøbing Falster	52	53	56
Næstved	57	57	61
Køge	61	62	66
Copenhagen central	100	100	100

Source: Hedonic price function for the Hamburg-Fehmarn region (see Table 7)

tural investments, since such investments tend to trigger new property developments, new commuting patterns, and therefore a new spatial redistribution of socio-economic groups.

Other housing attributes have also been standardised prior to the calculation of the house price indices in Table 10. Throughout we have assumed a standard dwelling with a floor area of 111 square metres, a building age of 16.4 years, and average quality and condition attributes. Since structural attributes are not independent of location, this reinforces the interpretation of the indices as being derived almost exclusively from accessibility considerations. There is, however, a possibility that some unknown attributes have had a minor influence, as well as the certainty that localised accessibility – for example to central Lübeck – have not been taken into account. The implication is that the results are reliable in general terms, but that there may be localised land value effects that may add or subtract one or two percentage points as regards each location in each scenario. Such effects will, however, have a uniform effect across scenarios, given a specific location.

SUMMARY

Housing and land values are determined by accessibility, environmental conditions, as well as other factors that are associated with location. The price of land and other immovable property also represents the expected future development of rental values. Hedonic property price models make use of a consistent and theoretically grounded methodology to evaluate the benefits of investments in transport infrastructure. In hedonic models, improved access to major labour and service markets is expected to raise property prices.

Hedonic price models have been used extensively to evaluate investments in transport infrastructure within regions, but until recently there have been very few evaluations of the impact of major inter-regional links such as the Fehmarnbelt link. However, some recent large-scale transport investments in Asia have been evaluated using hedonic price models that measure the impact of improved accessibility on house prices in the sub-regions that are influenced by the new infrastructure. The large-scale transport investments in Hong Kong and the very large-scale tunnel, road, and express train systems that connect the north, south, and east of Taiwan are pertinent examples of how hedonic price models can be used to evaluate the long-term benefits of inter-regional infrastructure investments that have many similarities with the new Fehmarnbelt link project.

We have estimated the impact of accessibility on house prices using an extensive sample of asking prices from the corridor that encompasses the Hamburg region and Eastern Holstein, including the island of Fehmarn. Our estimates confirm that there is a substantial and statistically significant positive impact of relative accessibility on house prices. The house price elasticity with respect to accessibility is estimated to be approximately -0.13 for owner-occupied housing and approximately -0.18 for rental housing. These estimates are in the same range as most other comparable studies, including the Asian studies described in this chapter. The estimated accessibility effect implies that a 10 per cent increase of the accessibility (i.e. a 10 per cent reduction in the time distance to the centre) would increase the prices of all owner-occupied housing in the affected area by 1.3 per cent.

With the help of three realistic scenarios, we applied our hedonic estimates to analyse and evaluate the impact of the improved Copenhagen-Hamburg connection via the Fehmarnbelt link:

- Scenario 0 is a minimum cost scenario, in which the only improvement is the investment in the connection across the Fehmarnbelt. In this scenario, our hedonic estimates imply that there will not be any measurable impacts on house prices on either the German and Danish side that could be attributed to the Fehmarnbelt link.

- Scenario 1 assumes that there will both be an investment in the Fehmarnbelt link itself as well as complementary investments in the rail link that allows for an average passenger train speed of 100 km per hour (including delays at stops). In this scenario, our estimates imply an increase of house prices in the municipalities with train stations of close to 2 per cent.

- Scenario 2 assumes an investment in a TGV-type high-speed train connection with an average speed of 165 km per hour, which includes delays associated with stopping at a total of eight stations, including the Copenhagen and Hamburg terminals. In this scenario there would be an increase in house prices of between 7.5 and 8.5 per cent in municipalities with stations. These estimates do not take other future dynamic changes into account, such as new property developments or new commuter preferences. An increase of 8 per cent in the prices of an average house on the German side corresponds to an absolute increase in 2009 prices by EUR 16,000. The estimates for the Danish side are somewhat more uncertain but could be expected to fall within the same range. Using data for the housing market of the municipalities with rapid train connections gives a total increase of residential housing values of EUR 1.6 billion on the German side of the new Fehmarn connection. 80 per cent of this increase is attributable to the housing market of Lübeck with its 81,000 standardised housing unit, where a standardised housing unit corresponds to a dwelling with a floor area of 100s square metres. The total increase for the local housing markets of Nykøbing-Falster, Næstved and Køge on the Danish side would amount to a minimum of EUR 1.4 billion, if the German estimates are extrapolated to the Danish side of the link.

The total minimal increase – assuming a high-speed rail connection – thus amounts to EUR 3 billion in 2009 prices, assuming an unchanging economic structure in Denmark and Germany. It must be stressed that these values are uncertain because of our lack of knowledge about the exact size and structure of the future housing stocks within station catchment areas. A more reliable projection would require a substantially more detailed study than the current one. In such a study the consequences for the commercial property market should also be included.

In this study, we have only analysed the possible effects of infrastructural investments on the price of residential housing. There are, of course, other obvious positive impacts from improved accessibility, such as price increases for holiday homes in Sweden or inter-regional accessibility effects that primarily affect commercial and industrial property. Inter-regional accessibility improvements may also change the patterns of industrial logistics in ways that may have substantial economy-wide benefits. Our analysis is thus limited to intra-regional benefits as they impact regional housing and labour markets. Prospective inter-regional benefits must be studied separately and be added to the possible benefits that affect housing markets.

REFERENCES

M. A. Al-Mosaind, K. J. Dueker & J. G. Strathman, '*Light Rail Transit Stations and Property Values: A Hedonic Price Approach*', Transportation Research Record, 1993, 1400, 90-4

Å. E. Andersson & D. E. Andersson, '*Requirements for the Region's Economic Development,*' National Atlas of Sweden: The Stockholm-Mälaren Region, Gävle, Kartförlaget, 2008

D. E. Andersson, '*The Spatial Nature of Entrepreneurship,*' Quarterly Journal of Austrian Economics, 2005, 8, 21-34

D. E. Andersson, O. F. Shyr & A. Lee, '*The Successes and Failures of a Key Transportation Link: Accessibility Effects of Taiwan's High-speed Rail,*' paper presented at the Annual Congress of the European Regional Science Association, Lodz, Poland, 2009

D. E. Andersson, O. F. Shyr & J. Fu, '*Does High-Speed Rail Accessibility Influence Residential Property Prices? Hedonic Estimates from Southern Taiwan*', Journal of Transport Geography, 201, 18, 166-74

D. E. Andersson & O. F. Shyr, '*The Impact of High-Speed Rail on Accessibility and Land-Price Variability: The Case of Two Taiwanese Regions*', in B. Andreosso-O'Callaghan & B. Zolin (editors), '*Current Issues in Economic Integration: Can Asia Inspire the 'West'*? Aldershot, Ashgate, 2010

D. Banister, '*Sustainable Transport: Challenges and Opportunities*', Transportmetrica, 3(2), 2007, 91-106

R. C. Bollinger & K. R. Ihlanfeldt, '*The Impact of Rapid Rail Transit on Economic Development: The Case of Atlanta's MARTA*', Journal of Urban Economics, 1997, 42, 179-204

A. Börsch-Supan, F. Heiss & M. Seko, '*Housing Demand in Germany and Japan*', Journal of Housing Economics, 2001, 10(3), 229-52

R. Cervero, '*Rail Transit and Joint Development: Land Impacts in Washington, D.C. and Atlanta*', APA Journal, 1994, 83-93

R. Cervero & J. Landis, '*Twenty Years of the Bay Area Rapid Transit System: Land Use and Development Impacts*', Transportation Research A, 1997, 31(4): 309-33

D. N. Dewees, '*The Effect of a Subway on Residential Property Values in Toronto*', Journal of Urban Economics, 1976, 3: 357-69

D. Forrest, J. Glen & R. Ward, '*The Impact of a Light Rail System on the Structure of House Prices*', Journal of Transport Economics and Policy, 1996, 30(1): 15-29

D. H. Gatzlaff & M. T. Smith, '*The Impact of the Miami Metrorail on the Value of Residences Near Station Locations*', Land Economics, 1993, 69(1): 54-66

J. Henneberry, '*Transport Investment and House Prices*', Journal of Property Valuation and Investment, 1998, 16(2), 144-58

O. F. Shyr & D. E. Andersson, *'The Role of the Xueshan Tunnel in the Enlargement of the Taipei Metropolitan Area'*, paper presented at the Annual Meeting of the Asian Real Estate Society, Los Angeles, California, 2009

H. M. So, R. Y. C. Tse & S. Ganesan, *'Estimating the Influence of Transport on House Prices: Evidence from Hong Kong'*, Journal of Property Valuation and Investment, 1997, 15(1), 40-47

C. Y. Yiu & S. K. Wong, *'The Effects of Expected Transport Improvements on Housing Prices'*, Urban Studies, 2005, 42(1), 113-25

CHAPTER 10
THE CULTURAL POTENTIAL

BIRGIT STÖBER

"Culture and creativity touch the daily life of citizens. They are important drivers for personal development, social cohesion and economic growth. But they mean much more: they are the core elements of a European project based on common values and a common heritage – which, at the same time, recognizes and respects diversity. Today's strategy promoting intercultural understanding confirms culture's place at the heart of our policies".

José Manuel Barroso, President of the European Commission

The following pages focus on the subject of culture. Culture as a local factor, culture as a way of communicating between people, culture as a national concern and finally, the cultural opportunities and challenges within the Fehmarnbelt Region.

To define this subject, experiences, opinions and impulses were collected from people with long-standing records for working with, or taking an interest in, Danish/Swedish/German affairs. This work was undertaken between May 2009 and January 2010 and the people interviewed ranged in age from their late 20s to mid 60s:

- Her Royal Highness Princess Benedikte of Denmark
- Dr. Johann Christoph Jessen, German Ambassador to Copenhagen since 2008
- Dr. Christoph Bartmann, Director of the Goethe Institute in Copenhagen between 2000-2007
- Dr. Bernd Henningsen, Professor of Scandinavian Studies and Director of the Northern Europe Institute at the Humboldt University in Berlin
- Uffe Andreasen, Cultural Attaché at the Royal Danish Embassy in Berlin until 2010
- Gerda Hempel, Director of Artlab (Danish Musicians Union) and leader of the Copenhagen think-tank "Creative Forum"

- Pia Allerslev, Mayor of Culture for Copenhagen since 2008
- Journalist Kerrin Linde from the Danish news agency Ritzau
- Jenny Kornmacher, German cultural researcher and project coordinator for Kultur Skåne and the cultural administration in Hamburg
- Anette Vedel Carlsen, Senior Advisor, the Øresund Committee
- Pia Walter, Danish translator and co-initiator of the Nordic Film Days. Resident in Lübeck
- Burkhard Stein, Chief Administrative Officer and Deputy Artistic Head of Schleswig-Holstein Music Festival
- Gert Haack, Head of Culture at Schleswig-Holstein Ministry of State
- Rosi Gerlach, the Scania cultural administration
- Jacob Fabricius, Director of the Malmö Konsthall
- Birger Olofsson, former Head of the Øresund Committee

In addition to the interviews, which lasted between 35 and 80 minutes each, a series of informal conversations was conducted with relevant individuals. Studies of existing cultural relationships were also undertaken. A literature study on the subject of culture and (border) regions completed the material.

Before the presentation of selected cultural activities of importance to the Fehmarnbelt Region, the following will give a brief presentation of the relationship between culture and regional development, as currently discussed in academic literature.

CULTURE AND REGIONAL DEVELOPMENT

Since the mid-1990s, several voices throughout Europe have advocated that the cultural sector is of importance to several trends that are not directly related to culture in themselves. As a result, the proponents of this view suggest that municipalities, regions or countries should now "put their trust in culture" (Mittag & Oerters, 2009).

On the one side, this should be seen on the backdrop of the relatively successful restructuring processes that have taken place in former industrial areas such as Sheffield in the UK or the German Ruhr area, both of which have made conscious efforts to create cultural facilities and experiences. On the other hand, the American professor Richard Florida's thesis has also significantly influenced European cultural economic and urban planning debates in recent years. According to Florida's thesis, a city's or region's economic growth depends on "its cultural powers of innovation that, in turn, are linked to creative minds and attractive places" (Quenzel, 2009). In other words, "culture as a local factor for corporate location, as a driver of job creation, as a magnet for attracting highly qualified labour as well as forming the basis for tourist development." (Quenzel, 2009). Within this context, culture becomes instrumentalised and reduced to a tool for development and economic growth. Other "cultural" dimensions such as "the development of the individual and of society's cohesiveness" (see Barroso) are, therefore, pushed into the background.

In the case of the Fehmarnbelt Region, it soon becomes clear that the area is not a previously densely populated industrial area or known for its cultural attractions. Since the current regional project is hardly directly comparable to other regions, such as the Ruhr or the Øresund Region, the visibility of and communication about the geographical structure is of particular significance. "Visibility and the emotionalisation of a region can drive regional development forward," wrote Diller (2009) pointing to culture as "an excellent instrument for creating visibility and emotionalisation."

Although culture and, by extension, creativity are perceived by many as factors that must be taken seriously in relation to regional development, urban planning and marketing of the area in question, it is often unclear what type of culture is being referred to and whether, in fact, there are measurable links between culture and development.

The following pages present a kind of status of the Fehmarnbelt Region's current cultural life.

PAST CULTURAL ACTIVITIES

Since the end of 1991, Danish and German partners have received financial grants under the EU INTERREG community initiative in order to strengthen co-operation across the national border. These grants have also applied to the cultural sector. One example that should be mentioned here is the project "A Cultural Bridge across the Belt" from 2003. Within the framework of the INTERREG IIIA programme, the project focused on the historical relations between Danes and Germans and consisted of a touring archaeological exhibition. To date, over 70 projects have received financial support from INTERREG I-IIIA, most of which relate to promotional activities for business and industry, education, the labour market and tourism.

Since 1999, regional politicians from Germany, Denmark and Sweden have been working with the same geographic division of the south-western part of the Baltic region under the so-called STRING project. The aim of this extensive network project is to develop common strategies where the partners' potential can be developed and promoted within the context of a rapidly growing global economy. One result of this process-oriented partnership is the first Joint Declaration from 2006 in which the partners agreed to support, develop and undertake projects in research and innovation, infrastructure, tourism as well as regional development and culture. In this way, the parties involved in cultural co-operation are committed to supporting co-operation between cultural institutions and festivals during planning and execution and realising community projects and exchange programmes.

At the end of 2008, and independently of the previously mentioned initiatives, representatives from Region Scania and Hamburg signed a letter of intent aimed at stimulating and strengthening co-operation within the fields of dance, film, music and art.

Despite several project initiatives, Sabine Hackenjos from the Chamber of Industry and Commerce in Lübeck (Lübecker Industrie- und Handelskammer), in connection with a STRING conference in mid-2009, described contacts across national borders as "rare".

According to Sabine Hackenjos, the few notable examples within archaeology, tourism and water sports had so far "failed to change much" because there "is no common profile for a cultural region". At the same time, she noted that "culture as a driver of psychological bridges" is extremely important. And the desire for co-operation within the cultural area really seems to exist.

This interest has also been observed, and since the end of 2008 supported by the Danish Embassy in Berlin, which with the concept of a Southern Danish-Northern German Cultural Bridge – Fehmarnbelt Kulturbro – has become an important point of contact. Inspired by the Danish-Swedish cultural partnership, The Culture Bridge, in the Øresund Region, the "Fehmarnbelt Kulturbro" should be seen as an "initiative to a self-initiative" (Tine Bredo). In this, the Danish Embassy's role lies primarily in providing a platform for information exchange and networking. Around 100 stakeholders attended the first joint conference in May 2009 in Fuglsang, Lolland. The second conference was held in Salzau in Schleswig-Holstein in September 2010 with about 80 Danish and German participants. On the backdrop of the existing STRING project and (according to the Embassy's estimates) the relatively well-functioning cooperation between players in major cities like Hamburg, Copenhagen and Malmö, the main interest is in creating support for smaller players. With regard to geographical demarcation, it is notable that there are few clear geographical boundaries except that Region Scania is not included. It is largely assumed that the Fehmarnbelt Region is defined by Lübeck, Plön and Eastern Holstein and Lolland, Falster and Zealand (excluding the Copenhagen Capital Region).

Another project initiated in 2009 is the "Mental Bridges" project which runs for two years. Co-funded by INTERREG, this project is based on a partnership between Roskilde University (RUC), Ernst-Moritz-Arndt University in Greifswald and the Northern Europe Institute at Humboldt University in Berlin. The project's main areas are linguistic and intercultural skills regarded as pre-requisites for "flexible, nuanced and mutually rewarding communication between Danish and German partners in business, administration, education and culture." More specifically, this is about communicating the importance of language skills and specific Danish-German intercultural competencies in relation to key personnel in the region. Within this context, the Fehmarnbelt Region is geographically limited to Zealand and Schleswig-Holstein, i.e. that within this context Scania is not regarded as being part of the Fehmarnbelt Region.

The fact that almost all these projects have received initial funding from the European Commission in one form or another can be seen as an important acknowledgement. However, several interviewees noted the risk that many of the activities may fade away once the financial support ceases.

Regardless of the geographical boundaries, all attempts to define the Fehmarnbelt Region share a common feature: that a large proportion of the area is sparsely populated and that the major population concentrations are found in the peripheries rather than centrally in the region.

AN EXAMPLE: SCHLESWIG-HOLSTEIN MUSIC FESTIVAL

"The need for culture is certainly present. Especially in the extensive land area of Schleswig-Holstein, it is quite important to offer culture throughout the region and not just in some major cities." (Stein).

The idea that art should not only be experienced in cities and in official localities designed for such purposes, but is brought directly to people in rural areas was, in the 1980s, considered to be new and daring in the German cultural landscape. Even so, with the formation of the Schleswig-Holstein Music Festival in 1985, Schleswig-Holstein launched an experiment by performing classical music outside established concert halls in such diverse venues as barns, stables, churches, shipyards, old industrial buildings and stately homes and castles. Most of the more than 160 concerts are performed in July and August in Schleswig-Holstein with some individual performances taking place in Hamburg and Lower Saxony outside Schleswig-Holstein's borders. According to Burkhard Stein, Denmark, as the immediate neighbour, also plays a role. The German organisation in North Schleswig (Bund der Deutschen Nord-Schleswiger) and Sønderborg Municipality have also shown considerable interest in hosting the festival's concerts.

Burkhard Stein emphasises that Schleswig-Holstein Music Festival "strongly thrives on local audiences. When, for example, we organise a concert in Hanover, it is more difficult. Here in Schleswig-Holstein, we have an audience that knows the festival and there is a special festival atmosphere that ultimately leads to ticket sales. This is difficult to achieve elsewhere as we have to create similar local enthusiasm." (Stein). Part of the festival is based on cooperation with numerous volunteers that manage many of the practical tasks locally. The number of visitors demonstrates that the concept of decentralisation works. In 2010, when, like last year, the opening concert was held in Copenhagen, the organisers counted some 130,000 visitors – more than ever before. On this occasion, the German Ambassador in Copenhagen highlighted the historical relations between Kiel and Copenhagen and the positive, symbolic nature of the opening concert in terms of Danish-German relations in the light of the planned fixed link project across the Fehmarnbelt. In a recent interview, Ambassador Jessen, however, also pointed out that the completion of the fixed link between Denmark and Germany does not in itself mean "we're actually getting closer."

While there is an "apparent confidence" between the government leaders and administrative bodies that frequently meet together, this does not necessarily have an immediate impact on local people.

The following presents some answers to questions about the planned fixed link's significance for the region.

THE SIGNIFICANCE OF THE FIXED LINK

"A connection between two rape fields". This, according to the weekly magazine Der Spiegel, is how critics refer to the planned fixed link across the Fehmarnbelt (Der Spiegel, 2009). Professor Henningsen used a similar term in an interview: "A link between two meadows". Henningsen, however, is not necessarily a critic of the project, but refers only to the sparsely populated areas on both sides of the belt and the enormous challenge that the fixed link project poses in that it has to be something more than just an infrastructure project.

HRH Princess Benedikte of Denmark expresses a markedly more positive view: "I'm very positive. I'd like to say so right away. I've long been a supporter of the fixed link, because I know how much it means. Just look at the Storebælt and Øresund Bridges. Clearly, we must also have a Fehmarn fixed link – not just for Danish-German trade, but also for Swedish-Danish-German trade relations and Swedish-German trade via Denmark. There are so many pluses."

In addition, HRH Princess Benedikte points to the fixed link's cultural significance: "The link is also a culture builder between Denmark and Northern Germany. I think we should say Northern Germany because Germany is such a large country that there are differences between north and south. This also applies to religion and faith. If you are a Protestant you can be a Calvinist or a Lutheran in the north. In the south, there are more Catholics."

A major advantage of the fixed link, according to Princess Benedikte, is that motorists will no longer be restricted by the ferry timetable. "Once you have a fixed link, it doesn't matter when the ferry departs. You can just leave. I think it will make people more curious – curious to learn about the other side. And this sort of interest can perhaps be stimulated. There's no need to play it down. You can encourage it – sow some seeds."

On the other hand, Burkhard Stein points out that "on closer inspection, the project may also be subject to some criticism." As a representative of Schleswig-Holstein Music Festival, he welcomes "all initiatives that lead to attracting more people to Schleswig-Holstein. If the project can contribute to this, it's all well and good. Whether this is the case with the Fehmarn project is another question. And a toll fee will, of course, be an impediment. Moreover, if the total time saving is no more than 30 minutes, this is not very effective either."

By extension, the question of what connotations are associated with the concept of the Fehmarnbelt Region is interesting.

ASSOCIATIONS WITH THE FEHMARNBELT REGION

"Nobody knows that there is a Fehmarnbelt Region – the idea would never have occurred to me," says Christoph Bartmann. To Jacob Fabricius, head of Malmö Konsthal since the beginning of 2008, the concept of the Fehmarnbelt Region is equally new. "In fact, I'm surprised at the concept," he admits.

Denmark's cultural attaché in Germany, Uffe Andreasen, also admits that his first associations with the concept of a Fehmarnbelt Region were "barren land" and "boredom". He has, however, revised his views thanks to contact with people in the region who show great commitment and interest in sharing experiences and relationships.

"The Fehmarnbelt Region: I don't think of it as a dynamic region unless you include Hamburg. This is clearly a region that has been asleep for years. If I have to mention something, it must be the immediate picture. It's not certain that it's correct. I also know that besides Hamburg there are other cities, some of them quite large. Of course, there is a lot of potential there. I know that. But it's not very apparent to us here in Denmark. We also know that the Danish side of the Fehmarnbelt Region has had major problems with jobs and so on. I understand that, too. At the same time, building the fixed link will create the opportunity to try something new. A new negotiation situation, for instance, has arisen for the region to perhaps get something from the state. Even so this is not a real city region as the one at Øresund." (Anette Vedel Carlsen).

Similar concerns are also heard on the German side in the area around the belt. On Fehmarn, officials express concern that, in the long term, the fixed link may damage tourism and will hardly contribute to an economic upturn. By contrast, in Schleswig-Holstein the state government sees the fixed link as an opportunity to be part of a growth axis between economically strong regions. In December 2009, Minister-President Peter Harry Carstensen said: "We don't want to be a transit country through which masses of traffic rushes through." (NDR, 2010).

Regarding the Fehmarnbelt Region concept, Rosi Gerlach from Scania's cultural administration, thinks of "holidays, freedom and beauty" and a region of great potential in respect of nature, culture and skills within education and employment. Copenhagen's Mayor of Culture's associations are generally positive:

"I think of it as a powerhouse, a huge area that suddenly brings us closer to Germany. By "us" I mean Copenhagen and Zealand where before it was mainly the South Jutlandians that had the benefit of a good working relationship with the northern part of Germany. And now I believe that there is suddenly the possibility of creating closer links between the two regions just like we did with Øresund. (…) So first and foremost, I think in terms of a new powerhouse that will generate new things if you tackle everything properly from the start and use the experiences from Sweden. (Allerslev).

This does not mean that the Øresund Region should just be copied – rather it should serve as an inspiration. According to Kerrin Linde, no direct comparisons can be drawn between the Øresund Region and the Fehmarnbelt Region:

"With regard to the Øresund Region, a capital and Sweden's third largest city were located opposite each other. (…) There is now more flow, but it's still two large cities, not two rural and structurally weak areas with few people in them. And those who live there have no jobs so it's really something else. You can't compare them." (Linde).

For Birger Olofsson, the technical concepts "sustainability, entrepreneurship and science" are the cue to the Fehmarnbelt Region. Nevertheless, he argues that you cannot assume that you can build a common labour market comparable to that of the Øresund Region.

The view that there are limited opportunities for making comparisons with the Øresund Region recurs in several interviews. Moreover, Ambassador Jessen refers to the political and structural differences and challenges: "I don't see this as German-Scandinavian. I see cities-cities, "gemeinden"-municipalities, districts-regions. We have one problem, however, and that is that there are no direct relations. We have completely different state structures. Thus, for example, the Minister-President of Schleswig-Holstein has no point of contact. There are some problems here and we have to organise something." (Jessen).

Although some interviewees perceive the concept of a Fehmarnbelt Region as somewhat artificial, the German Ambassador emphasises: "Of course, there is a Fehmarnbelt Region. It's taking shape. It's an evolutionary process and it represents an opportunity for the Fehmarn population. It's also a tremendous opportunity for Falster. (...) I believe that the people of Fehmarn will have the chance of a tourist boom partly because visitors will drive there to view the construction. So Fehmarn must make sure that the island gets something out of the traffic and economic opportunities that will stem from the fixed link, including the easier access for tourists." (Jessen).

However, it remains unclear exactly what type of tourism would be interesting (and important) for Fehmarn. Or whether the target group should be day-trippers or summer holidaymakers who are visiting the island for longer periods. With regard to cultural tourism, it is clear that the island has so far played no significant role. "Fehmarn? – it has nothing at all to do with culture – apart from the fact that some holidaymakers may go there." (Linde).

This is where the question of how the concept of "culture" is interpreted and what the term means for individuals.

WHAT IS CULTURE?

Given the diverse use of the term culture in different social contexts, culture can be described as a "contemporary magic formula" (Hofmann et al., 2004). According to the Eurobarometer survey of 2007, "it is clear that culture plays an important role in most Europeans' lives" (European Commission, 2007).

When asked how important culture is for the individual, 77 per cent of respondents in Denmark said that they regard culture as important. In Sweden, 76 per cent declared that culture is important to them, and in Germany the figure was 65 per cent. "With regard to culture's inner soul, it must be maintained that the word culture is most often associated with the arts, i.e. both performing and visual (...). Other frequently mentioned associations are literature, traditions, language, customs and habits (...)".

All interviewees were asked to comment on the concept of "culture". The following section presents some views on this.

"Culture is a concept we cannot live without" (Henningsen). "Culture is a social mirror" (Kornmacher). "Culture is something indispensable to our kind of society, to any kind of society. Culture is a necessity, compelling, an automatic component. If you define culture as a luxury, it has negative consequences for everyone. (...) In as much as culture is an engine for the whole community (...) it should be treated as a development factor and not regarded narrowly as a luxury item. " (Stein).

While Rosi Gerlach from Scania's cultural administration more or less equates the term "culture" with artistic manifestations such as theatre, dance, music, visual arts and cultural heritage, Princess Benedikte describes the concept as follows: "Yes, it's a broad concept. But culture is not just cultural events. I believe that social and socio-cultural issues are part of it. It's not only about art, it's also about society (...)."

For Copenhagen's Mayor of Culture, culture is "something that is both broad and narrow. (...). If you ask the Danes in general, I think many will mention the national anthem, the national team, the Eurovision Song Contest and The Royal Theatre (...). I also think that people will say that culture is important – that it is important to have something that binds us together in one way or another. That we have something that provides a common identity." (Allerslev).

For Uffe Andreasen, the Danish Cultural Attaché in Berlin, "Culture" consists primarily of experiences, experiences within nature as well as new experiences in urban spaces, surprises, music and architecture. Pia Allerslev agrees: "This is what culture is to me. To give people some good experiences that they weren't expecting."

Anette Vedel Carlsen says that over the past 10 years, culture has gained another dimension: "People are beginning to see culture more as a business". This is reflected in the fact that most Danish municipalities and even villages are currently promoting their "culture" – branding themselves through culture. This phenomenon – place branding – is not restricted to Denmark, but can be found in many locations around the world.

After more than one year, Mayor of Culture Pia Allerslev admits: "I've discovered that everything is about culture and everything about culture is also about money. However, unfortunately, money does not grow on trees."

NATIONAL CULTURES

To the question as to whether there are significant differences between Danish, German and Swedish culture, most of the interviewees answered in nuanced terms. Indeed, HRH Princess Benedikte said that German culture can more or less be divided into North German and South German: "North German culture is not that different while there is a big difference in respect of South German culture. (…) But, of course, there are differences between German and Danish so perhaps we should not call it culture, but mentality. Again, that's slightly different."

"Obviously there are differences between Danish and German mentality and culture, but that's also the case between Copenhagen and Hirtshals. There will always be differences between cities and countries. That's what makes culture exciting because you can challenge preconceived ideas and influence people to change their opinions – or at least reflect on them. " (Allerslev).

Kerrin Linde, who was born in Schleswig and raised in Flensburg and attended Danish nursery school and Danish school, believes "That Danish culture has inherited much of Germany's culture – which may not always be accepted." (Linde).

Rosi Gerlach highlights the artistic dimension of culture and refers to Germany's cultural diversity that, in her experience, is not found in Denmark and Sweden. That aside, Berlin and Copenhagen have a more experimentally-oriented cultural environment than Stockholm. In respect of art, primarily contemporary art, Jacob Fabricius detects a greater openness in Germany than in Denmark. "In Germany, we see art in the smallest of towns and even small towns are open to contemporary art. Danes are too conservative and narrow-minded." Even in his daily work in Malmö, he sees a greater openness than in Copenhagen.

Some interviewees also mentioned the different conflict cultures. While the Danes "have a no conflict culture, a consensus culture," the Germans "tend to have a culture of conflict" (Jessen). Or to put it differently: "Danes are not suited for conflict, Germans are not suited for consensus" (Henningsen). "That's why we in Germany have had more heated discussions about the Fehmarnbelt fixed link than the Danes. That's hard for them to understand." (Jessen).

CULTURAL CO-OPERATION ACROSS NATIONAL BORDERS

Culture across borders, according to Henningsen, is "tough work" that is particularly person-related and, therefore, negatively affected by rapid personal change. According to Henningsen, successful cultural exchange between nations requires "more professionalism and better management."

According to Anette Vedel Carlsen, cultural work across municipal boundaries is often a challenge for many of those involved. "And when they have to look all the way across Øresund to the Swedish side or to Germany, this may seem overwhelming. (...) I would also say that the sense of relevance is not always there. It all feels awfully difficult" (Vedel Carlsen). However, according to Jenny Kornmacher, the point is to "stop thinking of borders" but to think in terms of wider horizons and to define opportunities for action.

One of the biggest challenges, Anette Vedel Carlsen says, is to formulate a common policy framework. "I think this is really difficult because cultural policy is national policy. (...). In terms of culture, it's so difficult because culture is (...) about value policy. There's no doubt about it. So no-one really wants to let go of it. "On the other hand, it's very important to approach and adjust to each other. "The cohesion of a region is primarily dependent on practical partnerships that subsequently create networks." (Vedel Carlsen). But there has to be a genuine interest in the issues – and for the neighbours. Producing cultural events in order to create flow or to ensure that the fixed link's capacity is utilised will, predicts Christoph Bartmann, fail.

THE POTENTIAL FOR A "FEHMARNBELT REGION" – PROPOSALS WITHIN THE CULTURAL AREA

When asked about cultural opportunities for the Fehmarnbelt Region, Princess Benedikte responded: "I think you have to start with something that is understandable, such as the theatre. Take ballet, for instance, the Hamburg Ballet, John Neumeier, who is also a big name in Denmark. He loves being there and working with the Royal Ballet. He would be an obvious bridge-builder because he's very fond of Denmark and of working there. It's about finding things that are not too difficult and then proceeding step-by-step. Then you can go into more detail later on. But my advice would be to find things that are not too difficult or too complex because both regions, indeed both countries, have to take some steps. I would take many small steps that could develop into something big. Try to meet others without too much scepticism."

Together, visual art and music (...) are ideal for tying people together – with no language barriers" and therefore integrating projects across borders, says Burkhard Stein. "I have an expectation that we'll be inspired by German artists, and that we'll be able to inspire them in return. Maybe this will not become a major business generating largescale growth but merely being made aware of another country a few kilometres from the Danish border is exciting. I'm under no illusion that Copenhageners in large numbers will stream across the fixed link. Perhaps, you can hope that some Germans from the area will be drawn to Copenhagen "(Allerslev).

"I believe that it will only work properly if there are real attractions, i.e. attractors. You cannot just create something artificial in Lolland, for example, which creates lasting interest or attention and therefore entices the audience. There must be something real that relates to existing or new cultural locations." (Bartmann). Birger Olofsson also points out that there should be focus on existing cultural forms and activities. Otherwise the costs will be excessive.

Many interviewees agree that one has to think boldly and in terms of visions. Jacob Fabricius, who was awarded the Statens Kunstråd's "Formidlingsprisen 2009" and was praised as "a transcender of borders and a bridge builder – between people and art, between art and reality, between Denmark and other countries" highlights the importance of cultural institutions and events of high quality to the new region. "I don't think of this as a region at all. If some good institutions were to emerge, it would be good. Otherwise it would be no more than a transport corridor. There must be a reason to stop. If there were sufficient funds, you could build a new Louisiana or something similar to the Guggenheim Museum in Bilbao. I'm not a supporter of promoting cultural tourism but it's still impressive to see how the Bilbao area has changed as a result of a new building.".

There are, however, alternatives. Jacob Fabricus mentions the concept of joint exhibitions which, as Director of Malmö Konsthal, he tried out with the Danish Gammel Holtegård Museum in early 2010 and which could also be applied to other artistic institutions. The creation of a "biennale" across national borders could also provide culturally weak areas with solid content. Gert Haack points out, however, that there "is a long distance between the few museums in the region." Even so, Uffe Andreasen recommends using museums as key contact points. In his opinion, "museums plus cafés" as an attraction should not be underestimated.

Moreover, there should be more offers in respect of music and festivals, especially for young people. And "everything should be linked to transport," says the Danish Cultural Attaché. Burkhard Stein of the Schleswig-Holstein Music Festival also points out that accessibility to cultural institutions or events must be available, preferably by train or other public transport.

According to many interviewees, there are only limited opportunities for inspiration from cultural activities in the Øresund Region, in particular Scania. Opening artist studios to the public, as happens in connection with the annual initiative "Kunstrunder i Skåne", is difficult because of the low population density and the small number of artists.

"Numerically, I would think that artists living in the country are very few compared to those living in big cities. Whether you can build a movement based on them, I don't know. But, of course, there could be some tourist-related aspects and some experience trips where you can observe the artists in their workshops or something. If this is enough, and whether it's a unique selling point because all good tourist offices do this anyway, I don't know (Hempel).

According to Uffe Andreasen, a more far-reaching idea is to establish artist residencies – both to support professional artists and to create a cultural life in culturally weaker areas and consequently make them more interesting. At the same time, grants could be given to provide co-funding for concerts, exhibitions, workshops etc. Since 1998, Eckernförde in Schleswig-Holstein has had an international artists' house that could provide inspiration. This idea has the support of Anette Vedel Carlsen: "You could have a retreat in Rome and that would be fantastic to have. You could have retreats in many places. It's about who else is there. And again, you could collaborate with Hamburg and Copenhagen and Scania in making "artist in residence" programmes. Why not do this if you could get some interesting people from the outside to organise a programme encompassing the whole region?" Pia Allerslev also welcomes the idea of artist residencies and not only for rural areas. "Yes, this could, in fact, be the most concrete contribution I could make because we have one funded apartment in Copenhagen. I just wish that we had three to four at least so we actually had something to offer. It would also be good if the apartments were together so the artists who come here would feel they are a part of something in common." Jesper Fabricus also refers to the many artist houses in Europe and points out that success depends greatly on the design of this, in itself, welcome initiative. "You'll have to do something for those who come there. They shouldn't feel alien." Within this context, Fabricius demands a high degree of professionalism and ambition. To prevent the individual artist from feeling isolated, he suggests that more than one artist is invited at the same time. In addition, he sees artist residencies as places of production.

Another important area is, according to Uffe Andreasen, to facilitate access to information on existing and future cultural offerings, including the creation and maintenance of websites. Birger Olofsson suggests that broader news coverage in the media is indispensable and refers to a type of "cultural diary" for the German-Danish-Swedish region. Whereas projects across national borders have, so far, focused on official media partnerships between established radio and television channels, it could be relevant to focus on new media like the internet and related social media (Kornmacher).

The necessary infrastructure to enable different forms of information exchange is also important to Pia Allerslev. She points to the potential for establishing a "contact agency" for communicating the fact that "the region is interested in making all this as flexible and anti-bureaucratic as possible and that the relevant governments share this view. If we want to create a powerhouse, it's also important to communicate that we want to make things work smoothly."

Commitment from politicians is crucial, emphasises Anette Vedel Carlsen, based on her experiences from the Øresund Region: "To make things happen, there must be real commitment. I think it will be difficult to go to business and industry and say that "we want to do something with culture." (Vedel Carlsen). The economic and political conditions for cultural projects are currently "particularly bad", Gert Haack says. "This applies equally within individual countries and across national borders. Within this context he is referring not only to the global economic and financial crises, but also to the "weak structure" that has characterised much of the region for so long.

The business aspects of cultural life are referred to by many interviewees. Princess Benedikte, for instance, comments: "This is something that must go hand in hand. I believe that it will be difficult to do something culturally-related if we don't involve industry. And industry can benefit from culture. I believe that we have to be flexible – have an open mind and try to see some opportunities and exploit them in a partnership with industry. Anette Vedel Carlsen points out that in some cases, this may also lead to a more efficient allocation of resources. "What we see as the main challenges is that we need better coordination of cultural offerings and joint use of the arenas." (Vedel Carlsen).

In summary, one can conclude that most interviewees acknowledged and mentioned the opportunities within the cultural area in the Fehmarnbelt. At the same time, however, there is a demand for concrete action from the worlds of politics and business.

"I believe that the potential is there. It's all about selling it – delivering something good. Well, it's about getting it delivered as something good, something attractive." (Allerslev). Similarly, Anette Vedel Carlsen lists the need for specific communication strategies: "To articulate the region's agenda as such is the general challenge in everything we do (...). Everywhere. The more people who talk about a particular matter, the easier it is to promote it and make it self-perpetuating. (...) It's interesting to see who can help articulate some opportunities and involve as many people as possible in articulating them. I think this is what has to be done at Fehmarn. " (Vedel Carlsen).

CHALLENGES

For most interviewees, it appears to be important that the transparency of – and communication about – the region is not translated into simplified marketing activities based on the principles of a self-perpetuating rhetoric or self-fulfilling prophecy.

Burkhard Stein draws attention to the risk that "something will be blown out of proportion. This is a wonderful project that, image-wise, sounds brilliant and which has seductive qualities." Specifically, he is referring to his practical experience of getting the public from Flensburg to Sønderborg. "A train from Flensburg stops directly in front of the Concert Hall in Sønderborg. (...). Still, we couldn't get many people to travel from Flensburg to Sønderborg and vice versa. (...) It's probably because people would rather stay where they are." (Stein)

"Mobility", according to Haack, "is one of the basic pre-conditions for cultural participation." And this mobility, which must be present both with those creating cultural events and the public, is closely related to the psychological and economic aspects. This makes Gert Haack himself question whether "the fixed link can really open new doors and if so for whom?" Those who take an interest in culture and art are already moving across, or around, the region. But getting those who have so far been more or less immobile could be an important challenge. Once gain, Gert Haack points to the toll fee issue and the price level and says that the cost of crossing the fixed link could be an equally significant obstacle for some people as the current cost of a ferry crossing.

Most of the interviewees regarded toll fee levels as crucial. If the cost of crossing the fixed link is too high, it may impede the development of a vibrant, emerging cultural scene. This assessment is supported by a study conducted in 2009 on behalf of the rural districts of East Holstein, Stormarn, Herzogtum Lauenburg, Segeberg, the city of Lübeck and the Chamber of Industry and Commerce in Lübeck. The study concludes that "too high a toll fee for the fixed link could hinder the integration/partnership process". Similarly, it is noted that cross-border cooperation is highly dependent on external funding (mainly INTERREG), which is considered a risk (George & Ottenströer, 2009).

"Identity" is presented as yet another difficult area. "I don't believe that you have to work with some of the regions to create an "Øresund identity" or a "Fehmarn identity" or anything like that. If you do that, I think you'll have lost before you start. (...). I think that this is, and remains, a postulate because our identities are constantly subject to negotiation." (Vedel Carlsen). Although Birger Olofsson highlights the true importance of feelings and positive associations for a successful regional project, he also warns against focusing on a "shared identity" because such an approach is bound to fail. Moreover, the existing cultural differences can be exciting and rewarding and we should not try to eliminate them.

Another difficult topic that may prove challenging is mentioned by Gerda Hempel in connection with "cooperation versus competition. "I think it's terribly difficult. If we stand together, what is it that we're standing against? The big advantage, as I have understood the political project, is that you must be strong together to stand up to some other regions.

And here you can say that culture, arts and cultural institutions must show solidarity with themselves before showing solidarity with a region. And this means that a cultural institution in, for instance, the Fehmarnbelt Region could benefit more from collaborating with Berlin (which Hamburg at least sees as a rival). They will, of course, do that because they need to survive, get artistic inspiration, export opportunities etc." (Hempel).

During the many interviews, it became clear that there is a diversity of interests and ideas relating to culture and the Fehmarnbelt Region. On the one hand, there seems to be a generally sceptical wait-and-see attitude while, on the other, there is an undoubted desire for cultural activities and collaboration across national borders. Here Birger Olofsson asks for more professionalism and consistency since, in his experience, it is not sufficient that decision-makers meet only once a year to consider strategies.

According to Anette Vedel Carlsen, it is right to exercise caution in respect of excessive expectations and instead aim "for smaller victories as you go along." It would be wonderful to have some major strategies that would get you off to a good start. But I don't believe this will be possible because interests go in many different directions. "Within this context, time is an important factor that should not be underestimated," notes Jesper Fabricius. One of the key issues mentioned by many interviewees can be summarised by a quote from HRH Princess Benedikte, "Yes, you have to be optimistic."

SUMMARY (AND PERSPECTIVE)

The completed interviews do not create any clarity about the specific geographical boundaries of the Fehmarnbelt Region. There seems to be general doubt as to the expediency of a clear territorial definition.

Those who primarily see the project in terms of the area immediately adjacent to the fixed link, seem to take a more sceptical approach to the project than those who think of a region stretching from Hamburg to Southern Sweden.

The fact that culture plays an important role for the local population and for the region's development is not questioned by any of the interviewees. Culture is perceived as a tool to link geographical entities together and to experience a sense of community. At the same time, however, "culture" must not serve as an alibi for the political project "region."

Concerning the significance of culture, the concept of geographical identity emerges in many interviews. At the same time, however, there is broad consensus that this is a somewhat problematic issue that should best be avoided. Establishing an identity for the Fehmarnbelt Region should not be attempted.

Since the geographical – or another – definition of the Fehmarnbelt Region does not comprise a former densely populated industrial area or a previously known cultural region, communications relating to the geographical structure are seen as having particular significance. Several interviewees emphasised the importance of verbal communication and a visual profile of the region while also pointing out the risk of empty rhetoric and pure marketing.

Regarding a direct comparison with the Øresund Region, respondents considered such comparisons to be problematic and inappropriate. On the one hand, this is because of the widely differing population densities and on the other hand, because of the weak business structures that characterise much of the Fehmarnbelt Region.

Even so, lessons from the Øresund Region were frequently referred to, not least that statements of commitment by politicians are crucial and have to be followed up by concrete action. At the same time, attention was drawn to the complexities of a cultural policy which, on one side, is partly determined by different nation-state interests and, on the other, by current uncertainties concerning long-term planning and financing. According to a press release in late May 2010, Schleswig-Holstein has to save one million euros from its cultural budgets for 2011 and 2012. As a result of these savings, the Cultural Centre in Salzau, the Festival JazzBaltica and the Norddeutscher Filmpreis will no longer receive public money. (Kulturrat 2010).

The fact that many of the initiated and implemented cross-border projects have received initial funding from the European Commission in one form or another, involves (according to several interviewees) a risk that many such activities will not be maintained once the project aid runs out.

During the interviews, a number of specific proposals aimed at enhancing cultural life in the so far culturally fragile area were collected. These included the proposal for artists' residencies in rural areas as cultural venues/meeting places, the concept of joint exhibitions across national boundaries and the proposal to deliberately focus on the fields of visual arts, dance and music as none of these areas is hampered by language barriers. Emphasis was also placed on fast and timely exchange of information within the region through efficient use of new media. Many of the interviewees highlighted the need for accessibility to rural areas in addition to the establishment of the fixed link. For many, public transport is of major importance.

According to Haack, "a basic pre-requisite for cultural participation is mobility." This, however, should not only be considered in the narrow sense of the physical aspect of transportation, but also include psychological mobility and the financial possibility of moving around in the area. For this reason most of the interviewees mentioned the level of toll fee for the fixed link to be crucial to a vibrant cultural life in the Fehmarnbelt Region.

REFERENCES

P. Bethge, '*Brückenschlag in die Provinz I*', Der Spiegel, 2009, no. 25, 34-35

C. Diller, '*Potenziale und Grenzen von regionalen Kooperationen im Kulturbereich*' in P. S. Föhl & I. Neisener (eds.), „*Regionale Kooperationen im Kulturbereich. Theoretische Grundlagen und Praxisbeispiele*', Bielefeld, 2009, 47-65

Georg & Ottenströer, '*Zwischenbericht. Regionales Entwicklungskonzept in Folge einer festen Fehmarnbelt Querung*', Hamburg/Berlin, 2009

J. Mittag & K. Oerters, '*Kreativwirtschaft und Kulturhauptstadt: Katalysatoren urbaner Entwicklung in altindustriellen Ballungsregionen?*' in G. Quenzel (Hg.), '*Entwicklungsfaktor Kultur. Studien zum kulturellen und ökonomischen Potential der europäischen Stadt*',Transcript Verlag, Bielefeld, 2009, 61-94

B. Henningsen, '*Dänemark*', Munich, 2009

M. L. Hofmann, T. F. Korta & S. Niekisch, '*Culture Club*', Suhrkamp Verlag, Frankfurt, 2004

Ministerium für Justiz, Arbeit und Europa des Landes Schleswig-Holstein, '*Grenzüberschreitende Kooperation mit Süddänemark*', Kiel, 2008

G. Quenzel, '*Entwicklungsfaktor Kultur*', Transcript Verlag, Bielefeld, 2009

Der Spiegel, 2009, no. 25, 34-35

European Commission (eds.) '*Eurobarometer Spezial 278, Werte der europäischen Kultur*', 2007, http://ec.europa.eu/culture/pdf/doc960_de.pdf

Kulturrat, 2010, 02/06/2010, www.kulturrat.de,

Landesregierung Schleswig-Holstein, http://www.schleswig-holstein.de/wirtschaft/De/standortmarketing/wirtschaftsland/wirtschaftslandarchiv/pDFs/themenpDFs/ausgabe11__2006/titel__gutFuersimagegutFuersgeschaeft, templateid=raw,property=publicationFile.pdf

NDR, 2010, 26/2/2010, www.ndr.de/nachrichten/dossiers/fehmarnbeltbruecke/fehmarnbelt146.html

CHAPTER 11
GENERAL VALUES AND ATTITUDES AMONG YOUNG PEOPLE

INGVAR HOLMBERG

In 1989, the Institute for Future Studies (Sweden) launched a number of surveys among teenagers with the purpose of studying their thoughts about the future. The survey was inspired by the World Values Survey initiated by the political scientist Ronald Inglehart in 1977. However, whereas the target group in the World Values Survey was people of all age groups, the Swedish survey targeted young people between the ages of 18 and 20 attending their last term of upper school. The choice of age-group was based on Inglehart's theory that values and attitudes of adolescents stabilise around this age.

In 1992, the plans to build a fixed link between Sweden and Denmark in the Øresund Region were becoming more concrete. In order to investigate young people's attitudes and views on this project, the survey was extended to cover the Danish side of Øresund.

The construction of a permanent link between Sweden and Denmark led to a heated debate, especially on environmental issues. It was, therefore, regarded as interesting to investigate the extent to which this debate was reflected in the attitude among young people and to determine how their views related to their general values and attitudes. This also provided an opportunity to study young Danes and Swedes' respective value systems as well as their knowledge about their neighbouring country and their interest in studying, working or living in that country.

In general, the survey established that gender differences in values and attitudes exceeded national differences. Furthermore, there was a considerable asymmetry in their knowledge about the other country as well as large differences in their propensity to study, work or live in countries other than their country of nationality. Young people from Scania knew more about Denmark and Copenhagen than young Danes knew about Scania and Malmö. Young Swedes were also considerably more interested in working or living in Denmark compared to young Danes in respect of Sweden (Matthiessen & Andersson 1993).

In 2009, when the link was about to celebrate its 10th anniversary, a similar survey was aimed at exploring the effects of the new link and establishing the extent to which the integration of the regions on both sides of Øresund had improved.

Preliminary results show that general knowledge about the neighbouring country on the other side of Øresund had increased considerably, as had an interest in studying, working and living on the other side (Andersson, Andersson & Holmberg, 2010).

Today, when the planning of a fixed link across the Fehmarnbelt has commenced, it is essential to establish whether a similar asymmetry exists with regard to knowledge about

TABLE 1.
TOTAL SAMPLE BY GENDER AND COUNTRY

	Number			Per cent	
Country	Women	Men	Total	Women	Men
Denmark	189	87	276	68.5	31.5
Sweden	173	198	371	46.6	53.4
Germany	67	80	147	45.6	54.4
Total	429	365	794	54.0	46.0

the countries on each side of the Fehmarnbelt among young Danes, Germans and Swedes. It will also be of interest to explore the differences in attitudes towards studying, working and living in the neighbouring country amongst young Swedes, Danes and Germans. Such information could be crucial to investments in infrastructure, house building, the educational system and the labour market.

For this purpose, a survey was carried out in late 2009 and early 2010 among students in their final year of schooling – aged 18-20 – in the Fehmarnbelt Region, which includes Scania in Sweden, the Zealand archipelago and Bornholm in Denmark and Hamburg and Schleswig-Holstein in Germany. In the report, the three regions are referred to by their respective country names.

Around 800 young people were interviewed in the three countries. With respect to the original intent of interviewing a total of 1,000, the non-response rate was less than 20 per cent which should be regarded as acceptable. The survey was carried out partly as a traditional paper-and-pen survey and partly as an internet survey provided by Entergate, Sweden. Gender and country are divided as indicated in Table 1.

In relation to the target of between 300 and 250 interviews from each country, only Sweden meets the requirement. Denmark falls short of the target by around 10 per cent while Germany is 50 per cent below. In both countries, contacts were established with an appropriate number of schools, which promised to deliver the required number of interviews. Despite numerous reminders and an extension of the response period, it was not possible to obtain more answers.

FROM MATERIALISTIC TO POST-MATERIALISTIC VALUES

It is said that the future belongs to the young. Within 10 to 15 years, the young people who are currently in their late teens will be tomorrow's decision-makers and will exert a strong influence on society. A study of their attitudes and values will, therefore, play an important role when analysing the development of our society.

In the 1970s, the political scientist Ronald Inglehart (Inglehart, 1977) formulated a theory about changes to the value structure and their relation to economic development. According to Inglehart's theory, every person has a certain number of basic values formed during childhood and which stabilise around the ages of 18-19. Such basic values may undergo minor changes with age, but tend to remain the basic elements of their personal identity.

On the basis of a worldwide survey in the early 1980s (World Values Survey, first wave 1981-1984), Inglehart maintains that certain basic values are shared by people from all parts of the world. These values relate to physical security, material security and personal development.

The importance of these values is reflected in the way people from different societies prioritise them. This internal prioritisation reflects to some extent people's experience during their first 18-20 years of life. The period of adolescence represents a stable foundation for the individual's own values and a basis for consumption preferences. Statistical analysis of value structures from different parts of the world shows that there is a strong relationship between the prioritisation of values and the socio-economic environment during adolescence.

A child that grows up in wartime or under other violent conditions will prioritise physical security whereas a child that experiences material shortages will prioritise material security. Conversely, children that grow up in societies with physical and material security will focus on "soft" values as a potential for personal development, quality of life and diversity.

The materialistic value structure with its focus on security and survival is prevalent in newly industrialised societies while a post-materialistic value structure characterises highly educated, prosperous people in Western Europe, North America and Australia whose focus is on quality of life. Since the Second World War, there has been a trend towards the steady transformation from materialistic to post-materialistic priorities in the Western world. This transformation reflects the fact that an increasing proportion of the population experienced both physical and material security during adolescence. The transformation, therefore, is more of a generational effect than a life cycle effect. As a consequence, political priorities are no longer what they used to be. In typically materialistic societies like China, which according to World Value Survey is the world's most materialistic society, the common political priorities are economic growth and law and order. This means that political conflicts are related to the distribution of material resources and income.

The political priorities are significantly different in societies where the proportion of post-materialistic values is increasing, especially among the young and well-educated elite. Such post-materialistic values are environmental issues, aesthetic values and freedom of speech. Furthermore. nationalistic, ethnic and religious loyalties tend to become less important and will be replaced by cosmopolitan attitudes and a more widespread desire for freedom to choose a personal lifestyle and ideology.

Post-materialistic values do not only have political implications. On the contrary, Inglehart maintains that the new value structure influences a large number of important personal attitudes such as choice of occupation, family creation, religion and sexuality. He believes that this transformation is far reaching and will lead to an institutional revolution in Western societies. In this respect, the post-materialistic value structure has replaced protestant ethics.

A large number of surveys carried out among young Swedish students between the ages of 18-19 in the 1990s, have shown very consistent results. Young women from metropolitan regions studying theoretical subjects tend to represent the most post-materialistic segment of the population (Andersson, Fürth & Holmberg, 1997), whereas men from peripheral regions studying vocational subjects represented the most materialistic segment.

Typically, post-materialistic values are positive in relation to mobility, creativity and independence. Women with post-materialistic attitudes are also against hierarchies both in working life and in society in general. Focus on equality in the distribution of material resources seems to have been replaced by social equality.

When he started to measure post-materialism in the World Values Survey (first wave 1981-1984), Inglehart used only one question to do this. The respondents had to consider different priority targets for their native country for the next 10 years and to choose two out of the following four alternatives:

Question 1

1	Maintaining order in the country
2	*Giving people more say in important government decisions*
3	Fighting rising prices
4	*Protecting freedom of speech*

Note: Alternatives in italics are post-materialistic priorities

On the basis of the answers, Inglehart created a post-materialistic index which is the difference between the proportion choosing alternatives one or three and the proportion choosing two or four.

According to Inglehart's index, Denmark and Sweden are two of the most post-materialistic countries in the world together with Canada, Australia, and Norway. At the other end of the scale, we find Japan, Poland, India and China, countries with strong materialistic value structures.

In later versions of the World Values Survey (third wave 1994-1999), Inglehart extended his index of post-materialism to include the results from two further questions

Question 2		Question 3	
1	A high level of economic growth	1	A stable economy
2	Making sure this country has strong defence forces	2	*Progress toward a less impersonal and more humane society*
3	*Seeing that people have more say about how things are done at their jobs and in their communities*	3	*Progress toward a society in which ideas count more than money*
4	Trying to make our cities and countryside more beautiful	4	The fight against crime

Note: Alternatives in italics are post-materialistic priorities

This means that the new index was based on three questions, each with four different alternatives to be prioritised. Four alternatives were regarded as representing post-materialistic values, six alternatives were materialistic values while one alternative did not relate to either (attempting to beautify our cities and nature). In this case, the index becomes the difference in the proportion of respondents that chose three or four post-materialistic alternatives and the proportion of respondents that chose only one or none.

With this extended index it is possible to carry out a deeper analysis of post-materialism and materialism on the one side and a number of differently related variables by applying the information from the present survey in the Fehmarnbelt Region.

TABLE 2.
POST-MATERIALISTIC INDEX (QUESTION 1) BY GENDER AND COUNTRY

Country	Women	Men
Denmark	19.1	0.6
Sweden	-9.4	-15.6
Germany	26.7	18.0

TABLE 3.
INDEX OF POST-MATERIALISM IN DENMARK, SWEDEN AND GERMANY (BASED ON QUESTIONS 1-3)

Number of post-materialistic alternatives chosen	Denmark		Sweden		Germany	
	Women	Men	Women	Men	Women	Men
0	1.1	3.4	1.7	8.1	0.0	0.0
1	8.5	14.9	13.3	19.8	9.0	8.8
2	27.0	29.9	34.1	34.5	28.4	26.3
3	31.7	28.7	34.1	28.4	32.8	37.5
4	21.7	19.5	15.6	7.6	25.4	22.5
5	10.1	3.4	1.2	1.5	4.5	5.0
Total	100.0	100.0	100.0	100.0	100.0	100.0
Post-materialistic index	22.2	4.6	1.7	-18.8	20.9	18.8
Number of observations	189	87	173	197	67	80

POST-MATERIALISTIC AND MATERIALISTIC VALUES AMONG YOUNG PEOPLE IN THE FEHMARNBELT REGION

The simple index of post-materialism based on the single question (Question 1) shows that post-materialistic values are very strong among Danish women and Germans (both men and women). Danish men are more neutral while Swedish men are strong materialists.

One problem with this index is that the majority of the respondents tend to choose both post-materialistic and materialistic values at the same time. Only around a third of respondents have selected purely post-materialistic or materialistic alternatives. For that reason, the

more refined index based on three questions (Question 1 to Question 3) will provide a more realistic picture of young people's values.

The following tables give a general overview of post-materialism in the three sub-regions of the Fehmarnbelt Region:

According to this calculation, Germans (both men and women) and Danish women have the highest rate of post-materialistic values while Swedish men are the most materialistic and Swedish women are almost neutral.
The most interesting finding is that young Swedes who are generally assumed to be among the most post-materialistic in Europe rank quite low compared to young people in the other two countries. A more thorough investigation within the three countries may give further details on possible differences:

Table 4 shows strong materialistic values among men in all regions while women are either neutral or have weak post-materialistic values (other cities in the region than Malmö).

Corresponding data for Denmark are shown in Table 5. The overall picture is that Danish women, especially in Lolland-Falster, have very strong post-materialistic values

TABLE 4.
INDEX OF POST-MATERIALISM IN SUB-REGIONS OF SWEDEN
(BASED ON QUESTIONS 1-3)

Number of post-materialistic alternatives chosen	Malmö		Other large cities		Other municipalities	
	Women	Men	Women	Men	Women	Men
0	0.0	11.4	1.2	5.8	5.0	10.3
1	14.9	14.3	12.8	25.0	12.5	13.8
2	42.6	34.3	31.4	32.7	30.0	37.9
3	27.7	20.0	37.2	28.8	35.0	32.8
4	12.8	17.1	16.3	6.7	17.5	3.4
5	2.1	2.9	1.2	1.0	0.0	1.7
Total	100.0	100.0	100.0	100.0	100.0	100.0
Post-materialistic index	0.0	-5.7	3.5	-23.1	0.0	-19.0
Number of observations	47	35	86	104	40	58

while men from Bornholm are the only materialistic group. Corresponding data for regions of Germany are shown in Table 6.

It is often said that a post-materialistic value system is a metropolitan phenomenon. But young people from Lübeck/Kiel are clearly much more post-materialistic in their views than young people from Hamburg although the latter remain on the post-materialistic side.

GENERAL VALUES AND ATTITUDES

Since the majority of young people's fundamental values are shaped during adolescence, it is important to identify them in order to ascertain the future values of people of an older age. Such fundamental values are important determinants of what young people regard as important today and in fifteen years. The young of today are the adults of tomorrow.

To explore these fundamental values, the survey comprises two different questions: in the first the young people had to choose four alternatives out of a total of 19 in relation to being with family and friends, activities such as travelling abroad or receiving a good salary and desired life objectives such as being healthy or qualifying for further education. The respondents had to consider these alternatives in relation to the near future (today) and within a time frame of 15 years. In another set of questions, they had to consider whether they agreed with statements on more general aspects of social life in their society.

TABLE 5.
INDEX OF POST-MATERIALISM IN SUB-REGIONS OF DENMARK
(BASED ON QUESTIONS 1-3)

Number of post-materialistic alternatives chosen	Copenhagen		Zealand		Lolland-Falster		Bornholm	
	Women	Men	Women	Men	Women	Men	Women	Men
0	0.0	5.0	3.3	0.0	0.0	2.9	2.7	5.3
1	7.5	5.0	13.3	15.4	5.8	14.3	10.8	26.3
2	30.2	35.0	23.3	38.5	27.5	25.7	24.3	26.3
3	34.0	30.0	30.0	23.1	24.6	34.3	43.2	21.1
4	17.0	25.0	10.0	15.4	34.8	20.0	13.5	15.8
5	11.3	0.0	20.0	7.7	7.2	2.9	5.4	5.3
Total	100.0	100.0	100.0	100.0	100.0	100.0	100.0	100.0
Post-materialistic index	20.8	15.0	13.3	7.7	36.2	5.7	5.4	-10.5
Number of observations	53	20	30	13	69	35	37	19

TABLE 6.
INDEX OF POST-MATERIALISM IN SUB-REGIONS OF GERMANY
(BASED ON QUESTIONS 1-3)

Number of post-materialistic alternatives chosen	Hamburg		Lübeck / Kiel		Neumünster	
	Women	Men	Women	Men	Women	Men
0	0.0	0.0	0.0	0.0	0.0	0.0
1	16.7	8.7	0.0	6.7	0.0	25.0
2	30.6	32.6	27.3	20.0	22.2	0.0
3	27.8	39.1	36.4	33.3	44.4	50.0
4	19.4	17.4	31.8	30.0	33.3	25.0
5	5.6	2.2	4.5	10.0	0.0	0.0
Total	100.0	100.0	100.0	100.0	100.0	100.0
Post-materialistic index	8.3	10.9	36.4	33.3	33.3	0.0
Number of observations	36	46	22	30	9	4

FIGURE 1.
IMPORTANT TO YOUNG WOMEN TODAY

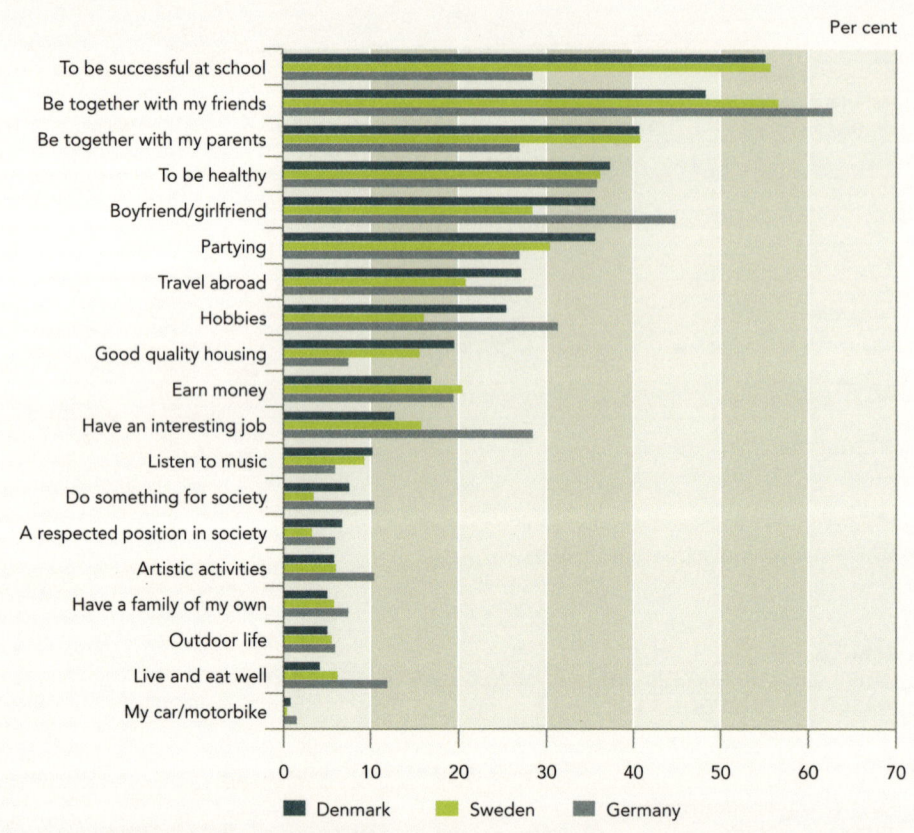

IMPORTANT TODAY – AND IN 15 YEARS

Ever since The Institute of Future Studies began its series of surveys among students in their final year of school there has been an extremely stable pattern in what the young regard as important.

FIGURE 2.
IMPORTANT TO YOUNG MEN TODAY

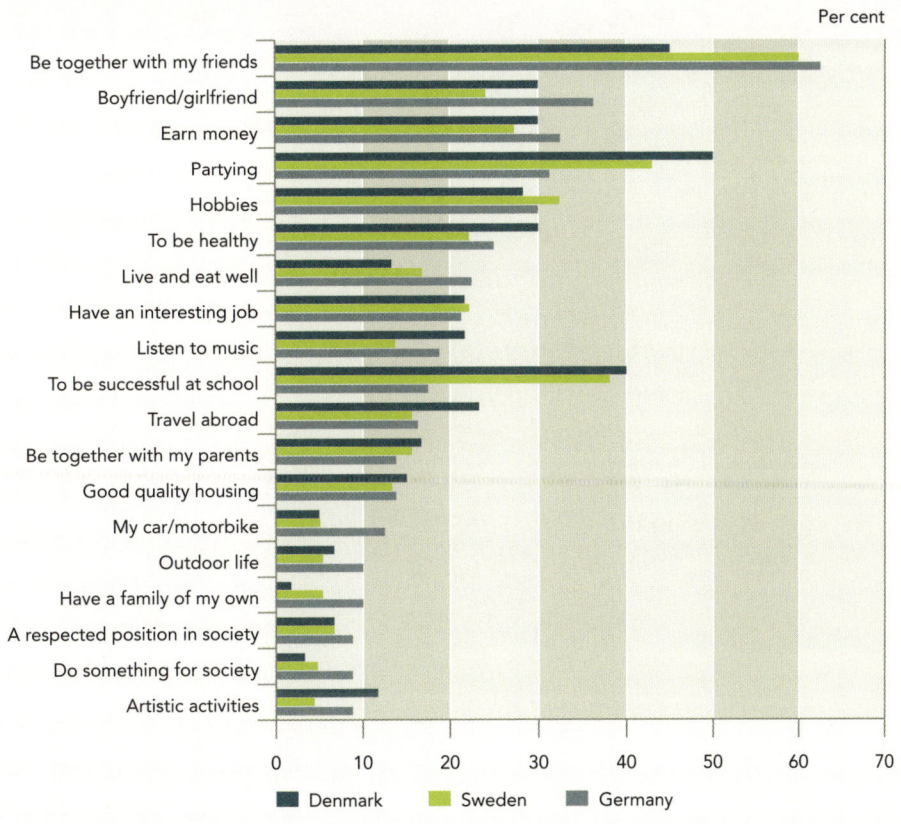

In the current survey, the respondents had to select four out of 19 alternatives they thought were the most important "today" and would be most important in 15 years.

The diagrams in Figures 1 and 2 show the order of the alternatives for the three countries and for women and men respectively. The ranking in the diagrams is based on the percentage of respondents for each of the alternatives.

THE TOP FIVE ALTERNATIVES IN THE THREE COUNTRIES ARE SUMMARISED BELOW

	Women			Men		
	Denmark	**Sweden**	**Germany**	**Denmark**	**Sweden**	**Germany**
	To be successful at school	Be together with my friends	Be together with my friends	Partying	Be together with my friends	Be together with my friends
	Be together with my friends	To be successful at school	My boyfriend	Be together with my friends	Partying	Girlfriend
	Be together with my parents	Be together with my parents	To be healthy	To be successful at school	To be successful at school	Earn money
	To be healthy	To be healthy	Hobbies	To be healthy	Hobbies	Partying
	My boyfriend	Partying	To be successful at school	Earn money	Earn money	Hobbies

Apart from some small changes in the ranking, the same alternatives are top priorities among young women in all three countries. Family relationships and relationships with boyfriend/girlfriend are very important while earning money is important to young men. Partying and hobbies are important to men in all three countries – less so among women. This aside, the same themes are more or less important to young people irrespective of country.

FIGURE 3.
IMPORTANT FOR YOUNG WOMEN 15 YEARS FROM NOW

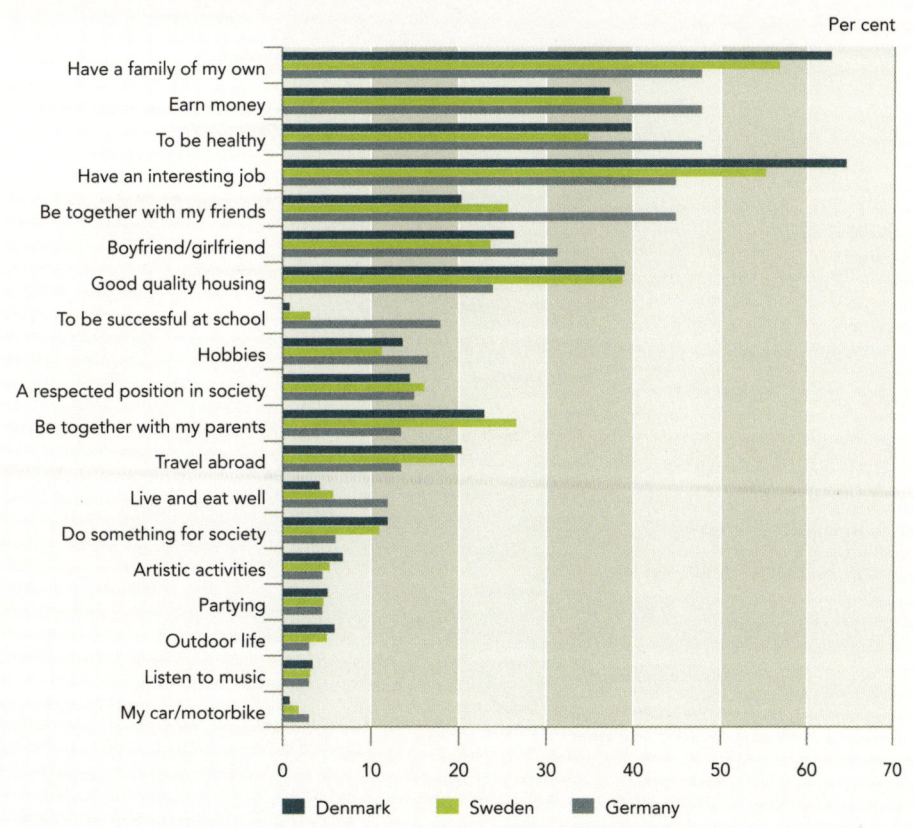

Top priorities after 15 years are shown in Figures 3 and 4.

The important issues are almost the same in all three countries. The list of priorities above provides a clear picture of the family breadwinner. Today's young people expect to have started a family within 15 years, live in good quality housing and have an interesting job. To achieve these goals they also need to be healthy and well paid.

FIGURE 4.
IMPORTANT FOR YOUNG MEN 15 YEARS FROM NOW

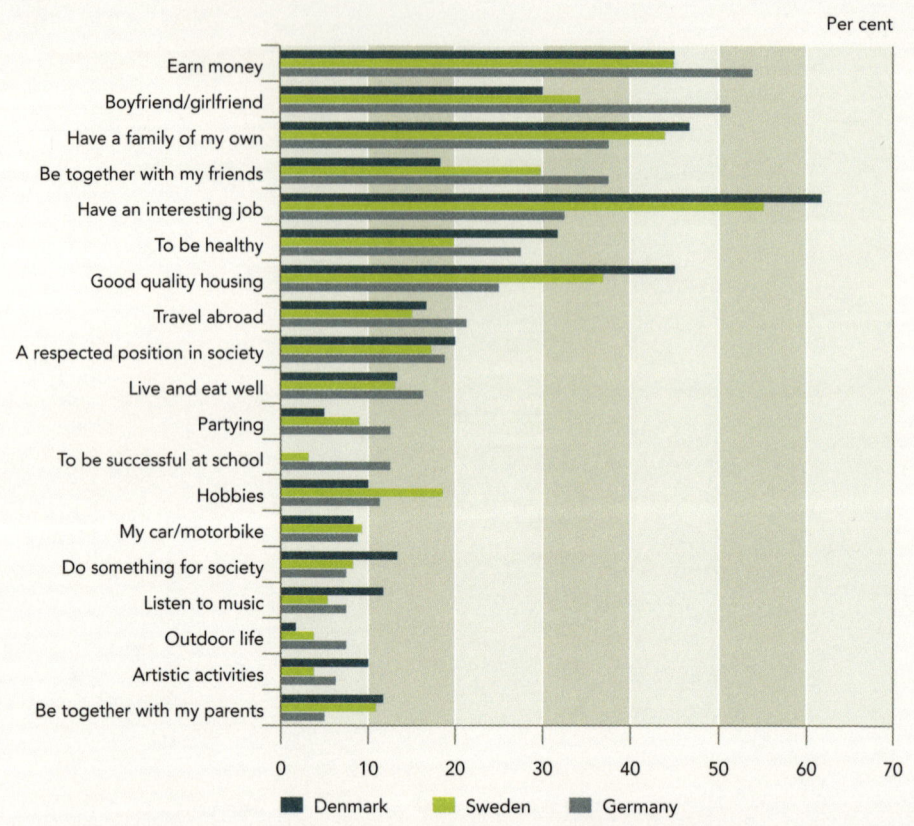

The result of this survey is in line with a trend observed since the beginning of the 1990s. In the first Swedish surveys, young people seemed to be ready for adult life and emphasised having a family, finding a proper job and earning money soon after finishing school. Towards the end of the century, the emphasis gradually shifted to a more hedonistic life

TOP FIVE ALTERNATIVES IN THE THREE COUNTRIES

	Women			Men		
	Denmark	Sweden	Germany	Denmark	Sweden	Germany
	Have an interesting job	Have a family of my own	Have a family of my own	Have an interesting job	Have an interesting job	Earn money
	Have a family of my own	Have an interesting job	Earn money	Have a family of my own	Earn money	Girlfriend
	To be healthy	Good quality housing	To be healthy	Good quality housing	Have a family of my own	Have a family of my own
	Good quality housing	Earn money	Have an interesting job	Earn money	Good quality housing	Be together with my friends
	Earn money	To be healthy	Be together with my friends	To be healthy	Girlfriend	Have an interesting job

style during the period immediately after finishing school – the period of adolescence extended well into their 20s (Fürth, Holmberg, Larsson & Raaterova, 2002). When this "Sturm-und-Drang" period is over in 15 years, young people are ready to live a normal family-oriented life although being with friends is still important.

GENERAL VALUES

Another aspect of general values derives from a direct question about values and attitudes. In this question, the young people were asked to grade their agreement with a number of statements on a scale from 1 (= don't agree at all) to 7 (=completely agree).

To compare the attitudes to these nine statements, an index was created where a value of 100 indicates that everybody agrees fully with the statement (they all chose the scale value 7) and a value of 0 if all respondents chose the scale value 1. See the following two diagrams.

A simple statistical test of these nine statements shows major differences between the countries but also some differences between the sexes. The differences between the countries are particularly apparent with regard to seven of the statements where there are gender differences with regard censorship, criminality, self-esteem, and ethnic diversity. Furthermore, there is complete agreement with respect to abortion among both men and women and in the three countries.

FIGURE 5.
GENERAL VALUES AMONG WOMEN

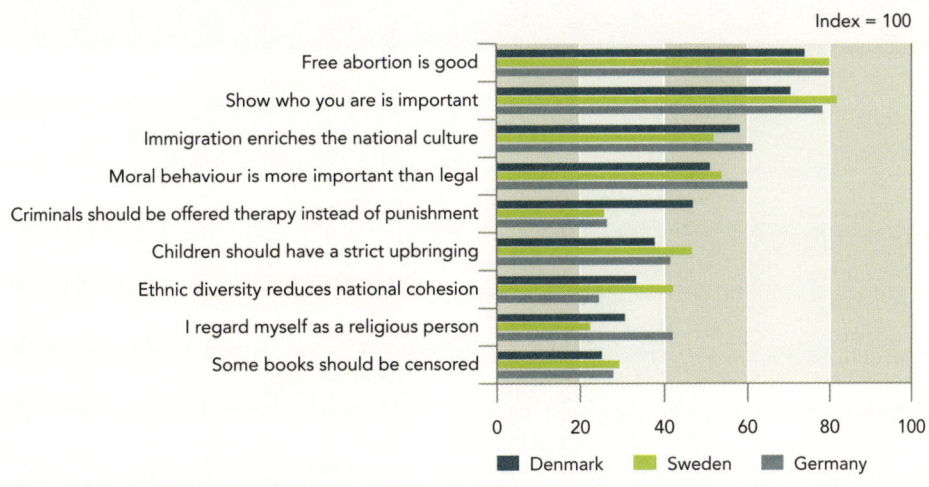

FIGURE 6.
GENERAL VALUES AMONG MEN

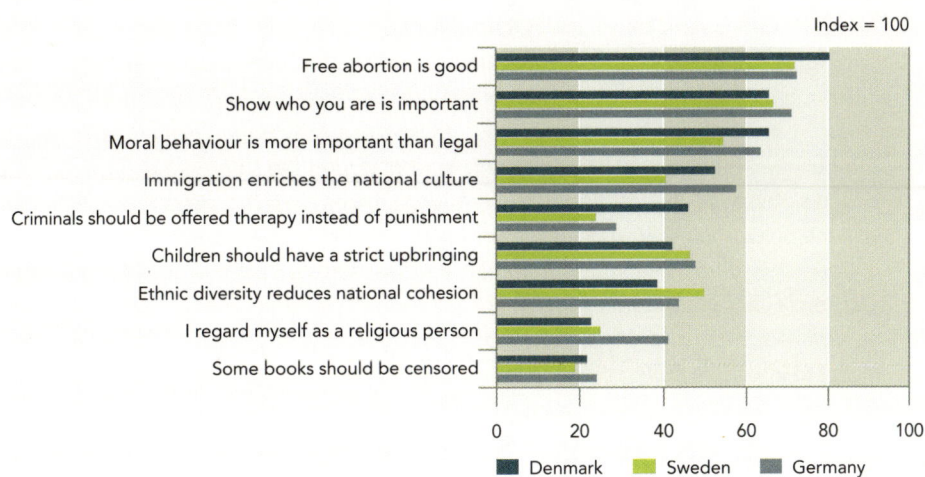

FIGURE 7.
PROPORTION OF WOMEN AND MEN WHO WORK DURING THEIR SUMMER HOLIDAYS AND AFTER SCHOOL

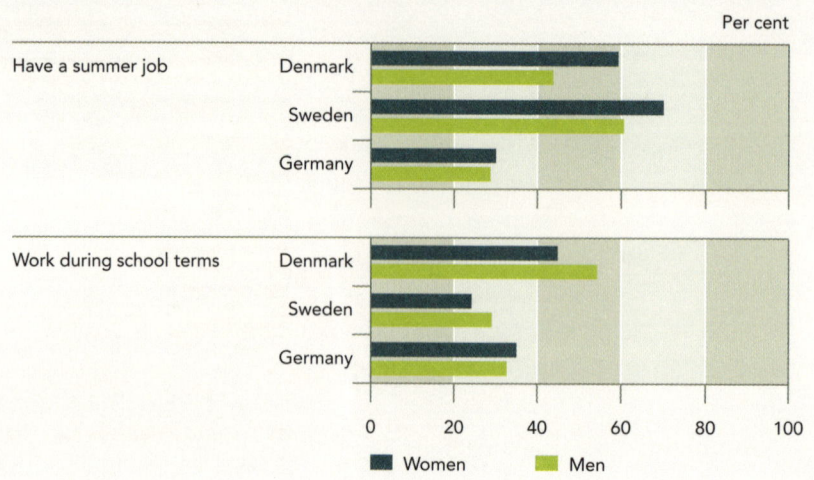

YOUNG PEOPLE AND THE LABOUR MARKET

Do teenagers in their final year of school know anything about the labour market? Do they really have opinions as to what is important in terms of their future jobs? It looks that way because the majority of young people have worked regularly during term time as well as during holidays. Eight out of 10 young people work during the summer holidays and one third works after school according to the previous studies of young people. In the current survey, the proportion that works is slightly lower, as given in the diagram in Figure 7.

Around two thirds of women in Denmark and Sweden have summer jobs and the same proportion of Danish women work after school. Among German women, these figures are much lower – around one third. Among men, the picture is as follows: men have a lower tendency to work both during the summer holidays and during term time, but the proportion is still over 50 per cent for Danish men. The conclusion that young people have formed an opinion about their requirements for future jobs is certainly valid.

FIGURE 8.
IMPORTANT JOB ISSUES FOR WOMEN

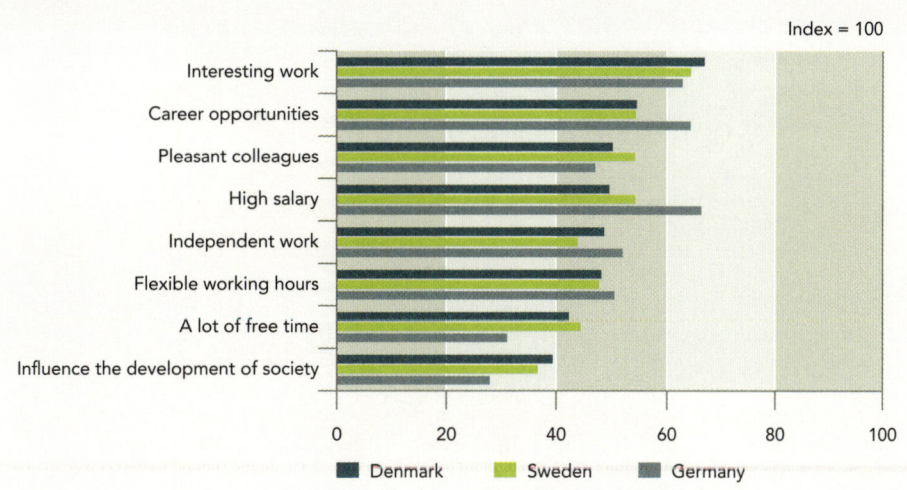

IMPORTANT JOB CHARACTERISTICS

In the current survey, young people were asked to rank eight different job characteristics by importance from 1 (don't agree at all) to 7 (completely agree).

To facilitate comparisons, the order of choices in the current survey was converted to an index that ranges from 100 (all respondents place the alternative at the top) to 0 (all respondents place it last). Figures 8 and 9 show the ranking of these alternatives by women and men in the three countries:

The ranking of key job characteristics is one of the few areas with some national differences. Young people from all three countries place a high salary and interesting work as their top priorities. What comes next, however, differs both in order and importance. Among Swedish men, there is clear prioritisation, with high salary at the top followed by interesting work, pleasant colleagues and career opportunities. German women also place a high salary at the top followed by career opportunities and interesting work. Pleasant

FIGURE 9.
IMPORTANT JOB ISSUES FOR MEN

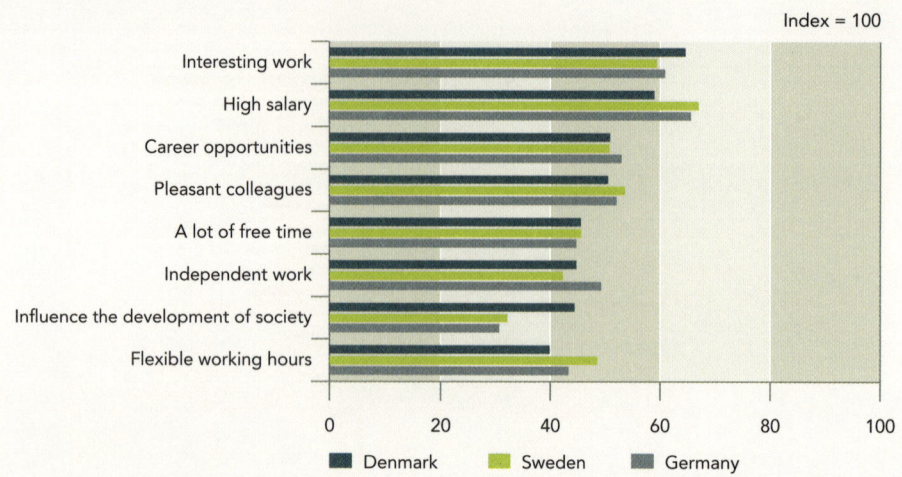

colleagues come, however, come far down the list (6th). For all other gender/nationality groups there is, in general, little difference in the ranking.

Closely related to the results in the previous ranking is the important and sometimes controversial question of job security. For this question, young people were asked to grade their agreement on a scale from 1 (=don't agree at all) to 7 (=completely agree). The Figures 10 and 11 illustrate the distribution between men and women.

Job security is very important to women from all three countries. By contrast, job security is only important to young Swedish men. Young German and Danish men are fairly indifferent.

MOST SOUGHT AFTER JOBS

The young people were presented with a list of 28 different occupations that covered the majority of the labour market. They were asked to select from among these the three most desirable occupations.

This selection clearly demonstrates the gender differences with regards to education. In general, men select jobs involving technology and computers while women prefer socially related jobs such as nursing or police work. Teaching at upper school level ranks higher among both men and women in Denmark than in Sweden.

FIGURE 10.
IMPORTANCE OF JOB SECURITY TO WOMEN

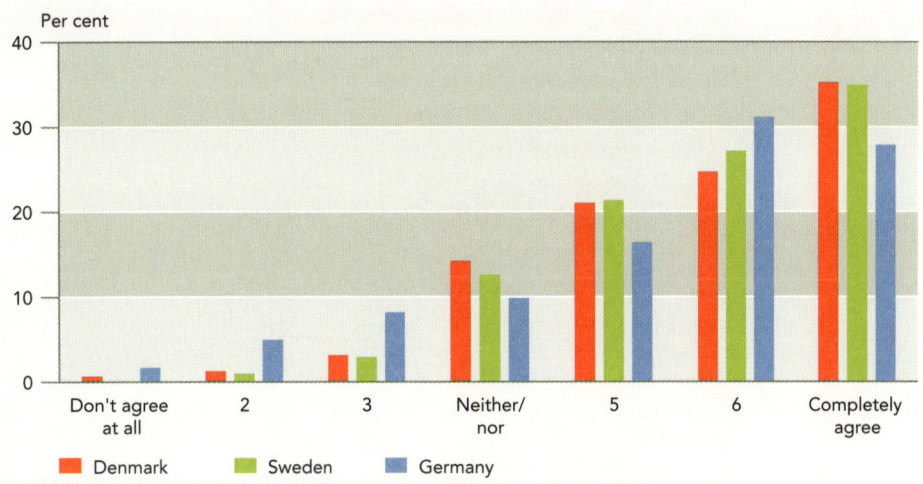

FIGURE 11.
IMPORTANCE OF JOB SECURITY TO MEN

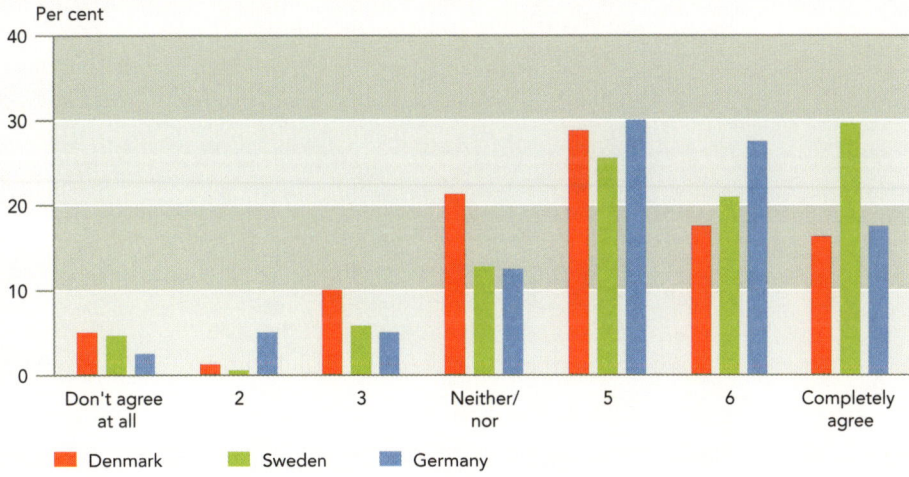

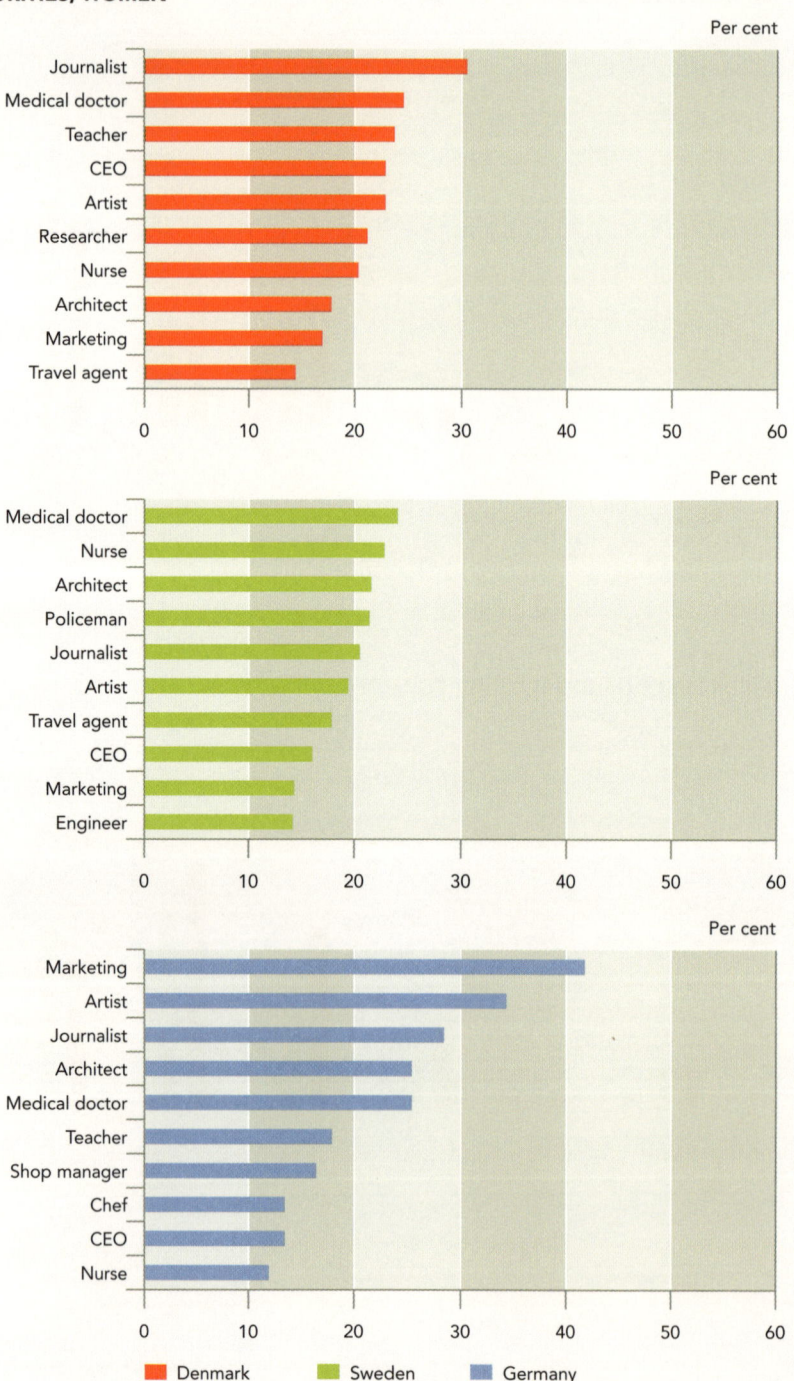

**FIGURE 12.
TOP JOB PRIORITIES, WOMEN**

FIGURE 12. (CONTINUED)
TOP JOB PRIORITIES, MEN

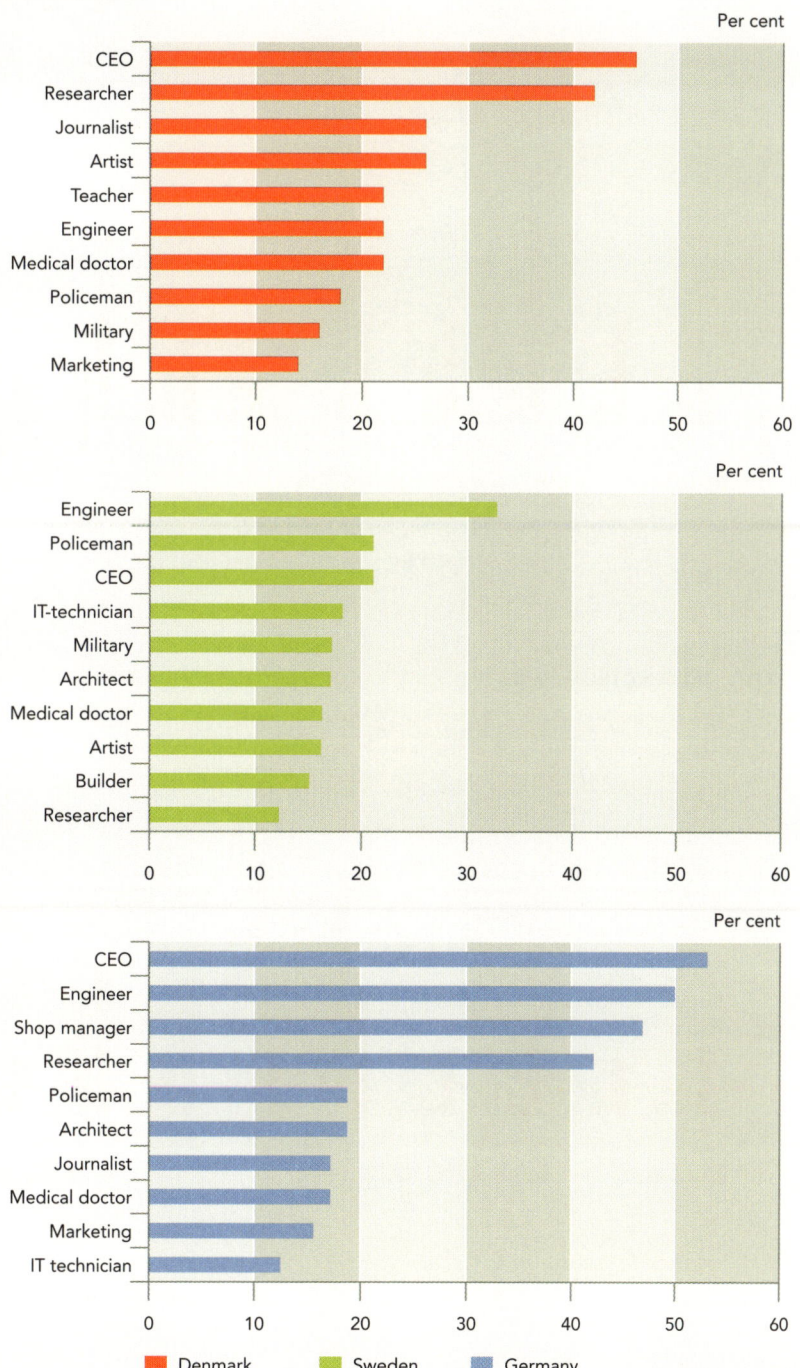

THE FEHMARNBELT FIXED LINK: REGIONAL DEVELOPMENT PERSPECTIVES

**FIGURE 13.
POLITICAL SPECTRUM, WOMEN**

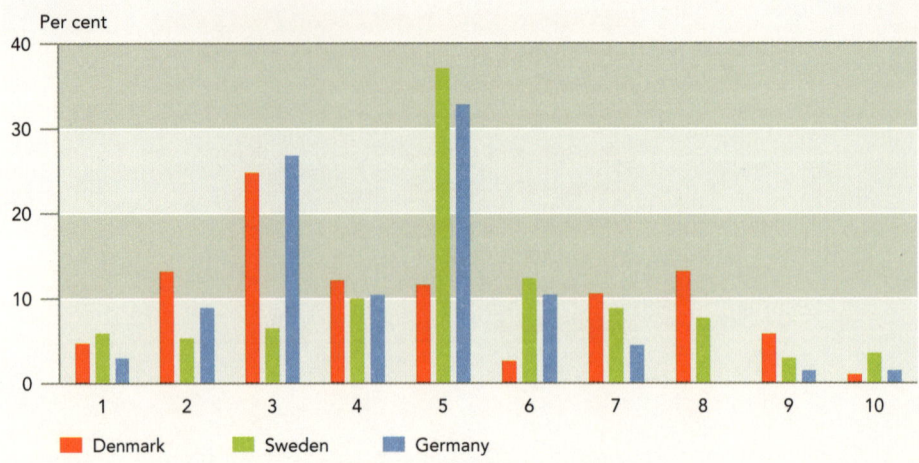

**FIGURE 14.
POLITICAL SPECTRUM, MEN**

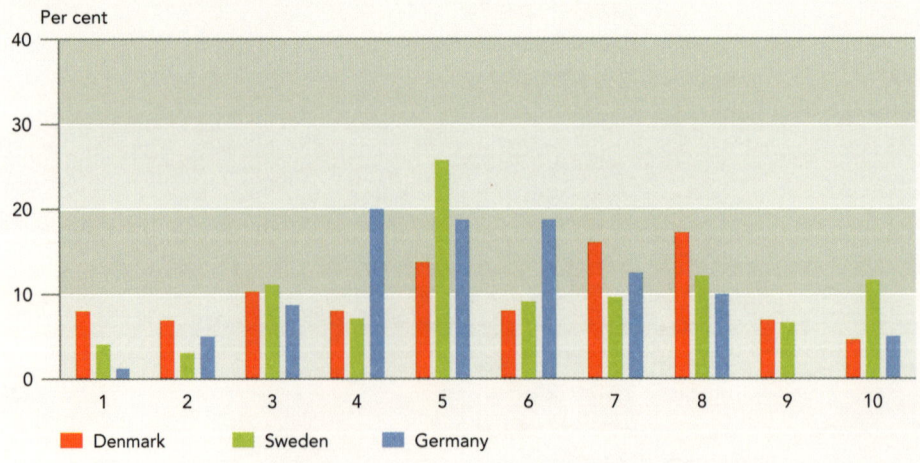

FIGURE 15.
POLITICAL INTEREST TODAY AND IN THE FUTURE, MEN AND WOMEN

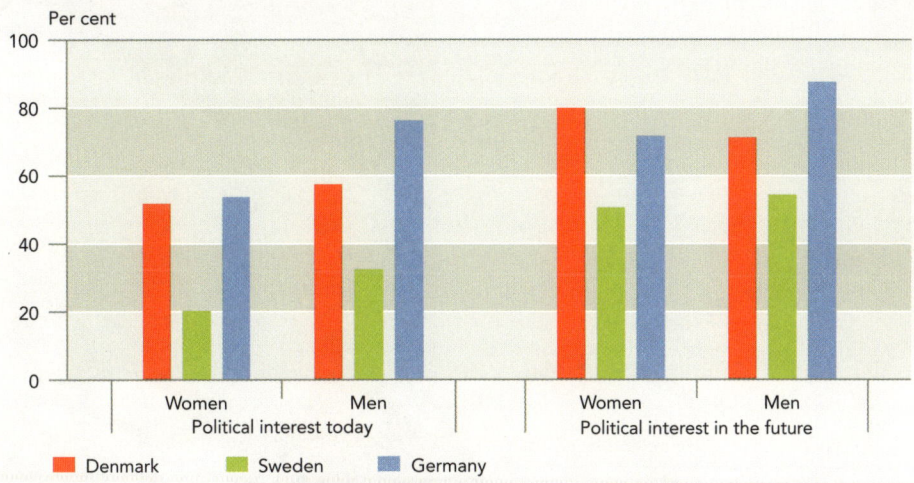

POLITICS AND SOCIETY

Young people are not interested in politics. This is the general perception and is largely true, albeit with some qualification. Figures 13 and 14 illustrate the political spectrum among young people in the three countries.

There are distinct differences in the political spectrum between men and women and that difference is expressed most clearly on the right side of the spectrum. There is a much higher proportion of men among right extremists, while women tend to gather at the centre or to the left of the spectrum.

Among Swedish women, there is a clear dominance at the centre while German women exhibit a bifurcated distribution with an additional peak towards the left. Danish women also show a bifurcated distribution, but in this case the two peaks are to the left and to the right.

Many previous Swedish surveys on young people have revealed a lack of interest in political issues among both men and women. The current survey is no exception: political interest is much higher among young people from Denmark and Germany than among young Swedes both "today" and in the future. Young Danes and especially young Germans take a much stronger interest in politics than do young Swedes.

Interest in politics is also reflected in questions regarding the importance of other political dimensions than the left/right spectrum. Among young Swedes, between half and two thirds have no views about this issue. This applies to less than half of the Danish and German women. By contrast, the majority of Danish and German men consider this important.

FIGURE 16.
POLITICAL INTEREST; OTHER POLITICAL DIMENSIONS THAN THE LEFT/RIGHT SPECTRUM ARE IMPORTANT

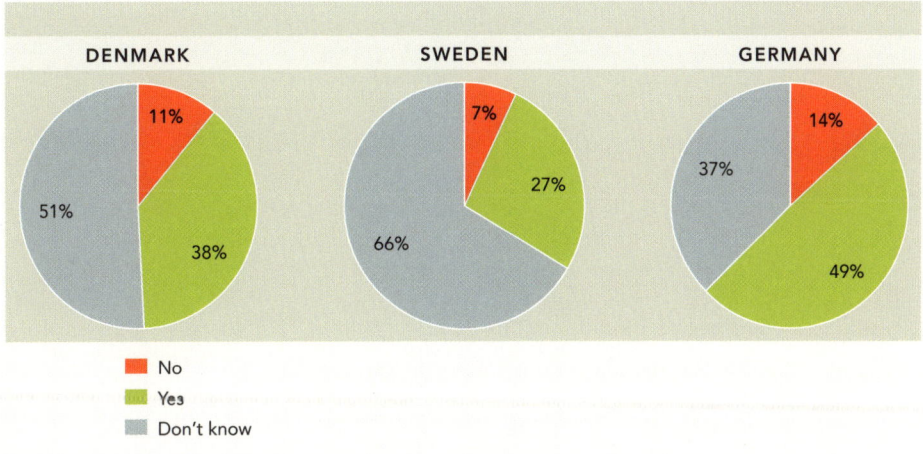

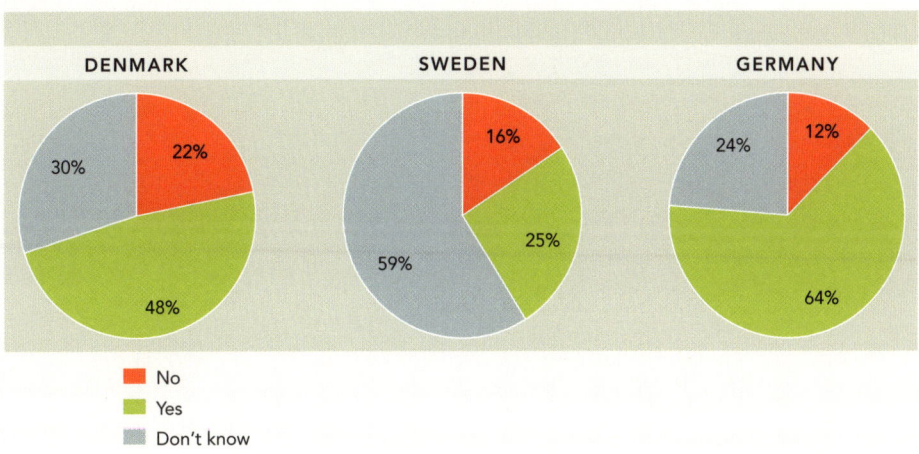

FIGURE 17.
TYPE OF FUTURE SOCIETY

WOMEN

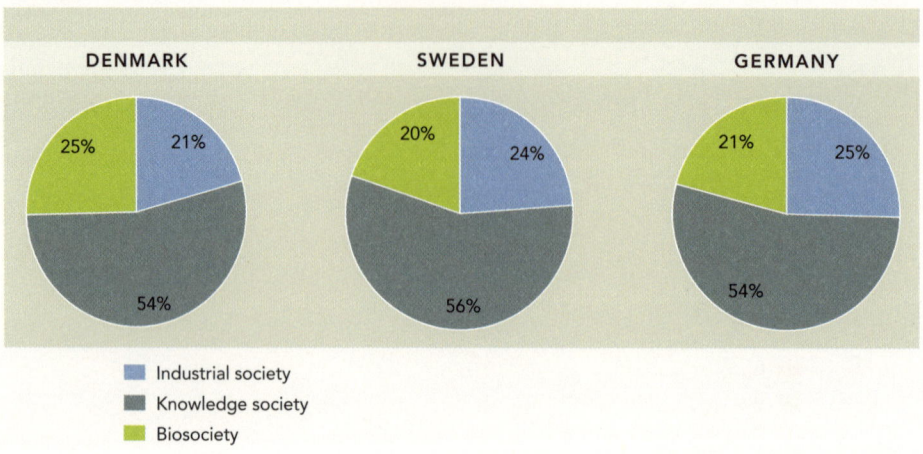

MEN

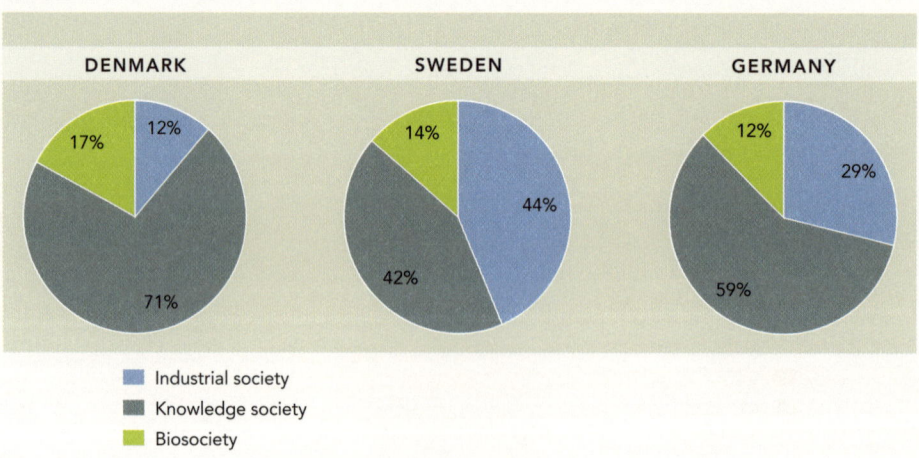

THE ENVIRONMENT AND THE SOCIETY OF THE FUTURE

The type of society we would like to have in the future is an important issue because the path to the future is defined by what we do today. You would expect this to be important to today's young people. The young people, therefore, were asked to answer questions about which type of society they would be most attracted by. They could choose between three alternatives:

1. The Industrial Society. Most people work within industry or the public or private sectors. In contrast to the agricultural society of before, the majority of the population are wage earners. Society is characterised by production technology.

2. The Knowledge and Information Society. This is a society in which most people work with information, communication and knowledge. Instead of producing goods, knowledge is produced and exported. The foundation of society is the ability of man to cultivate knowledge and communicate with the outside world.

3. The Biological or Ecological Society. Everything in society is focused on ecology and biology. Production processes are largely based on biological technology. Achieving ecological balance in society and the world in general is important and dominates man's perception of the world.

Swedish men's more materialistic views are confirmed by their considerable interest in industrial society. The knowledge society, on the other hand, seems to be the most sought after type of society for all other sub-groups – around 50 per cent of young people in Sweden. For young Danes the figure is two thirds.

FIGURE 18.
SOLUTIONS TO THE ENVIRONMENTAL PROBLEMS AMONG MEN AND WOMEN

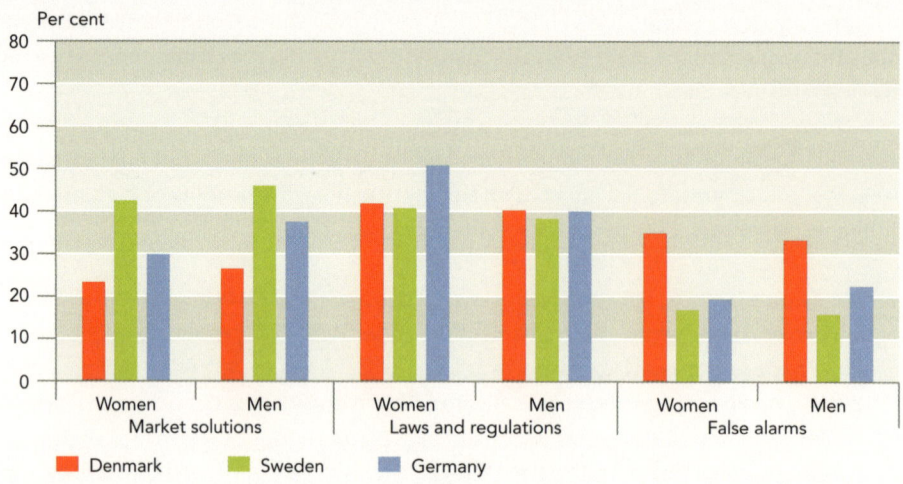

The question about the desired future society was supplemented by a further question concerning how to solve environmental problems. Three alternatives were presented: market solutions, legislation and regulations and "false alarm." See Figure 18.

With regard to environmental issues, there is an interesting national difference, but only a minor difference between men and women. Young Swedes believe in the market economy. A well-functioning market economy will influence companies to become more environmentally aware and thus generate resources for solving environmental problems. Young Germans, on the other hand, believe in a strong state that forces people to change their lifestyle through laws and regulations. Young Danes, however, tend to believe the debates on environmental problems are characterised by "false alarms."

FIGURE 19.
TYPE OF HOUSING AFTER 15 YEARS DESIRED BY MEN AND WOMEN

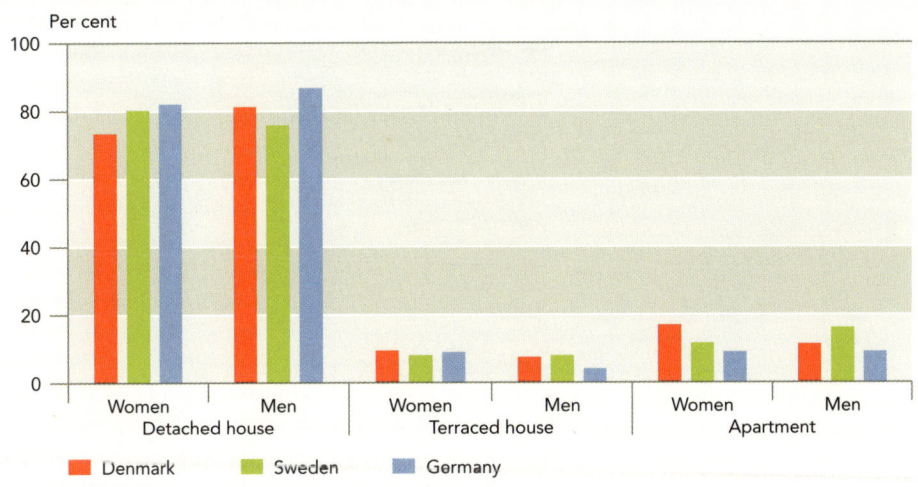

HOUSING AND CULTURE

Answers to housing issues – both immediately after finishing school and within a longer-term perspective – were included in the surveys and the answers were largely identical. Initially, young people want a cheap flat in an apartment block in the city centre. Later when starting a family, a detached house or a semi-detached house in pleasant surroundings was the first priority. Figure 19 presents the results from the current survey.

The result is quite extreme in that a detached house is clearly the first choice within a 15-year perspective. Only around 15 per cent would prefer to live in an apartment block. This difference between demand for housing and actual supply has been a problem for many years and will remain so in all three countries although the situation may have improved in recent years. In 2009, for example, 68 per cent of newly built homes in Demark were single family houses. In Sweden, this was as low as 41 per cent.

FIGURE 20.
DESIRED AMENITIES IN THE HOUSING AREA "TODAY" ACCORDING TO WOMEN

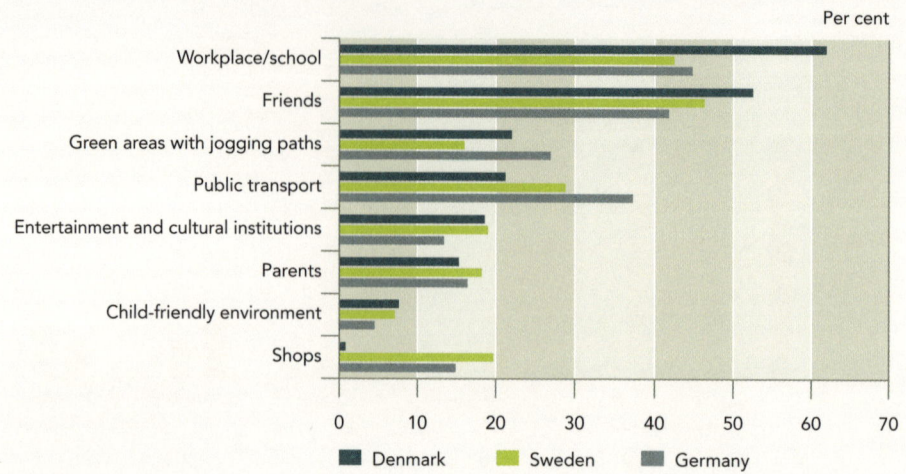

THE HOUSING ENVIRONMENT

In addition to the type of housing, amenities are the second most important factor in the local area. The answer, apparently, reflects a uniform assessment of the future.

Immediately after leaving school, the most important nearby amenities are friends, workplace, further education facilities and public transport. Later on, in a 15-year perspective, most young people expect to have a family which means that a child-friendly environment is important as well.

According to Figures 20 and 21, two alternatives dominate what is desired in the housing area in the years ahead: workplace/school and friends. The difference in order of preference is quite small for all remaining alternatives, with public transport in the third place. At this stage of their lives, a child-friendly environment plays a minor role.

FIGURE 21.
DESIRED AMENITIES IN THE HOUSING AREA "TODAY" ACCORDING TO MEN

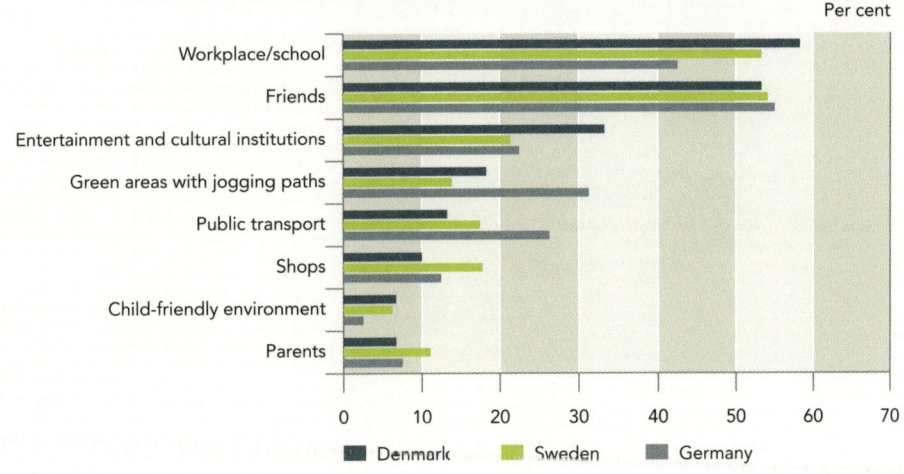

After 15 years the two alternatives continue to dominate, i.e. a child-friendly environment and workplace/school. German men, however, have a slightly different prioritisation of alternatives. Workplace/school remains the top priority, but then follows green areas with jogging paths, friends and only in fourth place, a child-friendly environment. Do they need an extended period of freedom from their commitments? It is also interesting to note that young people do not want to live near their parents – a sign of independence?

This selection of alternatives is quite consistent with earlier findings. The period immediately after school is clearly a time for having fun, with no commitments.

FIGURE 22.
DESIRED AMENITIES IN THE HOUSING AREA "15 YEARS FROM NOW" ACCORDING TO WOMEN

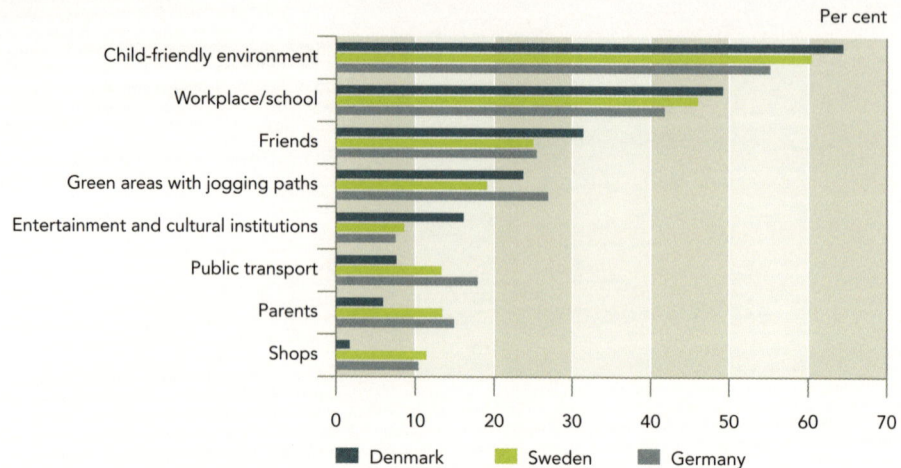

CULTURAL LIFE

Closely connected to the preferred type of housing and living conditions are young people's views on the availability of cultural opportunities.

The modern concept of culture differs significantly from that of the old industrial society. Young people are more open than politicians to changes in the social structure. Spontaneous movements are constantly emerging within the younger sections of society, which could not be accommodated by the old institutions. Typical examples are the wide range of festivals that did not fit into traditional cultural life. Previous surveys of young people support such recent trends. There is little support for traditional cultural institutions like museums, symphony orchestras etc. Instead the young choose events like music festivals, film festivals, temporary art exhibitions etc.

As seen in Figure 24, support for permanent cultural institutions is quite weak and generally below 50 per cent – in Denmark even below 20 per cent.

FIGURE 23.
DESIRED AMENITIES IN THE HOUSING AREA "15 YEARS FROM NOW" ACCORDING TO MEN

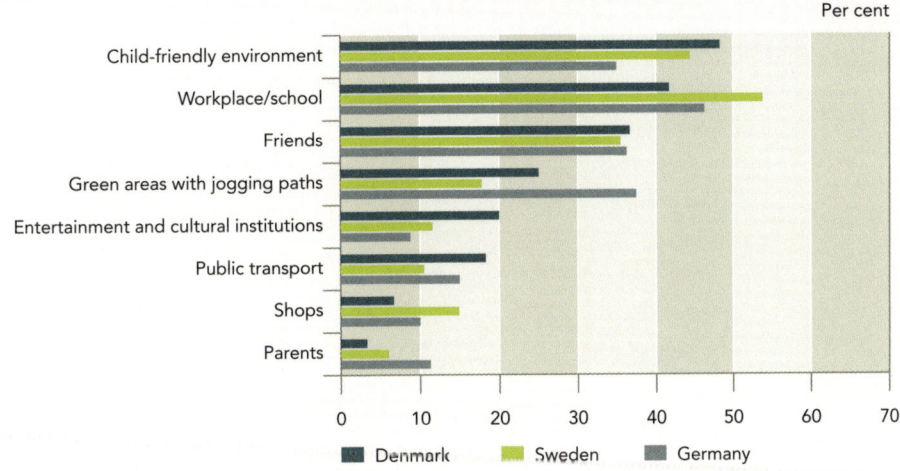

FIGURE 24.
DESIRED ORGANISATION OF CULTURAL LIFE AMONG WOMEN AND MEN

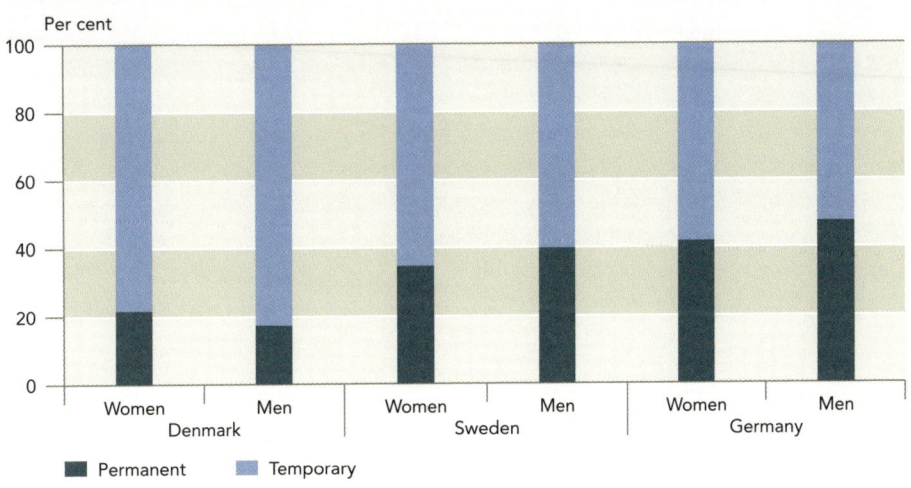

FIGURE 25.
PREFERRED TEMPORARY CULTURAL EVENTS BY WOMEN

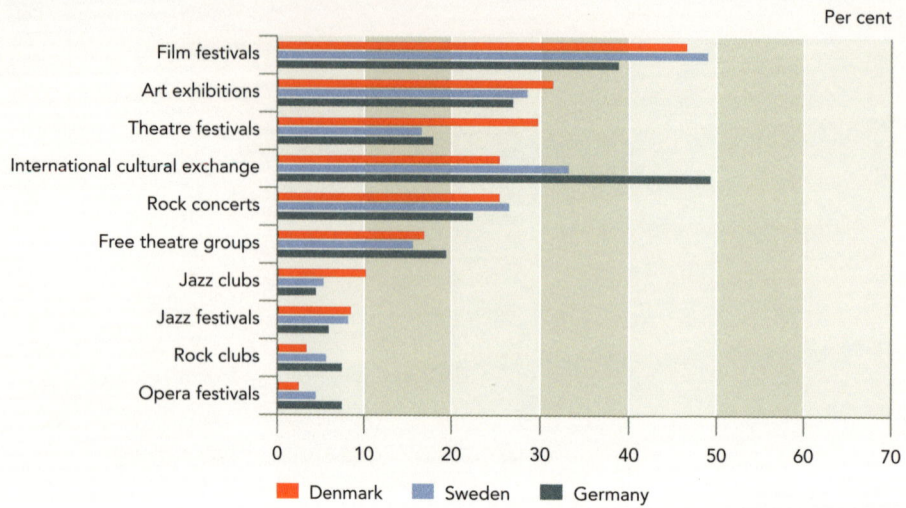

Figures 25 and 26 illustrate what type of temporary cultural events are preferred by young people:

It is commonly accepted that women have a deeper and broader interest in culture than men. This belief is confirmed by many Swedish surveys of young people during the 1990s and by this survey. Looking at the two figures that represent cultural interests in the three countries, we find some minor differences. Women prioritise a broad spectrum of cultural activities. German and Swedish women go for international cultural exchange, film festivals and art exhibitions, while Danish women also prioritise theatre festivals – six out 10 prioritise cultural activities fairly highly. The pattern is different among men who prefer film festivals and rock concerts followed by international cultural exchange (in the case of Denmark we may add art exhibitions as well).

FIGURE 26.
PREFERRED TEMPORARY CULTURAL EVENTS BY MEN

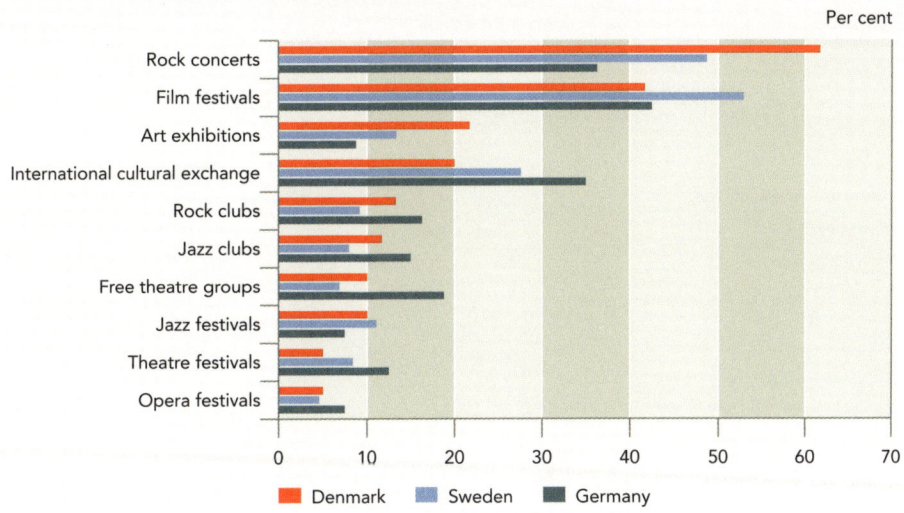

CONTACT WITH THE NEIGHBOURING COUNTRIES

What do young people in the Fehmarnbelt Region know about their neighbouring countries and what kind of contacts do they have? These questions were addressed under the headings: types and number of contacts and attitudes towards studying, working and living in the neighbouring country.

Contact with – and knowledge about – the neighbouring countries was measured by four different questions: number of visits over the past year, knowledge about tourist attractions, watching TV or having friends or relatives in the neighbouring country. To obtain a clearer picture of the answers, an index was developed showing the difference in intensity for each country pair divided by the sum of the intensity. The index thus varies from -100 (= 100 per cent of the young people in the second country of the pair and 0 per cent in the first country have, for example, visited the neighbouring country) to +100 (= vice versa).

TABLE 7.
INDEX OF NEIGHBOURING COUNTRY CONTACTS

	Denmark-Sweden		Denmark-Germany		Sweden-Germany	
	Women	Men	Women	Men	Women	Men
Visited the neighbouring country						
At least three times	-10.3	-12.8	63.8	60.0	95.4	90.3
At least once	-8.8	-5.7	-28.2	-5.5	46.7	33.1
Know tourist attractions						
Yes, several	-78.4	-47.5	-35.8	-86.8	-	56.9
Yes, at least one	-65.0	-45.5	-44.9	-60.3	66.9	70.0
Watch TV from the neighbouring country						
Yes, often	6.1	23.1	100.0	-	100.0	100.0
Yes	-0.6	-5.9	29.4	26.9	62.0	47.8
Know people from the neighbouring country						
Yes, both family and friends	11.9	-47.5	71.5	50.8	-	54.2
Yes	18.7	6.7	11.7	14.6	7.5	11.7

Both young Danes and Swedes visit Germany fairly often. This, however, does not mean that they have any particular knowledge of Hamburg. Only a few can list tourist attractions in the city. The Hagenbeck Zoo, for instance, is mentioned by two Swedes and one Dane and the port area is mentioned a couple of times. Neither do they watch German TV (less than 20 per cent). Even so, one in three knows at least one person in Germany. In respect of Denmark, the situation is different. Copenhagen, the Danish capital, attracts young people from both Sweden and Germany and the tourist attractions in Copenhagen are well known: Tivoli, Strøget and the Little Mermaid are mentioned by a large proportion of young visitors from both Sweden and Germany although the list is much longer. Slightly more than one in three young Swedes watches Danish TV and knows at least one person in Denmark. Young Germans on the other hand neither watch TV from the other two countries nor know any tourist attractions in Malmö although at least one in three knows at least one person in Sweden. Danish-Swedish relations are not as intense as Swedish-Danish relations, but the Danes are familiar with some tourist attractions in Malmö: The Turning Torso is, of course, hard to miss, but the old town and the castle are mentioned several times. Half the young Danes know at least someone in Sweden and one in three watches Swedish TV.

All this means that there is a high level of asymmetry in the relations between the three countries – as is expressed in Table 7. In many relations, Danish-Swedish relations are more balanced than Danish-German and Swedish-German relations because young Germans generally lack insight into the two Scandinavian countries.

STUDYING, WORKING AND LIVING IN THE NEIGHBOURING COUNTRIES

Interest in studying, working and living in the neighbouring countries was measured by direct questions: studying in one of the major university regions of Copenhagen, Malmö/Lund or Hamburg, working in one of the three regions if the pay were better or living permanently in one of the two other countries. The results are displayed in Table 8.

Both Swedish and German young people show a strong interest in studying, living and working in Denmark and many young Swedes perhaps already work in Copenhagen. The same can be said for young Germans vis-à-vis Sweden. By contrast, young Danes show little interest in studying or living in Germany (less than 10 per cent) while close to one in three could consider working in Germany. Among Swedish men, the interest in studying, living and working in Germany is lower, but not as low as in Denmark.

TABLE 8.
INDEX OF NEIGHBOURING CONTACTS

Do you want to:	Denmark-Sweden		Denmark-Germany		Sweden-Germany	
	Women	Men	Women	Men	Women	Men
Live	-18.2	5.2	-77.5	-47.5	-56.0	-30.0
Study	-30.7	5.9	-66.9	-65.6	-46.2	-41.0
Work	-25.2	-11.5	-44.9	-28.9	-19.0	-9.1

This significant asymmetry in the relations between the countries leads to large negative values in German relations with the two other countries. The interest among young Germans in studying, working or living in the other two countries is much higher than vice-versa. In Danish-Swedish relations, this asymmetry is only found among Swedish women while the views of men are almost in balance.

CONSEQUENCES OF THE FEHMARNBELT FIXED LINK

A final question was put to young people in Germany and Denmark, which referred to the perceived consequences of a permanent link across the Fehmarnbelt. The result is summarised in Figures 27 and 28.

The question regarding the possible consequences of a fixed Fehmarnbelt link was only answered by young Germans and Danes. More detailed questions regarding the Fehmarnbelt Region in all three countries will be considered elsewhere.

There is one striking difference of opinion – possibly under the influence of Danish experience with the Øresund bridge. Young people in Germany are more concerned about the environment than young Danes. The low level of concern among young Danes may be due to the fact that the construction of the Storebælt and Øresund bridges did not cause any of the environmental damage as was feared before the start of construction.

In the 1992 Danish-Swedish survey, 51 per cent expressed concern about the environmental consequences, 12 per cent believed in the economic opportunities and 2 per cent in the cultural potential. The current survey shows that compared to men, women remain uncertain as to the benefits of large infrastructure investments. On the other hand, they see possible cultural benefits. When it comes to environmental problems, young Germans are more in doubt.

FIGURE 27.
CONSEQUENCES OF THE FEHMARNBELT LINK ACCORDING TO YOUNG GERMANS

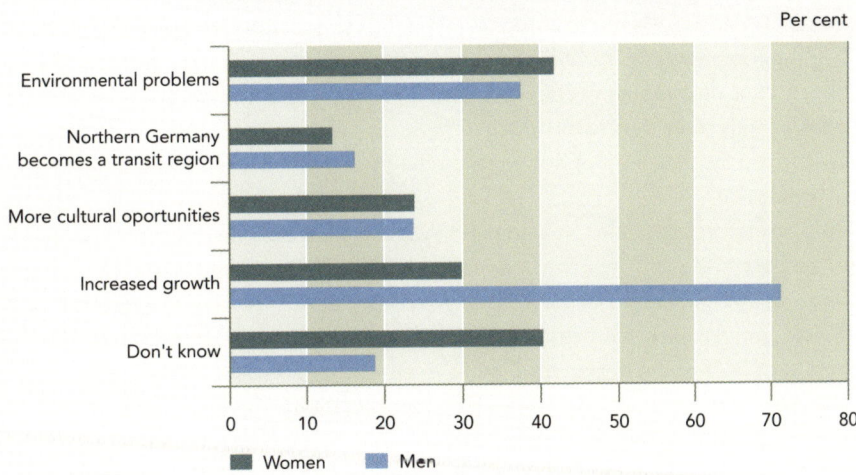

FIGURE 28.
CONSEQUENCES OF THE FEHMARNBELT LINK ACCORDING TO YOUNG DANES

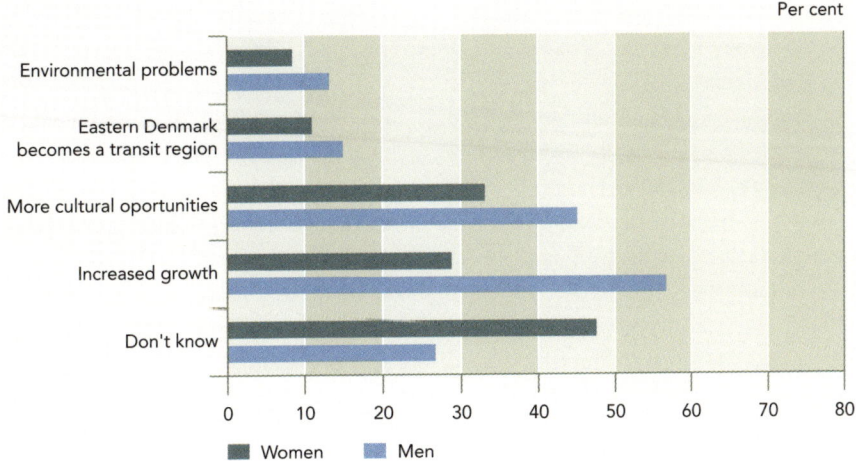

SUMMARY

In order to obtain a "baseline" study of the attitudes in the three countries involved in the new geography around the fixed link across the Fehmarnbelt, a survey was carried out in late 2009/early 2010 among students in the final year of their schooling (aged 18-20) in the Fehmarnbelt Region. The survey reveals comsiderable asymmetry in terms of knowledge about their neighbouring countries. Despite this, interest in studying, working or living permanently elsewhere in the region is fairly high among young people (except that young Danes and Swedes are not attracted by the idea of living or studying in the German part of the region).

An important revelation in the survey is the differing views of young people from the three countries with regard to general values and attitudes towards the labour market, housing and culture, politics and environmental issues. In general, it appears that the main dividing line for these themes lies between the sexes and not so much between the countries. Young people of the region have more in common in respect of their general values and attitudes than there are differences that separate them.

The topics covered in the survey, which comprised 800 young people, were:

- Values and attitudes in general
- Attitudes towards the labour market
- Future society and politics
- Environmental issues
- Housing and culture
- Interaction between the countries
- Consequences of a permanent Fehmarnbelt link

Young Danish women and young people from Germany have the highest rate of post-materialistic values while Swedish men are the most materialistic; Swedish women are neutral. An interesting finding is that young Swedes who are generally regarded as the most post-materialistic in Europe are much less post-materialistic than young people from the other two countries.

Important values "today" are much the same among young people in all three countries. Family relationships and relationships with boyfriends/girlfriends are very important, as is earning money among some sub-groups. A happy life with parties to go to and hobbies to enjoy are important to men in all three countries – but a bit less so among women. Enjoying life has great appeal at this stage of life.

The list of priorities 15 years from now gives a very clear picture of "responsible breadwinners". Young people of today expect to have started a family within 15 years, to have good quality housing and an interesting job. To achieve these goals, they need to be healthy. We also noticed that earning money has become considerably more important with regard to the future than is the case today. When it comes to more general values like censorship, abortion, ethnic diversity and religion, the major differences are between countries rather than gender.

Traditional job characteristics are ranked almost in the same order by young people from all three countries: young Germans are slightly more materialistic when it comes to working conditions, while young Swedes and Danes regard work not only as a means of earning a living, but also as part of their social life. Job security is very important to women of all three countries. Job security is only important to young men from Sweden. Young Germans and Danes are fairly indifferent.

When it comes to career, answers clearly demonstrate the gender gap. Men in general opt for technical and computer jobs while women prefer jobs that are people-oriented. The list of chosen jobs is similar in the three countries, with only a few exceptions. A teacher at "gymnasium" level (i.e. 16-19 year olds) is much more highly rated in Denmark among both men and women than in Sweden.

There are distinct differences in political attitudes between men and women and these differences are most evident to the right of the spectrum. There are more men among right extremists whereas women tend to gravitate towards the centre or the left. It can be concluded that political interest is much higher among young Danes and Germans than among young Swedes – now and in the future.

When asked about their ideal future society, the more materialistic attitudes among Swedish men are reflected in their strong interest in an industrial society. By contrast, a knowledge society seems to be the preferred choice for all other sub-groups – around 50 per cent of all young people (two-thirds of young Danes) opt for this type of society.

Another important issue relating to the future is how to solve our current environmental problems. We have found a striking difference between the countries in respect of alternatives: young Swedes are in favour of market solutions, young Germans prefer laws and regulations while young Danes think that environmental issues are of unnecessary concern.

With regard to future housing, there is complete unanimity. Eight out of 10 young people declare that they would prefer a detached house. After finishing school, however, the most important nearby amenities are friends, workplace, higher education and public transport. Within a 15-year perspective, most young people expect to have started a family, which makes a child-friendly environment important as well.

One of the main issues addressed in this survey is a possible asymmetry in knowledge about the respective neighbouring countries. The results from the survey clearly demonstrate the existence of such asymmetry. Contact with, and knowledge of, the German part of the region is rather limited. Contact between the three countries is mainly in the form of visits by young Danes and Swedes to Germany (on their way to holidays perhaps) but not the other way round. The Danish part of the region, including Copenhagen, is very well known to young people from both Sweden and Germany while young Danes and Swedes know almost nothing about Hamburg. Only a few young people from the two countries are able to mention tourist attractions in Hamburg. Young Germans' knowledge of Malmö is equally limited.

When it comes to studying, working or living in the neighbouring countries, contact between Denmark and Sweden is well established and interest is quite high. In relation to Germany, interest among young Germans in the other two countries is much higher than the other way around. Young Danes and Swedes are not interested in living or studying in Germany, but see working there as an interesting possibility. Young Germans, on the other hand, are interested in both studying and living and, to a very high degree, of working in one of the two countries.

REFERENCES

D. E. Andersson, Å. E. Andersson & I. Holmberg, *'Värderingar bland ungdomar i Skåne och på Själland'*, 2010

Å. E. Andersson, T. Fürth & I. Holmberg, *'70-talister. Om värderingar förr, nu och i framtiden'*, Natur och Kultur, Stockholm, 1997

T. Fürth, I. Holmberg, O. Larsson & M. Raaterova, *'90-talisterna kommer; Om kollektiva egoister, självuppoffrande livsnjutare och andra ungdomar'*, 2002

R. Inglehart *'The silent revolution'*, Princeton University Press, Princeton, 1997

C. W. Matthiessen & Å. E. Andersson, *'Øresundsregionen: Kreativitet, integration, vækst'*, Munksgård, Copenhagen, 1993

World Values Survey, http://www.worldvaluessurvey.org/

12

GLOSSARY

Agglomeration effects	The benefits that market participants obtain when locating near each other
Central place theory	Cities are service centres in relation to the surrounding hinterland which is defined by natural and man-made resources. The cities are part of a hierarchical system where cities at the top level dominate cities at a lower level which, in turn, dominate cities on the next level. Interaction between the cities is determined by the hierarchy. The same applies to flows of people, goods, information, energy and money.
Cohesion policy	EU policy aiming at diminishing the disparities between different regions
Commuter	Regular traveler between place of residence and place of work
Commuter flow	Number of commuters along a specific route

Concave curve	A curve with decreasing slope
Convex curve	A curve with increasing slope
Cross-border commuter	Commuter who crosses a national border to reach the place of work
Gravity model	A model of spatial interaction that contains some elements of mass and distance, a metaphor of physical gravity.
(Active) daytime population	The working population in an area, i.e. the workforce minus those who commute out of an area but including those who commute into an area.
ESPON	European Spatial Planning Observation network. EU's analysis unit for urban and regional development and planning, observation network.
Hedonic price	The price an actual buyer and user will pay for goods or services.
Hedonic price model	Mathematical model for calculating the hedonic price.
Intermodal transport	Transport solutions that combine different modes of transport.
Labour market integration	Reduction of impediments for labour mobility between regional or national labour markets
Lo-lo	Lift on, lift off – loading and unloading of a ship's cargo using cranes, c.f. ro-ro.
MEGA	Metropolitan growth area.
Multinomial model	An econometric model (e.g. a least-squares-regression) where the dependent variable can take only few specific values (e.g. 1-full-time employed, 2-part-time employed, 3-self-employed, 4-unemployed).
Multi-variate statistical method	Statistical analysis method which deals with many variables at a time; many dimensional analysis method.
Nodality	The ability to co-ordinate a system.
Node	Co-ordinating network centre.

Ordinary least-squares regression	A method for estimating the unknown parameters of a linear relationship between the dependent variable and the explanatory variables.
PDI	Pre-delivery inspection.
Postponement	Delay, i.e. to defer investment to maximise benefits and minimise risks e.g. Build-To-Order Concept (Dell).
Ro-ro-transport	Roll on, roll off – loading and unloading of ships by vehicles, c.f. lo-lo. The ro-ro system requires ramps as used on car ferries.
Science Citation Index	Comprehensive database which registers all papers in the most cited international scientific publications in the world.
STRING	Southwestern Baltic Sea Trans-regional Area Implementing New Geography.
Triple helix	Collaboration between the public sector, private companies and universities and the scientific world.
Øresund City	The metropolitan region in the Øresund Region: Copenhagen-Malmö-Lund-Helsingborg.

ABOUT THE AUTHORS

David Emanuel Andersson (1966), Associate Professor of Economics, Institute of Public Affairs Management, National Sun Yat-sen University, Kaohsiung, Taiwan

Åke E. Andersson (1936), Professor of Economics, Jönköping International Business School, Jönköping, Kungliga Tekniska Högskolan, Stockholm

Petra Aulin (1981), MSc., Research Assistant, Femern A/S, Copenhagen

Dr. Johannes Bröcker (1950), Professor, Chair of International and Regional Economics and Director of Institute for Regional Research, Christian-Albrechts-Universität zu Kiel, Kiel

Søren Find (1948), Head of Department, Technical University of Denmark, Lyngby

Dr. Hayo Herrmann (1949), Senior Researcher, Institute for Regional Research, Christian-Albrechts-Universität zu Kiel, Kiel

Ingvar Holmberg (1939-2010), Associate Professor, Institute for Demografi, University of Gothenburg, Gothenburg

Zoltan Kettinger (1966), MBA, M.sc., Ph.D. student, Department of Business Management, National Sun Yat-sen University, Kaohsiung, Taiwan

Dr. Artem Korzhenevych (1981), Institute for Regional Research, Christian-Albrechts-Universität zu Kiel, Kiel

Christian Wichmann Matthiessen (1945), Professor of Geography at the University of Copenhagen

Jacek Rokicki (1981), Research Assistant, Femern A/S, Copenhagen

Patrik Rydén (1973), Managing Director, Øresund Logistics, Copenhagen

Signe Schilling (1980), MA, Femern A/S, Copenhagen

Annette Winkel Schwarz (1944), Director of Development, Technical University of Denmark, Lyngby

Oliver Feng Yeu Shyr (1973), Ph.D., Assistant Professor, Department of Urban Planning, National Cheng-kung University in Tainan, Taiwan

Birgit Stöber (1969), Ph.D., Associate Professor in Cultural Geography, Department of Intercultural Communication and Management, Copenhagen Business School, Copenhagen

Lars Rostgaard Toft (1982), MSc., Research Assistant, Department of Geography and Geology, University of Copenhagen

Dr. Emmanouil Tranos (1979), Urban Systems Modelling, Newcastle University, Newcastle

Morten Vedby (1981), MSc., Research Assistant, Department of Geography and Geology, University of Copenhagen

Publisher
Femern A/S
Vester Søgade 10
1601 Copenhagen V
Denmark
T +45 33 41 63 00
E info@femern.dk
www.femern.com

With Syddansk
Universitetsforlag

Print run: 1,500
ISBN-13 978-87-92416-16-2

Editors
Christian Wichmann
Matthiessen &
Marianne Worm

Authors
Christian Wichmann
Matthiessen
David Emanuel Andersson
Åke E. Andersson
Petra Aulin
Johannes Bröcker
Søren Find
Hayo Herrmann
Ingvar Holmberg
Zoltan Kettinger
Artem Korzhenevych
Jacek Rokicki
Patrik Rydén
Signe Schilling
Annette Winkel Schwarz
Oliver Feng Yeu Shyr
Birgit Stöber
Lars Rostgaard Toft
Emmanouil Tranos
Morten Vedby

Photographers
Airbus, Claus Peucket,
Colourbox, ESS AB,
Herzog & de Meuron /
www.elbphilharmonie.de,
istock, Københavns
Lufthavne, Københavns
Universitet, Lunds Universitet,
Nordic, Scanpix, Shutterstock,
Stefan Nilsson / SJ,
Universität Hamburg,
Wonderful Copenhagen,
Øresundsbro Konsortiet

Illustrations
Femern A/S

Design
BGRAPHIC

Print
Nofoprint